Organizational Patterns
of Agile Software Development

It's hard to believe that a decade has come and gone since I first heard the word "pattern"—used in the special way I now use the word. The person who helped me understand what that word really meant was Jim Coplien. He was my mentor and, not only that, he held the torch for all us sitting in the "patterns cave" so we could see dimly what we knew in our hearts we wanted to try to do—make the world a little bit better. Cope and Neil have done amazing things to bring us this collection of, yes, pattern languages! I'm happy to see old friends like Take No Small Slips, but excited to see the photos and the new information. We expected great things from these two and they have not disappointed. Thanks from all of us, guys! Having this book means that these patterns will reach even more people who need their wisdom.

—Linda Rising
Consultant
Editor of *The Pattern Almanac*

This is a remarkably wise book, full of pragmatic advice drawn from real projects. Ultimately, software development is a human experience, and Jim and Neil have captured the essence of that experience in this work. The tapestry of patterns they have woven is positively brilliant, and each thread therein is a delight to read.

—Grady Booch
IBM Fellow

I think of patterns as "concentrated knowledge pills" that make you stronger (smarter). The best patterns can be taken many times over the course of a project, a job, or a career. This carefully researched (nothing artificial), artfully described (no sugar added), and extraordinarily useful (no harmful side-effects) catalog of organizational patterns gives every software development manager a lifetime's supply of knowledge pills that should be taken many times throughout their career. Recommended dosage: as many as you need, as often as you need. Refills? As many as needed. Expiration Date? None—the wisdom in this book is timeless.

—Luke Hohmann
Hohmann Consulting
Author of *Beyond Software Architecture*

As soon as I had worked through these patterns, I realized that several of my clients engaged in process definition projects could make good use of them.

—Ian Graham
Technical Director, trireme.com

I am working on a project to develop Principles and Patterns within the Network Domain for a Canadian Government Department. I stumbled across your work and can't get out of it. I was truly inspired with the clarity and insight that you built into the organizational patterns and this has helped me tremendously.

—Doug McLean
Public Works and Government Services, Canada

Organizational Patterns of Agile Software Development

James O. Coplien

Neil B. Harrison

PEARSON
Prentice
Hall

Upper Saddle River, NJ 07458

Library of Congress Cataloging-in-Publication Data

Coplien, James O.
 Organizational Patterns of Agile Software Development / James O. Coplien, Neil B. Harrison.
  p. cm.
 Includes bibliographical references and index.
 ISBN 0-13-146740-9
  1. Computer software--Development. I. Harrison, Neil. II. Title.

QA76.76.D47C668 2004
005.1--dc22

2004044606

Vice President and Editorial Director, ECS: *Marcia J. Horton*
Publisher: *Alan R. Apt*
Associate Editor: *Toni Dianne Holm*
Editorial Assistant: *Patrick Lindner*
Vice President and Director of Production and Manufacturing, ESM: *David W. Riccardi*
Executive Managing Editor: *Vince O'Brien*
Managing Editor: *Camille Trentacoste*
Production Editor: *John Keegan*
Director of Creative Services: *Paul Belfanti*
Art Director and Cover Manager: *Jayne Conte*
Director, Image Resource Center: *Melinda Reo*
Manager, Rights and Permissions: *Zina Arabia*
Manager, Visual Research: *Beth Brenzel*
Manager, Cover Visual Research and Permissions: *Karen Sanatar*
Image Permission Coordinator: *Cynthia Vincenti*
Managing Editor, AV Management and Production: *Patricia Burns*
Art Editor: *Gregory Dulles*
Manufacturing Manager: *Trudy Pisciotti*
Manufacturing Buyer: *Lisa McDowell*
Executive Marketing Manager: *Pamela Hersperger*
Marketing Assistant: *Barrie Reinhold*

© 2005 Lucent Technologies
Published by Pearson Prentice Hall
Pearson Education, Inc.
Upper Saddle River, NJ 07458

Printed in the United States of America

10 9 8 7 6 5 4 3 2 1

ISBN: 0-13-146740-9

Pearson Education Ltd., *London*
Pearson Education Australia Pty. Ltd., *Sydney*
Pearson Education Singapore, Pte. Ltd.
Pearson Education North Asia Ltd., *Hong Kong*
Pearson Education Canada, Inc., *Toronto*
Pearson Educación de Mexico, S.A. de C.V.
Pearson Education—Japan, *Tokyo*
Pearson Education Malaysia, Pte. Ltd.
Pearson Education, Inc., *Upper Saddle River, New Jersey*

To Lisa, whose wisdom, competence and patience
continue to amaze me.

—NBH

To Moody Ahmad, who led me to the human path,
to the hundreds of colleagues whose stories these patterns tell,
and to those many friends who've toiled together with us
in this labor of love.

—JOC

Preface

We are satisfied by doing real work. Software is like a plant that grows: You can't predict its exact shape or how big it will grow; you can control its growth only to a limited degree. There are no rules for this kind of thing—it's never been done before.

—Charlie Anderson, Architect, Borland Quattro Pro for Windows

You will find no books on the bookshelf here that tell you how to start up a new discipline. Software has been seeking its own way as a relatively young discipline for the past 40 years. Every new discipline struggles to find practices suitable to its survival and growth. Sometimes this struggle is incremental. Sometimes disciplines undergo more substantial shifts in process, structure, and values that break with the past to explore new ground. Charlie Anderson's quote about Borland Quattro Pro for Windows (QPW) in particular applies to the rhythms of software development in general. It warns us: Get ready for change, for it will come tomorrow.

The most exciting advances in science go hand in hand with radical social change. The move from classic physics to quantum physics precipitated from a crisis in physics. We talk about the software crisis, yet no individual crisis in software—let alone *the* software crisis, whatever that might be—has precipitated the same kinds of change that we associate with great advances in science. Software development perhaps has yet to face its first true crisis, which may lead to the first true industry-wide systemic change.

But that doesn't mean that software is static. We can identify different faces of change in software development over the past five decades. Our interest in this book focuses on what software development has learned about itself in that time from an organizational and a social perspective. Software development is perhaps working in its fourth *social* style of system development. Yet what is really interesting about these social styles is their ties to technical advances in the art of computer programming. The first style of software development goes back to the first computers that were programmed manually with console switches. The second style came with the advent of programming languages that allowed scientists to work individually or in small teams and to interact with machines through a language. In the third style, what we learned from hardware design and manufacturing carried over into the design of software. Formal processes drove development, management was visible and explicit, and both the system and the organizations that worked on the system were highly hierarchical. Now we are in the fourth style, one that breaks down hierarchy, features dynamic social structures and communication paths, and values immediacy. This fourth style often bears the label *agile*, but that is just one of many characterizations of a broad new way of developing software that has emerged over the past decade.

Yet, human endeavors tend to take the same shape century after century. Human endeavors all share common elements of human nature, which to some degree limits the range of human undertakings. For example, most organizations have leaders, and cliques, as well as their own rituals, their own nuances of meaning for terms of the trade, their own correspondence between physical space and organizational structure, and hundreds more. The organization of any major human endeavor follows basic laws of efficiency of communication, span of control, xenophobia, specialization, and other sociological forces that drive similar undertakings to implement similar practices and structures. Much has been made of the similarity between vernacular housing architecture and the construction of software systems [Coplien Devos 2000]. The same may be true for the organization of any social animals, but we leave verification of that claim to readers better tooled in those disciplines than we are.

Going deeper yet, the systems of nature have common rhythms and trends that underlie their emergent complexity. These properties come from the *structure* of their organization: the deeply held relationships that define the organization as a social entity. Senge [Senge 1990] popularized this aspect of social behavior in a discipline he called *systems thinking*, a concept that goes beyond our everyday disciplines that are based on a straightforward relationship between cause and effect. Many early attempts at software process improvement relied on this simplistic cause-and-effect relationship, particularly as the third style of software development started to take hold in the industry. Most ISO 9000 process improvement efforts were run this way: discover what we're doing wrong, identify the place in the process where the error has occured, and make it right. There was rarely any notion that the process as a whole might be wrong and that, for example, a step-by-step process should be replaced by a more reactive, much more agile process. And it was considered heresy to conjecture that strict formalism may pose problems and that the process itself might not capture the crucial properties of efficient, effective systems.

When we started this work in the early 1990s, we started with documented research that showed serious shortcomings in process-based approaches such as ISO 9000. We asked ourselves: if process isn't the answer, then what is? We chose organizational structure—and, in particular, the structure of relationships between roles—as the basis for system understanding. All systems are about relationships, and most disciplines that study systems study the relationships in those systems. The idea worked. What's better, the technique didn't displace the process-based approaches in existing organizations (it's always hard to tell an organization to stop doing something they think is helpful, anyhow), but instead complemented them by adding insight into deep structure that explained behavior at the process level. So if you already have a process improvement program in place, this book can add an enriching dimension that builds on your own culture and helps develop your peoples' insights into that culture.

Patterns provide a way to capture both the broad, invariant practices of socially built artifacts and the specialized practices of individual disciplines, as well as providing an understanding of how those practices build on each other. Long before Alexander started using patterns for the field of architecture, anthropologists were using them to describe human social structures [Kroeber 1948]. The pattern languages in this book combine the timeless human structures that transcend disciplines with the best practices of contemporary software development. These patterns are all empirical: they capture the major rhythms and structures of successful software-intensive organizations today. Many of the patterns come from our own research, but we have also incorporated patterns from other authors working in the same field. This is a collected work that in many ways reflects a community-wide effort.

There are two equally valid views of this book: it is a guide to organizational improvement, and it is a record of the "best typical" software development structures of the fourth social style of software development. Most readers will use the book as a guide to organizational improvement. However, it is our hope that this book reflects a well-enough grounded view of contemporary software development to serve as a touchstone that records what life was like in software development organizations in the late 20th and early 21st centuries. Fifty years from now, will this book provide a sobering admonishment to the industry? Will we simply chuckle at how things used to be? Or will time leave this fourth-generation culmination of software progress largely untouched? In that spirit, we greet those rare readers who find an archival copy of this tome on a dusty bookshelf in the middle of the 21st century, and we salute their efforts to use the information in this text to further improve the lot of the organizations of their time and place.

Our sense of history extends in the other direction as well. Christopher Alexander's book includes a picture at the beginning of every pattern, and each picture sets a broad tone for the pattern that follows [Alexander 1977]. We wanted to capture that same feeling for this book, and we strove to include a picture for each pattern. We initially felt that the social network diagrams would suffice as pictures, but these diagrams gave the book an "academic" feel that left a bad taste in our mouths. Paul Bramble pointed us to the prints and photographs division of the Library of Congress (http://lcweb.loc.gov/rr/print/catalog.html), which provided a wealth of vintage photos. Most of the photos come from a collection of Depression-era photographs sponsored by the Farm Services Administration. Some of the photos are strikingly poignant or relevant to the patterns, which is surprising since the photos come from an era that predates the software culture that is such a large part of this book. But we feel that the age and the human element of the photos lend an overall charm to the book that totally would be lacking in the social network diagrams. The photos also give us a sense of the timelessness of the basic human issues facing organizations of any culture, era, or ideology. This book is not about ideology, but about human nature. Finally, the pictures might help make the patterns more memorable: pictures are powerful association tools.

Many of the pictures have a military theme. Please remember that the purpose of patterns is human quality of life and comfort and that patterns help us capture as much learning from history's tragedies as from its moments of peak culture. Also remember that the earliest patterns of human organizations (such as [SunTzu 1989]) have roots in military organizational structure.

Acknowledgments

In doing this book, we view ourselves as editors and chroniclers of others' work and ideas. There are literally thousands of people who contributed to this book through their participation in the empirical studies from which we mined the patterns. We haven't listed all of their names here, but we are thankful to all of them for contributing their time and energy. Especially noteworthy were the Borland QPW Group, coordinated by David Intersimone; a remarkably productive project at AT&T led by Judy Tschirgi; highly effective projects at Schlumberger in Oslo, where we were hosted by Lise Hvatum; and the group managed by Richard Gabriel at ParcPlace Systems, which was undergoing a sobering restructuring at the time that we visited.

Other people put even more of their own energy into this book by building things for us and doing things with us. Brendan Cain was one of the original members of the Pasteur research effort at Bell Laboratories, and he wrote many of the original analysis tools. Anthropologist Peter Bürgi, another early member of the research team, contributed many of the insights on schismogenesis and on other direct parallels between the corporate world and the more "traditional" world of cultural anthropology. Tom Burrows' early work on the GIL and Romana programming environments at Bell Labs provided a platform for many of the early tools. We are grateful to Steve North for the **dot** tool that not only provides good supporting visuals that map out the pattern languages, but that also was a key research tool in its own right.

We are particularly indebted to authors who let us reproduce their patterns here. Pieces of the patterns of Alistair Cockburn, Ward Cunningham, Bruce Whitenack, Brian Foote, and Steve Berczuk have all made their way into this collection. Thanks for sharing, folks. Gerard Meszaros wrote several patterns, including Artifact Ownership, Architecture Definition Team, and Architecture Organization, whose contents filtered into many patterns in these pattern languages.

Other people steered us in the right direction. Diane Grinnell pointed us to references on organizational incest and its parallels to dysfunctional constellations in family therapy. Tom Stone, then at Addison-Wesley, directed us to some dynamite references on organizational learning, in particular the studies that came out of Royal Dutch Shell. Bindu Rama Rao of Lucent pointed us to the work by Kroeber, which gave us strong ties from patterns back to the world of anthropology. Urvashi Kaul of Allstate developed pattern taxonomies that shaped how we organized these patterns into pattern languages. But most of all, we're grateful to Moody Ahmad, who gave us our first hint back in the mid-1980s that software development research should investigate not just technical issues, but human issues as well.

Dozens of people reviewed these patterns in writers' workshops at pattern conferences and in local pattern groups. In addition, we enjoyed the feedback of a team of focused and thorough reviewers who weren't afraid to give us the benefit of their opinion in places where they felt we were misguided. They were usually right. Gerhard Ackermann at Siemens in Vienna offered a wealth of firsthand insights on organizational growth and repair. Paul Bramble and Ian Graham were our two main manuscript reviewers for the late versions of the manuscript, and they offered a lot of useful advice on the organization of the book. Joshua Kerievsky pioneered the conversion of these patterns to Alexandrian form with his outstanding editorial efforts on SOLO VIRTUOSO (4.2.5), SIZE THE ORGANIZATION (4.2.2), and SELF-SELECTING TEAM (4.2.11). And many thanks to our favorite Mercenary Analyst, Betsy Hanes Perry, for her contributions to PUBLIC CHARACTER (4.2.17). Jay Stagnone, Shalom Reich, and Luke Hohmann were also key early reviewers.

Others worked with us as partners along the way, and their editorial feedback and suggestions were fundamental to the shape of the book. Martine Devos (then of Argo in Belgium and currently of Avaya Labs) and Steve Berczuk invested much of themselves in this work, and we are grateful for their energy and dedication.

We enjoyed a good technical and organizational infrastructure to support our work. At Bell Labs, the research organizations managed by Eric Sumner, Mary Zajac, and David Weiss actively supported this work for over a decade. Ten years is a long time not only in Internet years, but even by research project standards. We honor their vision, patience, and forbearance. David Weiss continued to support this work in a similar capacity at Avaya Labs. Many thanks to Universität Karlsruhe for hosting the Wiki that we used to develop the book manuscript, and in particular to Dr. Helmut Goos. The support came in part under the auspices of the Information Society technologies (IST) 1999-14191 EasyComp joint research project of the European Community, and we are grateful for that support. Research Chair John Roddick and fellow professor Paul Calder sponsored the infrastructure and time for this work while Jim Coplien spent a summer (or was it winter?) at Flinders University in Adelaide, Australia.

And of course, where would we be without our editorial support? Alan Apt has always been there in the wings, supporting us in mighty ways and not bugging us too much. It has been a joy working with him. We are also grateful to John Keegan, who acted as a FIREWALL for us against many of the details of book production.

This book was generated automatically from a Wiki website using tools that generated a MIF file for transmission to the publisher.

Contents

Organizational Patterns
of Agile Software Development

PART I

History and Introduction

This book is about people—people who write software. No, this book doesn't offer a Dilbertesque look at our profession or an analysis of the minds of cult figures in the profession. Instead, it is about teams of real people who write real software. You see, over the last 10 years or so, we have studied how people work together to create software. And we have seen that these organizations have a lot in common, whether they are writing software for telephone systems, banks, or oil exploration. The people issues shine through, regardless of what application is being developed. And that is comforting in a way.

At the same time, though, it is disconcerting. For even though organizations are inanimate, they nonetheless take on a life of their own. We see that organizations grow, learn, and sometimes even get sick! Yet they can heal themselves and become healthy again. Of course, we are most interested in the characteristics of healthy organizations; perhaps other organizations can learn from their experiences.

These notions of healing, repair, and growth are the foundations of Agile development. O.K., we'll be frank: we chose "Agile" for the title out of marketing concerns. It seems to be the current term of choice for the kinds of things we describe in this book. It is a term that rolls off the tongue more easily than other clever names that clamor for your attention on today's bookshelves. This manuscript has been evolving piecemeal for more than a decade, and the early prepublication manuscripts have been a foundation and source of inspiration for many contemporary popular approaches. For example, Jeff Sutherland notes that an early publication on this work, related to the Borland case study in this book, was one early influence on SCRUM, an Agile software development process [Sutherland 2003]. Ken Schwaber notes that the early backgrounds of these pattern languages "were the genesis of some of the agile processes" [Schwaber 2003]. Gabriel's early article [Gabriel 1994] and later book [Gabriel 1996] discuss the successful application of these techniques at ParcPlace Systems as a key part of a broader effort that transformed the organization. And these patterns have the dubious distinction of earning the criticism of one notable software consultant who was the primary reviewer of the first published version of these patterns. He noted that anyone who worked on organizational issues was avoiding real work (which by his own admission was limited to anything directly related to Smalltalk programming). He would later go on to be one of the founders of Extreme Programming (XP)—a discipline that builds in part on the patterns that have been in this pattern language [e.g., DEVELOPING IN PAIRS (4.2.28)] for almost a decade.

Yet this book covers topics broader than so-called agile development. We are really concerned with effective software development—the ability to produce good software efficiently, time after time. Many of the organizations we studied and learned from would not be considered "agile," but they were highly effective. The 5ESS® development in AT&T, for example, would fit nobody's definition of agile. But year after year, AT&T produced software for one of the largest and most reliable software systems in the world. While many of these patterns contribute to agility, our chief aim is effectiveness.

We have captured the good things organizations do, and we have recorded them as patterns. We hope these patterns will be as interesting and useful to you as they have been to us. Many others have found them useful: At conferences, for example, we find that these patterns are the foundation of improvement programs in many companies worldwide.

We have divided this book into four parts:

- Part I: History and Introduction, the section you are reading
- Part II: The Patterns themselves
- Part III: Foundations and History
- Part IV: Case Studies

Here in the introduction, we provide background material that will help you better understand the core of the book, which is the patterns themselves. It is an ideal goal that each pattern should convey everything you need to know to touch the resources within you that will allow you to apply it. But more practically, experience has shown that a knowledge of the history behind the gathering and publication of patterns can help the reader better understand the patterns' scope and applicability. For example, John Vlissides' book *Pattern Hatching*, a reflection on the seminal Design patterns book [Gamma 1995], offers commentary that takes the pattern practitioner to a new level of depth in understanding both the strengths and limitations of various techniques [Vlissides 1998]. Here, we package both parts into the same book. Furthermore, we present the ideas up front as a foundation for what follows.

After you read the patterns, the case studies follow to reinforce the principles and practices that the patterns offer. The appendices include miscellaneous supporting material.

CHAPTER 1

An Overview of Patterns and Organizational Patterns

The authors of this book know that you really wanted to first open the book to How to Use This Book (Chapter 3), but we thought it would be good to introduce the topic a bit before taking you there. Having a bit of terminology in hand will provide context for the most powerful application of the patterns in this book. For this same reason, we kindly urge you to read all of Part I before moving into the patterns in the following sections.

1.1 What Are Patterns?

A *pattern* is an element of design that is most commonly ascribed to architect Christopher Alexander, who uses a pattern-based approach to the construction of towns, neighborhoods, and buildings ([Alexander 1977], [Alexander 1979]). Each pattern solves a problem by adding structure to a system. The main tenets of the pattern approach to system construction include incremental repair and piecemeal growth, building on experience, and attentiveness to quality of life. Alexander's ideas were adopted by the software community, and in particular by the object-oriented programming community, in the early 1990s.

The concept of a pattern is difficult to understand; it is plagued by even more misunderstandings than to understand such terms as *object* and *function* of the 1970s and 1980s. There are aspects of the definition that are intuitive—"a solution to a problem in a context"—yet a pattern is much more than that. In this book, your intuition about the meaning of the term *pattern* will take you far as you build and repair your organization. But a deeper knowledge of patterns will make it easier for you to extend the pattern language with your own patterns and to experience the joy that comes with the freedom of playful and insightful organizational design.

To fully understand what a pattern is, you must first understand what a pattern language is. A pattern doesn't exist apart from a pattern language; in fact, its first purpose is to establish connections to other patterns in the language ([Alexander 1977], p. xii). But to understand pattern languages, you must first understand what a pattern is. We know this concept is recursive, and to understand recursion, you must first understand recursion. We must start somewhere, and we start here: with patterns.

Here is a short and necessarily incomplete definition of a pattern:

> A recurring structural configuration that solves a problem in a context, contributing to the wholeness of some whole, or system, that reflects some aesthetic or cultural value.

Some of these aspects of a pattern don't come out in the popular literature, and you may not find them all in the same place in Alexander's definitions. But they are the key elements of what makes a pattern a pattern and of what makes a pattern different from a simple rule. A pattern *is* a rule: The word *configuration* should be read as "a rule to configure." But it is more than just a rule; it is a special kind of rule that contributes to the overall structure of a system and that works together with other patterns to create emergent structure and behavior.

Let's jump into an example. Consider the pattern TEAM PER TASK (4.1.21). Let's discuss each section of the pattern in turn interleaved with explanatory commentary.

Team Per Task **

That's the *name* of the pattern. We try to make pattern names descriptive and sometimes even evocative. The name is a shorthand by which we'll refer to the structure, forces, solution, etc., of the pattern as a whole, and it's important that patterns have good names to support good communication between you and your colleagues as you evolve your organization. The two stars after the name are a confidence level for the pattern. Each pattern can have zero, one, or two stars associated with it, depending on how often we have seen the pattern applied and depending on our sense of confidence about the pattern's value.

> ... a big diversion hits the team, threatening to disrupt ongoing work and temporarily halt progress.

This is the *context* in which we find the problem. The context tells us something about the current structure of the system and may give us a hint about what other patterns already have been applied. After this prologue is the following delimiter, which leads into a discussion of the *forces*, or trade-offs, behind the pattern:

> **Large distractions (usually called crises) must not be allowed to stop a project, even for a short time.** Crises are inevitable, and they can occur frequently. If the project members take time to respond to each crisis, they will soon find themselves spending so much time performing crisis management that the real work doesn't get done.
>
> Of course, the diversions are real. A previous release needs an emergency bug fix. New people must be trained. The ISO audit will happen. But these diversions must be handled in such a way that the project still moves forward.

At this point, we have a sense that this is a tough problem! These forces draw out the considerations that must be balanced in the solution. They point to the nub of the problem and, in summary, provide a statement of the problem itself. In this pattern form—called Alexandrian form, after Christopher Alexander—there is no separate problem statement. We can interpret the boldfaced part of the forces to summarize the problem, but it is *all* the forces together that cause the problem.

The problem isn't context-free; it is not a law of nature, but instead arises in a cultural context. Each culture has its own aesthetics about what is acceptable and what is not and about what is constructive and what is not. Patterns honor this human element of design.

Next, we present the solution after a ceremonious "Therefore":

> Therefore:
> **Let a subteam handle the diversion, which allows the main team to keep working.**
>
> One approach is to split the team. Sort the activities so that each team has a primary task with additional, sympathetic activities. Sitting in meetings, answering phone calls, and writing reports, for example, are nonsympathetic to designing software. Arrange it so that each team can focus on its primary task and so that each task has at least one dedicated team member.

We close off the solution with another set of stars and then go into some discussion about why the pattern works: how it balances the forces, what its strengths and liabilities might be, and so on:

> As a result, important distractions are handled almost entirely by specialized teams, thus allowing the main team to continue uninterrupted.

> However, one must be careful not to overdo it. Carried to extremes, this pattern results in single-person teams. In addition, while solving a crisis is important, be careful not to heap praise too lavishly on the crisis teams. Otherwise, crisis management becomes the glamor job, and the team focuses on putting out fires rather on than building the building. [See COMPENSATE SUCCESS (4.2.25)].

Aha! And there is a link to another pattern. We can also add sections to make such links explicit:

RELATED PATTERNS:

This pattern treats each task both as an activity and as a deliverable. Therefore:

OWNER PER DELIVERABLE (10.5.19) - addresses the general form of ownership and accountability.

FUNCTION OWNER AND COMPONENT OWNER - establishes a team for each artifact and addresses the task of designing each artifact.

. . . .

And so forth. For the full pattern, see TEAM PER TASK (4.1.21).

A good pattern takes the reader on an emotional journey. We want you to feel what it might be like to be on such a team, focused on one task. One goal of the forces is to touch those experiences within you that cause you to say "Aha!" and to identify with the pattern.

Patterns tend to be small, local things. There is no "organization structure" pattern or anything like that. Patterns work together in rich and complex ways to generate emergent structure and behavior. An individual pattern captures locally related concerns; a pattern is an encapsulation of related forces. When we apply patterns, we can do so without undue concern for other patterns in the language. In application, they are decoupled; however, in the broader scheme of things, they are always part of some whole that gives them context. Patterns are like the cells in a plant; the resulting organization is like the tree or the forest that results as the cells grow, divide, and specialize. The structure for putting the patterns together in this way is called a *pattern language*.

1.2 What Are Pattern Languages?

Patterns come from pattern languages. We use the term *language* as an analogy. English is a language, and as a language it comprises words and the rules to put words together in meaningful ways. A pattern language is a language that comprises patterns and the rules to put patterns together in meaningful ways and in a certain sequence. It tells how to build a whole, a *system*. Patterns encapsulate related forces so you can focus on local trade-offs using local thinking. Pattern languages are about emergent behavior in systems.

Actually, a pattern language is an outline of many ways that patterns may be put together. How they are put together depends on *context*. When we apply a pattern, the context changes.

When someone joins the organization or when the organization decides to build a new product line, the context may change. Depending on the context at any given time, different patterns might or might not apply.

So while a pattern language is a roadmap, there are paths to organizational growth. The exact path one takes depends on circumstances and on progress—and, of course, on the choices that people make in shaping the organization along the way. Sometimes people make bad choices, and that may mean that the organization needs to back up a bit or take a detour on the journey. And bad choices sometimes result in insights that lead to new patterns and to new structures in the pattern language.

Consider that you are working in the PROJECT MANAGEMENT PATTERN LANGUAGE (4.1). You already have PROGRAMMING EPISODES (4.1.19) in place, and you've decided that you need the pattern SOMEONE ALWAYS MAKES PROGRESS (4.1.20) to keep the project from getting "stuck" or distracted, particularly by diversions. SOMEONE ALWAYS MAKES PROGRESS seems like the right idea since you have many tasks that go awry. But now the question is how to tailor SOMEONE ALWAYS MAKES PROGRESS to the particular situation. You could derail the entire team to address the problem, but that would be overkill.

So you look at SOMEONE ALWAYS MAKES PROGRESS where you find that you can employ one of a broad range of particular solutions and tactics depending on the exact forces to be resolved. The following specializations are example refinements of this pattern:

- DEVELOPING IN PAIRS (4.2.28)—allow one person to take the keyboard.
- TEAM PER TASK (4.1.21)—separate tasks into sympathetic sets.
- SACRIFICE ONE PERSON (4.1.22)—assign only one person to the distraction.
- DAY CARE (4.1.23)—separate the training task from that of producing software.

You home in on TEAM PER TASK as being a good response to the concerns raised by trying to fit SOMEONE ALWAYS MAKES PROGRESS (4.1.20) into the organization. So you design a team into your organization to address the problem.

How do you staff the team? You move onward in the language and find that SACRIFICE ONE PERSON (4.1.22) or DEVELOPING IN PAIRS (4.2.28) might be a suitable solution to the problem. Or you might look at INTERRUPTS UNJAM BLOCKING (4.1.25) as another refinement of TEAM PER TASK: connect the team with a manager who can get the team off top dead center if the team becomes stuck on the problem too long.

Each of these pattern selections follows a natural progression through the pattern language. Most patterns can be applied one at a time. However, it pays to know the patterns in advance, and it pays to reflect upon several patterns to proceed from instinct to the right action. Good advice from peers and, even more so, from the stakeholders in the decision can also help guide the decision. Having the patterns at hand provides a foundation for discussion and analysis of the problem and its potential solutions.

Four pattern languages in this book build four "wholes." These languages are a Project Management Pattern Language (4.1), a Piecemeal Growth Pattern Language (4.2) for growing the organization incrementally, an Organizational Style Pattern Language (5.1), and a People and Code Pattern Language (5.2). Note, though, that the "wholes" aren't distinct, but instead are different views of the same organization. In other words, a healthy organization exhibits patterns from all four of these pattern languages simultaneously!

1.3 Organizational Pattern Languages

1.3.1   The Structure of Social Systems

An organization is a system and, like most systems, it has structure. In particular, it is a social system. What does it mean for a social system to have structure?

The study of human organizations goes back thousands of years, and many of the schools of this nascent organizational science looked at structure. The Chinese classics like *The Art of War* [SunTzu 1989] talk much about organization structure as it applied to the organization of armies, some of the earliest large groups of people that needed guidance from organizational principles. The primary structure in a classic militia is one of hierarchy, authority, and top-down control. These tenets form the core of most other military structures.

These structures are part of culture [see ANTHROPOLOGICAL FOUNDATIONS (CHAPTER 7)]. A friend of ours at Siemens-Nixdorf claims to be able to trace the hierarchical structure of the company back to its founders, who were military officers in the Bismarck era in Prussia—a very hierarchical culture. One finds such overt hierarchy in much of German culture and in its companies.

But there are other kinds of culture that reflect different kinds of structure, and that structure comes about from the patterns that generate it. Another extreme is the contemporary Linux culture in software, an extremely shallow and broad hierarchy. This structure, in turn, leads to different processes [see BEYOND PROCESS TO STRUCTURE AND VALUES (7.2)].

Culture is important. While engineering organizations traditionally seek out technical missteps in their postmortem analyses, the contributions of culture are usually ignored. If we are *in* a culture, it's hard to *see* the culture, which can cause us to miss the important cultural roots of failed projects again and again. But we are getting better at it. The Columbia Accident Investigation Board lays blame for the Columbia disaster on NASA's culture. Elements of that culture included its value system of funding, schedule, and safety [Recer 2003]. We don't need to wait for disaster to strike to take proactive steps to grow and repair corporate culture. That's what organizational pattern languages do.

1.3.2   The Multiple Structures of Social Systems

Organizations are complex; we might define *complexity* as proportional to the number of distinct, meaningful views of a system. In software, we sometimes use the word *architecture* to describe the articulation of system structure. We can also talk about the organization as a system that can be described by an architecture that comprises the structures in the organization and the relationships between them. The *structures* are patterns, and each pattern documents its relationships to the other patterns in the language. In this book, we talk about four interrelated architectures of an organization. Each one has its own pattern language:

- PROJECT MANAGEMENT PATTERN LANGUAGE (4.1): This pattern language has to do with the work of the organization and the manner in which that work is structured. It focuses on schedule, process, tasks, and in particular the structures needed to support good work progress.

- PIECEMEAL GROWTH PATTERN LANGUAGE (4.2): This pattern language describes how to grow the organization and process together. It is reminiscent of concurrent engineering approaches that grow the process and product together.

- ORGANIZATIONAL STYLE PATTERN LANGUAGE (5.1): This pattern language looks at the structure of role relationships in the organization and examines what these relationships portend for different organizational styles.

- PEOPLE AND CODE PATTERN LANGUAGE (5.2): This pattern language is an expansion of the famous Conway's Law, which states that there is a close relationship between the structure of an organization and the artifacts it builds. The pattern language offers further insight on organizational structuring in light of growing insight into the system architecture.

Each of the pattern languages reflects a domain. These domains come from our analysis of the patterns. We grouped the patterns according to the way in which they work together in sequences and, after eliminating a small number of pattern duplications, we ended up with four groupings. There's nothing magic about the number four, but it's a nice and manageably small number.

In practice, one uses all of these pattern languages in parallel. Each one describes a different architecture of the organization, and each of these architectures must be tended to. There are, of course, relationships between the pattern languages; in particular, some patterns are common to more than one pattern language. In this book, we present each pattern only once, in the pattern language where it best seems to belong, and the other pattern languages make reference to that presentation of the pattern, where appropriate.

These patterns come from a wide variety of organizations, large and small. As such, we feel that most of the patterns can be considered for most organizations, large and small. Large organizations almost always comprise several smaller organizations. Almost all of these patterns were collected from identifiable groups that were cohesive in their own right, though these groups all had effective established relationships with external agencies, organizations, and individuals. The PEOPLE AND CODE PATTERN LANGUAGE (5.2) is particularly applicable to small organizations, and those readers who have a particular interest in small team dynamics might find that chapter particularly useful. (However, neither of us believe in the existence of "large teams." The word *team* means something, and the spirit and effectiveness that come with the word *team* can't be sustained across large populations.)

1.3.3   Pattern Languages and Sequences

With each pattern language we provide a story—from real life—that illustrates how patterns from the pattern language might fit together to achieve organizational growth, improvement, or maturity. These stories are a form of what we call *sequences*. A sequence is an architect's tour through the structure about to be built. It is a path through the pattern language; when you use the patterns in a given order, you follow a sequence. For example, one may begin a new project by appointing an architect to design the overall product [ARCHITECT CONTROLS PRODUCT (5.2.3)]. Because it is a big project, the architect gets help [ARCHITECTURE TEAM (5.2.4)], and then the team members sequester themselves to come up with the initial architecture [LOCK 'EM UP TOGETHER (5.2.5)]. This summary shows only a small piece of a typical sequence of a new project. A given path, or sequence of patterns, results in a particular system, or whole. At the beginning of each of the four languages, we share a story that illustrates a sequence through the pattern language.

These sequences should help you get a feel for what the language is trying to build and for what it's trying to achieve. They should give you a better feel for what pattern languages in general are about and help you see the patterns' interconnection and interdependence. As you read the pattern languages and consider your own experiences, you will be able to see sequences through the pattern language—your own stories.

Of course, all possible sequences are implicit in the structure of the pattern language. You can and should generate your own sequence by going from pattern to pattern, working your way through the language. The pattern language diagrams presented at the beginning of each pattern language can provide guidance. And sometimes you may find a place to apply a pattern in a way that's a bit out of sequence. As long as the context is suitable for the new pattern, let common sense rule and try the pattern if your instinct leads in that direction.

Near the end of the book, we also present some case studies. These studies are like the sequences in the stories we present with each pattern language, only they are less structured. The case studies come from organizations we have studied and modeled, so we have less insight into their process of growth than we do for the examples given with the pattern languages. But one can still imagine what process might have taken place, and one can still see the interworking of the patterns in those stories.

CHAPTER 2

How the Patterns Came to Us

We didn't make up these patterns. No one invents a pattern (or at least no one should). Patterns are out there waiting to be discovered and documented. We took it upon ourselves to find the latent patterns of the domain of organizational maintenance and to document them. This book is the result.

This chapter briefly looks at the techniques we used to find and organize the patterns. You should read this chapter if you are interested as much in the methodology behind the patterns as you are in the patterns themselves. However, the section on How to Use This Book (Chapter 3) provides a summary of what you'll need to know to understand most of the patterns that follow.

We can summarize our research approach as follows:

1. Gather data from identifiable teams using team interviews.

2. Analyze the data using social network techniques to build organizational models.

3. Present the analysis results to the team, note team reactions, and adjust the model as necessary.

4. Catalog the analysis results and look for common patterns, identifying the problem, forces, and solution for each pattern.

5. Capture the patterns in pattern form.

6. Look for links between the patterns that form meaningful sequences for applying the patterns.

7. Organize the sequences into pattern languages.

We started with team interviews and largely relied on social network analysis tools to look for patterns in the data from around 100 organizations. Those organizations ranged in size from 5 people to 100 people, but most of them were organizations of 20 to 40 people working on a common software project. By *organization* here, we mean a social unit such as a department or project or work location where people depend on each other and work together. This sense of organization may (or may not) resemble that shown on corporate organizational charts. Often, each organization would be responsible for one or more *processes* in the sense that the term is used in ISO 9000 certification.

We studied organizations in Europe, America, the Middle East, and Australia. Our models unfortunately do not build on any substantial data from Japan, China, Singapore, or other countries of the Pacific Rim. It is possible that cultural differences (in the vernacular sense) might limit the application of some of these patterns in Pacific Rim settings. However, we have found remarkable commonality across organizations in Western Europe, the Nordic countries, the United States, and the Middle East.

Given that background, here's a more in-depth description of how we gathered and analyzed the organizational data.

2.1 Gathering Organizational Data

This work draws on data gathered as part of the Pasteur process research program at AT&T Bell Laboratories. In the Pasteur program, we studied software development organizations in many companies worldwide, covering a wide spectrum of development cultures. The Pasteur analysis techniques are based in part on organizational visualization. Many of the patterns in this pattern language have visual analogues in the Pasteur analyses. We sometimes use visualizations to illustrate a pattern.

Two kinds of pictures are used in the Pasteur studies. The first is a *social network diagram*, also called an *adjacency diagram*. Each diagram shows a network of roles and the communication paths between them. The roles are situated according to their coupling relationships: Closely coupled roles are close together, and decoupled roles are far apart. Roles at the center of these pictures tend to be the most active roles in these organizations, while those nearer the edges have a more distant relationship with the organization as a whole.

The second kind of picture is an *interaction grid*. The interaction grid is a communication matrix for the organization, structured in a way that makes it easier to find clusters of communication, of engaged and disengaged roles, and of other patterns in the communication network. We present an overview of these tools in READING THE PATTERNS (3.1) and describe them in more detail in SOCIAL NETWORK ANALYSIS (7.4).

The pattern texts in this book often make reference to documents or projects that typify the pattern, particularly in the design rationale section of the patterns. One of our most important case studies was a 1993 evaluation of Borland's QuattroPro for Windows development, also called *QPW* in the text. This research is further discussed in the proceedings of BIC/94 [Coplien 1994], in a column by Richard Gabriel [Gabriel 1994], and in an article in *Dr. Dobb's Journal* [Coplien 1994b]. The case study appears in this book as BORLAND QUATTRO PRO FOR WINDOWS (CHAPTER 8).

2.1.1 Introspection in and Analysis of Organizations

We launched our work on process and organization as ISO 9000, STD 2167a, and other standards broadened their influence on software development in the late 1980s and early 1990s. These standards focused on process reproducibility, striving to reduce organizational performance variation rather than to raise the mean. Such baselining is important to the quality techniques popularized by W. Edwards Deming [Deming 1986], which are based on statistical process control. A process can be improved if it can be understood; it can be understood only if it has a consistent structure [Senge 1990]; and its structure can be consistent only after the first steps of process improvement have reduced process variability. We found that the process culture in most contemporary organizations has a strong focus on the development of process documentation, but have also found that the documented process often does not resemble day-to-day practice. The process cultures often ignored important variations in organizational behavior that are key to dealing with market uncertainties or the uncertainties that arise in any process rooted in human intellect and instinct.

2.1.2   Shortcomings of State of the Art

Most process-intensive organizations look to a process specification document as the final word on development activities. We noted three problems with this approach in practice: lack of empirical conformance between practice and process specifications, incompleteness of process models, and inability to capture long-term stable process abstractions. Many processes exhibited such broad variation in behavior that it was difficult for process specifiers to agree on a process that represented the typical scenario. Many organizations informally built process specifications from anecdotal process experience instead of developing the baseline process model with empirical models and data. Many organizations we studied created an ideal specification instead of capturing empirical practices [Coplien 1993], and organizations used these specifications as a baseline for improvement despite the mismatch. Because many process specification models were divorced from empirical practice, they could not reliably drive real development practice.

Second, process models were often incomplete and inconsistent. Most process models focused on the task and event perspective, leaving artifacts, roles, actors, and agents as secondary abstractions. Much of this task perspective was driven by a preoccupation with interval prediction and reduction on one hand (management of the overall interval by focusing on individual intervals) and quality on the other (methodical reviews form obvious task/event benchmarks). Task models fit well with the waterfall-based development model that predominates in most development cultures. Furthermore, task models held up the promise of process automation (e.g., [Krishnamurthy Rosenblum 1991]). We note that the disconnect between process tasks and the artifacts they produce continues to plague most of the organizations we work with today.

Third, many organizations built their process-improvement programs around the task or event dimension of process. Well-understood processes (e.g., bug report flow) often can be regularized, but the core processes of software architecture, design, implementation, and validation are poorly understood from a task perspective. We have found that task ordering changes rapidly in a high-technology development organization, so it can't be counted on as a stable component of process structure. One large organization we studied surveyed its developers and found that 80 percent of them were working under officially granted process waivers instead of the official common process, largely because the project's process standard didn't capture the essential stable structure of the process. One reason that task chain models don't capture the stable structure is because of the high degree of concurrency present in modern software development. It is interesting to note that iterative and incremental design cultures were demonstrating success at about the same time that process consciousness was growing. Project managers still find it difficult to reconcile iterative and incremental techniques with process standards that prescribe process steps [Archibald 1993]. Many organizations we studied exhibited concurrent engineering practices, where requirements, design, and implementation activities proceeded in parallel [Hartley 1992]. Few organizations intentionally applied concurrent engineering. In fact, many organizations using concurrent engineering (as we discovered empirically) remained stalwart about the accuracy of their waterfall design methods (as stipulated in project process documents). We felt that a role-based model would be a better match for these concurrent engineering organizations than would models based on tasks and events.

There is growing recognition that even if process models could represent interesting aspects of an organization, they aren't terribly useful as a guide for carrying out the work of the business. In *Contextual Design* ([Beyer Holtzblatt 1998], p. 41), Beyer and Holtzblatt note the following:

> In Contextual Design, we always try to build on natural human ways of interacting. It is easier to act, not out of a long list of rules, but out of a simple, familiar model of relationship. A list of rules says, "Do all these things"—you have to concentrate so much on following the rules you can't relate to the customer. It's too much to remember. A *relationship model* says, "Be like this"—stay in the appropriate relationship, and you will naturally act appropriately.

And this position, in turn, builds on long-standing observations of human behavior. Beyer and Holtzblatt cite Goffman's work from almost a half-century ago as a foundation for this position [Goffman 1959]. We sought to counter the problems of an explicitly process-based approach to organizational improvement with an explicitly role-based modeling approach.

We wanted to adopt process formalisms that would allow us to compare iterative processes with traditional waterfall models, which meant going beyond task and event models. While many aspects of process might be automatable, we found that productive processes emphasized the creative value added by the people in the process. In general, this suggested that we should study many dimensions of process, such as artifacts, organizational roles and structure, personal skill sets, and many other factors. Together, these diverse properties define a process architecture. *Architecture* is a partitioning of a system that results from applying a set of partitioning principles, together with the relationship between the parts that result from that partitioning. Since our resources didn't allow us to study all of these concepts at once, we decided to focus on organizational structure in order to balance the investment most organizations had made in task models. The industry has a fascination with the relationship between development organizations and the software they create (see [Fraser 1994a] and [Fraser 1994b]), so we felt there would be interest in such research.

The organizations we studied didn't necessarily correspond to formal organizational structures, but instead arose as communities of interest developed within a project. The "real" organizations in any culture can be defined in terms of coupling between actors or roles brought together by a common interest or objective. Such organizations are called *instrumental organizations* and should be distinguished from the formal organization structure. An instrumental organization is the "instrument which regulates organizational behaviour" ([Swieringa Wierdsma 1992], p. 10). These two structures line up in some organizations (see [Swieringa Wierdsma 1992]).

2.1.3   The CRC Card Methodology

The Pasteur research program was an empirical research program based on real-world experience. Research on human subjects is notoriously difficult. We were wary of any results that would simply reduce people to numbers; instead, we wanted results that were intuitive. We wanted to build on the insight of our subjects at least as much as on the insights that we as researchers would develop. One of the few constraints we wanted to apply to the data we collected is that it be based on roles, and we felt that roles were a general enough representation so as to not interfere with the gathering of insights from the study subjects. This section describes how we used CRC (classes, responsibilities, and collaborators) cards to capture the data about organizational roles that would serve as input to our analyses.

We set out to build instrumental organizational models from first-hand accounts [Cain Coplien 1993]. Since process works at the level of the engineers doing the day-to-day design, coding, and firefighting, why not build the models from their perspective? We chose CRC cards as the tool we would use to analyze organizations. CRC cards had been developed as a software design tool by Beck and Cunningham to support their work on software architecture and implementation in the mid-1980s [Beck 1991]. In CRC design, each index card represents an object in the system. The card is used to note and track a *c*lass's set of *r*esponsibilities and *c*ollaborations (hence the name *CRC*) in a role-playing exercise.

Subsystem Coord.	
Validate MR lists	Subsystem coord.
Build group products	Change committee
Administer ENVY	Designers
Resolve physical deps.	system test
	Tool vendors

FIGURE 2.1 A CRC Card

In our organizational analysis, each index card represents a role. We also captured responsibilities and helping relationships in our role play; however, the resulting model captures the structure not of an object-oriented program, but of an organization.

CRC cards fit our needs in several respects. First, they support a highly participatory information-gathering technique—something that would help us get at empirical behavior. This level of participation allowed people to retain an accurate history of day-to-day events.

Second, CRC cards made it possible to gather data in a group setting. Role-playing is a powerful technique that can help people recall past events, particularly in the company of the original players. Sociometric research by Bernard, Killworth, et al., has shown that informant accuracy is less than 50 percent when people report individually on their interactions ([Wasserman 1994], p. 57). However, there is something about acting out one's memories that makes the memories almost tactile. Role-playing can help one draw out further detail and recall context that helps keep the data faithful to actual practice. This enactment unfolds in a *sociodrama*, a kind of play that recalls the reality of life in the organization. Our subjects were the actors; we were the audience. Of course, the subjects were also unwitting members of the audience, and the technique owes much of its power to that fact. Bringing group members together helps recall corporate memory. It is also an opportunity to plant the seeds of group learning [Senge 1990], as we will discuss later.

Third, CRC cards were a good fit for the domain we were studying. Each card could be used to model an organizational role. Further, the "responsibilities" captured the responsibilities of each role to the organization, and the "collaborations" captured the dependency relationships. At this early juncture, we were naive about social network theory and sociometric diagrams, but we would find that the CRC model would serve us well to support social network formalisms.

Fourth, CRC cards balanced important aspects of several techniques commonly used in social network data gathering ([Wasserman 1994], p. 19, p. 44). There are many different kinds of modeling units, and examples include actors, dyads, triads, and others. Our primary modeling unit was *roles*, a generalization of related actor responsibilities. In dyadic data gathering, actors are asked about their interactions with other actors. In triadic data gathering, one actor offers an opinion on how a second actor interacts with a third. The CRC modeling technique focuses on dyadic data by helping role actors focus on their interactions with others. However, group discussions led to the collection of triadic data, particularly for controversial or problematic interactions. It was possible to gather data from an entire organization in one or two sessions of a few hours each.

We have used CRC cards to gather data from about 100 organizations, almost all of which serve the software industry. We focused on large system development efforts, including development organizations in AT&T and other telecommunications companies, companies producing software development environment products, aerospace organizations, financial firms and medical software development firms. We also have data points from areas as diverse as government administration projects and consumer software. Most of these groups have been software development organizations, the folks who design, implement, and test software. We have a smaller sampling of organizations that interface the market to the development organization and that perform other assorted functions.

You can read more details about the CRC technique, particularly from the perspective of research methodology, in CRC CARDS AND ROLES (7.5.1).

2.1.4   Analyzing Roles and Relationships

We analyzed the data from the CRC cards and from notes taken during the role-playing in various ways. We analyzed the data from the CRC cards quantitatively. Over time, three meaningful quantitative measures emerged: number of roles, communication saturation, and communication intensity ratio.

> *Number of Roles:* The number of roles in the organization, not the number of people.

> *Communication Saturation:* Each role has the potential to communicate with every other role. The communication saturation is the percentage of the potential communication paths that are actually used.

> *Communication Intensity Ratio:* Not every role has the same number of communication paths to other roles. In many organizations, one role has the lion's share of the communication paths. The communication intensity ratio is the ratio of the number of communication paths of the busiest role to the average number of communication paths in an organization. It measures how much the communication is concentrated in a single role.

These measures helped form some of the patterns, and you will see the measures mentioned later in the patterns themselves. The patterns will explain the implications of the measures.

Besides the quantitative analysis, we found that *looking* at the data from the CRC cards yielded some interesting—and sometimes surprising—insights.

The first "picture" of the data we use is called a *sociogram,* which is best explained by a metaphor. At the conclusion of a session with an organization, we have a deck of cards, one for each role. We take the cards back home to our laboratory. We begin by rubbing each card through our hair, thus imparting a weak positive charge to the cards (and a negative charge to our hair). We deal the cards out on a frictionless table. Then we reach for our jar of protons and very carefully place one proton in the middle of the table, which causes all of the cards to move away from the center and away from each other. But then we hook the cards that communicate with each other together with rubber bands. In fact, we have three strengths of rubber bands, representing the different strengths of communication. These strengths show up as lines of different thicknesses. We have noticed that the more rubber bands that a card gets, the darker it is shaded.

Finally, we step back, let the cards settle down, and view the resulting patterns. As you can imagine, cards that communicate strongly with each other clump together. Some cards are left pretty much alone, whereas the cards with the most overall communication end up in the middle. In the sociodiagram shown in Figure 2.2, for example, you can see that a role called "SPM" is central to the entire organization. On the other hand, the factory role is largely isolated from the rest of the organization.

With practice, we were able to learn many things about an organization, literally at a glance. These diagrams led to other patterns. Figure 2.2 is representative of the HUB SPOKE AND RIM (5.1.17) pattern.

The second diagram we use is called an *interaction grid.* Figure 2.3 shows a simple interaction grid for the same organization depicted in the Figure 2.2.

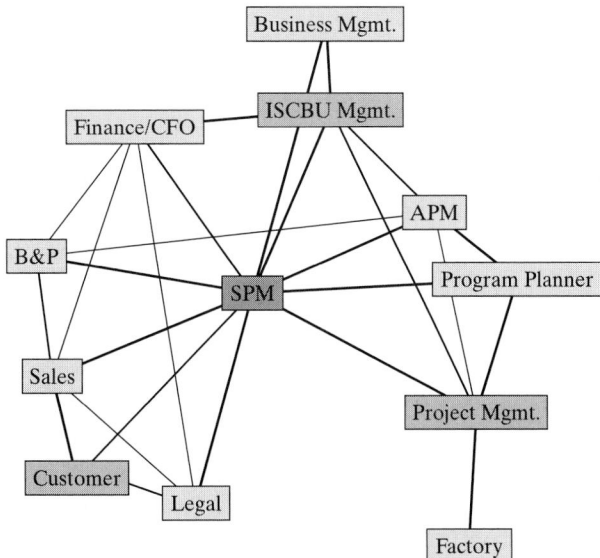

FIGURE 2.2 Sociodiagram

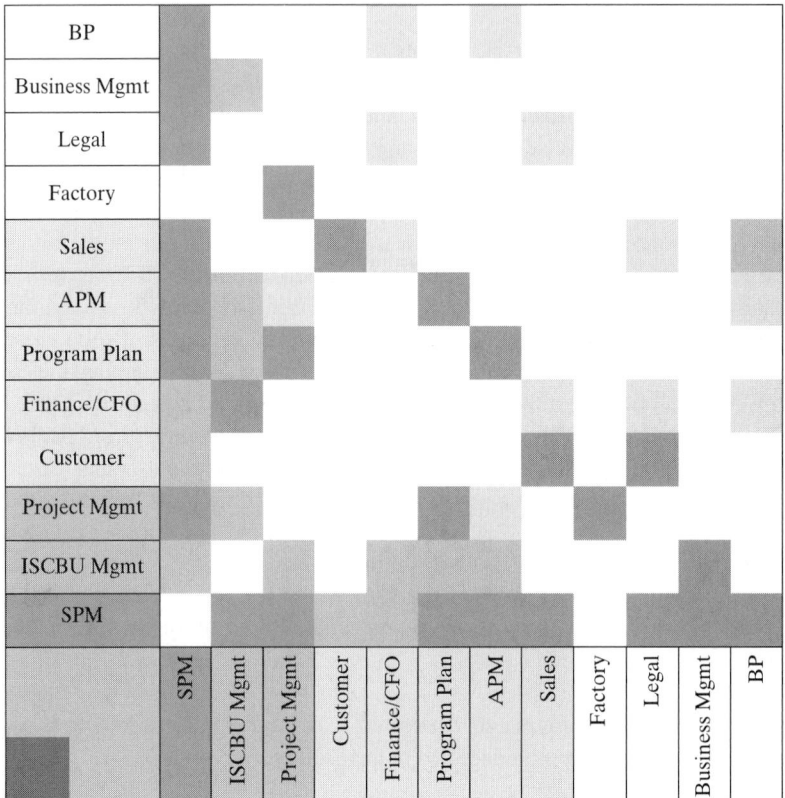

FIGURE 2.3 Interaction Grid

This diagram shows both communication and direction—which roles initiate communication to other roles. The roles shown along the bottom of the grid (the *x* axis) initiate communication with the (same set of) roles along the left side of the grid (the *y* axis). The shading represents the intensity of the communication, just as in the sociogram.

These visualizations have their roots in social network theory. For those of you who are interested, we explore the origins of this theory and the tools used to create the pictures in SOCIAL NETWORK THEORY FOUNDATIONS (7.5.2).

2.2 Creating Sequences

2.2.1   Why Sequences Are Important

The pattern languages themselves in this book are static. Organizations are always changing, and the way they change isn't always predictable. So where do the dynamics come from?

The dynamics come from the application of the patterns and from the order in which one applies them. What is the right order, then? One might speculate that one follows the structural relationships between the patterns [as in the sections PROJECT MANAGEMENT PATTERN LANGUAGE (4.1), PIECEMEAL GROWTH PATTERN LANGUAGE (4.2), ORGANIZATIONAL STYLE PATTERN LANGUAGE (5.1), and

PEOPLE AND CODE PATTERN LANGUAGE (5.2), where the relationships are shown graphically]. But it doesn't always work that way.

Alexander believes that order in any system fundamentally depends on the process used to build the system, which is why the fundamental process is important [see PIECEMEAL GROWTH (6.2)]. It is important that each step preserves structure and gradually adds local symmetries and that the organization unfolds over time. The process thus involves step-by-step adaptation with feedback. Simply following the pattern language doesn't give you a clue about how to handle the feedback. So that's why the fundamental process exists: to give complete freedom to the design process to attack the weakest part of the system, wherever it may be.

However, the fundamental process cannot work on a human scale without some kind of cognitive guide that is built on experience and that can foresee some of the centers that must be built. That's what patterns are: essential centers.

If unfolding is important, how do you know in what order to unfold things? The sequence is crucial. You want a smooth unfolding that preserves the structure and that doesn't feel like "organizational design."

So, a sequence does the following:

- Preserves structure.
- Keeps you doing one thing at a time.
- Takes the whole organization into account at each step.
- Allows itself to be repeated tens of thousands of times.

Sequences take you into unpredictability and into circumstances you handle with feedback, always in the context of the whole organization. Sequences are where generativity comes from.

2.2.2   **Our Sequences**

We have created sequences for each pattern language here. Each of these sequences is one of millions of sequences one could hypothesize for each pattern language; in other words, there are many meaningful paths through each pattern language graph.

Sequences unfold as stories, and so that's how we present them. These stories are sanity checks on the set of patterns they refer to. If these patterns really do belong together, then we should be able to come up with a story that flows through the patterns. (And note that this is not necessarily a temporal flow through the patterns.) The story may point out patterns that don't quite fit where they are or that don't fit well in the group at all. We might also use the story in the book as an illustration of how the patterns work together. Look at these sequences in the book:

- A STORY ABOUT PROJECT MANAGEMENT [in PROJECT MANAGEMENT PATTERN LANGUAGE (4.1)]
- A STORY ABOUT PIECEMEAL GROWTH [in PIECEMEAL GROWTH PATTERN LANGUAGE (4.2)]
- A STORY ABOUT ORGANIZATIONAL STYLE [in ORGANIZATIONAL STYLE PATTERN LANGUAGE (5.1)]
- A STORY ABOUT PEOPLE AND CODE [in PEOPLE AND CODE PATTERN LANGUAGE (5.2)]

These sequences are real. They come from our experience, and we thought they typified the rich ways in which patterns build on each other, as well as the way in which the language can become alive.

Of course, each of the case studies could also have a sequence written for it. Each sequence selects patterns that themselves form a small language. That language describes the culture of the organization.

2.3 History and Related Work

The bulk of the organizational patterns in this book draws on the Pasteur research project at Bell Laboratories. The earliest work on that project sought alternatives to ISO 9000 series approaches as a means to baselining organizational quality. That work dates back to about 1991, and the first paper published from that work was [Cain Coplien 1993]. The key idea of using roles dates back to that work.

That first research program started using patterns to capture organizational structures in late 1993. This body of patterns grew, and the first draft of those patterns was presented for review at the first conference on Pattern Languages of Programs (PLoP) in 1994. The organizational pattern language that was eventually published in the first book in the Pattern Languages of Program Design (PLoPD) series [Coplien 1995] was one of the first pattern languages in software. That pattern language dealt with recurring structures—configurations of roles—in software development organizations as a reaction against the predominate organizational literature of the era that was based on development process, ISO 9000 series standards, and the Capability Maturity Model (CMM).

A contemporary language that dealt closely with process and organizational issues was Bruce Whitenack's RAPPeL pattern language [Whitenack 1995]. RAPPeL focused largely on the requirements process in order to, as Whitenack notes, "build systems that do the right things." His view of prototyping contributed heavily to the BUILD PROTOTYPES (4.1.7) pattern in this book. It is perhaps regrettable that few of his other patterns appear here, but we decided they make a good pattern collection in their own right, with loose enough coupling to other organizational issues that it would be best to keep the two collections separate.

Another contemporary pattern language was Norm Kerth's "Caterpillar's Fate" [Kerth 1995], which also appeared at the first pattern conference and is published in the first PLoPD book. It looks at the transition from analysis to design, and there are many good organizational insights in his patterns, the result of years of consulting and experience. Like RAPPeL, the patterns look at organizational structure as a secondary concern, so we elected not to incorporate them into the patterns here.

Since then, several other efforts have come on the scene and have matured over the years. Steve Berczuk wrote patterns about developing software with distributed teams that are strongly technical, but that have interesting organizational overtones [Berczuk 1996]. Some of these ideas have evolved into the excellent book by Berczuk and his co-author, Brad Appleton [Berczuk Appleton 2002].

Another follow-on was Ward Cunningham's *Episodes* pattern language. *Episodes* reflected long-standing experience in the Smalltalk community on small projects that extended all the way back to Ward's experience at Wyatt Software. His work included patterns such as PROGRAMMING EPISODE (4.1.19) and its subtending patterns, and provided much of the foundational material for Extreme Programming (XP). *Episodes* was first published in the PLoPD-2 book [Cunningham 1996].

Other follow-on work in this vein came from Alistair Cockburn in 1998 and showed up in his book *Surviving Object-Oriented Projects: A Manager's Guide* [Cockburn 1998]. His patterns include DAY CARE (4.1.23), SACRIFICE ONE PERSON (4.1.22), and many other practical project management patterns.

Joseph Morabi and colleagues studied the design of organizations [Morabito Sack Bhate 1999] and their work provides insights that complement the work here.

Scott Ambler wrote some patterns of developing software from the process perspective [Ambler 1999]. Though they are written in pattern form, these ideas neither form a pattern language nor are grounded in an articulated research program.

You can find more research foundations and related work in ANTHROPOLOGICAL FOUNDATIONS (CHAPTER 7), and particularly in PATLETS FROM OTHER PATTERN LANGUAGES (10.5).

CHAPTER 3

How to Use This Book

How should you use this book? Just read the patterns and apply them in your organization! But of course, it isn't that easy. In fact, it isn't easy at all. But right now, the big question for you is how to get started. Here is what we recommend.

3.1 Reading the Patterns

First, read the patterns. We have attempted to put them in the logical order of a typical sequence through each of the languages. So begin by reading them in order.

3.1.1 The Form

We use Alexandrian form, a stylized format for organizing the important components of a pattern. The body of each pattern starts with a statement of the context in which that pattern applies. A problem may arise in that context; accordingly, the problem description comes next in the pattern. Then, the pattern elaborates the problem with a description of the forces that define the problem. Last, the pattern presents a solution that we have validated across a spectrum of development organizations, followed by a rationale that describes why the pattern should be successful.

3.1.2 Understanding the Models Behind the Patterns

In How the Patterns Came to Us (Chapter 2), we gave a detailed description of the methodology and research technique behind the patterns. We told you that the chapter was optional reading. Nevertheless, it's important to go into the rest of the book with some level of understanding of the source of the patterns, so we will give you a summary here.

All of these patterns came out of empirical research. Most of the patterns were distilled from observations gleaned from organizational analysis exercises we conducted on dozens of

organizations worldwide. These exercises were used to build organizational models. The *role* is
the basic building block of these models. Every organization has roles, such as developer, manager, systems engineer, tester, and many more. Roles get their work done by interacting with
other roles, and an organization owes much of its success to how effectively roles can exchange
information and work together. Each model attempts to capture these interactions between roles.

We gathered the data for the models in role-playing exercises where each participant
tracked the interactions between their role and other roles in the model as the role-play pro-
gressed. We used CRC cards—a technique borrowed from object-oriented design—as the tool
for capturing these interactions.

These data were fed into a tool to visualize the interaction structure of a given organization. We discovered many of these patterns by looking at diagrams of the communication structures between roles or individuals in the organizations. It was easy for us to notice important
features and anomalies in these pictures, and it will be easy for you to do so as well.

For example, consider the organizational model shown in Figure 3.1 (called a *sociogram*)
that we cite frequently in this book. The roles near the center are more closely coupled to the
organization as a whole than are those nearer the outer edge. Further, roles that are near each
other are more closely coupled to each other than they are to more distant roles. Finally, roles
with more coloring are more closely coupled to other roles than are roles with less coloring.

We can see many patterns in this picture. We can see that the roles in this organization Dis-
TRIBUTE WORK EVENLY (5.1.13), since the amount of work—reflected by the shading of the roles—
is spread around rather than being centralized in a handful of roles. We can see that the
ARCHITECT CONTROLS PRODUCT (5.2.3), being central to the organization. We can validate that
the ARCHITECT ALSO IMPLEMENTS (5.2.10) because of the proximity to the Coder role. Of course,

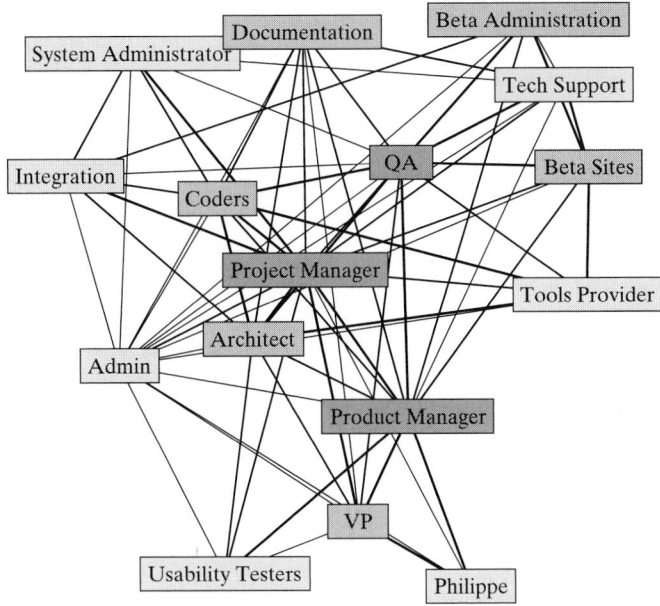

FIGURE 3.1 Organizational Model I (Sociogram)

when we wrote the patterns, we had additional information that led us to these conclusions, information that came from the organization's process sequences. However, these diagrams serve to substantiate and illustrate those observations.

(Don't worry that you don't yet understand these patterns; we'll get to them later on.)

The Sociogram is just one kind of visual model that we can build. Figure 3.2 shows another model of the same organization. The axes of the interaction grid span the roles in the organization, which are ordered according to their coupling to the organization as a whole. If a role at ordinate position p initiates an interaction with a role at coordinate position q, we put a point at position (p, q). The point is shaded according to the strength of the interaction. In the preceding model, we can see that there is a dense network of communication between roles. There aren't very many large "holes" in the communication structure of the organization. Compare the grid of Figure 3.2 with the grid shown in Figure 3.3.

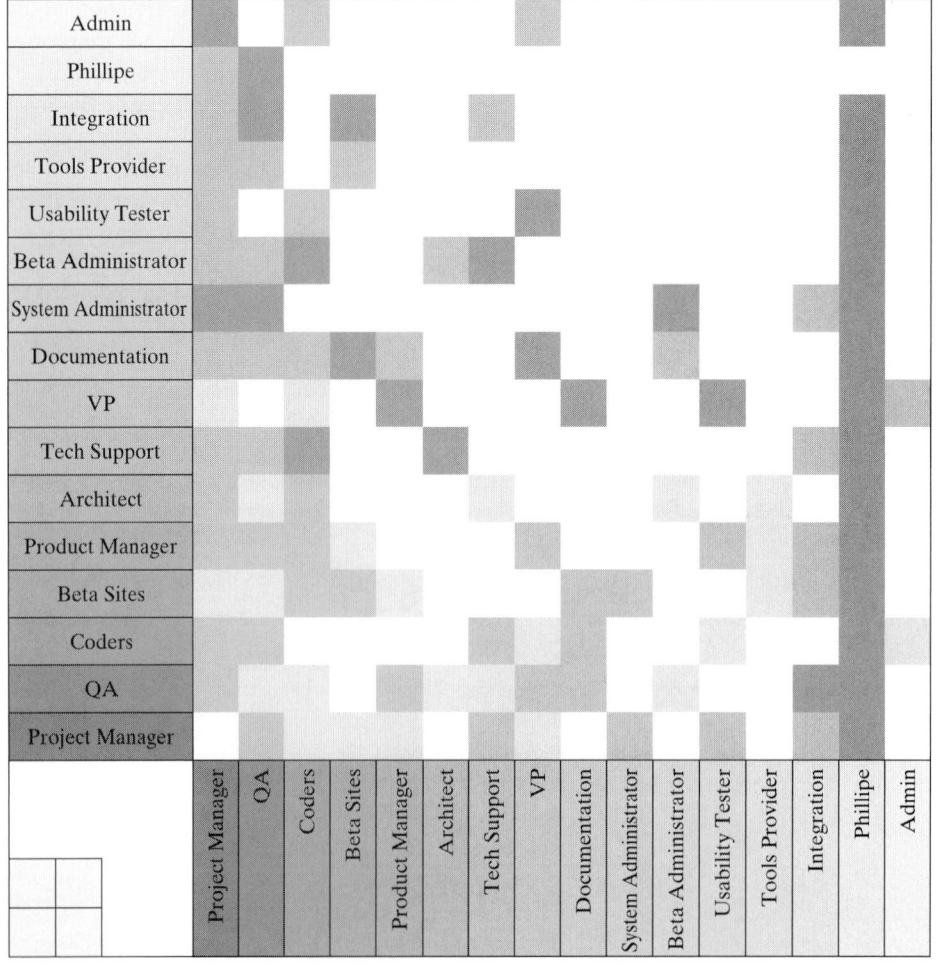

FIGURE 3.2 Organizational Model 2 (Interaction Grid)

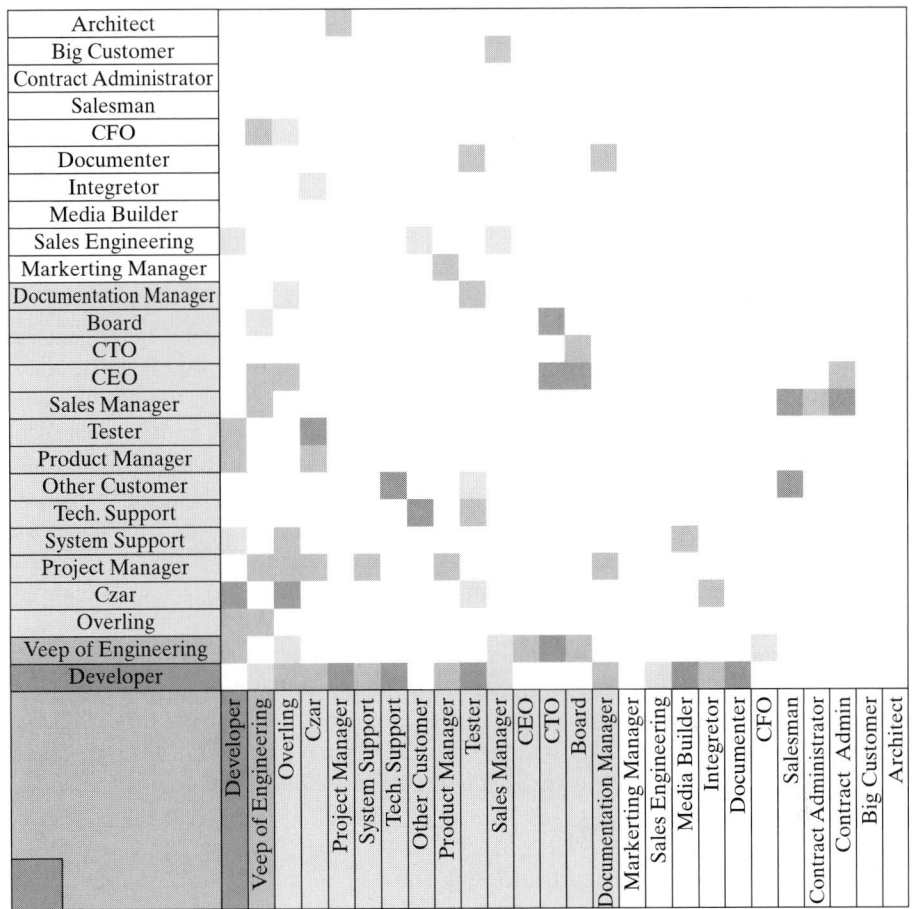

FIGURE 3.3 Organizational Model 3 (Another Interaction Grid)

This picture tells a tale of a much different management style, one where a few core managers initiate interactions across the rest of the organization. Barring those management-initiated interactions, there just isn't much interaction between roles.

Many of the patterns in this book use these pictures as aids to understanding the context and forces described in the patterns. We describe the diagrams in more detail in SOCIAL NETWORK THEORY FOUNDATIONS (7.5.2), and we recommend that you take a quick look at that section before exploring the patterns in depth. For more on our research techniques, you can read HOW THE PATTERNS CAME TO US (CHAPTER 2).

3.1.3   Stories and Pictures in the Patterns

Many of these patterns are derived from stories we have picked up throughout our travels—stories of real problems in real organizations and of the real solutions those organizations applied. Many of our patterns start with what we believe to be a particularly poignant or appropriate selection from among such stories.

Each pattern starts with a picture. The pictures are sometimes fun, sometimes somber, and sometimes thought provoking. Each one strives to underscore the human dimension of the pattern and to serve as a tool to help make the pattern memorable.

3.1.4   Finding Your Way

You will soon see that patterns point to other patterns, though not necessarily in the sequence presented, which one would expect since there are many paths through a language. So you may find it more useful to read the patterns in a different order than that in which we present them. Feel free to do so.

Each pattern is designed to be understandable and applicable in isolation, even though each pattern gains much of its power by reinforcing the patterns around it in the pattern language. When you read the patterns, focus on understanding each one individually, and don't worry unduly about the sequence. Allow yourself to get lost, to explore, to play. Of course, if you're a more linear thinker, you may want to follow a specific sequence to order your thoughts. In short, do what is comfortable for you. There are many paths to understanding these patterns.

If you need to get a quick overview of a pattern, just read the bold text, which provides the pattern name and describes both the problem it solves and the solution. For convenience, a quick reference summary of the patterns, called *patlets,* is located at the end of the book. In the patlets, the problem and solution are distilled into a single sentence. Therefore, they are best used as a reference, as a reminder of what each pattern is about.

Whatever order you read the patterns in, you will find some patterns that seem particularly relevant to your organization. Some will jump out at you, and you will say to yourself, "Now here's a pattern that our organization can really use." So mark these patterns with a little yellow sticky note. One or more of these patterns will probably become your organization's entry into the pattern language. Of course, the patterns you mark must be not only helpful, but also feasible in your situation.

3.2 Applying the Patterns

Now for the hard part: getting the organization to actually use any of the patterns. Changing the culture of an organization is tricky, difficult, sometimes painful, and sometimes even dangerous. We cover this topic in more detail in ORGANIZATIONAL PRINCIPLES (CHAPTER 6), and it is important to read that chapter before actually trying out any of these patterns in your organization. PIECE-MEAL GROWTH (6.2) gives particularly important advice that can be boiled down to the following: *apply one pattern at a time, and if it doesn't feel right, back out.* Until you read ORGANIZATIONAL PRINCIPLES, here are some tips to get started.

3.2.1   Sequences

You should apply the patterns in a *sequence*. Though you can *understand* the patterns individually in almost any sequence, they gain much of their power by building on each other in the right order. Each particular organization is built from a sequence of patterns whose order is suggested by the succession of unbalanced forces each pattern leaves for the ensuing one. At the beginning of each pattern language chapter, we offer some example sequences.

For more on sequences, see CREATING SEQUENCES (2.2).

3.2.2 Which Patterns?

There is no prize for using the most patterns. Using the sequences as a guide, choose the patterns that solve problems that you actually have. Do you feel the pattern's forces in your organization? If so, then the pattern is worth considering. Otherwise, don't oblige yourself to use the pattern. *There is nothing intrinsically good about any pattern in isolation; instead, each one is good only to the extent that it resolves the forces that actually exist in your organization.* Pay specific attention to the patterns you have marked with yellow sticky notes. Remember: patterns don't tell you what to do; instead, they help you discover what you knew how to do all along.

3.2.3 Human Concerns

Organizations comprise people, so it should be no surprise that you will need to deal with "people issues" as you unfold a pattern language in an organization. Let common sense and sensitivity be your guides. Here are a few tips to guide you.

First, remember that nearly every organization has some awareness of its own failings. People may not be able to put their finger on a particular problem, but they know when they have troubles. However, we tend to be our own worst critics, and we usually think that things are worse than they are. So recognize this tendency toward self-awareness and self-criticism. You may wish to begin with patterns that the organization already does well and then introduce the patterns the organization can easily adopt.

Language and conversation are keys to successful change. In other words, people need to learn what the patterns are and then begin to use the names of the patterns in their conversations. So teach people about the patterns you have selected. Naturally, we think it would be grand if everyone in the organization had their own copy of this book to refer to!

Finally, recognize that no matter who your are, *you* can't change the organization. People must change themselves. So enlist allies. Make sure you read the following patterns: GATEKEEPER (4.2.10), PATRON ROLE (4.2.15), PUBLIC CHARACTER (4.2.17), LEGEND ROLE (4.2.20), and WISE FOOL (4.2.21). These patterns describe some of the key movers and shakers in an organization. Identify them in your organization and approach them first. Once they get excited about these patterns, it is likely the rest of the organization will come along. By the way, which of these patterns fit *you*?

3.3 Updating the Patterns

We certainly didn't foresee all possible details of organizational structure in this book! Your business almost certainly has detailed needs that beg for new patterns or for different versions of the patterns here. Make the patterns your own. That's OK, we won't mind—really! Until you make a subset of these patterns your own, you won't really be in control of your organization. Take control by letting your instinct guide you in tailoring these patterns.

By the way, we are interested in your updates, if you care to share them with us. Your experiences expand, correct, or substantiate these patterns. In a very real sense, these patterns do not belong to us, but to the software development community as a whole. So write us—we would love to hear from you!

3.4 Who Should Use This Book?

Let us say a few words about the intended audience for this book. What kind of organization can use these patterns? Who should be responsible for applying the patterns in these organizations?

These patterns come from studies of a wide range of organizations, most of which are software development organizations. These organizations ranged from small individual companies of a couple dozen people to organizations embedded in companies with hundreds of thousands of employees. In turn, we have used these patterns in improvement efforts in a similar range of organizations. While a few of the patterns may be more suitable to teams of a particular size, almost all of them are generic.

While the patterns often exhibit ties to software development, they apply to other kinds of organizations as well. Project managers, testers, marketing people, secretaries and clerks, business planners, and a host of other roles figure as strongly or more strongly than the designer and coder in software development. There is something in this book for every member of a software enterprise. And many of the patterns generalize into other businesses, so long as the patterns are applied with insight and discretion.

Many of the patterns require some authority to implement, so first- or second-level managers are a natural audience for this book. But the funny thing is that we predict that many of the people who read this book will not be managers, but developers. So we think there is a good chance that you, dear reader, are a developer. But not just any developer. You probably feel an extra concern for the function of your organization. In fact, you are probably a key person, one of the roles we mentioned above: GATEKEEPER, PATRON ROLE, PUBLIC CHARACTER, LEGEND ROLE, or WISE FOOL. You may have more influence on your organization than you think you do.

So what is a GATEKEEPER or a WISE FOOL? We've talked enough about the patterns. Now it's time to learn about the patterns themselves.

PART II

The Pattern Languages

Finally, the patterns themselves! Thank you for patiently reading the introductory material, for it will help you use the patterns.

We have divided the patterns into four interrelated pattern languages:

1. Project Management: the organizational aspects of managing projects.
2. Piecemeal Growth of the Organization: the ways in which an organization grows and develops over time.
3. Organizational Style: the general approach to the way the organization works.
4. People and Code: the ways in which people affect code—and the ways in which the design of code affects people!

Each pattern language presents patterns in a sequence that allows the patterns to build on each other. Sometimes a pattern recurs in multiple pattern languages, but we present the pattern only in the pattern language with which it is most strongly connected, and we include a reference to that appearance in other appearances of the pattern. In practice, you will use all four of these pattern languages together, weaving patterns together to solve problems and to strengthen your organization one pattern at a time.

The first two pattern languages are design pattern languages; the second two are construction pattern languages. Chapters 4 and 5 are dedicated to these two kinds of patterns, respectively. Alexander makes the same distinction in his pattern language, separating the act of design from the engineering considerations of construction.

Design patterns are those that lay the foundation of the entity to be built—buildings and towns for Alexander, and software development organizations for us.

Construction patterns deal with the nuts and bolts of creating the thing. Organizations need to be built just as surely as buildings need to be built.

The appendix Summary Patlets (Appendix A) presents summaries of all of the patterns in *patlet* form. A patlet is a terse summary of a pattern's problem and solution. You may find this reference useful as you set about putting the patterns into practice.

CHAPTER 4

Organization Design Patterns

The term *design patterns* has unfortunately come to mean the collection of 23 patterns that appears in the book *Design Patterns: Elements of Reusable Object-Oriented Software* by Erich Gamma, Richard Helm, Ralph Johnson, and John Vlissides [Gamma 1995]. Here, we use the term in the same sense Alexander does in his classic text *A Pattern Language* [Alexander 1977]. In Alexander's sense, a design pattern is something you use to understand the geometry of a building and to understand the major relationships between parts. It is a definition that most of us recognize as applying to the word *architecture* in software.

Once you design an organization, the organization comes to life through organizational *construction patterns.* Construction patterns discuss the materials and processes used to put the conceptual design into practice.

The distinction between these two kinds of patterns isn't as clear in organizational design as it is in the design of buildings, and even there the difference isn't formal or clean. We separated the two kinds of patterns based less on their characterization as "design" or "construction" patterns than according to their affinity for each other. The so-called "construction patterns" can be found in the chapter ORGANIZATION CONSTRUCTION PATTERNS (CHAPTER 5).

4.1 Project Management Pattern Language

Project Management is a crucial part of organizational design. Many organizations have a project manager role, but in fact project management is a much broader function—so broad that it covers almost a quarter of the patterns in this book.

The patterns here do concern themselves with all of the things a project manager worries about. We start out with COMMUNITY OF TRUST (4.1.1), followed by SIZE THE SCHEDULE (4.1.2). In today's markets, time to market is everything. In the classic view of project management, which suggests that there are three resources one can trade off against each other—

staff, functionality, and schedule—schedule is most often the strongest invariant. Past years have seen functionality fall from this first-place position as software development enterprises have come to realize the difficulty in both capturing and meeting detailed a priori requirements. Customers have come to the realization that it's better to get *something* that works in a finite amount of time than to spend a seeming eternity getting it right the first time. Instead, we tend to defer correctness to later releases.

The Pattern Language

Figure 4.1 depicts the patterns in the pattern language and the connections between them. The connections are as much a part of the language as the patterns themselves. Each pattern provides a possible context for any patterns that appear below it. The figure depicts the dependencies between the patterns that govern the order in which they are to be applied. You start at the top

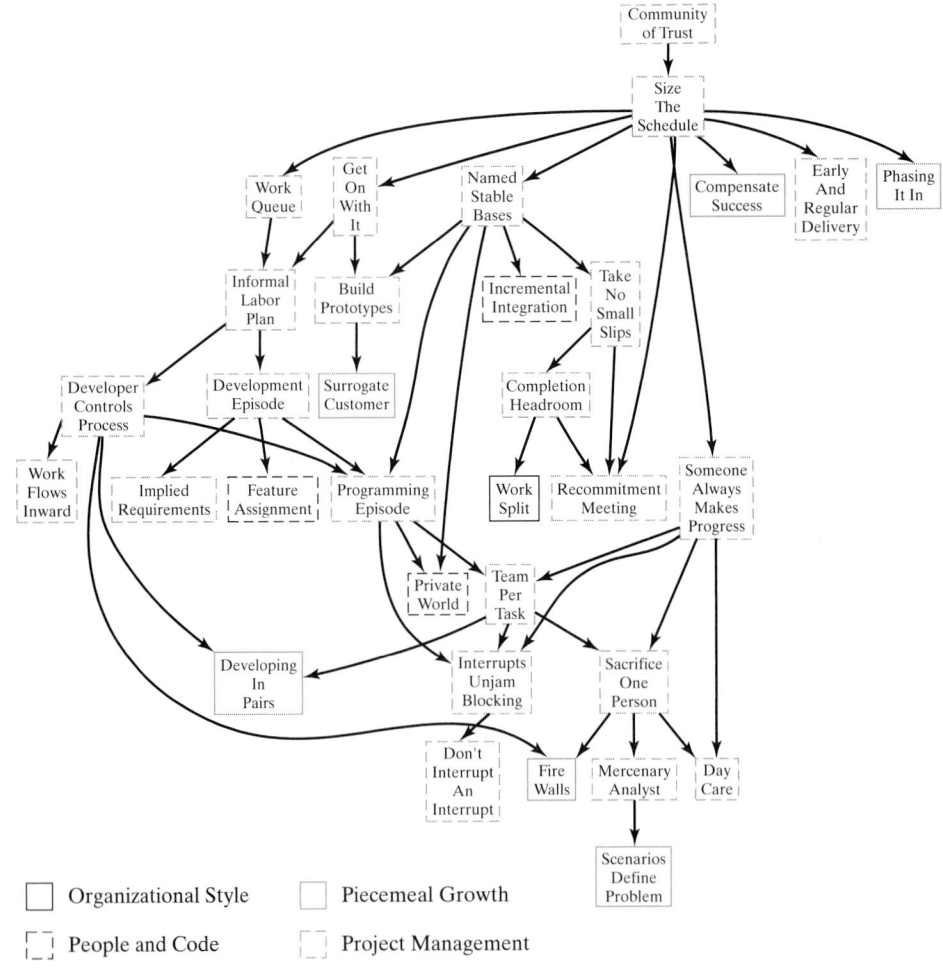

FIGURE 4.1 Patterns and Connections

and work your way toward the bottom. If a pattern has several subtending patterns, you can apply as few or as many of them as you like, and in any order.

The pattern language is based on empirical study of organizations that develop software, most of which deliver some software artifact to a customer. However, the pattern language has little to do with software per se. We believe these patterns reflect management principles that are deeper and broader than principles applied to software alone. Software development organizations can learn from these broader principles.

Here is a real story about a real project that features many of the patterns in this pattern language. Think of this story as a sequence of application of the patterns.

A Story about Project Management

In the mid 1980s, my group embarked on an ambitious project. We took a successful product and adapted it to new technology. We began by testing the concepts in prototypes [BUILD PROTOTYPES (4.1.7)], and their success gave us the confidence to SIZE THE SCHEDULE (4.1.2).

Because we were building on an existing product, it was easy to have NAMED STABLE BASES (4.1.4) of code, and we continued them throughout the project. These stable bases made it possible—and necessary—to provide developers with a way to have their own view of the system, a PRIVATE WORLD (4.1.6). There was ample tool support for these views.

Although the project was large, the project was basically centered on the developers. For example, we decided on our own coding standards [DEVELOPER CONTROLS PROCESS (4.1.17)], which certainly had a feel of WORK FLOWS INWARD (4.1.18). Developers had some latitude about how to organize their work, and WORK QUEUE (4.1.13), INFORMAL LABOR PLAN (4.1.14), and PROGRAMMING EPISODES (4.1.19) were common.

Unfortunately, we had problems. One of the biggest was that we did not allow COMPLETION HEADROOM (4.1.10). As the technical difficulties intensified, the schedule became tighter. Finally, the head of the project called everyone together, announced a single large schedule slip [TAKE NO SMALL SLIPS (4.1.9)], and asked everyone to commit to the new schedule [RECOMMITMENT MEETING (4.1.12)].

We continued to struggle with technical challenges, some of which became crises. We created teams to deal with these crises [TEAM PER TASK (4.1.21)], and even had to SACRIFICE ONE PERSON (4.1.22) on at least one occasion. However, no crisis stopped everyone [SOMEONE ALWAYS MAKES PROGRESS (4.1.20)], in part because the architecture of the system allowed some progress to be made regardless of the struggles we encountered.

In the end, we met the slipped date. But the technology was moving in such a direction that it made no sense to deploy it. However, pieces of that project were used in later projects for years to come.

4.1.1   Community of Trust **

In high school, I went to music camp one year. During one orchestra rehearsal, my section was struggling with a particularly difficult passage. The conductor asked about it, and I said, "Don't worry. We will have it tomorrow." He said, "OK," and continued with the rehearsal. By the next day, we had indeed learned the passage.

... once an organization has been established, interpersonal relationships have a significant positive or negative impact on the effectiveness of the team.

It is essential that the people in a team trust each other; otherwise, it will be difficult to get anything done.

Communication is essential to the smooth working of any team. For example, software developers must constantly talk to each other to coordinate interfaces, builds, and tests. If individuals do not trust each other, communication will not be smooth.

If people do not trust each other, they will spend time in defensive mode. For example, if I don't believe you will provide me with a certain interface on time, I might go to great lengths to code around it, thus costing extra work and time.

Design reviews can foment distrust. All too often, design reviews become contests among the reviewers to show who is the most clever and thus do not provide helpful suggestions to the designer. One alternative is for people to put on their best social behavior in reviews; however, such behavior can dampen the energetic discussions that lead to the best insights in group discussions.

The organization might have policies that seem distrustful. For example, one may have to jump through hoops to be allowed to submit code to the project base.

The perception of trust or mistrust becomes the reality, regardless of the intention.

Therefore:

Do things that explicitly demonstrate trust. Managers, for example, should make it overtly obvious that they facilitate the achievement of organizational goals, rather than playing a central role to assert control over people. Take visible actions to give developers control over the process.

The key here is that the actions must be visible and obvious, particularly if these actions involve the removal of onerous rules and processes. Shortly before I went to work at a certain company, for example, the company dispensed with time clocks for research and development personnel. My co-workers spoke fondly of the time clock smashing ceremony they had.

This pattern is different than the oft-cited "empowerment" strategy. Empowerment is a conscious abdication of control to lower levels [see THE OPEN/CLOSED PRINCIPLE OF TEAMS (6.1.4)]. In a COMMUNITY OF TRUST, progress is more often made by bilateral agreement than by unilateral directions. If people feel they have a voice and have influence over decisions, they are more likely to trust those who make the decisions. By the same token, they are likely to be more responsive in carrying out responsibilities they have committed to themselves than in carrying out responsibilities that have been assigned to them. In fact, you can't give someone responsibility; you can only hold someone accountable. Responsibility is taken, not given. One of the most demoralizing things a manager can do is to give accountability in the absence of resources to responsibly carry out the task.

Trust must be built between the customer and all team members in order to lay out project plans that extend from SIZE THE SCHEDULE (4.1.2) in the PROJECT MANAGEMENT PATTERN LANGUAGE (4.1). The same is true for role differentiation. Encouraging a sense of pride and individuality in every team member can contribute to trust, as in SIZE THE ORGANIZATION (4.2.2) and its subtending patterns in the PIECEMEAL GROWTH PATTERN LANGUAGE (4.2). Build trust by starting small with FEW ROLES (5.1.2), and let this principle guide the ORGANIZATIONAL STYLE PATTERN LANGUAGE (5.1). To keep people from working defensively, one needs a team spirit, which is true of ARCHITECT CONTROLS PRODUCT (5.2.3) and subtending patterns relating to the PEOPLE AND CODE PATTERN LANGUAGE (5.2).

COMMUNITY OF TRUST provides a foundation for many other patterns, such as UNITY OF PURPOSE (4.2.12), PATRON ROLE (4.2.15), FIREWALLS (4.2.9), DEVELOPER CONTROLS PROCESS (4.1.17), RESPONSIBILITIES ENGAGE (5.1.14), and more.

So why is COMMUNITY OF TRUST a separate pattern? It has a specific structural impact: it is about nurturing communication paths, and it also has some positional impact (in particular, it encourages manager roles to shift away from the center). Second, the visible nature of the actions is important, and we haven't captured this visibility in any of the other patterns.

Trust is contagious, and it spreads most effectively through an organization from the top down.

4.1.2   Size the Schedule **

Software engineers determining the next schedule.

... the product is understood and the project size has been estimated.

Both overly ambitious schedules and overly generous schedules have their pains, either for the developers or the customers.

If you make a schedule too generous, developers become complacent, and you miss market windows. But if a schedule is too ambitious, developers become burned out, and you also miss market windows. And if the schedule is too ambitious, product quality suffers, and compromised architectural principles establish a poor foundation for future maintenance.

Conventional wisdom says that you can trade off staff, schedule, and functionality. While principles such as Brooks' "adding people to a late project makes it later" [Brooks 1995] cast doubt on the place of staff in this equation, it's clear that schedule and functionality trade off against each other. Ward Cunningham says in his pattern COMPARABLE WORK, "Every project must commit to delivery on a few hard and fast dates. This is actually fortunate because it is about the only way to get out of work that is going poorly" [Cunningham 1996]. In a reasonable business climate, it is much smarter to hold the schedule constant and to negotiate functionality than it is to extend the schedule. The customer believes you can cut functionality, but a promise of having the yet unattained functionality at some future date leaves the customer much less comfortable. And projects without schedule motivation tend to go on forever or to spend too much time polishing details that are either irrelevant or that don't serve customer needs.

Therefore:

Reward developers for negotiating a schedule they prove they can meet with financial bonuses [or at-risk compensation; see COMPENSATE SUCCESS (4.2.25)] or with extra time off. Keep two sets of schedules: one for the market, and one for the developers.

The external schedule is negotiated with the customer, whereas the internal schedule is negotiated with development staff. The internal schedule should be shorter than the external schedule by 2 or 3 weeks for a moderate project (this figure comes from a senior staff member at a well-known software consulting firm). If the two schedules can't be reconciled, customer needs or the organization's resources—or the schedule itself—must be renegotiated [RECOMMITMENT MEETING (4.1.12)].

Help delineate the schedule with NAMED STABLE BASES (4.1.4). Grow the schedule as needed with PHASING IT IN (4.2.3). Define initial targets with WORK QUEUE (4.1.13). Make sure SOMEONE ALWAYS MAKES PROGRESS (4.1.20).

The forces come from the Massachusetts Institute of Technology (MIT) project management simulation and from studies of projects such as Borland Quattro Pro for Windows. Another manager suggested that the skew between the internal and external schedules be closer to 2 months than 2 weeks because slippage usually reflects a major oversight that costs 2 or 3 months.

De Marco talks about rewarding people for accuracy of schedules (see [DeMarco Boehm 1986]). Also, read about the place of promptness in [Zuckerman Hatala 1992].

You don't need a full schedule—or perhaps any schedule at all—to get started. See GET ON WITH IT (4.1.3) and BUILD PROTOTYPES (4.1.7).

4.1.3   Get On with It **
Alias: PARTIAL EVALUATION

Get ready ...

Go!!!!!

> During one study, I asked the organization to describe how they develop software. "Well," they said, "project management gives us a list of features they want estimates for. So we start working on the features we think are the most important. Over time, they ask for more detailed estimates, and the features we are working on have smaller estimates because they are underway. Those features generally make the cut. By the time we get official approval to begin development, we are nearly finished."

... you have a good idea of a market need and, furthermore, a good idea of how to get started on parts of the project. You're eager to get started, but you want to proceed deliberately and by the path that will be both expedient and productive.

You can't wait until you have every last requirement to get started.

Team members are sitting idle because their upstream tasks have not been completed. On the one hand, you want requirements to be developed carefully. On the other hand, you have some information, and some people are sitting idle.

Therefore:

As soon as you have some confidence about project direction, start developing areas in which you have high confidence. These areas may involve hardware development (or procurement), algorithm development, database schema development, etc. Let each subgroup work according to an INFORMAL LABOR PLAN (4.1.14) as if the group were in full-swing development.

Note that "high confidence" refers to project direction and requirements, not to technology. It's perfectly all right, and in fact desirable, to work on the technologically risky areas first [see BUILD PROTOTYPES (4.1.7)].

Give yourself some room to retrench later as requirements become more clear.

In many projects, behavioral requirements are one of the last things that designers get right. Many projects ship a first release that meets only basic requirements, with economically more significant requirements being met in subsequent releases. Telecommunications systems often follow this pattern, offering basic communications systems in early releases and more advanced features later. In fact, the impact of behavioral requirements on the overall structure of the system is often overrated. The code that meets behavioral requirements often lives in application code that is added very late to a robust stable base. This base thus reflects deep domain knowledge more than it reflects behavioral requirements. Much common code can be developed early on with high confidence, code that supports common domain functionality that is part of most systems for a given market. This code can often be started or acquired before requirements are firm.

This pattern can increase rework, but it is more in the spirit of piecemeal growth architecture than is a master-planned system that precipitates from complete requirements. It is likely that any false starts will also be educational at the enterprise level. In fact, as a risk-management measure one can consciously decide not to commit to the results of such an activity. On the enterprise level, this pattern becomes the pattern SKUNKWORKS (4.2.14); at the project level, it is BUILD PROTOTYPES (4.1.7).

There are two occasions in which you cannot tolerate that rework. First, if the task is the process bottleneck, it must work at peak efficiency, and rework should be minimized. Very infrequently, the rework will take longer than the original task, and in such cases this pattern should not be used.

Teams need good communication with their upstream colleagues through the use of patterns like RESPONSIBILITIES ENGAGE (5.1.14) and HALLWAY CHATTER (5.1.15).

A process that does not constrain the overall system can afford to be done inefficiently and in parallel with other processes. It is often the case that the analysts, designers, and programmers can get started right away even if they lack finalized requirements. Serializing their work will take longer than doing 10-20 percent rework. One database group we studied constrained the process: They could not afford rework and had to work in the most efficient way possible. Therefore, they did not start official development early, but instead waited until their requirements were stable. The designers/programmers had enough extra time that they could afford to prototype some test databases for themselves, which were thrown away when the database designers did their final design.

See [Goldratt Cox 1986].

EXAMPLE:

Each team had one requirement and analysis person and two to three designers/programmers. Database design was understaffed and constraining the process, so it was made into a special service group and given final requirements only (the counterforce). A first cut at the requirements had been done earlier, so a rough set of requirements was available. The system was pretty much the same throughout.

The designers/programmers quickly got ahead of the requirements people, who were busy in meetings trying to nail down details of the requirements. If they had waited until the requirements were solid, they would not have enough time to do their work. They were able to guess quite closely what the requirements would be, even without knowing final details, so they started design and programming right away. The requirements people gave them course corrections after each meeting. The amount of time it took to incorporate those mid-course alterations was small compared to the total design time.

This pattern comes from Alistair Cockburn's original pattern ALL AT ONCE (A.5.3) [Cockburn 1996], which was later modified and renamed GOLD RUSH [Cockburn 1998]. The alias name "PARTIAL EVALUATION" comes from the inspiration that this pattern is a temporal form of DIVIDE AND CONQUER (5.1.6). GET ON WITH IT (4.1.3) arose when we discovered that the name the pattern bore at that time—JUST DO IT—conflicted with another pattern written by Jeff Garland. Garland suggested the current name.

Shalom Reich writes:

> The "ALL AT ONCE" pattern appears to be a typical Project Management "crash project" approach. In a "crash project" one must be careful to identify true predecessors for each task with the goal of reducing the "critical path." This allows parallel efforts to proceed which will all "come together" at the last possible moment. I have found that project plans often contain *false* linkages between

tasks. For example, in one large project we had a "specification" phase. I was able to break the project into several smaller projects which each had its own specification phase. This allowed me to juggle my limited resources and have coders working on the part that went first through the specification phase at the same time that the analysts were working on the specifications for the second sub-project [Reich 2001].

4.1.4   Named Stable Bases *

A stable base with a name on it ...

... the project schedule has been laid out, and development has started.

❖   ❖   ❖

It is important to integrate software frequently enough so that the base doesn't become stale, but not so frequently that you damage a shared understanding of what functionality is sound and trusted in an evolving software base.

If you try continuous integration, developers struggle to follow a moving target, and there is no shared sense of quanta of functionality at any given time or quanta of progress from week to week. But if it's too long between integrations, developers become blocked from making progress beyond the limits of the last base.

So, while stability is a good thing, the project must always make progress—and, more importantly, the stakeholders must *perceive* that progress is being made.

Therefore:

Stabilize system interfaces—the architecture—about once a week. Give the stable system a name of some kind by which developers can identify their shared understanding of that version's functionality.

The names need not be elaborate; they can, for example, simply be a load number. The names should, however, be easy to remember, easy to identify with the correct version of software, and easy to distinguish from each other. The idea is to provide some sort of handle that people can use to communicate about a stable base.

Other software can be changed (and even integrated) more frequently.

A prototype can be an expedient for one of the NAMED STABLE BASES [see BUILD PROTO-TYPES (4.1.7)].

The project has targets to shoot for and benchmarks whose accomplishments can be trumpeted to customers. These targets and benchmarks affect the Customer view of the process and have strong ramifications for the Architect as well.

The pattern was initially pointed out by Dennis DeBruler at AT&T.

The main point of the pattern is that a project should schedule change introduction so the effects of changes can be anticipated. It is less important to publish the content of a change (which will go unheeded under high change volume) than to ensure that the development community understands that change is taking place. It is important not to violate "the rule of least surprise."

It can be helpful to have, simultaneously, various bases at different levels of stability. For example, one AT&T project had a nightly build (which is guaranteed only to have compiled), a weekly integration test build (which is guaranteed to have passed systemwide sanity tests), and a (roughly) biweekly service test build (which is considered stable enough for quality assurance (QA) system testing).

PROGRAMMING EPISODES (4.1.19) is an example of this pattern in the small.

4.1.5   Incremental Integration **

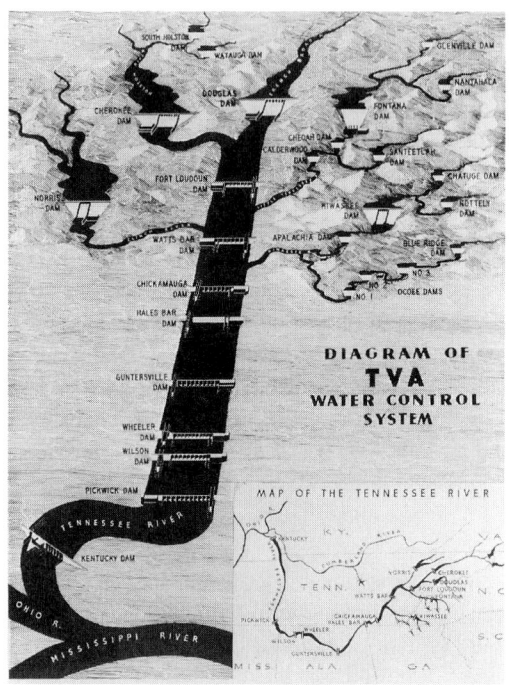

*Contribute to software one piece at a time, gradually, avoiding
waterfalls and other precipitous changes.*

... some organizations have infrequent integrations that reflect large changes, which can
make it difficult for the integration release to work as expected, complicate the process of work
integration, and make NAMED STABLE BASES (4.1.4) difficult to achieve when modules do not
work together. Because we often develop with one OWNER PER DELIVERABLE (A.5.19), there will
be occasional mismatches between development units.

**For iterative development to work well, it is necessary to make sure that components
work together.**

Subsystems are developed at different rates. Developers work in a PRIVATE WORLD (4.1.6).
We need to find a way to make it possible to integrate without surprises.

Therefore:

**Provide a mechanism to allow developers to build all of the current software periodi-
cally. Developers should be discouraged from maintaining long intervals between check-ins.**

Developers should at any time also be able to build against any of the NAMED STABLE BASES (4.1.4) or the newest checked-in software.

❖   ❖   ❖

Assign the task of building the entire software system periodically. NAMED STABLE BASES (4.1.4) suggests intervals that are no more frequent than 1 week. This periodic build should be checked for interface compatibility (does it compile?) and tested (does it still work?).

Encourage developers to build from files that are likely to be in the release in order to anticipate and allow time to correct for incompatibilities. The goal is to avoid a "big bang" integration and to allow the developmental build to proceed smoothly.

This pattern can be combined with PRIVATE WORLD (4.1.6) to ensure that the changes integrate with a copy of the current development system. There are issues relating to the size of the software system (some systems take quite a while to build, making frequent integrations difficult). Address these issues with PRIVATE VERSIONING (5.2.16) to allow the developer some leeway on deciding when to integrate new code into the environment, but do not put the issues off for too long.

EXAMPLE:

The developer's work space could be updated (at the developer's request) to a named stable base from the project repository on approximately a weekly basis. The developer will also retrieve the current files from the repository to anticipate how the current changes in the work space will integrate with files that may later be in the baseline.

This pattern was derived from INCREMENTAL INTEGRATION in [Berczuk Appleton 2002].

4.1.6   Private World **

... an organization is creating NAMED STABLE BASES (4.1.4), and developers can build against these versions, integrating their own code with the latest other code [INCREMENTAL INTEGRATION (4.1.5)].

How can we balance the need for developers to use current revisions, based on periodic baselines, with the desire to prevent developers from experiencing undue grief by having development dependencies change from underneath them?

It is important for developers to work with current versions of software subsystems in order to keep up with the latest enhancements, avoid running into bugs that have already been fixed elsewhere, and avoid getting out of synch with interface changes.

Introducing new software into an environment while debugging may cause grief by introducing new behavior and providing distractions. Because of the time spent resolving integration issues in some cases, code may no longer compile due to interface changes.

However, we must balance the need to keep up to date with the need of developers to maintain a stable environment for feature development/bug fixing.

Some organizations facilitate INCREMENTAL INTEGRATION (4.1.5) by having a shared baseline of code, libraries, etc. Unfortunately, changing a code base, even in a different subsystem, can cause problems when there are interface changes, for example. You want to avoid hearing stories about developers leaving a problem at night in order to view it in the morning with a clear head, only to find that the test environment does not compile in the morning.

Therefore:

Provide a mechanism where developers can maintain a PRIVATE WORLD development environment. In their PRIVATE WORLD, they can control the rate of integration, which allows them to avoid having an integration step interrupt work in progress. The environment should represent a snapshot of all of the software being developed in a system, not just the code the developer is modifying. Try to ensure that the private development area is not used as a means of avoiding integration issues.

❖ ❖ ❖

A starting point for the independent development area would be one of the NAMED STABLE BASES (4.1.4) that have been previously released. Developers then build their software and any related software that depends on their software. Alternatively, you can provide a capability that allows developers to perform a private system build from source code (and other artifacts).

While allowing developers the freedom to decide when to allow changes into their space, you need to make sure that the developers update their code as often as possible to avoid integration surprises. So, encourage developers to integrate their code frequently, perhaps by providing a mechanism for easily backing out of a difficult change.

Depending on the details of implementation, one consequence of using this pattern might be that project disk space requirements may grow quickly, since developers will have their own copies of the source code. But the costs of personnel always exceed the cost of an extra disk. A modification to this approach is that stable and distantly related subsystems can be used by reference, but one should be made aware when changes are imminent. In this case, the configuration management system should provide access to prior NAMED STABLE BASES (4.1.4) as well.

Developers can simply refrain from advancing to a new instance of the NAMED STABLE BASES until the current problem is solved.

A variation of a PRIVATE WORLD is a shared integration machine. In this case, the developers move their new code to a system that has a current version of the system.

The pattern simulates SOLO VIRTUOSO (4.2.5). See also PRIVATE VERSIONING (5.2.16).

EXAMPLE:

A developer is working on a problem. The developer's work space is self-contained with all of the files needed to build the system. The developer's work space is updated after the problem is solved in the context of the current NAMED STABLE BASES and only at the developer's request.

NOTES:

Brad Appleton points out:

> Sun's NSE (Network Software Environment) had this type of thing built into it.
> I think that the more recent TeamWare product may also have preserved some of

these concepts. NSE let you create work spaces that it called "environments." There were three kinds of environments you could create:

- Independent Development Environments: for Independent Development.
- Independent Integration Environments: for integrating (importing and merging) and reconciling changes and integration building and testing.
- Independent Release Environments: for release builds, system test, and other release engineering and software product deployment activities [Appleton 2001].

PRIVATE WORLD captures the spirit of all these environments.

An environment would insulate developers, but would not isolate them. There was an event-notification and registration mechanism for broadcasting events in one or more other environments to interested parties (maybe this is a more general configuration management event-notification pattern of which things like baseline publishing and change publishing are concrete variants).

This pattern was derived from PRIVATE WORLD in [Berczuk Appleton 2002].

4.1.7   Build Prototypes **

... you are trying to gather requirements necessary for test planning, as in the pattern
APPLICATION DESIGN IS BOUNDED BY TEST DESIGN (4.2.30), and for the architecture, as in the pattern ARCHITECT ALSO IMPLEMENTS (5.2.10). Some of these requirements come from the customer,
but some are design decisions that come from the structure of the solution itself. For example,
you may be building a user interface, developing some new database or network technology,
working on a new, critical algorithm, or lacking an understanding of your project domain.

**A project must test requirements and design decisions in order to reduce the risk of
wasted cost and missed expectations.**

You need knowledge to proceed on development, and you must move forward; yet,
requirements (or your understanding of them) are always changing.

You're missing information about the product (not the process), you have a best guess you
can use to move forward, and you want some way to evaluate the result of your best guess.

Written requirements that are gathered once at the beginning of a development cycle with
the hope that they can drive development are usually too ambiguous.

You want to get requirements changes as early as possible, and you want an understanding
of requirements to lead deployment as much as possible.

Designers and implementors must understand requirements directly—the fact that the
requirements have been captured in a document isn't enough. And the ability of designers and

developers to understand requirements implies that they must understand the implementation ramifications.

Therefore:

Build an isolated prototype solution whose purposes are to

- **Understand requirements, including latent needs**
- **Validate requirements with customers, as in ENGAGE CUSTOMERS (4.2.6)**
- **Explore human/computer interactions for the system**
- **Explore the cost and benefits of design decisions**

The prototype is a small system that explores a small number of issues in isolation using best current knowledge. By examining that small system, you can learn whether or not your current knowledge is correct and sufficient. Prototypes are particularly useful for external interfaces.

Throw the prototype away when you're done. This action is more important than it may sound. Since the purpose of prototyping is to gain knowledge, prototypes can (and should) ignore details necessary in production software. Yet, such details (e.g., scale, performance, and robustness) cannot be incorporated into prototype-based software without the result resembling the proverbial bowl of pasta.

You will decide if your current knowledge is sufficient. If it is, adapt that small system's design (not its code!) to your larger system (incorporate it entirely if it was built to production specifications). If not, decide if you now have enough information to safely proceed or if you need to develop another prototype.

It's good to use DEVELOPING IN PAIRS (4.2.28), particularly if one of the pair represents the customer interests or is a customer per se.

Prototypes are a good supplement to use cases to help assess requirements more thoroughly. For one thing, prototypes help bring unstated requirements into the open. This pattern nicely complements ENGAGE CUSTOMERS (4.2.6) and SCENARIOS DEFINE PROBLEM (4.2.8).

The visualizations used for DEVELOPER CONTROLS PROCESS (4.1.17) and the pattern ENGAGE QUALITY ASSURANCE (4.2.29) come from processes based largely on prototyping.

Continued prototyping without convergence means that the design is constantly shifting and that the team is not learning enough to reach a conclusion. If other teams that depend on the prototyping team do not get the stable interface they need, it is time to get out of prototyping and either implement the system or ENGAGE CUSTOMERS (4.2.6) [RECOMMITMENT MEETING (4.1.12)] to evaluate current project directions and priorities.

There are subtle organizational overtones to building prototypes. It is important that the ARCHITECT CONTROLS PRODUCT (5.2.3), instead of the prototype controlling the product. Therefore, the prototyping team should be kept separate from the Architect and the ARCHITECTURE TEAM (5.2.4). Instead, the prototyping activity helps enhance the DOMAIN EXPERTISE IN ROLES (4.2.22). And one of the positive effects of building a prototype is that it reduces the risk of the unknown. The prototype helps to define the scope of the problem, as well as to offer a possible solution.

RELATED PATTERNS:

- EARLY AND REGULAR DELIVERY (A.5.11)—adds knowledge about your development process.

- MICROCOSM (A.5.18)—returns measurable data about process and technology.

Another related pattern is Alistair Cockburn's CLEAR THE FOG (A.5.7) [Cockburn 1998], which one might view as a generic version of this pattern. In that pattern, he recommends, "Do something (almost anything) that is a best initial attempt to deliver some part of the system in a short period of time" in the interest of SOMEONE ALWAYS MAKES PROGRESS (4.1.20). He gives the following as his rationale: "The difficulty is that you don't know what it is that you don't know. Only by making some movement can you detect what it is you don't know. Once you come to know what it is you don't know, you can pursue that information directly." And he adds an interesting admonition: "If you only 'clear the fog' and 'clear the fog' and 'clear the fog', you will not make real progress. You will have lots of little experiments and no deliverable results."

Bruce Whitenack's RAPPeL pattern language also presents a PROTOTYPES (A.5.23) pattern ([Whitenack 1995], p. 288). He adds the admonition:

> The dark side to prototyping is that solutions can be hacked together with the software inadequately robust and not well designed. It takes maturity, discipline, and a very good programming/design environment to reengineer quality back into a product. Without rigor and discipline a product is in serious risk of failure when features are continually added. As more prototyping and evaluating are done, there will be the need to modify the requirements. Iteration between prototyping and use-case modeling occurs during requirements analysis. In addition, user expectations have to [be] kept realistic as a prototype is not a product. Customers must realize that what they are seeing is a product simulation — not the product itself.

He also distinguishes between *low-fidelity prototypes* and *high-fidelity prototypes*:

> Work with the customer to build (initially) low-fidelity prototypes ... using paper widgets, drawings, self-stick notes, and index cards. (These are true throwaway prototypes.) Or, if the necessary skills and tools are available, build high-fidelity prototypes. (You do not want to spend more than 10 percent of your time on how to use the tool instead of focusing on the actual prototype, however.) Alternate between prototyping and use-case modeling. Prototyping provides more user involvement, and use case modeling provides rigorous analysis. Augment the use case documentation with references to prototype versions (product simulations).

> The high-fidelity prototypes that are developed with a tool capable of generating useful code may be used for evolutionary development. It may not be a throwaway prototype, but it should be developed in the spirit that it will be thrown away, which means making sure that all on the project—especially managers—understand that the prototype *may* be thrown away. It has been my experience with Smalltalk development that if developers have a good design in mind and if they are experienced, the prototype will probably contain code that is very usable for a production version. Be sure to plan for training of beta users and for creating a number of prototypes for prospective users.

Building and demonstrating prototypes is an art in itself. See the excellent pattern language DEMO PREP (A.5.9) by Todd Coram [Coram 1996] for guidance on the building, administration, and demonstration of prototypes. See also an earlier work by Ian Graham [Graham 1991].

The risk to your project of a small, throwaway effort is a small schedule delay. The risk of making a poor technical choice is a poor product or perhaps a commitment to a technology that simply will not work.

Be careful not to be seduced by the siren song of a successful prototype. Prototypes almost never can demonstrate capacity, reliability, or performance, which are often the most troublesome issues in development. The danger is that we see a prototype working and naturally assume that it will scale gracefully, run for weeks without rebooting, or perform nimbly under a customer's typical load. A working prototype does not imply that these problems are solved.

Contrast this pattern with SKUNKWORKS (4.2.14), which many think of as prototyping on a larger scale, but which is actually a little bit different in its forces and intent.

"The best friend of the architect is the pencil in the drafting room, and the sledgehammer on the job." — Frank Lloyd Wright, quoted in [Jacobs 1978].

4.1.8   Surrogate Customer

See section 4.2.7.

4.1.9   Take No Small Slips **

Boarding house, Washington, D.C., 1942, morning bathroom line. Small slips in the bathroom schedule build up, causing unfulfilled expectations downstream and leading to discomfort and dissatisfaction on the part of others.

Our project was in trouble. Everybody knew it. And then our project manager left the company. When our new project manager arrived, he called us all together. "I believe in taking one schedule slip," he said. Then he announced a 3-month slip. We all returned to work and redoubled our efforts. It was a challenge to meet the revised schedule, but he (and we) stuck to it, and we ultimately completed our development without incurring another slip.

... development is underway, and progress must be tracked, thus avoiding major surprises to both the customer and the enterprise.

It's difficult to know how long a project should take, and it's even more difficult to recover when the guess is wrong.

If you guess pessimistically, developers become complacent, and you miss market windows. If you guess optimistically, developers become burned out, and you also miss market windows. Projects without schedule motivation tend to go on forever or to spend too much time polishing details that are either irrelevant or that don't serve customer needs.

Therefore:

Prefer a single large slip to several small slips. ([Brooks 1995], page 24.)

As Paul Chisholm notes, "We found a good way to live by TAKE NO SMALL SLIPS from ... [Frederick Brooks'] *The Mythical Man-Month.* **Every week, measure how close the critical path (at least) of the schedule is doing. If it's 3 days behind schedule, track a 'delusion index' of 3 days. When the delusion index gets too ludicrous, then slip the schedule.** This helps avoid churning the schedule" [Chisholm 1994].

This pattern helps support a project with a flexible target date.

Dates are always difficult to estimate. DeMarco notes that one of the most serious signs that an organization in trouble is a schedule worked backward from an end date [DeMarco 1993].

A single large slip is important for the morale of the team. If you continually take small slips, nobody believes the schedule anymore, which hurts morale, reduces the sense of urgency, and encourages people to stop caring. On the other hand, a single large slip preserves at least some of the believability of the schedule, and people tend to be more willing to work toward a revised schedule.

Much of the rationale is supported in the MIT project management simulation, the Borland Quattro Pro for Windows case study, and Brooks' seminal work [Brooks 1995].

Most sane projects are managed this way.

See also RECOMMITMENT MEETING (4.1.12).

4.1.10   Completion Headroom **

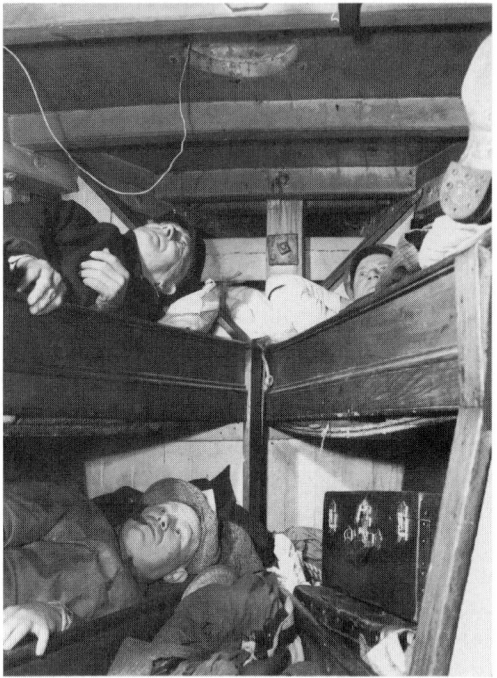

Speaking of headroom ...

... work is progressing as the software unfolds and as the team learns more about the system from the customer and from the behavior of the system itself. Things are far enough along to start thinking about making a delivery to the customer on the agreed delivery date.

Every project must commit to delivery on a few hard and fast dates. This commitment is actually fortunate because it is about the only way to get out of work that is going poorly. It's also usually more important to deliver *something* on a specified date than to deliver everything at a later date: *When* is often more important than *what*. A WORK SPLIT (4.1.11) provides such a graceful exit by allowing the portion of work that is not understood or that is going poorly to be deferred while saving the part that does work or that will help the organization save face. A WORK SPLIT does require some advance notice since some portion of the work must still be completed by the deadline.

Therefore:

Project work group completion dates from remaining effort estimates in the WORK QUEUE REPORT [Cunningham 1996]. Compare the largest of the earliest completion dates for each work group to any hard delivery date that may apply. The difference is your COMPLETION HEADROOM.

Any group has an obligation to make their efforts visible through what becomes the ultimate trouble signal, low COMPLETION HEADROOM. Headroom disappears when developmental activities fail to match those of COMPARABLE WORK [Cunningham 1996].

In order for COMPLETION HEADROOM to work, it must be calculated from the beginning and recalculated often, at least weekly. Watch for trends. Headroom will often shift plus or minus a day or two from week to week. But steady evaporation of headroom for any WORK GROUP (A.5.30) is a sure indicator that management attention is needed. You can reorder the WORK QUEUE (4.1.13), possibly defer entire items to a later release, use the WORK SPLIT (4.1.11) pattern already mentioned, or face the public embarrassment of a RECOMMITMENT MEETING (4.1.12).

A common problem is the well-meaning escalation of requirements by people who are too close to a problem. If you track COMPLETION HEADROOM, you are in a better position to assess the impact of adding these requirements to the project.

See also TAKE NO SMALL SLIPS (4.1.9).

A version of this pattern first appeared in [Cunningham 1996].

4.1.11   Work Split *

... a WORK GROUP (A.5.30) commits to resolve and deliver IMPLIED REQUIREMENTS (4.1.16) in the most timely and satisfactory way they can find. They are not committed to specific dates.

A work group has an obligation to make its efforts visible through what becomes the ultimate trouble signal, low COMPLETION HEADROOM (4.1.10). Headroom disappears when developmental activities fail to match those of COMPARABLE WORK. A common problem is the well-meaning escalation of requirements by people who are too close to a problem.

Therefore:

Divide a task into an urgent component and a deferred component such that no more than half of the developmental work is in the urgent half. Defer more work, if required, to acquire sufficient COMPLETION HEADROOM (4.1.10). Defer analysis and design of parts that won't be implemented (this advice runs counter to conventional wisdom).

❖   ❖   ❖

Often, a split is just a way to get back to the basic work that had been originally planned. Trust architecture and requirements substitutions to cover for omissions and inconveniences caused by incomplete up-front work. Both halves of the split will appear in the WORK QUEUE (4.1.13) with distinctly different urgency levels.

The split should be based on clear business priorities or should otherwise be rooted in agreed values. Ian Graham has written patterns that combine to form a small pattern language (drawn from a larger pattern language) to address this issue. See the patlets for BUSINESS PROCESS MODEL (A.5.6), ESTABLISH THE BUSINESS OBJECTIVES (A.5.12), and GRADUAL STIFFENING (A.5.14).

A version of this pattern first appeared in [Cunningham 1996].

4.1.12   Recommitment Meeting *

... each development group is managing its schedule using WORK SPLIT (4.1.11), but additional scheduling problems seem to keep coming up.

If a product initiative is in jeopardy because IMPLIED REQUIREMENTS (4.1.16) cannot be met through schedule and WORK QUEUE (4.1.13) adjustments, then it is unlikely that any other development-initiated activity will help. Management up to at least the level that began the initiative will suddenly take an interest in all circumstances leading up to the current situation. Some of this analysis is natural and appropriate. However, this period won't be a time of high productivity, and it shouldn't be allowed to continue too long.

Therefore:

Assemble a meeting of interested management and key development people. In the meeting, review the history of the situation until all present agree that simple adjustments (e.g., working weekends or adding staff) won't help. Eventually a solution appears, usually expressed as a question of the form: What is the least amount of work required to do X? (X is one person's idea of the most important part of the initiative.) The question should be answered quickly and confidently by consulting a recent WORK QUEUE REPORT [Cunningham 1996].

The process may repeat for plans Y and Z. Ultimately, a plan will be selected. Then, the remainder of the meeting is devoted to talking through the implications of the decision and getting all parties' commitment to the new plan and/or schedule.

This pattern, of course, is another form of episode. The decisions are ones of business resource allocation and thus belong in upper management. However, all present can and should contribute in a frank, honest, nondefensive, and constructive way.

See also TAKE NO SMALL SLIPS (4.1.9).

A version of this pattern first appeared in [Cunningham 1996].

4.1.13   Work Queue *

    ... IMPLIED REQUIREMENTS (4.1.16) suggest deliverable program enhancements that will have various necessities, dependencies, risks, and rewards. Deliverables may be ill-defined, being represented more by a vision or desire than by anything concrete or measurable.

❖   ❖   ❖

    It is difficult to perform linear, monochronic scheduling in light of IMPLIED REQUIRE-MENTS (4.1.16).

    If we were to work up a conventional schedule, we would probably begin with a block of requirements analysis for each item. From these blocks would be hung blocks of specification, design, implementation, and eventually integration and testing. Add to this structure some wild guesses and a few ordering constraints, and, presto, you have a 30-foot diagram showing what will be finished when and by whom. Such a document takes on a life of its own, striking fear in developers' hearts and generally distracting everyone else from the real scheduling task, which is to get better input, not larger output.

    Therefore:

    Produce a schedule that is simply a prioritized list of work. Use the list of IMPLIED REQUIREMENTS (4.1.16) (really just names) as a starting point and situate them into a likely implementation order, favoring the more urgent or higher priority items. When work can be factored from two or more entries, go ahead and do so, giving the common element a name that establishes its worth and implies its implementation precedence.

EXAMPLE:

1. Settlement-Data Positions
2. Settlement-Date-Based Tax Reports
3. Trade vs. Settlement Accounting Preference by Portfolio

Be prepared to reorder this list as unforeseen interactions surface or as business realities demand new priorities. Remove work from the list as that work is completed. Observed defects are not enough to return completed work to the list. However, independently scheduled repair activity may uncover omissions that are more appropriately removed from defect tracking and scheduled in competition with all of the other work in the WORK QUEUE (4.1.13).

A version of this pattern first appeared in [Cunningham 1996]. The pattern is similar to the later SCRUM pattern BACKLOG ([Beedle 1999], p. 643–644), which is summarized in ([Rising 2000], p. 146):

> To organize the work remaining on a project, maintain a prioritized list, the Backlog. The list is dynamic and updated at the end of each Sprint.

4.1.14   Informal Labor Plan **

Workers using an informal labor plan to construct an adobe building, Penasco, New Mexico.

We were discussing the introduction of new project management software. One project manager protested that it didn't provide the granularity she needed. It turned out that she wanted to track items that were fractions of days of effort.

... real development requires developers to work on several parallel tasks such as DEVEL-OPMENT EPISODES (4.1.15) that may have interdependent or even conflicting priorities and due dates.

A schedule of developer work tasks can both assist workers in planning their time and provide reassurance to stakeholders about scheduling expectations. The DEVELOPMENT EPISODE (4.1.15) presents an ideal that must be worked into the lives of people trying to get a big job done quickly. Developers often find themselves obligated to work on more than one in-progress DEVELOPMENT EPISODE at a time. The WORK QUEUE (4.1.13) offers one prioritizing method, though it ignores the many small trade-offs possible when the work is at hand.

Therefore:

Let individuals devise their own short-term plans. Accept that much of the group activity implied in a DEVELOPMENT EPISODE will take place between group members who find the time to tackle some issue together [DEVELOPING IN PAIRS (4.2.28)]. Avoid the temptation to call a meeting where a developmental climax is intended to happen. It won't. Instead, let individuals express interests and make commitments to each other. And let them revise these intentions on a moment's notice when the energy of some episode reaches an irresistible level.

Accordingly, there is a threshold of detail below which a project manager should not track. The threshold may vary depending on the project, but it is a safe bet that tasks that require less than a few days of effort should not be formally tracked. One might get a sense of excess detail by the amount of developer complaints about the relevance of the tracking.

The above mentioned practices lead to an organization where the DEVELOPER CONTROLS PROCESS (4.1.17). Not only does the developer suggest the overall structure of commitments, but the developer also becomes the focal point for day-to-day priority calls.

A DEVELOPMENT EPISODE is actually composed of a series of PROGRAMMING EPISODES (4.1.19), some of which must take place in (at least) pairs if any approximation of group consciousness is to form. Individuals' labor plans are the tools they use to make these connections happen. Pair programming facilities [Beck 1999] are configurations of the physical environment that can reduce this planning to an occasional HALLWAY CHATTER (5.1.15) promise.

A version of this pattern first appeared in [Cunningham 1996].

4.1.15   Development Episode *

A baseball game is divided into separate episodes, called innings.

... members of a WORK GROUP (A.5.30) have been selected based on needs inferred from the IMPLIED REQUIREMENTS (4.1.16).

It's important to build on the collective strength of an entire team and to build a true gestalt from the team members.

Each team member contributes specific skills that will be important at some point in the development. For this we can be thankful. However, if we overemphasize a team member's specific strength, we diminish the perception of everyone's general abilities, unnecessarily narrow the team member's focus to the application of that specialty, risk creating ambiguity as to who is responsible for nonspecialized tasks, and discourage the learning of new skills.

Therefore:

Approach all development as a group activity as if no one had anything else to do. Expect the activity to follow the usual course of an episode, where energy builds to a decision-making climax and then dissipates. At the height of the episode, purpose should be clear, terminology well understood, knowns well explored, and unknowns identified. It is at

exactly this point that individual strengths merge into a sort of common consciousness. Landmark decisions come easily. Breakthroughs are common. A creative act will have been shared.

Besides yielding better decisions, the collective episode has very positive effects on the participants. Looking back, people often have trouble identifying the actual source of key ideas. Nonspecialists gain invaluable insight into the thought processes of the specialist, whose ideas are demystified and shared throughout the group. Specialists will realize that this sharing will not diminish their own status within the group. The specialist may even delay sharing some insights, realizing that their actual recognition experience will be of tremendous value to the nonspecialists and a small loss to himself or herself. Seymour Papert called this an "Ah Ha" moment and admonished instructors not to "Steal the Ah Ha" [Papert 1980].

A version of this pattern first appeared in [Cunningham 1996].

4.1.16   Implied Requirements

Farm Security Administration (FSA) home supervisor Miss Harton helping some members of a borrower's family cut patterns and make their own clothes. Caswell County, North Carolina. Pattern parts such as sleeves are chunks of functionality that are well understood by the customer.

... a PRODUCT INITIATIVE (A.5.22) has identified the direction for further development, and a MARKET WALK-THROUGH (A.5.16) has explored the customer motivation and developmental possibilities behind that initiative. We expect positions and attitudes to be understood, but we have yet to make any commitments beyond everyone's general commitment to do a good job for the company.

A commitment implies an agreement between people. Development commitments generally obligate developers to meet some customer need in a timely and satisfactory way. The tension here is to define a need in sufficient detail so that commitments have meaning without exhausting up-front analysis or overconstraining a solution.

Therefore:

Select and name chunks of functionality. Use names that have meaning to customers and that are consistent with the PRODUCT INITIATIVE (A.5.22). Allow these names to imply customer requirements without actually enumerating requirements in the traditional sense.

❖   ❖   ❖

EXAMPLES:

- Year-End Tax Reports
- Dollar-Denominated Japanese Bonds
- High-Quality Printing
- Disconnected Operation on Laptops

These names will fill in the blank in recurring questions like the following: Who's handling the programming (or specification, or customer contact, or manual update, or release notes) for _____.

See also NAMED STABLE BASES (4.1.4).

A version of this pattern first appeared in [Cunningham 1996].

4.1.17   Developer Controls Process **

A journeyman devises effective and efficient processes for the manufacture of self-sealing fuel tanks during World War II.

... an organization has come together to build software for a new market in an immature domain or in a domain that is unfamiliar to the development team. Progress will be marked by an INFORMAL LABOR PLAN (4.1.14). The necessary roles have been defined and initially staffed.

A development culture, like any culture, can benefit from recognizing a focal point of project direction and communication. Successful organizations work in an organic way with a minimum of centralized control. Yet important points of focus, embodied in roles, tie together ideas, requirements, and constraints into an artifact ready for testing, packaging, marketing, and delivery.

Strict control is viewed by most development teams as a draconian measure. The right information must flow through the right roles. You need to support information flow across analysis, design, and implementation.

Because developers contribute directly to the end-user-visible artifact, they are in the best position to take accountability for the product. Of all roles, they have the largest stake in the largest number of phases of product development. And there should be no accountability without control. The manager has some accountability as well, to the extent that he or she indirectly supports delivery of the user-visible artifacts. These are process issues.

Therefore:

Make the Developer the focal point of process information. In the spirit of ORGANIZATION FOLLOWS MARKET (5.1.9) place the developer role at a hub of the process for a given feature. A feature is a unit of system functionality (implemented largely in software) that can be separately marketed, and for which customers are willing to pay. Responsibilities of developers include understanding requirements, reviewing the solution structure and algorithm with peers, building the implementation, and performing unit testing.

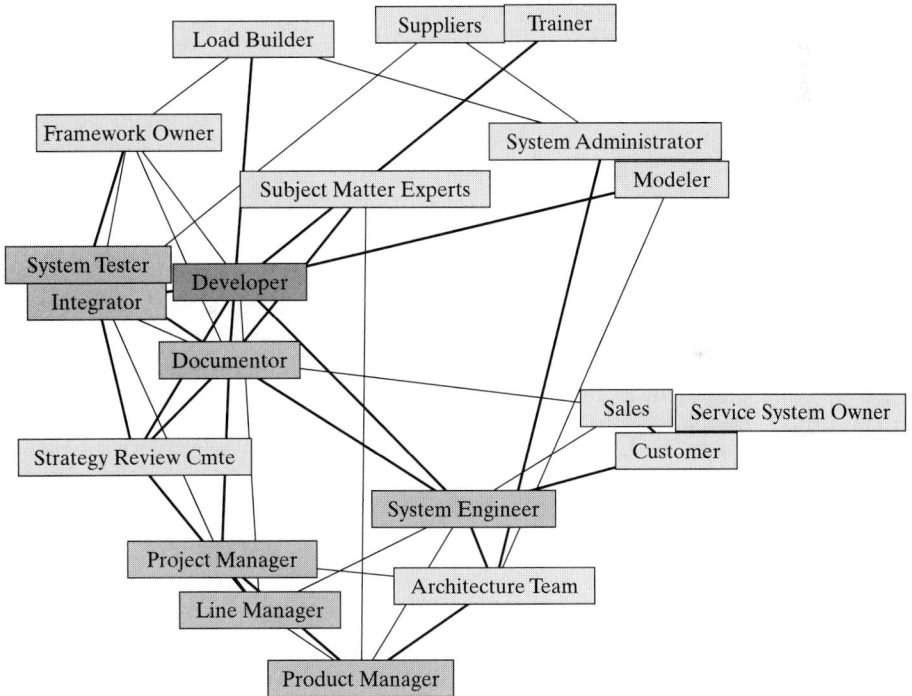

The developer is central to all activities of this end-to-end software development process.

Note that other hubs, such as a Manager role, may exist as well, though they are less central than the Developer role.

The Developer who is at the hub of a particular feature may be accorded that position according to FEATURE ASSIGNMENT (5.2.14), but, more generally developers should be at the communication hub of whatever process engages them in writing code for the customer. This pattern encourages a structure that supports its prime information consumer. The Developer can be moved toward the center of the process using the patterns WORK FLOWS INWARD (4.1.18) and MOVE RESPONSIBILITIES (5.1.18).

Though Developer should be a key role, care must be taken not to overburden that role. This pattern should be balanced with MERCENARY ANALYST (4.1.24), FIREWALLS (4.2.9), GATE-KEEPER (4.2.10), and more general load-balancing patterns like RESPONSIBILITIES ENGAGE (5.1.14), HALLWAY CHATTER (5.1.15), and MOVE RESPONSIBILITIES (5.1.18). The Developer should enjoy particularly strong support from the PATRON ROLE (4.2.15), and conflicts can be escalated to the PATRON ROLE when consensus breaks down.

If the Developer controls the process, then it's possible to implement the pattern WORK FLOWS INWARD (4.1.18).

Developers, of course, don't control the process unilaterally, but as a collective group, starting with DEVELOPING IN PAIRS (4.2.28).

We have no role called Designer because design is really the whole task. Managers fill a supporting role; empirically, they are rarely seen to control a process except during crises. While the Developer controls the process, the Architect controls the product. [In the figure, the Architect role is split across Framework Owner and ARCHITECTURE TEAM (5.2.4).] This communication is particularly important in domains that are not well understood, so that iteration can take place to explore the domain with the customer.

In a mature domain, consider HUB SPOKE AND RIM (5.1.17) as an alternative.

You can still write down your process as part of a process improvement program. But keep the documentation light; many organizations have found that one page per process is good enough. And make sure each process step meets a need that you can tie to your organization's value proposition. Most often, this value is or should be tied to the product you are producing for a paying customer. If it isn't obvious how the process step helps to achieve what you know the customer wants, then do the right thing instead.

4.1.18   Work Flows Inward **

Work (i.e., pears) flowing into a pear processing plant.

... an organization is in place and has been doing work long enough that it can introspect about its structure and workings. There is some management pecking order or hierarchical decision-making structure in the organizational network. Work instructions flow through this structure, with the possibility that each role makes decisions, adds constraints, or works to carry out decisions within some set of constraints.

An organization must seek a structure that best ensures that the most authoritative roles make the decisions and carry out the work that adds value directly to the product.

Some centralized control and direction are necessary. During software production, the work bottleneck of a system should be at the center of its communication and control structure. If the communication center of the organization generates work more than it does work, then organization performance can become unpredictable and sporadic. The developer is already sensitized to market needs through FIREWALLS (4.2.9) and GATEKEEPER (4.2.10) (no centralized role need fill this function).

Look at the following grid that depicts the directed flow of communication in an organization [see How the Patterns Came to Us (Chapter 2)]. In this organization, a core of roles at the center initiates interactions across the spectrum of most of the other roles.

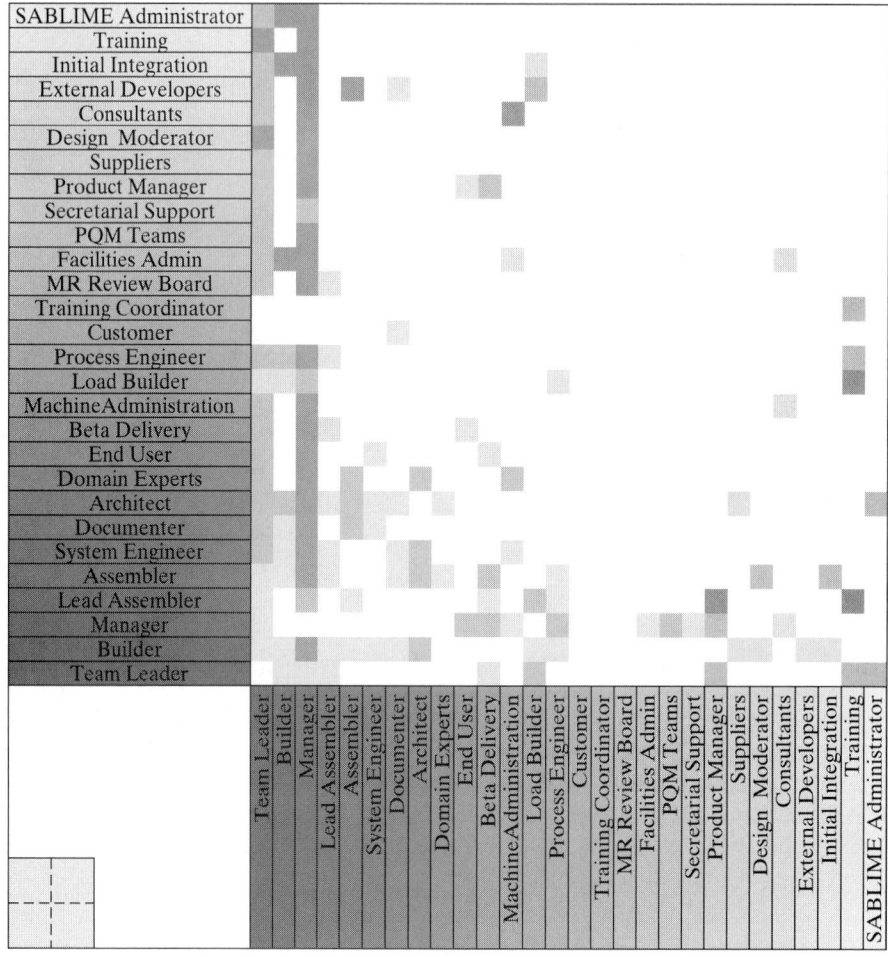

Yet, this core receives very little input from the rest of the roles in the organization, and this core is rife with management roles (Team Leader, Manager, Lead Assembler). It has an overloaded center, and work requests flow outward from this center, diffusing across the other roles. Core roles *make* work.

Katz and Kahn's analysis of organizations shows that the exercise of control is not a zero-sum game ([Katz Kahn 1978], p. 314).

Therefore:

Work should flow in to Developers from stakeholders, especially customers. Work should not flow out from managers.

Managers should not be situated at the center of the communication grid: They will become overloaded and make decisions that don't take day-to-day dynamics into account.

Consider the following picture, where work flows from the roles across the organization to the roles at the center: Developer, Architect, and Ambassador. The grid shows a healthy distribution of inward-directed inputs. And, in large part, the central roles *do* work, rather than *make* work.

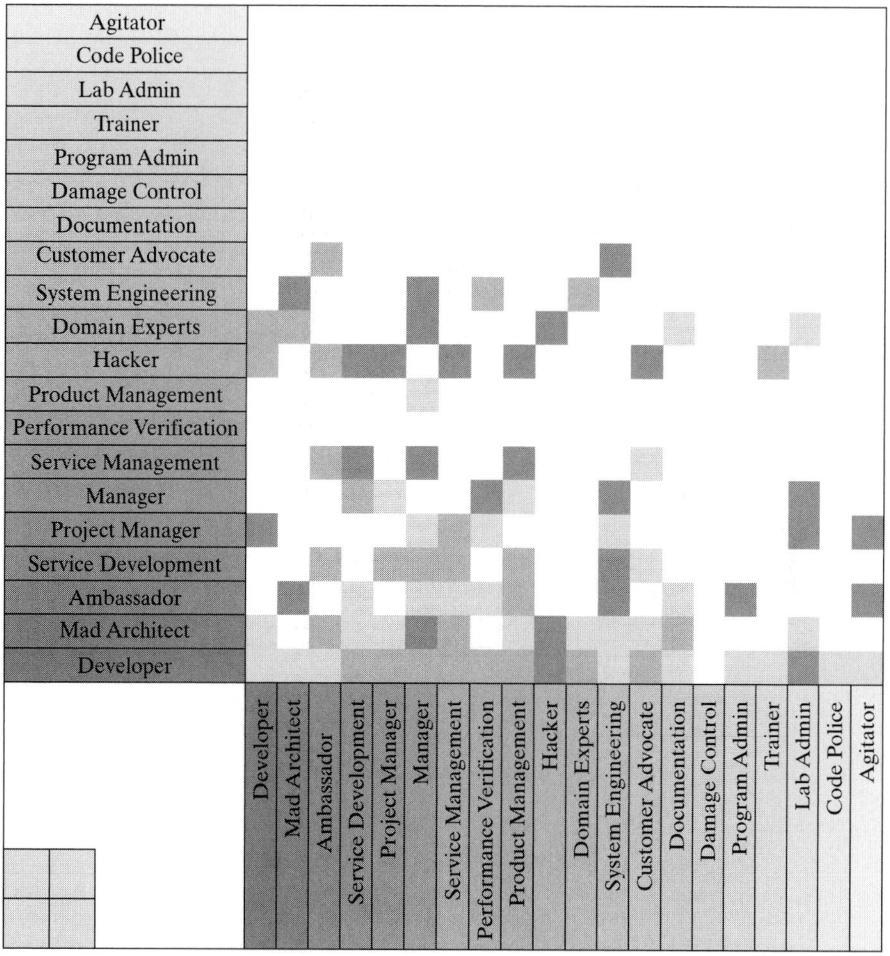

Grid rows (top to bottom): Agitator, Code Police, Lab Admin, Trainer, Program Admin, Damage Control, Documentation, Customer Advocate, System Engineering, Domain Experts, Hacker, Product Management, Performance Verification, Service Management, Manager, Project Manager, Service Development, Ambassador, Mad Architect, Developer

Grid columns (left to right): Developer, Mad Architect, Ambassador, Service Development, Project Manager, Manager, Service Management, Performance Verification, Product Management, Hacker, Domain Experts, System Engineering, Customer Advocate, Documentation, Damage Control, Program Admin, Trainer, Lab Admin, Code Police, Agitator

The result is an organization whose communication grid has more points below the diagonal than above it (as in the figure above).

The work should focus at the center of the process, and the center of the process should focus on value-added activities [DEVELOPER CONTROLS PROCESS (4.1.17)].

But consider this interaction grid:

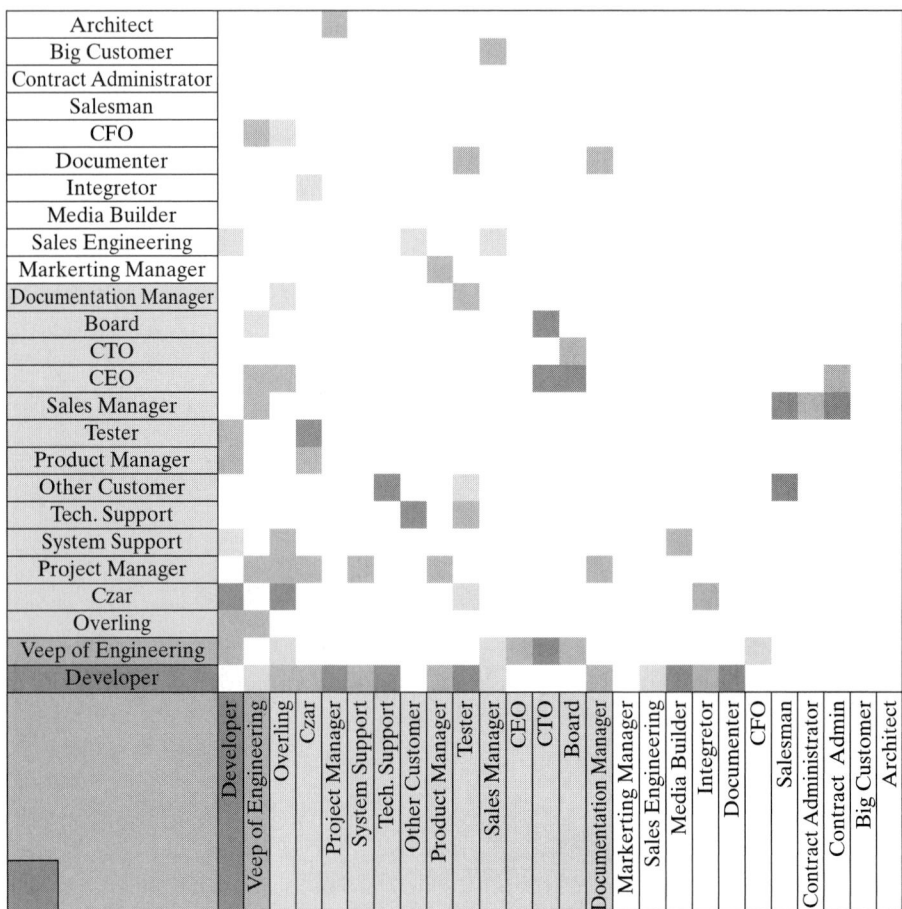

Superficially, the graph appears to show a WORK FLOWS INWARD pattern. But, in fact, most of the interactions directed from outlying roles to the developer are of an imperative nature rather than of an informative nature. The developer role is being pulled in many directions, and the organization health suffers greatly.

Organizations run by professional managers tend to have repeatable business processes, but don't seem to reach the same productivity plateaus as organizations run by engineers. In programmer-centric organizations, the value-added roles are at the center of the process [DEVELOPER CONTROLS PROCESS (4.1.17) and ARCHITECT ALSO IMPLEMENTS (5.2.10)]. The manager should facilitate and support these roles and their work [FIREWALLS (4.2.9) and PATRON ROLE (4.2.15)].

Mackenzie characterizes this pattern using *M-curves*, which model the percentage of task processes of each task process law level (planning, directing, and execution) as a function of the classification [Mackenzie 1986].

The rationale is supported with empirical observations from existing projects.

The broad goal of this pattern is to separate overhead work from central work. DAY CARE (4.1.23) is another pattern with a similar intent.

The Manager should still make day-to-day decisions for the business process and accept the responsibility to "keep the pests away" [FIREWALLS (4.2.9)].

In his new work *The Nature of Order*, Christopher Alexander speaks of *gradients* as one of the 15 structural properties of whole systems that emerge naturally in a process of local adaptation [Alexander 2003]. In WORK FLOWS INWARD, there should be a natural gradient of information flow toward the developer at the "center" of the organization—both in the sense of the social network diagrams and in the sense that Alexander uses the term "center" to describe a prominent feature of a system.

4.1.19   Programming Episodes **

Making the possible decision now: What kind of candy can I buy with my nickel?

... you have a good idea of where to start and perhaps even some fledgling pieces of code. Now you need to establish a rhythm of productive development that can engage and fuel the team.

Programming is the act of deciding now what will happen in the future, but it always seems like some parts of the future don't happen soon enough and other parts are always too far off and out of reach. A programming language offers an operationally precise way to encode decisions through a process called coding. Programmers reason about future behavior by interpreting previously coded decisions and integrating these decisions with their own decisions, their interpretations of other sources like technical memos, and the guidance of domain experts. The depth, quality, and value of programming decisions will be limited by the programmers' ability to concentrate.

Therefore:

Develop a program in discrete episodes. Select appropriate deliverables for each episode and commit sufficient mind share to complete these deliverables by making the possible decisions now and coding those decisions. Be aware of the rise in concentration as the episode progresses. Consider each source and consciously include or exclude its recommendations.

Fear often accompanies a decision that has not yet been made. Use this fear as a motivation. Try to compare your position within an episode with similar points in previously successful episodes.

EXAMPLE:

"I feel like we've been around twice now on the possible ways we can bind the six terms of this bond analytic to the four calculation classes we have in our library."

"Yeah, right now I'd be happy if we could place the four primary terms, look at the error cases, and see if all that gives us a hint as to how to proceed after lunch."

Push for the decisions that can be made. Don't abandon an episode; doing so will leave you feeling defeated and unable to achieve even the same level of concentration at a future time. Make the decisions that seem possible, code the decisions, and then review the code to be sure that the extent of your decisions and your confidence in them are apparent in the code. Coding occurs on the downhill side of a programming episode. Coding is the most direct way to promulgate programming decisions.

A version of this pattern first appeared in [Cunningham 1996].

4.1.20   Someone Always Makes Progress*

Room enough for everyone to work ...

... secondary tasks are dominating the team's time, keeping them from moving forward with their primary goal. There are common complaints about distractions.

It is important to keep a team moving forward and to avoid getting stuck on the obstacles. You need to pay attention to every task, including small diverting ones. But you also need to complete the primary task by an important date.

Therefore:

Ensure that someone on the team is making progress on the primary task at all times.

If you do not complete your primary task, nothing else will matter. Therefore, complete that task at all costs.

You can employ one of a broad range of particular solutions and tactics depending on the exact forces to be resolved. The following specializations are example refinements of this pattern:

- DEVELOPING IN PAIRS (4.2.28)—allow one person to take the keyboard.
- TEAM PER TASK (4.1.21)—separate tasks into sympathetic sets.

- SACRIFICE ONE PERSON (4.1.22)—assign only one person to the distraction.
- DAY CARE (4.1.23)—separate the training task from the task of producing software.

But, in any case, making progress on the primary task will always bring you closer to your final goal, which is not always the case when dealing with distractions.

The psychological effect of this pattern should not be underestimated. If the project is hit with many distractions, it can be demoralizing to see work grind to a halt. However, any visible progress will help the entire team stay focused and will encourage them to get through the crisis so that they too can once again make progress.

Carried too far, this pattern might lead you into trouble for not adequately addressing the distractions. However, too many distractions are usually a symptom of some other problem [see, for example, FIREWALLS (4.2.9)].

SAMPLE SITUATIONS:

A. Scylla and Charybdis. In The Odyssey, Odysseus has to sail past either Scylla or Charybdis. If Odysseus chooses to sail past Scylla, a six-headed monster, six of his crew members will be eaten, but the rest will survive. If Odysseus chooses to sail past Charydbis, a whirlpool, the entire ship will be destroyed. In this paradigmatic dilemma, Odysseus chooses to sacrifice six people rather than sacrifice his entire crew.

B. Atalanta. In the Greek story of Atalanta, Atalanta is assured by the gods that she will remain the fastest runner as long as she remains a virgin. So she tells her father, the king, that she will only marry the man who can beat her in a foot race; the losers are to be killed for wasting her time. The successful young man is aided by a god, who gives him three golden apples. Each time Atalanta pulls ahead, he tosses an apple in front of her. When she pauses to pick up each golden apple, he races ahead and eventually wins the race.

The moral of this story is that Atalanta should not have stopped to pick up the apples, which also illustrates the point of this pattern. I choose to view the story metaphorically; Atalanta represents distractions trying to beat you to your project's deadline. The apples are members of your team, whom you will separate from the main team one at a time to ensure success.

See [Csikszentmihalyi 1990] and [DeMarco Lister 1976].

A version of this pattern first appeared in [Cockburn 1998].

4.1.21   Team Per Task **

... a big diversion hits the team, threatening to disrupt ongoing work and temporarily halt progress.

Large distractions (usually called crises) must not be allowed to stop a project, even for a short time. Crises are inevitable, and they can occur frequently. If the project members take time to respond to each crisis, they will soon find themselves spending so much time performing crisis management that the real work doesn't get done.

Of course, the diversions are real. A previous release needs an emergency bug fix. New people must be trained. The ISO audit will happen. But these diversions must be handled in such a way that the project still moves forward.

The temptation is to throw everything you have at these high-priority items and to let the whole team work on the issues until they go away. However, such an approach confuses urgency with amount of effort. Some problems require only a small amount of attention, although that attention should be *immediate*. A stitch in time saves nine.

Therefore:

Let a subteam handle the diversion, which allows the main team to keep working.

One approach is to split the team. Sort the activities so that each team has a primary task with additional, sympathetic activities. Sitting in meetings, answering phone calls, and writing reports, for example, are nonsympathetic to designing software. Arrange it so that each team can focus on its primary task and so that each task has at least one dedicated team member.

As a result, important distractions are handled almost entirely by specialized teams, thus allowing the main team to continue uninterrupted.

However, one must be careful not to overdo it. Carried to extremes, this pattern results in single-person teams. In addition, while solving a crisis is important, be careful not to heap praise too lavishly on the crisis teams. Otherwise, crisis management becomes the glamor job, and the team focuses on putting out fires rather than on building the building. [See COMPENSATE SUCCESS (4.2.25).]

PRINCIPLES INVOLVED:

Increase flow time and decrease distractions, thus trading personnel parallelism for time-slicing. *Flow* is the quiet time in the brain when the problem flows through the designer ([Csik-szentmihalyi 1990] and [DeMarco Lister 1976]). It is when design alternatives are weighed and decisions are made in rapid succession as mental doors open. The problem, the alternatives, and the state of the decision process are all kept in the head. It is a not only a highly productive time, but it is also the only time when the designer feels comfortable making decisions.

It takes about 20 minutes to reach the internal state of flow and only a minute to lose it. Beyond getting into the flow, the designer must have time to actually make progress, which may take another 10 minutes. Any significant interruption within that half hour essentially causes the entire half hour to be lost. As it takes energy to get into the flow, so too a distraction costs energy as well as time.

To increase flow time, distractions have to be reduced. Certain pairs of activities are more mutually distracting that others. Fixing a bug requires flow in the old system and hence distracts from flow in the new system. Sitting in meetings, answering questions, and time on the telephone are major distracters to design flow. Therefore, the recommendation is to group tasks into sympathetic sets. Requirements and analysis involve attending meetings, reading, and writing. Design and programming require concentration on the implementation technology and the ability to keep a great number of details in the head.

Note that time-slicing, whereby each person will do design some part of the time, can be more attractive in terms of job satisfaction. The significant time needed to switch between tasks causes parallelism to be preferred in this case. Some of the people may adopt the new task as their profession [see SACRIFICE ONE PERSON (4.1.22), DAY CARE (4.1.23), and FIREWALLS (4.2.9)].

EXAMPLE:

Concurrent gathering of requirements and designing of software:

Project Winifred tried having each person gather requirements and perform analysis, design, and programming. We thought that the developers would enjoy the variation in activities and that the developers' multi-tasking would reduce the meetings and bureaucratic documentation exchanged between people.

What happened, however, was that the first two activities were so different from the latter two that people were unable to switch easily between them. After attending meetings and writing documentation for much of the day, people found it difficult to start working on design and programming. As with bug fixing/new development, every time a designer was pulled away from her or his work, it cost an additional hour to recover the train of thought.

We applied TEAM PER TASK and split the teams along task lines. Requirements gathering and analysis were assigned to designated people in each team, and design and programming were assigned to others. The result was that the requirements/analysis people sat in meetings, read and wrote specifications, examined interfaces, etc. They communicated their findings to the designers/programmers—orally, for the most part, since they were closely linked on the same team [HOLISTIC DIVERSITY (4.2.19)]. The designers/programmers stayed in their train of thought, getting fresh input from their requirements colleagues. Some of the people assigned to develop requirements really wanted to program, so their assignment was quite a sacrifice for them [SACRIFICE ONE PERSON (4.1.22)].

There are two things we did not do. We did not put the requirements/analysis people into a separate team [HOLISTIC DIVERSITY (4.2.19)]. Instead, each team was jointly responsible for a section of the system, from requirements to delivery. The splitting thus occurred within each team. We also did not force the requirements group to document their decisions for the designers' benefit (they did document their decisions for the project's benefit). The requirements and design people were in close contact at all times, and most information was communicated orally. There was, therefore, no "throw it over the wall" effect. These important teaming decisions were made earlier, and we were intent on preserving them.

RELATED PATTERNS:

This pattern treats each task both as an activity and as a deliverable.

OWNER PER DELIVERABLE (A.5.19)—addresses the general form of ownership and accountability.

FUNCTION OWNER AND COMPONENT OWNER—establishes a team for each artifact, and addresses the task of designing each artifact.

SOMEONE ALWAYS MAKES PROGRESS (4.1.20)—addresses the general distraction management pattern.

SACRIFICE ONE PERSON (4.1.22)—addresses specialization to lose only one person.

DAY CARE (4.1.23)—addresses training as a separate deliverable from the software.

SACRIFICE ONE PERSON (4.1.22).

READING:

See [Csikszentmihalyi 1990] and [DeMarco Lister 1976].

A version of this pattern first appeared in [Cockburn 1998].

4.1.22   Sacrifice One Person *

Alias: SACRIFICIAL LAMB

... during a typical project, there are always a host of small distractions.

Small distractions can add up and sap the strength of the team.

Even small distractions must be handled, but it is important to note that they take time away from the primary task. In particular, any distraction, even a small one, disrupts "flow" time, which costs significant additional time to regain.

Many small distractions involve less desirable jobs.

Therefore:

Assign just one person to the distraction until it is resolved.

This pattern is very much like TEAM PER TASK (4.1.21), except that the distraction is smaller. As such, it can seemingly be handled by one person half time to full time.

All but one member of the team moves forward distraction free. The person assigned to the distracting task may be unhappy, so try to get that person back on the team again as soon as possible. If you feel that one person is too much to sacrifice to this task and want to make it part time work, estimate the loss of flow time that would result from trying to address both this distraction and some other task.

If distractions keep happening, you will be left with no one performing the primary task, and you will need to examine why you have so many distractions in the first place.

OWNER PER DELIVERABLE (A.5.19) is the general ownership and accountability pattern. SOMEONE ALWAYS MAKES PROGRESS (4.1.20) is the general distraction management pattern. TEAM PER TASK (4.1.21) is the general form of this pattern at the team level.

Several patterns refine this pattern for specific contexts. DAY CARE (4.1.23) addresses training as a separate deliverable from the software and produces *mentor* as a profession. In FIREWALLS (4.2.9), the distraction is a series of requests from outside the team, so one of the developers is sacrificed to act as project manager (which can produce *project manager* as a profession). The MERCENARY ANALYST (4.1.24), usually a "hired gun," handles the distraction of documentation, leading to *technical writing* as a profession. And in GATEKEEPER (4.2.10), the constant inflow of technical information is the distraction, and one person is assigned to manage that information as a distinct, part-time task. GATEKEEPER is one of the major foundations for *manager* as a profession.

Don't forget the sacrificial lamb when it comes time to COMPENSATE SUCCESS (4.2.25).

PRINCIPLES INVOLVED:

As in TEAM PER TASK (4.1.21), the fact that handling the distraction looks like less than a full-time job illustrates the significance of the time spent getting into mental flow.

Maximum parallelism, profession, or sacrifice? If the people do not like the task, they consider it a sacrifice. If they like the task, it becomes their profession. Thus, FIREWALLS gives rise to the profession of project management, and DAY CARE gives rise to the profession of mentor.

EXAMPLES:

A. Updating the project schedule. On Project Winifred, the schedule was out of date. We thought it would be fair to let everyone on each team evaluate their own work in order to spread the experience, discomfort, and load. What really happened was that progress came to a total halt. When the design team got back to designing, a month had gone by with no design progress, and they had forgotten some of the design issues that had been in their heads. One of the teams used SACRIFICE ONE PERSON. They drew lots to choose one person to complete the whole team's estimation while the others got on with the main task. At the end of several weeks of estimation, that team had moved forward while the other teams were at a standstill. Thereafter, every team applied the pattern. The person working on the schedule really felt as if a sacrifice had been made. This pattern was originally called "Scylla," as described in the story of Scylla and Charybdis.

B. Simultaneous release to QA and development of the next release.

Project Winifred had one unit entering testing at the same time design was starting on the next. We optimistically thought the bug fixes would take a relatively small amount of time, and so we assigned the whole team to both fix bugs and perform new design.

Each fix broke a designer's train of thought for a period of time on the order of an hour, even though the fix itself took little time. Three or four bug fixes a day caused the designer to lose most of the day. Eventually, the designers gave up on the new release because they knew the next bug fix would arrive before they would have recovered their thoughts and made progress on the new design.

We applied SACRIFICE ONE PERSON, and assigned one person to fix bugs. We originally planned it as a half-time job, but found there was not enough time left over for the person to do any useful design. The person rejoined the new design team as soon as the release went through testing.

A version of this pattern first appeared in [Cockburn 1998].

4.1.23   Day Care *
Alias: PROGRESS TEAM/TRAINING TEAM

.. the project has just brought on several new people.

Your experts are spending all of their time mentoring novices.

You begin to hear things like "We are wasting our experts," or "A few experts could complete the whole project faster." Indeed, the experts are not proceeding at the rate you or they would expect because training the new people is draining their energy, time, and concentration. But the new people must be trained, by experts, of course.

At the same time, you must make progress on the project itself.

Therefore:

Put one expert in charge of all of the novices, and let the others develop the system.

Separate an experts-only "progress" team from a training team under the tutelage of one or more mentors. Select the mentors for their ability to teach design and programming (e.g., object-oriented design and programming) to novices. Let the progress team design 85-95 percent of the system, and let the training team deliver only 5-15 percent of the system and instead focus on quality training. Transfer people to the progress team as they become able to contribute meaningfully.

Make sure that the training team does not simply perform training exercises, but that they actually contribute to the final system in an ever-increasing way.

If you have many people to train (more than, say, six), you will have to design a series of tasks for them to attempt. Otherwise, you may give them a small, real part of the main system to design.

If the people in the training team are the ones who know the domain, you will have to make some further adjustment, or else the division of labor may cause conflict.

The result is that most of the experts can continue to make progress on the project. The novices contribute to a small part of the project that grows as they gain experience.

In extreme cases, though, you eventually have too few people to constitute a progress team.

How many people can one mentor train if the mentor performs training full time? A reasonable number is five. I have, however, heard of one person mentoring 15 people on five concurrent mini-projects.

PRINCIPLES INVOLVED:

The principles are synergy vs. distraction, the synergy of having a novice learn directly from an expert vs. the distraction experienced by the expert. Experts who have to answer novice questions are reduced to a fraction of their productivity, without particularly raising the productivity of the newcomers. Assigning one novice to work with an expert may cut the expert's productivity in half, assigning two may cut it to a third, and adding three may eliminate productivity altogether.

Assume X experts work at productivity 1 each and that a larger number of N novices work at n productivity each, with n being much smaller than 1 (on the order of 1/10 the productivity of the experts). If the experts could work together, they would have, in this simple model, a total productivity of (X).

If one expert is sacrificed to train the novices full time, that person has zero productivity. The group's total productivity using DAY CARE is

$$(X-1) + N*n$$

which is shown in the upper curve in the figure. If the experts and the novices are all mixed together ("Even Mix"), m=N/X novices per expert, each expert's productivity falls from 1 to something like 1/(m+1). The group's total productivity is now

$$(X*X/ (N+1)) + N*n$$

which is shown in the lower curve in the figure. The figure shows the productivity of DAY CARE versus the even mix. This graph shows the total productivity for the team in units of experienced people's productivity. As the number of novices increases, the even mix line shows the effect of training them. Let us check that the assumed productivity difference is not skewing the results. The lower figure shows the ratio of DAY CARE to even mix, for different productivity assumptions. Note that with five experts and five novices, the ratio is actually just below one, meaning that the experts are absorbing and making use of the novices. By two novices per expert, DAY CARE is already considerably more effective.

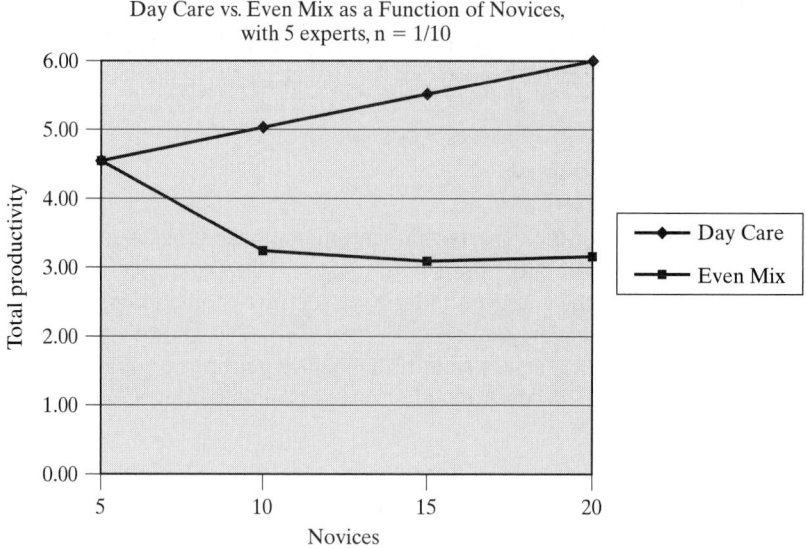

Day Care vs. Even Mix as a Function of Novices, with 5 experts, n = 1/10

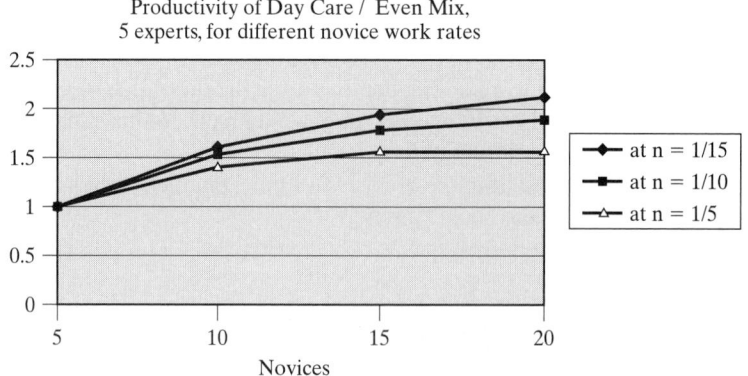

Productivity of Day Care / Even Mix, 5 experts, for different novice work rates

The nature of the training does not matter. Design and teaching are antagonistic tasks [as described in TEAM PER TASK (4.1.21)] that are better split into separate teams.

Treating the delivery of trained people as separate from the delivery of running software gives you access to OWNER PER DELIVERABLE (A.5.19). SOMEONE ALWAYS MAKES PROGRESS (4.1.20) protects the delivery of running software.

A. Mentoring.

The standard recommendation in the industry is to assign one to five novices to each trained expert. The consequence is that the experts spend the prime part of their energies training halfheartedly. Besides being drained of the energy needed to design the system, the experts typically do not have the personality, background, or inclination to actually teach the novices how to do design. They are torn between trying to get maximum productivity out of their trainees and trying to perform the maximum amount of development themselves. Thus, they neither develop the system nor train the novices adequately.

Some companies have developed dedicated "Apprenticeship" programs, in which novices are put under the tutelage of a dedicated mentor for 2 out of every 3 weeks for 6 months.

B. Adding staff.

In *The Mythical Man-Month*, Fred Brooks talks about the training costs of adding people to a project [Brooks 1995]. These new people drain productivity from the experts. The same suggestion applies: Put the newcomers in a separate team to learn the system and move them to the progress team as soon as they are up to speed.

In *Situated Learning: Legitimate Peripheral Participation*, Lave and Wenger describe the use of this sort of arrangement in apprentice-based work situations [Lave Wenger 1991].

A version of this pattern first appeared in [Cockburn 1998].

RELATED PATTERNS:

This pattern is a cross-specialization of several patterns: SOMEONE ALWAYS MAKES PROGRESS (4.1.20), TEAM PER TASK (4.1.21), SACRIFICE ONE PERSON (4.1.22), and OWNER PER DELIVERABLE (A.5.19).

See also APPRENTICESHIP (4.2.4).

4.1.24   Mercenary Analyst *

On one of his many journeys in the Appalachian Mountains, the itinerant folk song collector John Jacob Niles heard a woman singing a particularly beautiful song. He persuaded her to repeat the now-famous Christmas song "I Wonder as I Wander" until he had learned it himself. He later said, "I never saw her again."

... you are assembling the roles for the organization. The organization exists in a context where external reviewers, customers, and internal developers expect to use project documentation to understand the system architecture and its internal workings. (User documentation is considered separately.) Supporting both a design notation and the related project documentation is too tedious a job for people who are directly contributing to product artifacts.

Technical documentation is the dirty work required of every project. It's important to create—and, more so, to maintain—good documentation for subsequent use by the project team. But who writes these documents?

If developers create their own documentation, "real" work is hampered. Meeting software deadlines means money to the organization, and technical documentation is one of those things we tell ourselves that we can defer until there is time to do it. But the time often never comes, and an organization without good internal technical documentation of its system has a serious handicap.

Internal documentation is often write-only: it is rarely read after it is written.

Engineers often don't have good communication skills.

Many projects use tools like Rational Rose to do design. These tools produce pretty pictures. A good picture, however, is not necessarily a good design, and architects can become victims of the elegance of their own drawings (see the following rationale).

Therefore:

Hire a technical writer who is proficient in the necessary domains, but who does not have a stake in the design itself.

This person will capture the design using a suitable notation and will format and publish the design for reviews and for use by the organization itself.

The documentation itself should be maintained online if possible. It must be kept up to date (therefore, MERCENARY ANALYST is a full-time job), and it should relate to customer scenarios [SCENARIOS DEFINE PROBLEM (4.2.8)]. Note, though, that all team members need to provide input to keep the documentation current. The AD-HOC CORRECTIONS (A.5.2) pattern [Weir 1998] suggests that a master copy of the documentation be kept and that team members write corrections in the margin. One team member is assigned to periodically update the document.

The success of this pattern depends on the ability to find a suitably skilled agent to fill the role of mercenary analyst. If the pattern succeeds, the new context defines a project whose progress can be reviewed [STAND-UP MEETING (5.2.7)] and monitored by community experts outside the project.

If the MERCENARY ANALYST really is a "mercenary" who, as Paul Chisholm notes, "rides into town, gets the early stuff documented, kisses his horse, saddles up his girl, and rides off into the sunset" [Chisholm 1994], then it's good to retain some of the expertise by combining MERCENARY ANALYST with DEVELOPING IN PAIRS (4.2.28).

This pattern, uncommon though empirically grounded and effective, is found in Borland's Quattro Pro for Windows and in many AT&T projects (e.g., a joint venture based in New Jersey, a formative organization in switching support, and others). It is difficult to find people with the necessary skills to fill this role.

Rybczynski writes:

> Here is another liability: beautiful drawings can become ends in themselves. Often, if the drawing deceives, it is not only the viewer who is enchanted but also the maker, who is the victim of his own artifice. Alberti understood this danger and pointed out that architects should not try to imitate painters and produce lifelike drawings. The purpose of architectural drawings, according to him, was merely to illustrate the relationship of the various parts ... Alberti understood, as many architects of today do not, that the rules of drawing and the rules of building are not one and the same, and mastery of the former does not ensure success in the latter. [Rybczynski 1989, p. 121].

A passage from Manzoni's *The Betrothed* [Manzoni 1984] might amuse the MERCENARY ANALYST.

> The peasant who knows not how to write, and who needs to write, applies to one who knows that art, choosing as far as he can one of his own station, for with others he is hesitant, or a little untrusting. He informs him, with more or less clarity and orderliness, of who his ancestors were, and in the same manner tells him what to set down on paper. The literate person understands part and guesses at the rest, gives a few pieces of advice, suggests a few changes, and says "Leave it to me."

> He picks up his pen, puts the other's thoughts as well as he can in literary form, corrects them, improves them, embellishes them, tones them down, or even omits them, according to how he thinks best, because—and there's nothing to be done about it—someone who knows better than others has no wish to be a mere tool in their hands, and when he is concerned with the business of others he wants it to go a little in his own way.

Richard Gabriel [Gabriel 1995] notes the following are important traits of this role:

- Possesses strong skills as a meeting facilitator
- Likes things organized
- Possesses good attention to details
- Possesses written instructional material (for software)
- Lacks the ego to invest in the material being documented
- Is very smart and highly educated

In exceptional cases, the MERCENARY ANALYST can actually have a stake in the design. Betsy Hanes Perry writes:

> When I fill this role, I most definitely have a stake in the design: I want to make sure it's elegant, consistent, and clean. The architect has primary responsibility, of course, but I also suggest places in which the design conflicts with itself or may lead to future misunderstandings. As I see it, a software architecture is an idea. The designer/implementors are responsible for expressing that idea (or those ideas) as code; I express it/them as prose. Both are projections of the idea into a particular plane. When there's a conflict, the code is probably correct [Perry 1997].

Many projects put faith in tools and notations such as Unified Modeling Language (UML) to improve quality. But, as Perry points out, tools largely provide the forum and opportunity for a human being to engage in the processes and convey the insights that contribute to quality. For documentation to have added value as a quality tool, the documentation process must proceed in the spirit of this admonition.

Paul Chisholm offers the following about the history and rationale of MERCENARY ANALYST:

> MERCENARY ANALYST came from two sources:

> (1) Borland's Quattro Pro for Windows, which Jim Coplien identified as *the* most productive software development organization he's ever seen (average 1000 delivered noncommentary source lines of C++ per staff **week**), in large

part due to the fact that developers had people to write the development documentation for them).

Designer/coders have responsibilities that cannot be delegated. Some responsibilities, such as documentation, can be delegated. Besides, many excellent programmers and most average ones are less than stellar writers. (Richard [Gabriel] may disagree that this *is* the case, and will certainly disagree that this *should* be the case ...)

(2) A combination of two patterns. One, from Tony Hansen's group, is DISPOSABLE ANALYSIS: do analysis once, translate to design, throw away the analysis, keep only the design up to date with the code. The other is my observation that most CASE tools require significant experience in the method and the tool itself. If you have DISPOSABLE ANALYSIS (which few projects plan to do but many follow unintentionally), you should not develop local expertise in Computer-Aided Software Engineering (CASE) tool operation.

It's bad enough learning FrameMaker. CASE tools tend to have lousy user interfaces; it's a real pain to use them, or learn how to use them.

The "mercenary" in MERCENARY ANALYST comes from the "hired gun" quality a MERCENARY ANALYST might have: he rides into town, gets the early stuff documented, kisses his horse, saddles up his girl, and rides off into the sunset. That's the DISPOSABLE ANALYSIS model, not the Borland Quattro Pro for Windows model!

MERCENARY ANALYST plays well with DEVELOPING IN PAIRS (4.2.28).

Someone quoted by Jim Coplien wrote that "Mercenary Analyst is the professional technical writer who takes care of all the project diagrams and documentation so that the task of documentation doesn't get in the way of the architects."

Maybe not a "tech writer," and not "*all* the diagrams and documentation," but, yes, that's the idea.

What should be a MERCENARY ANALYST's education? Mastery of his or her tools (e.g., word processor, CASE tool) is beyond that of most users. Experience (perhaps expertise) in the "method" behind the documentation (e.g., an ObjecTime MERCENARY ANALYST would have to know ROOM well, someone writing requirements would need systems engineering and/or software development experience).

What is the MERCENARY ANALYST's motivation? To get the *software* (**not** the documentation) out faster!

How can one paint CASE diagrams without knowledge of software? I had some naive hope that a CASE tool MERCENARY ANALYST could be a highly skilled clerk. I've given up on that. There may be some way of combining MERCENARY ANALYST with DEVELOPING IN PAIRS (4.2.28) (or a variant for triples) to make MERCENARY ANALYST some sort of entry-level or apprentice position.

Domain Knowledge. While knowledge of the domain is important for a project [(DOMAIN EXPERTISE IN ROLES (4.2.22)]. I don't think the MERCENARY ANALYST needs it. (I hope not!)

Knowledge of software is important. Would you trust a driving instruction manual written by someone who'd never driven? [Chisholm 1994]

4.1.25   Interrupts Unjam Blocking **

During one project status meeting, it was reported that a critical piece of hardware was malfunctioning. Unfortunately, the expert on the hardware was on the other side of the country and was involved in his own work. However, the expert had the (mis)fortune to be on the meeting conference call, as was the project director, who informed the expert in blunt terms that his services were required immediately. He was on the next plane out.

... you are fine-tuning the scheduling for a high productivity design/implementation process or a low-latency service process. The scheduling problem is to be addressed on a small scale (i.e., this is not the scheduling for entire departments, but the work of cooperating individuals). You want to use INFORMAL LABOR PLAN (4.1.14), but you need additional criteria for individuals and small groups in order to plan their schedules. Local decisions may lack the scope necessary to avoid duplication of work, missed opportunities, and other unfortunate problems.

A comprehensive scheduling plan is difficult if not impossible to develop; yet, without some kind of plan it becomes easy to fall into thrashing: rushing from task to task without making any real progress.

The events and tasks in a process are too complex to schedule development activities as a time-linear sequence.

Complete scheduling insight is impossible. Even if it were possible to capture the entire picture of the project for an instant, that picture would change very quickly. The dynamics of project development mean that the best we can hope for is a high-level, approximate schedule.

The programmers with the longest development schedules will benefit if more of other peoples' code is done before they try integrating or testing later code, especially if their interval can't otherwise be shortened [see CODE OWNERSHIP (5.2.13)].

Therefore:

If a process is about to be blocked because a critical resource is unavailable, interrupt the role that provides that resource so that role can unblock that process.

The nature of the critical resource can vary. It may be a software module that is in the critical path. It could be the latest software integration. It is often critical knowledge, without which one cannot move forward. Whatever the resource, the approach is to interrupt the provider of that resource.

If the overhead is small enough, it doesn't affect throughput. It will always improve local latency.

The process should have a higher throughput, again, at the expense of higher coupling. Coupling may have already been facilitated by earlier patterns, such as WORK FLOWS INWARD (4.1.18), RESPONSIBILITIES ENGAGE (5.1.14), HALLWAY CHATTER (5.1.15), MOVE RESPONSIBILITIES (5.1.18), and COUPLING DECREASES LATENCY (5.1.22).

This pattern is intended to apply most frequently to cooperating developers working on a single project, a concept supported empirically from a high productivity process in AT&T. There are strong software engineering (operating system) principles at work here as well.

It may be useful to prioritize interrupts and to service the ones that would optimize the productivity of the organization as a whole. That is, it is better to unblock four people who are currently blocked than to unblock a single squeaky wheel. The decision-making process should be fast, and most of the time it should be distributed. Where arbitration is needed, apply PATRON ROLE (4.2.15). The simplest resolution is the pattern DON'T INTERRUPT AN INTERRUPT (4.1.26).

The PATRON ROLE (4.2.15) and manager roles can help the team audit the project for blocked progress, but they should defer to the Developers (or other directly impacted roles) to resolve the blockage whenever possible. Management intervention can be effective, but it may risk goodwill within the project.

Joe Maranzano notes that a corollary to this pattern is another pattern, which can be summarized as follows: Don't put too many critical tasks on one person [Maranzano 1992]. This pattern is related to MODERATE TRUCK NUMBER (4.2.24) and DISTRIBUTE WORK EVENLY (5.1.13).

This pattern is much less effective if the provider of the resource is not working on the same project as you are. In that case, the provider has little incentive to service your interrupt, and you risk alienating the provider if you engage in incessant pestering. This problem can be mitigated by adopting a policy of reciprocity, of fair and proactive exchange of value among partners. [Dikel 2001].

4.1.26   Don't Interrupt an Interrupt *

The original interruption device.

... you've applied INTERRUPTS UNJAM BLOCKING (4.1.25), but you notice that the organization is now thrashing, particularly in the end game or under heavy churn.

It's important to balance a desire that SOMEONE ALWAYS MAKES PROGRESS (4.1.20) with the thrashing that can accompany short-term priority calls. One worker will inevitably be blocked on you—you can't do both things at once. Complete foresight and perfect scheduling are unreasonable to expect.

Therefore:

If a developer is already working in "interrupt mode" on a critical issue, don't put that work aside until it is complete or until that issue itself becomes hopelessly tangled.

This pattern prevents the endless churn that can result from too much context switching. It also helps to ensure that SOMEONE ALWAYS MAKES PROGRESS (4.1.20). And it provides some "back pressure" in the process that can help temper irresponsibly quick reversals of position in the front end.

This is a simple, though somewhat arbitrary, rule that keeps scheduling from becoming an elaborate ceremony.

This concept relates to the "red zone" from Linda McLyman's analysis of the Satir change model [Satir 1991], which suggests that if a foreign element (problem) arrives before the organization starts to learn its way out of the last foreign element, recovery is difficult.

4.2 Piecemeal Growth Pattern Language

The Pattern Language

This pattern language offers patterns to strengthen and fine-tune an organization using feedback and insight. It is essentially a process of repair. Figure 4.2 shows the patterns and their connections to each other.

Note, perhaps surprisingly, that none of these patterns have fundamental ties to software development. They are applicable to any design activity that involves a group of people building something to solve a problem. They are as applicable to software services as they are to building product, to hardware development as they are to software development. They are patterns about human nature and human organizations, about the ways that people come together to solve problems.

A Story about Piecemeal Growth

When I started to plan the Q project, I wanted a small core team of architects, so I employed SIZE THE ORGANIZATION (4.2.2) with an eye to PHASING IT IN (4.2.3) through APPRENTICESHIP (4.2.4) with other staff later on. The project was too large for a SOLO VIRTUOSO (4.2.5) approach—though we would use that pattern later to flesh out a prototype. I put forward the opportunity and made it possible for people to sign up; there was no corporate or management compunction to join. Hence, it was purely a SELF-SELECTING TEAM (4.2.11), started as a SKUNKWORKS (4.2.14) beneath management radar.

My main job as project coordinator was to put up the FIREWALLS (4.2.9) to management until we had our act together. But my second job was to make sure we got a good group of people to the end of HOLISTIC DIVERSITY (4.2.19). We brought in Lalita for her work in scripting languages and their environments and Peter for his architectural expertise. Later, we decided we needed market domain knowledge, and that's when we brought on Jim and Beki in the interest of having DOMAIN EXPERTISE IN ROLES (4.2.22). The recruitment strategy always involved ferreting out matches of interest that would excite the players, amplified by the new nature and somewhat subversive approach of the opportunity. TEAM PRIDE (4.2.13) was an emergent property of this process. We also had our own value system and model of rewards: all team members would share credit for any patents that were issued, and, together, we would seize a leadership role in the organization. We also knew that we were catering to the organization's product interests and that the organization would COMPENSATE SUCCESS (4.2.25).

Beki served as the GATEKEEPER (4.2.10), bringing in ideas from the AOL Instant Messenger world, interviewing (child!) users of the system, and bringing in knowledge of the organization and market opportunities. She and I split the duties of PUBLIC CHARACTER (4.2.17) and MATRON ROLE (4.2.18).

We moved forward on design using CRC cards to formulate an architecture, employing SCENARIOS DEFINE PROBLEM (4.2.8) and GROUP VALIDATION (4.2.32). The goal was to get the project "running" on CRC cards and then to implement a first, simple cut in a 1- or 2-day programming session, DEVELOPING IN PAIRS (4.2.28) all together in one room. The CRC cards were given to the individuals best suited to those areas, exemplifying both DOMAIN EXPERTISE IN ROLES (4.2.22) and, to the degree one could talk about subsystems at that point, SUBSYSTEM BY SKILL (4.2.23).

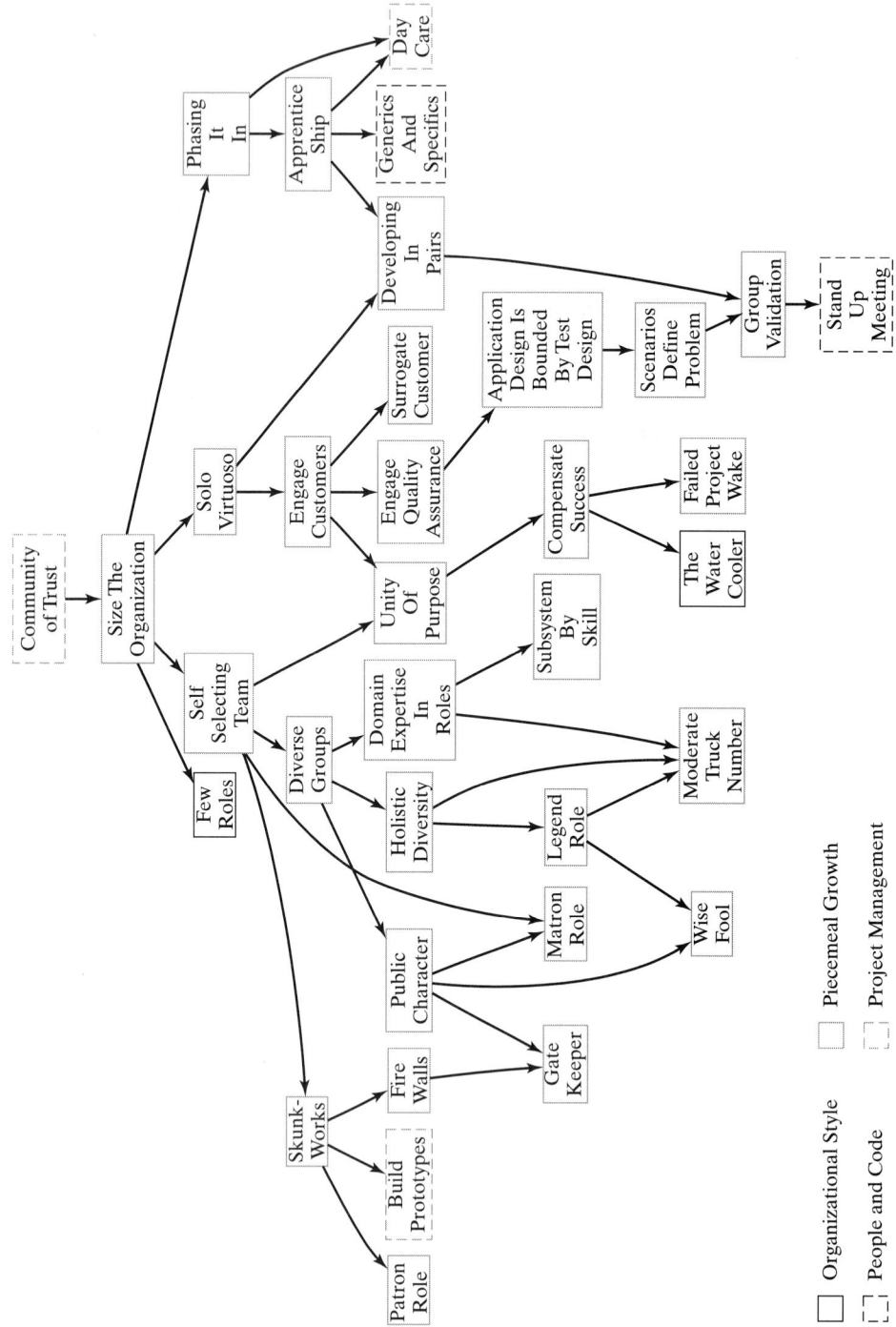

FIGURE 4.2 The patterns and their Interconnection

At our (frequent) meetings, we made sure that work was spread around evenly. We did most things in a group to make sure that the specialization didn't get out of hand. We occasionally traded off CRC cards, all in the interest of having a MODERATE TRUCK NUMBER (4.2.24).

At some point in the process, people felt that the CRC cards weren't enough and that we needed to document the scenarios. We used ping-pong diagrams, first on whiteboards and later using a formal documentation tool [SCENARIOS DEFINE PROBLEM (4.2.8)]. In order to create this documentation, we had to SACRIFICE ONE PERSON (4.1.22) and find a MERCENARY ANALYST (4.1.24) [we were too small to enlist a full-fledged MERCENARY ANALYST (4.1.24), but we faked it].

Lalita went away as a SOLO VIRTUOSO (4.2.5) to BUILD PROTOTYPES (4.1.7). The prototype failed to energize the team to take the next steps forward, and things came to an impasse, particularly in light of competing priorities on other development projects.

Dysfunction struck the organization due to the untimely departure of Beki and Peter from the project and, afterwards, to Lalita's promotion out of the project. Jim took the ideas forward into another project, but he took no other people with him. We did not have a FAILED PROJECT WAKE (4.2.26), though perhaps we should have. We didn't get so far as to run the development exercise as a team in a room, at which point INTERRUPTS UNJAM BLOCKING (4.1.25) and DON'T INTERRUPT AN INTERRUPT (4.1.26) would have become important.

4.2.1   Community of Trust

See Section 4.1.1.

4.2.2   Size the Organization **

... within a larger organization, usually that of a sponsoring enterprise or company, there need to be smaller organizations capable of creating large software systems [greater than 25,000 source lines of code (SLOC)] that meet competitive cost and schedule benchmarks. This pattern shows how the proper sizing of an organization is vital to the health of the project and to the productivity of its people.

❖   ❖   ❖

Large software projects (greater than 25,000 SLOC) are seldom delivered on time and within budget when the development team is either too large or too small.
Two arguments have led us to this conclusion:

1. There are limits to the size of software development teams that allow them to work effectively. A team can handle a larger problem than an individual can ([Beyer Holtzblatt 1998], p. 4).

2. The addition of people to a project late in the game rarely helps complete that project on time and within budget.

If a software development team is too large, you can reach a point of greatly diminishing returns. We have found empirically that an organization's size affects a deliverable nonlinearly. Communication overhead goes up as the square of the size increases, which means that the organization becomes less cohesive as the square of the size increases, while the "horsepower" of the organization goes up only linearly.

In addition, if the organization is too small, the team won't have critical mass, and productivity will suffer. Projects larger than 25 KSLOC can rarely be done by a SOLO VIRTUOSO (4.2.5), and overly small organizations have inadequate inertia and can easily become unstable.

However, experience has shown that a carefully selected and well-nurtured small team of around 10 people can provide a suitable critical mass with a capacity to develop a 1,500 KSLOC project in 31 months, a 200 KSLOC project in 15 months, or a 60 KSLOC project in 8 months.

Keeping the organization small makes it possible for everybody to have knowledge of how the project works (*global knowledge*). We have found empirically that most roles in a project can handle interactions with about six or seven other roles; with 10 people, you can almost manage total global communications (and a fully connected network may not be necessary).

Projects that do well have processes that adapt, and processes adapt well only if there is widespread buy-in and benefit. The dialogue necessary to ensure both buy-in and benefit can occur only in small organizations. Tom DeMarco has noted that everybody who is to benefit from process should be involved in process work and process decision making [DeMarco 1993].

Further study might evaluate the relationship between this pattern and Alexander's THE DISTRIBUTION OF TOWNS ([Alexander 1977], ff. 16) and related patterns. Here, we stipulate that the social organization must be small reflecting a SUBCULTURE BOUNDARY ([Alexander 1977], ff. 75) and an IDENTIFIABLE NEIGHBORHOOD ([Alexander 1977], ff. 80). Alexander emphasizes the grander architectural context that balances support for the ecology with the economies of scale that large towns can provide, while also supporting the xenophobic tendencies of human nature. Small organizations like that being built here rarely exist in isolation, but instead exist in the context of a broader supporting organization. This relationship to the larger organization invokes the PATRON ROLE (4.2.15).

Adding people late to a project rarely helps complete that project on time and within budget.

One manager writes: "On [one] project, I grew from 10 to 20 people to meet a customer contract ... with new people, [I] wound up three months late because of 'absorption' of new folks into the organization."

Many software development cultures support technical manager groups of up to 10 people. Adding more people to the group would force a group split, which can cause a large decrease in productivity, all other things being equal. We have also found that a single team is better than a collection of subteams. The faster a team breaks up into subteams that worry about their own responsibilities rather than those of the larger team, the less effective the enterprise will be as a whole.

Therefore:

By default, choose about 10 people to establish critical mass in the development of large software systems and avoid adding individuals late in the game or trying to work backwards from a completion date.

Experts vary on the exact number. The number 10 has a bit of tradition associated with it, but numbers like 6 or 7 are also common. A two-person group is too small, and a 13-person group is too big.

Starting a large project with 10 people can be overkill, but it avoids the expense and overhead of adding more people later. However, once a core team establishes an identity, it can grow graciously by PHASING IT IN (4.2.3) or using APPRENTICESHIP (4.2.4). The organization can generate knowledge early on by building and throwing away a prototype [see BUILD PROTOTYPES (4.1.7)]. To decide whom to hire into the nascent organization, use patterns like DOMAIN EXPERTISE IN ROLES (4.2.22) and ARCHITECTURE TEAM (5.2.4). SMALL WRITING TEAM (A.5.27) ([Bramble 2002], p. 31) suggests that two or three people write the use cases; the others will fill in other roles.

Astute readers might consider this pattern and remark, "You have a strange idea of what constitutes a large project! I can see this pattern working for projects that will grow to 30 or 40 people and maybe a few tens of thousands of lines of code. But does this pattern work for really large projects?"

First, it's important to understand that few real software development teams are larger than a few dozen people; larger projects almost always self-organize into subcommunities [DIVIDE AND CONQUER (5.1.6)]. But even the largest projects start with an idea, and an idea starts with an individual or a small group of people. This pattern says that a small group should take the project as far as they can before other staff are actively engaged. One must anticipate the point of diminishing returns for the seed team and seek people early enough so that they will be available and ready when they are needed. And, of course, people should be brought on gradually (see PHASING IT IN (4.2.3), DAY CARE (4.1.23), etc.). But start small, and stay as small as possible for as long as possible. Large systems grow from small systems that work.

Second, remember that it is imperative to have FEW ROLES (5.1.2). With 10 people, it is easy to define and fill half a dozen or so roles. But with a large initial team, people will at first be at a loss as to what to do until they receive assignments (and you can't give everyone an assignment all at once). So they will find something to do, and they will tend to invent roles for themselves. Unfortunately, this is a good way to create deadbeat roles.

Joe Walters said that a project shouldn't grow larger than the size of the auditorium of the building where the project is centered [Walters 1976].

Once the staff sizing is complete, the project can SIZE THE SCHEDULE (4.1.2).

4.2.3   Phasing It In **

... key project players have been hired or otherwise brought into the project. They cover the necessary areas of expertise [DOMAIN EXPERTISE IN ROLES (4.2.22)], but the project still needs more staff.

❖   ❖   ❖

Growing projects must figure out how to increase the number of long-term staff: whom to hire, how many to hire, and when to hire them. Projects must ramp up while minimizing the pains of growth.

You need enough people for critical mass. Yet you cannot just hire anyone off the street; staff are not plug compatible and interchangeable.

The right group of initial people [SIZE THE ORGANIZATION (4.2.2)] sets the tone for the project, and it's important to hire the key people first. You need a critical mass of key people early on. However, too many people too early creates a burden for the core team.

Therefore:

Phase the hiring program. Start by hiring people to meet the basic core competencies of the business and gradually bring on new people as the project needs to grow.

❖   ❖   ❖

The organization can staff up to meet development load. This pattern is closely related to APPRENTICESHIP (4.2.4) and MODERATE TRUCK NUMBER (4.2.24). DAY CARE (4.1.23) can be applied to help with the training and mentoring load that new employees place on the organization.

This well-known management technique allows the project to establish an identity early on and to grow graciously.

Larry Putnam points out that projects that grow very quickly at the beginning tend to be late. He advocates the idea of growing staff gradually [Putnam 1992].

In *The Mythical Man-Month,* Brooks states, "V. A. Vyssotsky of Bell Telephone Laboratories estimates that a large project can sustain a manpower buildup of 30 percent per year. More than that strains and even inhibits the evolution of the essential informal structure and its communication pathways" ([Brooks 1995], page 293).

What constitutes *core competencies*? It depends on the business you are in. If you are in finance, you want people who can develop financial software. The better people you can get early on, the better off you will be, and it is probably a good return on investment to spare no expense on talent at this early stage. Talent isn't limited to domain knowledge, though. You also need individuals who can put customers at ease, keep a cool head for strategic planning, "fill in the cracks" by performing the miscellaneous detailed tasks that others don't want to do or forget to do, etc. Many individuals have many of these talents. The key, then, is to cover the crucial needs early on with as few people as possible and to grow the organization once that organization has gelled [see STABLE ROLES (5.1.5)]. You can achieve these goals with HOLISTIC DIVERSITY (4.2.19) and DIVERSE GROUPS (4.2.16).

4.2.4   Apprenticeship *

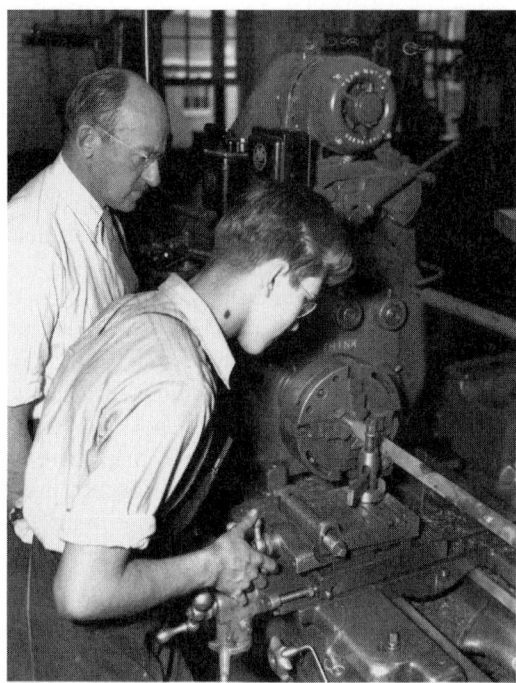

...the project is incrementally staffing up after the first round of experts have been brought on board.

❖   ❖   ❖

A project must balance its need for growth with its need to develop and maintain deep domain expertise. You need enough people for critical mass. However, staff are not plug compatible and interchangeable. And academic training and prior experience are rarely, in themselves, adequate preparation for competent work at a new task.

Therefore:

Turn new hires into experts [see DOMAIN EXPERTISE IN ROLES (4.2.22)] through an apprenticeship program. Every new employee should work as an apprentice (not just a mentee) to an established expert. Most apprenticeship programs will last 6 months to 1 year—the amount of time it takes to make a paradigm shift.

❖   ❖   ❖

It will be possible to maintain expertise in the organization. This pattern also reduces the organization's *truck number* by spreading knowledge around. The truck number is the number of people who possess unique critical domain expertise. If any one of these people were hit by a truck, the organization will have lost a critical resource [see MODERATE TRUCK NUMBER (4.2.24)]. By working to reduce the truck number, the experts feel valued, and the apprentices are given a good environment in which to learn.

Manage drain on expert staff resources with DAY CARE (4.1.23).

DEVELOPING IN PAIRS (4.2.28) is often used as an effective APPRENTICESHIP technique.

It is better to apprentice people than to put people through a "trial by fire" that may damage the project. The apprenticeship approach makes it possible to form domain-specific teams, and it is important to keep the team concept as a central part of organizational values.

4.2.5   Solo Virtuoso *

. . . we have described the optimal size of organizations needed to create large software systems on time and within budget [SIZE THE ORGANIZATION (4.2.2)]. The following pattern explains what to do for smaller systems (fewer than 25 KSLOC) when a product must still be created on time and within budget, but when rapid growth is not anticipated after the first release.

When a smaller software project (fewer than 25 KSLOC) is overstaffed, communication overhead increases, and talented individuals, who could produce the software entirely on their own, are bridled, their "horsepower" diminished.

We have said that organizational size affects the deliverable in a nonlinear manner [SIZE THE ORGANIZATION (4.2.2)]. We have also observed that communication overhead increases as the square of the size, which means that the organization becomes less cohesive as the square of the size, while the "horsepower" of the organization increases only linearly.

The question, then, is this: What organizational size works best for smaller software projects?

The answer depends on the individual(s) involved in the project. The productivity of a single individual can be higher than that of a collection of productive individuals. We have seen single-person developments generate 25 KSLOC of deliverable code in 4 months (e.g., for a craft interface for a telecommunication system) and two-person developments generate 135 KSLOC in 30 months. Many of these individuals adhered faithfully to all stipulated review schedules and verification steps.

Boehm [Boehm 1981] notes a 20-fold spread between the least and most effective developers. A telecommunications developer recently told me that "having the right expertise means the difference between being able to solve a problem in a half hour and never being able to solve the problem at all."

[Note: Boehm quotes Grant and Sackman ([Grant Sackman 1966] p. 667), who note a 26-fold spread.]

The result of using a SOLO VIRTUOSO is an organization limited to producing small development efforts. Though there is a single development role, other roles may be necessary to support marketing, toolsmithing, and other functions. The productivity of a suitably chosen single developer is sufficient for sizable projects; here, we establish 25 KSLOC as a limit.

Therefore:

Design and implement the entire system with one or two of your most effective developers.

❖   ❖   ❖

This pattern is not a "License to Hack." The work of a SOLO VIRTUOSO is still subject to technical reviews, validation, and verification at appropriate times in the development cycle [ENGAGE CUSTOMERS (4.2.6) and STAND-UP MEETING (5.2.7)]. This pattern works nicely with DEVELOPING IN PAIRS (4.2.28).

See also MODERATE TRUCK NUMBER (4.2.24), which raises concerns about the use of this pattern in risk-averse businesses.

4.2.6   Engage Customers **

Clerk measuring a customer for a suit of clothes, San Antonio, Texas.

A friend of one of the authors once designed and implemented the user interface for a large system. He received input from customers on how to make it useful for them. Unfortunately, the requirements writers had a different idea and made him remove the features the customers liked. However, when the customers asked for the missing features, the requirements writers were forced to relent. I guess the situation didn't help relations between my friend and the requirements writers.

... an organization is in place, and its QA function has been generally shaped and chartered. The QA function needs input to drive its work. Many people in the enterprise are concerned about quality issues.

It's important that the development organization ensures and maintains customer satisfaction by encouraging communication between customers and key development organization roles. This communication isn't the responsibility of any single "customer satisfaction" group; instead, the need pervades the entire organizational structure. Most organizations hesitate to allow direct contact between developers and customers, fearing that the developers are "loose cannons on deck" who will promise to deliver things that exceed the scope of a job.

Yet, you can't know all of the requirements up front, so developers need to keep going back to customers for more information. Customers, in turn, need to keep coming back to developers with their insights, particularly when developers BUILD PROTOTYPES (4.1.7). After all, requirements changes occur even after design reviews are complete and coding has started.

Many organizations depend on their marketing organization to provide them with requirements data. But marketing doesn't provide design data (Beyer Holtzblatt 1998], p. 30). The best that marketing can do (or *should* do) is to understand what will sell and why people will buy what you want to sell. Designers, in turn, must understand how people will use the product in a way that creates value for them. Good value sometimes leads to good market potential, but marketing usually looks at other factors (e.g., brand name recognition, product name, and posturing in the market) that designers care little about.

Missing customer requirements are a serious problem; in fact, most problems in software systems can be traced to requirements problems ([Daley 1977], [Boehm 1976]). Yet it seems like so much effort to elicit these requirements, especially when this work does not directly produce a marketable artifact. It seems like make-work.

Customers are traditionally not part of the mainstream development effort, which makes it difficult to discover and incorporate their insights. Yet, customer contact correlates with project success [Keil Carmel 1995].

Trust relationships between managers and coders are often strained, so you don't want them to be the sole intermediaries between developers and customers.

Therefore:

Closely couple the Customer role with the Developer and Architect roles, not just with QA or marketing roles. In short, developers and architects must talk freely and often with customers. When possible, engage customers in their own environment rather than bringing them into your environment.

Two things are necessary to allow this interaction to happen: opportunity and culture. Developers must have the opportunity (and the means) to communicate with customers. They should meet customers personally to establish trust and a free flow of communication.

But these visits will be superficial if the organizational culture builds walls between customers and developers. In particular, if system requirements must go through a lengthy formal process to be approved, the developer will be hamstrung, unable to respond to customer requests. Therefore, the organization must develop a culture where developers have some latitude to respond to customers. We are not saying, however, that all control of requirements should be relegated to the developer. Order is necessary.

Beyer and Holtzblatt note that "many common ways of working with customers remove [designers] from their work" ([Beyer Holtzblatt 1998], pp. 36–7). One way to solve this problem is by "putting designers and engineers directly in the customer's work context" ([Beyer Holtzblatt 1998], p. 20), which is particularly important if you are using customer engagement to create wholly new market directions for the enterprise, rather than simply refining existing work. Putting developers in the customer's work environment also trains developers' intuition about good design and good human interfaces, and this intuition can fill in when specific detailed requirements are unavailable ([Beyer Holtzblatt 1998], p. 35).

Language is a key element of culture that can ensure a smooth customer engagement if treated properly and smother it if treated badly. Don't make your customers learn UML or other technical notations; instead, do your best to learn *their* language and to communicate with them in the terms of *their* culture.

The QA team can monitor the relationship to keep the direction within contractual business limits, while allowing a free flow of insights back and forth between developers and customers. Such communication can often flow unimpeded; at other times, however, it cannot [see GATEKEEPER (4.2.10)].

Note that this pattern is all about relationships and culture. It is the culture of respect for and interaction with customers that makes the communication effective, such as during the writing of use cases, as described in PARTICIPATING AUDIENCE (A.5.20) ([Bramble 2002], p. 35).

❖   ❖   ❖

This pattern supports requirements discovery from the customer, as required by SCENARIOS DEFINE PROBLEM (4.2.8) and BUILD PROTOTYPES (4.1.7). Other patterns like FIREWALLS (4.2.9) also build on this pattern. The pattern RECOMMITMENT MEETING (4.1.12) is a more formal derivative of this pattern in a different context.

A good understanding of customer needs can help you to avoid rework after implementation is done. While it is also important to continuously engage customers through each development episode of iteration, early understanding helps launch the effort in the right direction. For example, a Navision team in Copenhagen felt that improvements in customer engagement helped save time on their development schedule [Pedersen 2002].

This pattern was prominent in the Borland Quattro Pro for Windows case study. Also, see [Floyd 1992] and, in particular, the works of Reisin and Floyd therein.

Some processes and methods are founded on customer engagement, such as IBM's Joint Application Development (JAD). Other methods are conducive to customer engagement, such as Cunningham and Beck's CRC design technique. Other methods, and especially most CASE-based methods, are indifferent or harmful to customer engagement.

Even some of the best customer engagement techniques tend to stop once they achieve some level of contractual agreement about what is to be delivered. Customer engagement in agile processes, however, goes far beyond this traditional stopping point. Developers need to assimilate the context in which their product will be used: This process is called *contextual design*. Contextual design means gathering data on customers' models of how they do their work rather than creating models of how the program will solve the problem (such as done in use case modeling). See [Beyer Holtzblatt 1998].

The pattern is called ENGAGE CUSTOMERS (in the plural) to support a domain view and to avoid the possibility of being blindsided by a single customer.

The project must be careful to temper interactions between Customers and Developers, using FIREWALLS (4.2.9), GATEKEEPER (4.2.10), and the QA organizational presence as in ENGAGE QUALITY ASSURANCE (4.2.29). A big part of interacting with customers involves learning how they want to interact with the project as the unfolding software uncovers problems in requirements and systems engineering [see APPLICATION DESIGN IS BOUNDED BY TEST DESIGN (4.2.30)].

Note that maintenance of product quality is not the problem being solved here. Product quality is only one component of customer satisfaction. Studies have shown that customers leave one company for another when they feel they are being ignored (20 percent of the time) or when the attention they receive is rude or unhelpful (50 percent of the time). If customers experience software problems that cost more than $100 to fix and if the company does not fix the problems, then only 9 percent of the customers would do business with the company again. 82 percent would do business with the company again if the problems were quickly resolved after they complained. (The source for the former pair of percentages is The Forum Corporation; the source for the latter pair of percentages is Traveler's Insurance Company [Zuckerman Hatala1992].)

Joe Maranzano [Maranzano 1992] notes that this pattern probably should come earlier in the pattern language. However, it is important that the project roles be defined first—particularly those that involve interacting with the customer, and those that are driven by customer input (e.g., QA). Said in another way, the organization exists to serve the customer, so the organization should be in place before the customer is fully engaged.

This pattern works only if customers are directly accessible to the development team. If such accessibility is impossible for business reasons or because of geographic separation, consider SURROGATE CUSTOMER (4.2.7).

4.2.7   Surrogate Customer *

Store dummy displaying Daniel Boone hat, Amsterdam, New York.

... the project is beginning to move forward. As architects and developers get deeper into the project, questions about requirements begin to surface.

It is important to exchange ideas and clarify issues with customers. However, customers may not be available.

There are several reasons that a customer may be unavailable. If the project is new, there may be no customers yet. In fact, the product might even create its own customers. Or, the organization may never have established relationships with existing customers, and now it may not be a propitious time to do so.

In some cases, customers might not have the time to meet right now. They're busy too. But you need answers immediately.

Some corporate cultures insulate the developers from the customers; the two groups just don't talk. We certainly aren't recommending such a scenario but it does happen.

Whatever the cause, there is a temptation for developers to make their best guess and go on. The problem is that developers are naturally biased and they often assume customer behavior that conforms to their own design. However, there are always other ways to think about the application, some of which may not mesh with the developer's view.

Therefore:

Create a Surrogate Customer role in the project and fill that role with someone who will try to think like the customer. Treat the Surrogate Customer like the real customer.

If the organization has human factors people, they make natural Surrogate Customers. Their emphasis may be on the human interface, but developing that interface is often much of the battle.

System test organizations are similar to Surrogate Customers, but there are important differences in intent. System testers tend to evaluate a product with respect to a specification in order to determine its readiness for market. Customers, real or surrogate, are interested in knowing if the product meets their needs and is easy to use.

Fellow developers tend to make poor Surrogate Customers. For the most part, developers think too much alike.

Of course, no Surrogate Customer will ever replace a real customer. But surrogates can allow the project to move ahead in the absence of more concrete information. For more reading on the limitations of the Surrogate Customer role, see [Constantine Lockwood 1999] and [Bramble 2002].

Perhaps the perfect ideal involves the developers themselves as customers or Surrogate Customers, if they can overcome the "nerdish groupthink" owing to their identity as developers. See Create Rather Than Conform (8.9) in the Quattro Pro for Windows case study.

Most organizations seat the Surrogate Customer with the development team; in fact, this role is often a member of the development team. Consider instead seating developers at the customer site to avoid the problem described in the book *Contextual Design* ([Beyer Holtzblatt 1998], p. 34):

> Many IT departments avoid these problems by stationing IT developers with the customer organization. This certainly succeeds in making IT more responsive to the customer, but brings a loss of control. The developers easily become focused on short-term problems and solutions—they tend to become the local fix-it man. The structure of the customer's work and long-term possibilities for improvement are no more visible to IT developers than to the customer, and without this perspective they, like the customer, focus on the immediate and most visible issues. And they are stationed in a particular department, so cross-departmental issues are as invisible to them as to their customers. They are rewarded for producing quick fixes to pressing problems. The usual result is dozens of small applications, each solving a single problem, that do not work together to support the work coherently.

4.2.8   Scenarios Define Problem *

Discussing a worst-case scenario ...

How do you know a programmer is extroverted?
He stares at YOUR shoes when he talks to you.

... you want to engage the customer, and you need a mechanism to support other organizational alliances between the customer and developers.

Design documents are often ineffective as vehicles to communicate the customer vision of how the system should work.

There is a sense of natural business distancing and mistrust between customers and developers. Communication between developers and customers is crucial to the success of a system.

Therefore:

Capture system functional requirements as use cases.

It is obvious that use cases help increase understanding of requirements, but a less obvious aspect of use cases is that they help set boundaries of a problem. The latter concept became clear as one of the authors consulted with a group who was writing patterns of use cases. When I questioned a member of the group about what problem use cases solve, I got an unsatisfying answer. I probed deeper by asking how the situation would look if one didn't apply use cases, and he responded, "[without use cases,] you wouldn't know where to start because the problem would be too broad." Interestingly, he had never thought about use cases as a tool to bound the problem until that point.

Use cases do not capture success scenarios alone: Instead, they capture all of the scenarios that the system must deal with. There is no such thing as an exceptional case; in other words, make the exception the rule. Interview enough constituencies to get full coverage of the expectations of users and other stakeholders. Use cases also can, should, and almost certainly must be augmented with nonfunctional requirements.

It is easy to see that capturing requirements as use cases is a good idea, but what does this have to do with organizations? One of the tensions in many organizations is that the developers are, well, geeks. Many don't have particularly good communication skills or, more precisely, aren't particularly interested in interpersonal communication. So it is difficult to communicate requirements to developers. However, scenarios work. So if you really want to ENGAGE CUS-TOMERS (4.2.6), this pattern makes the job much easier.

The problem is now defined, and the architecture can proceed in earnest. You can use scenarios as a means of dialogue and requirements clarification with your users, particularly when building and demonstrating a system or subsystem prototype. For more on this concept, see CAT-ALYTIC SCENARIOS in the DEMO PREP (A.5.9) pattern language from Todd Coram [Coram 1996].

Also read about the MERCENARY ANALYST (4.1.24), who captures scenarios and uses them for project documentation (both internal and external).

[Cockburn 2000] is one of the most acclaimed references on use cases. Also see [Goldberg Rubin 1995], which takes scenarios all the way to the front of the process preceding design, and [Hsia 1994].

4.2.9   Firewalls **

Nobody gets past this point without my permission!

"A manager should be like the sweeper in curling: The sweeper runs ahead of the stone and sweeps away debris from the path of the stone so that the progress of the stone will be smooth and undisturbed — does this sound like your manager?" [Gabriel 1996]

Unfortunately, heavy human use in this same area could lead to bear/human interactions which could injure humans and cause management actions against the bear. — Sign at an entrance to Boulder Mountain Parks, Boulder, Colorado

... an organization of developers has formed in a corporate or social context where they are scrutinized by peers and by funders, customers, and other "outsiders." Project implementors are often distracted by outsiders who feel a need to offer input and criticism.

It's important to placate stakeholders who feel a need to "help" by giving them access to low levels of the project, without distracting developers and others who are moving towards project completion.

Isolationism doesn't work because information flow is important. But communication overhead increase nonlinearly with the number of external collaborators.

Many interruptions are noise.

Maturity and progress are more highly correlated with being in control than with being effectively controlled.

Therefore:

Create a manager role who shields other development personnel from interaction with external roles. The responsibility of this role is "to keep the pests away."

The new organization isolates developers from extraneous external interrupts. To avoid isolationism, this pattern must be tempered with others, such as ENGAGE CUSTOMERS (4.2.6) and GATEKEEPER (4.2.10).

This pattern was present in both BORLAND QUATTRO PRO FOR WINDOWS (CHAPTER 8) and in A HYPERPRODUCTIVE TELECOMMUNICATIONS DEVELOPMENT TEAM (CHAPTER 9). See also the pattern ENGAGE CUSTOMERS (4.2.6), which complements this pattern.

GATEKEEPER (4.2.10) is a pattern that facilitates an effective flow of useful information; FIREWALLS restricts a detracting flow of (even potentially useful) information. You need a balance between the two. In the park in Boulder, people (customers) come to see nature, and bears are a part of nature. But if the customers interact too closely with the core contributors—to the point where they cause a distraction—things can get out of control. Developers need information, and they can take advantage of customer contacts and GATEKEEPERS to get the information they need. But they can also use managers as a shield. Furthermore, managers may need to step in to help developers who may be afraid to ask not to be bothered by customer contacts, or who are at risk of not fulfilling their own responsibilities if they are embroiled in customer matters.

Be warned that if the organization fills this role with someone motivated largely by personal power, the potential damage to the organization can be large. If other roles like GATEKEEPER maintain good contact with other organizations, communications are more likely to remain open, and FIREWALLS will more likely be called to account for self-serving actions.

As Sun Tzu notes, "He will win who has military capacity and is not interfered with by the sovereign" [SunTzu 1983].

4.2.10   Gatekeeper **

... an organization of developers has formed in a corporate or social context scrutinized by peers and by funders, customers, and other "outsiders."

A project must develop good interfaces with the many outsiders with whom it interacts or with whom it should interact.

Most software development professionals—particularly programmers—are more comfortable interacting with their software and working with technology than working with people. Yet, isolationism doesn't work because information flow is important. On the other hand, communication has a cost: Communication overhead increases nonlinearly with the number of external collaborators. That overhead wouldn't be so bad if so many interruptions weren't mere noise. And an organization should be in control of its external interactions rather than letting the external interactions control it. Such control is a hallmark of organizational maturity.

Therefore:

One project member, a PUBLIC CHARACTER (4.2.17) with an engaging personality, rises to the role of GATEKEEPER. This person disseminates leading-edge and fringe information

from outside the project to project members, "translating" it into terms relevant to the project. The GATEKEEPER may also "leak" project information to relevant outsiders.

❖   ❖   ❖

This role can also manage the development interface to marketing and to the corporate control structure.

This pattern provides balance for the pattern FIREWALLS (4.2.9) and complements the pattern ENGAGE CUSTOMERS (4.2.6) (to the degree that customers are still viewed as outsiders).

GATEKEEPER and FIREWALLS (4.2.9) alone are insufficient to protect developers in an organization whose culture allows marketing to drive development schedules. However, this role can be made explicit in large projects whose budget and staffing profiles provide funding and support for such a role. But the role can also thrive informally in the margins.

GATEKEEPER is a pattern that *facilitates* the effective flow of useful information; whereas the FIREWALLS (4.2.9) role *restricts* the flow of detracting information. As described in FIREWALLS, self-serving people who work their way into this role can do much damage. It is probably healthier for the organization if this role is filled by someone who is not part of the management establishment. In such a case, it is more likely that peer support will sustain that person in the role, and it is more likely that the person will remain responsive to his or her constituencies. However, respected managers can also make great GATEKEEPERS.

The GATEKEEPER pattern has empirical value. In the discussion of this pattern at PLoP 94, many of the reviewers noted that creating a GATEKEEPER role had served their organizations well.

Engineers are lousy communicators on the whole; as such, it's important to leverage the abilities of an engineer who is an effective communicator when such a person is found.

Alexander notes that while it is important to build subcultures in a society (as we are building a subculture here in the framework of a company or of the software industry as a whole), these subcultures should not be closed (MOSAIC OF SUBCULTURES, [Alexander 1977], ff. 42). Also see MAIN GATEWAYS ([Alexander 1977], ff. 276).

By analogy to Alexander's ENTRANCE TRANSITION, one might muse that the GATEKEEPER takes an outsider through any rites of passage needed to give that person intimate access to the development team ([Alexander 1977], ff. 548). In addition, GATEKEEPER can serve the role of "pedagogue," as in Alexander's pattern NETWORK OF LEARNING ([Alexander 1977], ff. 99).

Joe Maranzano notes that the same person often must fill both the MANAGER ROLE and GATEKEEPER role because of the relationships built with external people who need the information [Maranzano 1992].

If the GATEKEEPER (4.2.10) function starts taking on an aura of stability and legitimacy in its own right, it might point to the fact that key business issues cut across the existing organizations. Look at FUNCTION OWNER AND COMPONENT OWNER and UPSIDE DOWN MATRIX MANAGEMENT (5.1.19) as solutions that broaden the GATEKEEPER function to an organizational scope.

4.2.11   Self-Selecting Team **

Child coal miners, Circa 1910, the opposite of a Self-Selecting Team.

I had applied for a job in a different part of the company. It was forward-looking work on a small team. The manager was happy to take me, but it wasn't until the team had interviewed me that I got the job.

... SIZE THE ORGANIZATION (4.2.2) revealed the need for a small, select team. How do you staff such a team?

The worst team dynamics can be found in appointed teams.

There are no perfect criteria for screening team members. Yet broad shared interests (e.g., music and poetry) are an indicator that team players can work together successfully. Teams staffed with such individuals are often willing to take extraordinary measures to meet project goals.

However, when such interests are ignored or when team members are appointed, team dynamics can suffer, thereby greatly diminishing the productivity of a team.

Therefore:

Create enthusiastic teams by letting people select their own team members. Do limited screening on the basis of the team members' track records and broader interests.

Such teams often, though not always, come about of their own volition. Sometimes a PATRON ROLE (4.2.15) or other leader can seed the idea of such a team first as a rallying point for the formation of the team.

❖ ❖ ❖

A SOLO VIRTUOSO (4.2.5) or APPRENTICESHIP (4.2.4) role may self-select a team. FORM FOLLOWS FUNCTION (5.1.11) can give such a team its structure, DIVERSE GROUPS (4.2.16) can help in the screening process, and temporary SELF SELECTING TEAMS can come together to work on PROGRAMMING EPISODES (4.1.19).

A SKUNKWORKS (4.2.14) is a special kind of SELF-SELECTING TEAM that comes together to share high risk on behalf of the organization.

Self-selection can, and should, happen at finer granularity than teams, too [e.g., see DEPLOY ALONG THE GRAIN (5.2.8)].

Such teams are different from "empowered teams." Research has shown that empowerment leads to communication locales that can become blindsided to the broader context of surrounding teams and that can unnecessarily narrow the communication channels between teams, though communication may increase within the teams themselves [Yates 1995].

One danger to be aware of is that an exclusive group of friends may build a team from their own numbers, failing to take advantage of other people's skills. The PATRON ROLE (4.2.15), however, can monitor these dynamics.

4.2.12   Unity of Purpose **

... the team is beginning to come together. Team members may come from different back-grounds and *may bring with them many different experiences.*

Many projects have rocky beginnings as people struggle to work together.

Often, people have different ideas about what the final product should be. In fact, the final product may well be a pretty fuzzy concept. Yet people must have a consistent view of the product if there is any hope of it getting done.

Each person is different and has unique views and opinions. They come with different backgrounds and experiences, and they must learn to work together.

It is important to get off to a good start—initial impressions, good or bad, tend to be lasting.

Therefore:

The leader of the project must instill a common vision and purpose in all of the members of the team. This "leader," whether a manager, the Patron Role (4.2.15), or a customer advocate, should be someone who holds the team's respect and who has influence over the team's thinking. Gaining respect and influence requires overt action; you can't count on it happening automatically. The leader should make sure everyone agrees on the answers to the following questions: What is the product supposed to do? Who are the customers, and how will the product help them? What is the schedule? Does everyone feel personally committed to the schedule? Who is the competition?

An important component of these team unification exercises is to identify the strengths of the team and to use these strengths as rallying points. The team thus identifies the challenges and competition and unites to overcome and surpass them, respectively.

As time goes on, the UNITY OF PURPOSE continues to emerge from ongoing dialogue within the team and with customers and other stakeholders. While the team leader primes the pump, team dynamics take over and keep things going.

The obvious result is that the team is working together rather than working at cross purposes. But a more subtle yet probably more powerful effect is what healthy team dynamics can do for the morale of the team. The best teams tend to feel that they are somehow better than others—and they work to prove it!

This pattern relates to some deep-seated principles and values of organizational health. There may be no more important single property of an organization than that its members have a shared vision that they are motivated to achieve. Communication—which receives the bulk of the attention in this book—is just a means to achieving that shared vision. UNITY OF PURPOSE, thus, is a deeper principle than even effective communication; communication is just a means to UNITY OF PURPOSE.

RELATED PATTERNS:

SHARED CLEAR VISION (A.5.25) ([Bramble 2002], p. 80) notes the importance of a clear vision in creating unity, from the point of view of writing use cases. SELF-SELECTING TEAM (4.2.11) outlines how a team should come together, though this guidance alone is insufficient to achieve UNITY OF PURPOSE. LOCK 'EM UP TOGETHER (5.2.5) helps achieve unity, particularly unity of architecture. A GATEKEEPER (4.2.10) also can help the team become more unified in establishing the requirements needed to ENGAGE CUSTOMERS (4.2.6). This pattern sets up COMPENSATE SUCCESS (4.2.25): it's much easier to compensate success when everyone knows what success means. And, while UNITY OF PURPOSE is important in galvanizing the team, effective team dynamics can develop only if every team member is also valued as an individual. HOLISTIC DIVERSITY (4.2.19) comes to play here.

4.2.13   Team Pride **

Problems worthy
of attack
prove their worth
by hitting back.

—*Piet Hein (1905-1996)*

... you are about to embark on yet another challenging project. The work will be technically difficult, or maybe you'll have a very short schedule. But at least you have some idea of what you want to do, which can begin to give you a sense of UNITY OF PURPOSE (4.2.12).

❖   ❖   ❖

People are most successful when they feel good about their project and when they are confident. But there is a chicken and egg problem here: Confidence breeds success, but success creates confidence.

Pride perhaps goeth before a fall, but so does apathy.

Most software projects—sometimes even the fun ones—demand a lot of work. And the ones that aren't fun don't have much of a chance of seeing a victorious finish unless something pulls its people together and draws them on towards completion. The hard work feels even harder because of short schedules. Such projects demand the best everyone can give, so motivation is often a key to success.

If people consider the work to be "just a job," the results will reflect this attitude.

Team success tends to become a self-fulfilling prophecy: everyone wants to work on a winning team, so teams can pick the best people. On the other hand, teams with low performance tend to be stuck with low morale. People don't join such teams willingly; instead, people are stuck with them.

So how do you improve the attitude of such team members? it is important to give a team a winning attitude right from the start.

Therefore:

Instill a sense of elitism into the team. Teams that have a certain arrogance tend to work hard and accomplish what is put before them.

Really, one cannot give someone else a sense of team pride. A sense of team pride must come from within. But there are many things you can do to help it come to pass:

- Start with a worthwhile problem. Team members are more likely to feel elite if they have a challenging problem to tackle. It is especially good if the problem involves new technology; nothing excites a bunch of geeks more than working with the newest stuff.
- Apply SELF-SELECTING TEAM (4.2.11). If the team self-selects, they will try to choose the best people.
- Find some important strength of the team and make that strength a rallying point. Teach the team that they have skills in a particular area. Be sure to find a *real* strength; people can easily see through a manufactured strength. The strength should be a technical strength; while a team might rally around the idea that "they party better than anyone else," this skill won't get the software written.
- Provide some explicit separation from other projects. This separation can be physical (separate the team from others), organizational, or informational (share secrets with the group). It can also involve exemption from some of the rules that everyone else must follow. Just make it clear that they are set apart from other groups.
- COMPENSATE SUCCESS (4.2.25).
- Hope that the parent company is doing well enough so that it isn't a concern. This author was once on a team that felt it was elite until the company started doing very poorly. The company woes diverted our attention and sapped our morale.
- Use FIREWALLS (4.2.9) to help instill the idea that "top teams shouldn't be bothered by bureaucracy."
- Unite against a common enemy, as with UNITY OF PURPOSE (4.2.12).

By itself, TEAM PRIDE does not guarantee the success of a project. But Boehm and others have pointed out that people are the key success element of any project, and TEAM PRIDE helps nurture and encourage them. Such pride may even be able to overcome poor overall morale in the company.

4.2.14   Skunkworks *

At the end of college, I was interviewed for a job with Lockheed Aircraft Corporations famed "Skunkworks" division. They had a huge skunk painted on the wall at the entrance to their work area. Everyone said the same thing to me: "We can't tell you what we do, but we sure have fun." I ultimately went to work elsewhere, but I occasionally wonder what it would have been like to work there. I don't know what work I would have been doing, but I'm sure I would have enjoyed it.

... organizations have the freedom to iterate and innovate early in the lifecycle of their major products. As a project matures, the context becomes rigid, and innovation becomes "forced" and may appear in the guise of "innovation programs." While these programs are good at encouraging the divergent thinking component of innovation, they rarely do a good job of encouraging convergent thinking. The result is that novelty, valued for its own sake, finds its way into mainstream development where it incurs costs and leads to results that range from indifferent to disastrous. "Home runs" are rare, and the net result is most often negative.

❖   ❖   ❖

A project must accommodate major innovations while also keeping an eye on risk. It is too risky to innovate too much in project development. Some projects have "innovation programs" that value divergent thinking, and the fruits of these efforts often make their way into development. It is only rarely that an organization honestly evaluates whether such ideas actually added value; the value, instead, is often taken on faith. For example, the latest technologies are always held to have value in their own right; conversion to object-oriented (OO) design, to components, or to patterns is considered beneficial without even a second thought. Too often, these new ideas either have indifferent results or increase cost. They may decrease time to market or decrease cost, but if they decrease cost at the expense of time to market, then the overall effect is disastrous if time to market is the highest business priority. And, in fact, any new idea can increase both time to market and cost in ways that may never be noticed, in part because of the stock taken in the buzzword value of the idea.

Yet projects become dead if there is no way to incorporate paradigm shifts into them now and then.

Therefore:

Allow a limited-cost SKUNKWORKS to form [as a SELF-SELECTING TEAM (4.2.11)] in order to develop an idea outside the constraints of project development and to build confidence in the idea. Give the SKUNKWORKS organization ownership and credit for the idea.

The organization is sustained by strong FIREWALLS (4.2.9) that insulate it from the scrutiny of upper management and funders; in fact, the very existence of the SKUNKWORKS should be a secret. The idea is to keep the project off of management radar screens in order to foster the kind of innovation that leads to success before tradition and its constraints, as embodied in managers, can dampen innovation.

The success of the idea is assessed according to the fruits of the SKUNKWORKS effort: the ability of the resulting product to attract customers willing to invest time, money, or people in building the product or in otherwise furthering the idea. The product must *tangibly* show positive results that differentiate it from the mainstream product line. If it is to thrive over existing external *and* internal competitors, it must demonstrate distinguishing market superiority. Directly moving new ideas into existing business units rarely works. As a practical matter, this evaluation of success and the ensuing steps to act on it happen at unusual places in the management structure: at a higher level of management, in an organization that has venture funding, or in the marketing group, which can use the customer needs statements and customer commitments as leverage. However, the technology's chance of long-term success is much higher if the Skunkworks team includes developers who also have responsibilities in existing products. These developers can provide new development teams with ideas for new products or, they can be conduits for introduction of the new technology into development organizations. Therefore, this pattern also depends on a small set of interested developers having some limited amount of time to work with the SKUNKWORKS team in a GATEKEEPER (4.2.10) capacity.

The SKUNKWORKS organization itself rarely can take a product all the way into production. It usually lacks the infrastructure, and sometimes the skill set, to build a solid product. This phenomenon is at the root of the inability of many large companies to capitalize on their greatest inventions.

If the idea succeeds, the team should reap the benefits of developing the idea. The organization subsidizes some of the risk of the team under the sponsorship of a PATRON ROLE (4.2.15), so that the risk takers are guaranteed some minimum level of security even if they fail. However, these risk takers are not *guaranteed* the same level of rewards as people who succeed in lower-risk ventures [see COMPENSATE SUCCESS (4.2.25)].

❖   ❖   ❖

This pattern is a bit different from BUILD PROTOTYPES (4.1.7). Prototyping is one strategy for running a SKUNKWORKS operation; however, a SKUNKWORKS project may just buy an existing product and integrate it with existing products or market it differently without doing any prototyping.

This pattern does not integrate with the other scheduling and organizational structures in the pattern language because it's a decoupled effort. The effort should evolve into a product over time and eventually incorporate patterns like SIZE THE SCHEDULE (4.1.2) and SIZE THE ORGANIZATION (4.2.2), but only after it's on its feet and has proven itself.

It is important that the SKUNKWORKS be organizationally separate from the mainline organization, which allows so-called disruptive technologies to flourish within the company. (For further information on disruptive technologies, see works by Clayton Christiansen, [Christianson 1997].)

Though it's clear how SKUNKWORKS fits into a large organization, it is useful to note that it can work on a smaller scale in small organizations as well. A couple of team members can develop innovative ideas "in the margins" as a side activity. Such opportunities may provide particularly good outlets for employees whose skills are strong enough that they seek challenges beyond those offered by day-to-day business.

4.2.15   Patron Role **

... the development organization has come to the point where DEVELOPER CONTROLS PROCESS (4.1.17), and now additional roles are being defined.

It is important to give a project continuity. But centralized control can be a drag, and anarchy can be even worse. However, most societies need a king/parent figure, and an organization needs a single, ultimate decision maker. The time to make a decision should be less than the time it takes to implement it.

Therefore:

Give the project access to a visible, high-level manager, who champions the cause of the project. The patron can be the final arbiter for project decisions, thus providing a driving force for the organization to make decisions quickly. The patron is accountable for removing project-level barriers that hinder progress and is responsible for the organization's "morale" (sense of well-being).

Having a patron gives the organization a sense of identity, and a sense of focus for later process and organizational changes. Other roles can be defined in terms of the patron's role. The manager role is not one of total centralized control, but rather one of championing the team. That is, the manager's influence usually does not include those developing the product itself, but instead includes those whose cooperation is necessary for the success of the product (e.g., support organizations, funders, and test organizations). This role also serves as a patron or sponsor and sometimes even as a corporate visionary.

We have observed this role being implemented by Philippe Kahn in QPW; Ravi Sethi and others in early C++ efforts at AT&T; a manager of a high-productivity Network Systems project at AT&T; and others at another multilocation AT&T project.

This pattern relates to the pattern FIREWALLS (4.2.9), which in turn relates to the pattern GATEKEEPER (4.2.10). Patrons are central to the success of SKUNKWORKS (4.2.14). They also can help arbitrate the membership of SELF-SELECTING TEAMS (4.2.11) to guard against exclusivity.

Block talks about the importance of influencing forces over which the project has no direct control [Block 1983].

In a JAD session ([Kendall2002], pp. 132–135), one of the key roles is that of a "tie breaker" who is usually a manager who appears only occasionally at the meetings.

The etymology of the term *Patron,* as described in a dictionary of medieval terms is instructive:

> The term pattern comes from Middle English patron (and the more ancient French patron) which still means both 'patron' and 'pattern.' In the 16th century, patron, with a shifted accent, evidently began to be pronounced patrn, and spelt patarne, paterne, pattern. By 1700 the original form ceased to be used of things, and patron and pattern became differentiated in form and sense.

> ... 'The original proposed to imitation; the archetype; that which is to be copied; an exemplar' ... an example or model deserving imitation; an example or model of a particular excellence [Sane 1996]. aC. 1369 CHAUCER Dethe Blaunche 910 Truely she Was her chefe patron of beaute, And chefe ensample of al her werke.

4.2.16   Diverse Groups *

... a development team is forming, and birds of a feather tend to flock together.

❖   ❖   ❖

Homogeneous teams that comprise too many of the same kinds of people easily fall into groupthink-like dysfunction.

Design is the act of changing the structure of the world. In software, it usually means changing the literature of an author who had encoded a solution in a programming language. That author usually remains as part of the community that retains an interest in the code [see CODE OWNERSHIP (5.2.13) and the combination of CONWAY'S LAW (5.1.7) and ORGANIZATION FOLLOWS MARKET (5.1.9), which implies that architecture follows market].

Change is a process that has several phases, starting with complacency, which is upset by an opportunity or realization of an oversight. The struggle to identify and to realize solutions culminates in deployment.

Different people are more comfortable with some parts of this process than with others. Some people are good at identifying problems, and others are good at the innovative processes of identifying solutions. Yet others are good at focusing on implementation. The variance in comfort comes from a variance in experiences and individual backgrounds and temperaments. These variances are true even when programmers, in their role as designers who are making a change, are the same programmers who were the original authors of the code.

Therefore:

Consider temperaments and diverse experience backgrounds when assembling a team. This diversity sometimes corresponds with social classifications like age and gender, but more generally can be assessed on a personal level.

One source of variation is the variety of domains in the application itself [see DOMAIN EXPERTISE IN ROLES (4.2.22)]. There is an open question as to whether a SELF-SELECTING TEAM (4.2.11) prejudices a homogeneous group outcome; in any case, DIVERSE GROUPS can be a good audit of a SELF-SELECTING TEAM.

Another source of difference is the variation in roles. The vestigial pattern DIVERSITY OF MEMBERSHIP recommends building a requirements team from diverse roles:

> The team should include a developer, a user or user's representative, and a system tester (at least one of each). These individuals will work through the issues surrounding product requirements, often using small prototypes to identify the requirements and determine testing criteria. The user of prototypes can be closely tied to using use cases or similar usage scenarios as analysis and validation tools.
>
> One area in which this approach is especially useful is in the specification and design of the user interface. The developer creates mock-ups of the user interface, and the user and system tester examine them. In this way, this small subteam can go through many different designs of the user interface and select the best one [Harrison 1996].

See more about this kind of diversity in HOLISTIC DIVERSITY (4.2.19).

Sometimes teams form around mutual interests and talents in a domain, as in SUBSYSTEM BY SKILL (4.2.23), and diversity falls along other dimensions of interest.

Yet another kind of diversity is ethnic diversity. The oft-touted value of ethnic diversity is that it brings together people who can think about problems differently and from much different perspectives, which improves the chance of finding a good solution. But there are other subtle advantages. In a large multinational corporation, we found that each department had a few members of French national origin. The French people all ate lunch together, which provided a natural path of communication flow between departments.

One kind of person you want to include in the mix is a PUBLIC CHARACTER (4.2.17).

However, one must guard against stereotyping people (e.g., using personality instruments or other information to *limit* the roles of people in organizations). See [Kerth Coplien Weinberg 1998].

See the related pattern BALANCED TEAM (A.5.5) in [Bramble 2002].

4.2.17   Public Character *

... an organizational structure is emerging, both formally and informally, and frequent contact in the workplace cultivates friendships as well as a social context that begs for support of common social graces and functioning.

An organization is a social entity whose smooth functioning depends on more than professional relationships.

Much of what defines "culture" are the widely known but rarely spoken myths, tidbits, histories, and interpretations of stories about an organization and its people. However, most professional organizations are built around the exchange of more structured information in blatantly public forums: memoranda, meetings, explicit policies, and executive pronouncements.

Yet daily small pieces of information, details, and deep insights are the glue that hold the organization and its systems together. Furthermore, this information might include insights on shortcuts and other expediencies that serve the culture and its value system while falling short of the "letter of the law." The formal organization rarely has any organ that legitimizes the exchange of such information, yet such information is crucial not only to the smooth operation of the enterprise, but also to its very survival.

Such details include information that falls outside of the primary business goals, but which is nonetheless important to the support of the work environment (e.g., where to find a good place for lunch, how to find the boss when she's not in the office, and who knows how to fix the jam in the copy machine). It also includes metaknowledge about how to find the answers to certain kinds of information. For example, who would know how to find answers to questions about the web server machine? Who would know where to direct questions about personnel issues?

Therefore:

Ensure one or more people serve in the role of Public Character in order to help social processes both behind the scenes and at social events.

There may be sociotechnological role combinations. For example, an architect role might spend time passing information between development coordinators who otherwise wouldn't take the initiative to talk with each other [Coplien Devos 2000]. We wrote up this pattern as Shmoozing Architect at Object Technology (OT) '99.

❖   ❖   ❖

Gatekeeper (4.2.10) and Matron Role (4.2.18) are examples of Public Characters.

Jane Jacobs notes the following in *The Death and Life of Great American Cities*, [Jacobs 1961] p. 68:

> The social structure of sidewalk life hangs partly on what can be called self-appointed public characters. A public character is anyone who is in frequent contact with a wide circle of people and who is sufficiently interested to make himself a public character. ... His main qualification is that he *is* public, that he talks to lots of different people. In this way, news travels that is of sidewalk interest.

Jacobs goes on to say that, once the neighborhood recognizes a Public Character, people consciously share gossip with that person (e.g., regarding meeting dates and lost items) that they want propagated. A Public Character is a sort of living bulletin board, with highly advanced search capabilities.

One finds a similar function in the Maven role in *The Tipping Point* [Gladwell 2000].

In our experience, large software projects usually have at least one Public Character, and this person is critical to project success. When you want to know who understands the persistence layer, you don't ask the architects; they're too busy. Instead, you ask the Public Character, who won't know beans about the persistence layer, but who will know that Mary is a database expert and that she will either understand the persistence layer or will know who does.

One interesting form of Public Character is the Jester, or Wise Fool (4.2.21). In medieval courts, the Jester was a person who could give advice and make fun of the king with impunity. The king was not obliged to follow the jester's insights; rather, these insights simply provided food for thought. Jesters can incite the organization to engage in introspection; again, part of their qualification is that they are public figures. Such a person might be instrumental in facilitating workshops using creative techniques, such as visual meetings, system envisioning concepts, and games. The jester might also report on user fears and expectations and act as a change agent. This role is also reminiscent of the "laughing uncle" configuration Bateson talks about in his writings on Pacific cultures [Bateson 1958]. This uncle advised a child's father of feelings that the child might not have been able to convey to the father directly.

Project members are often penalized for being PUBLIC CHARACTERS. For example, some might say, "Oh, she never gets anything done, she's always gossiping." However, a PUBLIC CHARACTER is a vital part of an organization's ability to keep large projects connected and successful. In a number of cases, we have seen that the disappearance of a single public character caused a major turn in morale and culture in the organization, *to a much greater degree than the loss of a key technical person.* The role is essentially informal; a project manager can't successfully assign somebody to this role. Rather, the role is recognized and exploited when it is already present. Such recognition can help sustain the role.

If you see a team member who is always gossiping, consider whether the team member has become a PUBLIC CHARACTER. Ask the person a couple of team-related questions (e.g., "Where can I find out more about the garbage collection?" "Who understands the compiler tools"?). If the individual can handle these, as well as other more general questions (e.g., "Where's the best place to have lunch?" "How can I find Phil if he isn't at his desk?" "And what about... Naomi?"), then you've found your PUBLIC CHARACTER.

It is instructive to compare the PUBLIC CHARACTER role, GATEKEEPER role (4.2.10), and MATRON ROLE (4.2.18). In fact, the three roles are related, but different. The MATRON ROLE is concerned with nurturing the organization and is inward focused. On the other hand, the GATEKEEPER is outward focused, always looking forward to the next great direction for the organization to take. The PUBLIC CHARACTER is somewhat in the middle of these two roles, but separate from each. An ideal project has each of these roles filled by different people.

A good place for the PUBLIC CHARACTER to hang out is at THE WATERCOOLER (5.1.20).

4.2.18   Matron Role*

One of the members of my group was a woman named Anita. She was certainly technically competent, but I remember her more for the nontechnical things she did for the group. For birthdays, Anita was almost always the one who brought cakes, pies, or other treats to celebrate. Because she liked to cook, many treats were homemade; in fact, she occasionally brought in something just because she had tried out a new recipe. She did other things for the group too. She was often on picnic committees and helped to arrange "take your daughter to work" days.

Anita eventually moved on to another group, and our group has since been fragmented into other groups. But we still remember when we were a cohesive team, and Anita was a major part of the team.

... once a team is established, regular care and feeding is needed to maintain the unity of the team.

Teams do not survive simply because of the work they do. Some social activities are necessary to keep the team focused on the technical work.

"All work and no play makes Jack a dull boy," and the same holds true for teams. Unless teams play together some, they have trouble maintaining healthy interpersonal relationships, even in work situations.

But many people are not particularly adept at arranging social functions for their teams. This is particularly true in software organizations, which are dominated by introverts. In fact, some people are not even sufficiently aware of the importance such functions to be of any use in planning them.

Therefore:

Make sure that the team contains a Matron who will take charge of the social and interpersonal activities necessary to keep the team unified.

The Matron keeps track of birthdays and other occasions for celebration. The Matron is often willing to plan activities and usually serves as a member of party committees.

Note that you can't force this role on someone; some people are naturally Matrons, some are not. Therefore, you need to find one rather than manufacture one.

With a MATRON ROLE, the team is much more likely to be cohesive in good times and in bad.

Don Olson's PEACEMAKER (A.5.21) pattern ([Olson 1998], p. 168) is similar ([Rising 2000], p. 131):

> A peacemaker is a placeholder in an organization who tries to calm and hold things together until a leader can be found or a reorganization is complete. The peacemaker should be someone who is well liked but who is not necessarily technically proficient. Usually this individual has many years with the company, knows the political ropes, and can buy time for a team as well as the team's management.

MATRON ROLE is a broader version of the PEACEMAKER role.

The MATRON ROLE is usually a PUBLIC CHARACTER (4.2.17).

4.2.19   Holistic Diversity *

Even the manager pulls his weight in this small team, which is cooking up some new concoction.

... during the course of a project, groups of people begin to specialize. Teams are structured by specialty or by phase deliverables. This specialization leads to bureaucratic processes, lack of interteam communication, and a "throw it over the wall" style of development. As a result, teams don't trust each other, and product quality and efficiency suffer.

Development of a subsystem requires many skills, which can become a problem since people specialize.

Project development demands fast feedback, and fast, rich communication regarding decisions. Feedback slows with distance (e.g., room, floor, building, or city) and medium of expression (e.g., interactive face-to-face discussion, video teleconferencing, or writing).

Multiple skills are needed to develop a piece of the system, particularly the user functions, and it is hard to find people with those multiple specialties. In addition, people tend to specialize and even protect their own unique skills from others, as a natural self-preservation mechanism. Many teams thus tend to specialize.

So a project requires multiple skills, which tend to reside in separate teams. But this arrangement is not optimal. People within a team are more likely to help each other, whereas people on different teams are more likely to blame each other. Communication across teams tends to be inefficient and incomplete.

The obvious approach is to create one giant team for the project. This should solve the problem, right? But if the team is too large to fit comfortably in one room, it tends to fragment naturally—along lines of specialization.

Therefore:

For each function or set of functions to be delivered, create a small team (two to five people) that is responsible for delivering that function. That team can be seeded with or can evolve specialists in requirements gathering, user interface design, technical design and programming, databases, and testing. Evaluate the team as a single unit so there is no benefit to hiding within a specialty. Arrange the team location so the team members can communicate directly with each other, instead of by writing. The team has no internal documentation requirements, although they do have documentation responsibilities to the rest of the project. However they choose to split up their work is their choice.

Note that this leads to organizing teams along architectural lines in accordance with Con-way's Law (5.1.7). As a result, it is necessary to coordinate the teams to get consistency of deliverables (e.g., requirements document, user interface design, and software architecture) across teams.

Beware of making teams too small. If the team size is one person, that person will have difficulty in mastering all of the specialties and in changing mental context to perform well in the different specialties (meetings require a different temperament and more concentration than designing OO frameworks). [See Solo Virtuoso (4.2.5).] On the other hand, if the team size is too large, communication latency increases.

See also Owner Per Deliverable (A.5.19), which ensures that somebody owns each function, class, and required deliverable.

This pattern is similar to Diversity of Membership [Harrison 1996], which is used to ensure that requirements gathering teams include users.

Jim McCarthy [McCarthy 1995] wrote Feature Teams with much of the same intent.

It is hard to find single individuals who can master needed specialties and change work contexts as needed. Creating a small, co-located, mixed-specialty team with no written deliverables between them increases the communication bandwidth between people, while letting the individuals develop their strengths. Rewarding them as a team keeps them motivated to help each other deliver, rather than to hide behind their specialty.

There is a tight connection between the specialties. A designer or programmer may discover something that reveals that the requirements are more difficult than previously thought. The analyst may have a flawed view of the business, though the final code must be a valid business model. The suggested user interface may be impractical to implement, or perhaps the user interface designer knows best how to implement it. Putting diverse people on the same team speeds up the feedback loop between programming and requirements. Separating those same people and putting written deliverables between them slows that feedback.

Alistair Cockburn tells of his experiences with a project:

> Project Winifred was initially structured by function, which produced the trouble that many people were altering one class at any moment in time...

> It was next structured by phase deliverables and requirements. Analysts were separated from designers and programmers. The analysts produced ineffective models, communications between the people became sluggish, the analysts and programmers looked down on each other, and the analysts' designs did not match the final system design (the programmers ended up designing it as they needed to make it work).

> There was a very brief period of "everyone does everything." It did not last long because the mental load was too great on each person trying to do everything, and people rapidly fell into the specialties they could handle.

> The fourth, and successful arrangement, was HOLISTIC DIVERSITY [4.2.19]. Those who could do the requirements gathering and analysis went to meetings, interviewed people, and investigated interfaces and options. They communicated the results rapidly, face-to-face, with the people who navigated the class library and designed classes and frameworks. A function team consisted of a combined requirements gatherer/analyst with two to four programmer designers.

> The team used JUST DO IT to move rapidly through the design. They had no internal deliverables, but created the deliverables as required by the project for interteam communication and maintenance. Most of the communication within the team was verbal. They talked several times a day, either in one-hour mutual-education sessions, or in small, several minute interchanges to mention a recent discovery. This amount of communication could not have been handled through formal deliverables.

See also DIVERSE GROUPS (4.2.16).

This pattern was originally written by Alistair Cockburn [Cockburn 1996].

4.2.20 Legend Role *

Baseball legends George Sisler, Babe Ruth, and Ty Cobb

The hero Westley had returned in the guise of the Dread Pirate Roberts. He explained to Princess Buttercup that he had been trained by the previous Dread Pirate Roberts: "One day Roberts pulled me aside. I'm not the Dread Pirate Roberts, said he. And the man before me wasn't either. Then he explained that the name was important. You see, no one would surrender to the Dread Pirate Westley" (from The Princess Bride [Princess Bride 1987]).

... over time, certain people really excel at their jobs. They become masters, and they take on many important jobs on the project.

Certain individuals take on so many jobs and become so important to the project that when they leave, the project is in more than just serious trouble.

These individuals are generally the elder statesmen and women on the project. They have been around longer than most anybody else, and their depth of experience is invaluable. But because of their age, they are the ones most likely to retire.

Not all people are masters. These people are the ones who tend to pick up extra work and the associated expertise, so their absence is felt all the more. In fact, it seems like it would take two or more people to fill each of their shoes.

Therefore:

Name a role after the person, and make it an honor to fill that role. People will want to emulate the legendary person and to do just as good a job.

In many cases, the role named after the person will naturally emerge. Then it is a matter of formalizing the role a bit and filling it when the legend retires.

There *must* be training provided for the person filling the role. Ideally, it is offered by the LEGEND ROLE as part of the process of turning over the role to the new person. This training is as important as the naming of the role itself.

A software company we analyzed had a role named "Simon." They told us that Simon had been a key player on the project and had done seemingly everything. They used his name for the role involving the jobs he had done.

Some corporate cultures are built around archetypes. For example, electric power companies are built around the heroic acts of linemen working during threatening weather.

Emulation can be encouraged with an award. This author wrote some patterns of shepherding. Later, the Neil Harrison Shepherding Award was established, which encourages shepherds to excel at the work they do.

❖   ❖   ❖

Filling the LEGEND ROLE helps to maintain project knowledge and expertise over time, as well as helping to keep a MODERATE TRUCK NUMBER (4.2.24). Note that legend roles will fade over time, which is generally all right.

There is a subtle but important difference between having a legend *role* and having the actual legendary *person* on staff. In writing about his CULT OF PERSONALITY pattern, Don Olson ([Olson 1998], pp. 154–155) offers this advice:

> A tight schedule, poorly defined requirements, uneven distribution of skills among the development team, and new technologies have put a project in jeopardy. To save the day, bring in a legendary figure among the developers to take over the lead. Team members who are not impressed may need removal or reeducation.

LEGEND ROLE looks longer term and intends to be an inspirational rather than a remedial pattern. CULT OF PERSONALITY can work if the legendary figure offers true leadership and develops growth in the team, but then it is no longer a "personality cult" in the vernacular sense. It is dangerous for a team to develop too much dependency on a single power figure, because the team has difficulty adjusting to a new communication structure, authority and control structure, and culture when the legendary figure is gone. Also, the LEGEND ROLE could become a bottleneck under these situations [see DISTRIBUTE WORK EVENLY (5.1.13)].

This overreliance, in fact, was noted by Alistair Cockburn as being a problem in the XP-based [Beck 1999] C3 project, where he characterized XP as a high-discipline methodology and likened it to Humphrey's Personal Software Process [Humphrey 1995]. The following commentary comes from the WIKI WIKI Web [Wiki-Discipline 2001].

> I consider XP a HIGH DISCIPLINE METHODOLOGY, one in which the people will actually fall away from the practices if they don't have some particular mechanism in place to keep them practicing. Ron [Jeffries] is that mechanism at the moment. Should (when) Ron leave, then unless he is replaced in his role, I quite expect to see the team not following the practices properly in less than 6 months.

Ron did leave the project, and the following discussion appears on the CThreeProjectTerminated Wiki page [Wiki-Terminated 2001]:

> *... It wasn't "to live" it was to stop following all of the practices.*

- "unless [the coach] is replaced in his role, I quite expect to see the team not following the practices properly in less than 6 months. I think that is a fair test of a HIGH DISCIPLINE METHODOLOGY. — Alistair Cockburn"
- "I'm no longer on C3 full time. Alistair's six-month clock has started. — Ron Jeffries 6/25/99"
- "As of the first of February, 2000, the C3 project has been terminated without a successful launch of the next phase."

The coach, in fact, does figure strongly in the XP organization. The coach is "responsible for the process as a whole" and sometimes must intervene to the point of "rudeness ([Beck 1999], pp. 145–146)." However, XP as published recognizes both the danger and difficulty of interventions that are overly direct and immediate. But our study of several projects claiming to use XP practices found strong elements of a personality cult. In one case, the team leader on XP project at an insurance company became more assertively involved when the project got behind schedule (the project dutifully and effectively used the XP planning game).

If, instead, the legendary figure consults with the team, with the aim of helping the team members to grow, this approach can be effective. See [Weinberg 1986] for ideas.

4.2.21   Wise Fool *

I marvel what kin thou and thy daughters are: they'll have me whipped for speaking true, thou'lt have me whipped for lying; and sometimes I am whipped for holding my peace.

—*The fool, King Lear, act 1, scene 3*

... a team has been established and is functioning. It is faced with a continual barrage of technical and nontechnical challenges, about which it must make decisions.

Interpersonal dynamics often discourage good ideas from being aired and bad ideas from being weeded out.

Two dynamics are at work here, depending on the persons involved. Authority figures are often unchallenged: You might be reluctant to challenge your boss because of the perceived danger to your continued employment. People are also loathe to challenge the word of a respected elder in the organization for slightly different reasons. But this reticence tends to allow bad ideas promoted by authority figures to promulgate without sufficient challenge and discussion.

The other dynamic is the group itself. It is difficult to stand up to an entire group to challenge an idea. These days, such troublemakers are rarely tarred and feathered, but they might be ostracized or labeled as poor team players.

Yet somebody needs to be the catalyst of occasional group introspection. Someone needs to shout a warning when the group heads in the wrong direction.

Therefore:

Nurture the role of the wise fool who can raise uncomfortable truths with impunity.

The Wise Fool asks the questions that may be unpopular or that seem politically risky, but these questions make the team pause and reexamine decisions. Often, many people want to ask the same question, but they do not dare. The Wise Fool displays a mix of insight, candor, and foolhardiness.

The Wise Fool is legendary. The most famous Wise Fool may well be found in the story of the Emperor's New Clothes. In the story, only a small boy has the courage to point out the obvious.

The Wise Fool is much like a Public Character (4.2.17). However, the Public Character makes the group function smoothly, whereas the Wise Fool focuses mainly on the (mainly technical) outputs of the group. Like the Public Character, the Wise Fool is not designated, but emerges. A Wise Fool, though known for lacking tact, is usually highly respected technically and may be (or become) a Legend Role (4.2.20). They usually eschew managerial opportunities and may even show disdain for management. An acquaintance of the author was once honored with the following words: "In the face of management opposition, he charged ahead and did what was right."

Some organizations recognize the need for a Wise Fool. One organization we studied even included a role called "Agitator."

A Wise Fool needs to recognize the difference between asking legitimate questions and complaining incessantly. Questioning things that one has no control over is often construed as whining. Too many such questions can lead the court of public opinion to demote a Wise Fool to a Whiner rather quickly.

Organizations that have the good fortune to have a Wise Fool in their midst are likely to make fewer wrong decisions than other organizations. However, Wise Fools may not receive the recognition they deserve and may be perceived as troublemakers, a scenario that is slightly reminiscent of Sacrifice One Person (4.1.22). Managers should be sensitive to this possibility and make sure that Wise Fools are supported.

Note that the key here is that the organization itself must be willing to accept criticism from within. There will always be people around willing to fill this role, but only healthy organizations benefit from their insights. In fact, it often doesn't come naturally even to healthy organizations. Some organizations within Siemens, for example, hold workshops to help create a culture where people can speak out [Ackermann 2002]. However, unhealthy organizations may ignore or, even worse, actively suppress criticism. This climate of fear of speaking leads to widespread cynicism. In such cases, a few Wise Fools will refuse to be silenced and will become whistleblowers. When they report illegal conduct to authorities, they may even need laws to protect their actions.

4.2.22   Domain Expertise in Roles **

Naval air base, Corpus Christi, Texas. A top notch mechanic, Mary Josephine Farley, expertly rebuilds airplane engines. Although she's only twenty years old she has a private pilot's license and has made several cross country flights.

... you know the key atomic process roles [FORM FOLLOWS FUNCTION (5.1.11)], including a characterization of the developer role.

Matching staff with roles is one of the hardest challenges of a growing and dynamic organization. All roles must be staffed with qualified individuals. Just as in a play, several actors may be assigned to a single role, and any given actor may play several roles.

You'd like to use domain-inspecific qualification criteria like college grades or years of experience to qualify people for jobs. Such an approach gives the project flexibility in staff allocation and it helps it avoid being overly dependent on individual skill sets and experience. In short, the hope that such criteria might work provides project managers with a basis for keeping the project from becoming overly dependent on certain individuals who may leave or who may hold the organization hostage to gain higher salaries or to see their own policies implemented unilaterally. Nonetheless, successful projects tend to be staffed not with people who possess textbook qualifications, but instead with people who have already worked on successful projects.

Spreading expertise across roles complicates communication patterns. It makes it difficult for a developer or other project member to know who to turn to for answers to domain-specific requirements and design questions.

Therefore:

Hire domain experts with proven track records, and staff the project around the expertise embodied in their roles. Teams and groups will tend to form around areas of common domain interest and focus. Any given actor may fill several roles. In many cases, multiple actors can fill a given role.

Domain training is more important than process training.

Organizations can benefit from having local gurus in all areas from application expertise to expertise in methods and language.

This pattern is a tool that helps ensure that roles can be successfully carried out. It also helps make roles autonomous. Empirically, highly productive projects (e.g., QPW) hire deeply specialized experts. OLD PEOPLE EVERYWHERE ([Alexander 1977], ff. 215), talks about the need for the young to interact with the old. The same deep rationale and many of the same forces of Alexander's pattern also apply here.

This pattern also provides a systems principle that one finds in software development [Lea 1995].

A seasoned manager writes, "The most poorly staffed roles are System Engineering and System Test. We hire rookies and make them System Engineers. (In Japan, only the most experienced person interacts with customers.) We staff System Test with 'leftovers' after we have staffed the important jobs of architecture, design, and developer. [Anon 1997]"

Some roles [DEVELOPER CONTROLS PROCESS (4.1.17), MERCENARY ANALYST (4.1.24), ARCHITECT CONTROLS PRODUCT (5.2.3), and others] are prescribed by their respective patterns.

If expertise becomes too narrow, the organization is at risk of losing key expertise if a single person leaves, is promoted, etc. Temper this pattern with MODERATE TRUCK NUMBER (4.2.24).

Domain experts can naturally come together in PROGRAMMING EPISODES (4.1.19). The pattern APPRENTICESHIP (4.2.4) helps maintain this pattern in the long term. DIVERSE GROUPS (4.2.16) is, in some sense, a more general version of this pattern.

See also SUBSYSTEM BY SKILL (4.2.23) and UPSIDE DOWN MATRIX MANAGEMENT (5.1.19).

4.2.23   Subsystem by Skill *

... an organization of developers exists. They have different skills and specialties, but there is not yet any structure in the organization, or in the system architecture that reflects such specializations or interests.

Birds of a feather flock together. By CONWAY'S LAW (5.1.7), you want the architecture and the organization to match each other. Yet there are many possible principles of organizing both the software and the organization that builds it. One structure relates to domain knowledge and the system architecture. There is also a business structure and a geographic structure, as found in ORGANIZATION FOLLOWS LOCATION (5.1.8). But in ORGANIZATION FOLLOWS LOCATION, each location is largely autonomous and has its own organizational decisions to make, so the issue remains as to how to modularize the organizational structure locally. ORGANIZATION FOLLOWS LOCATION conveys global constraints that relate to business priorities and concerns; CONWAY'S LAW offers guidance in the large, but doesn't extend as well to the fine structure at the group level. And that structure—the primary low-level structure of the organization—relates to the subsystem structure. We need to enhance CONWAY'S LAW with a set of partitioning criteria.

Therefore:
Separate subsystems by staff skills and skill requirements.

This pattern, a refinement CONWAY'S LAW, indicates the criterion by which the structures of the organization should be aligned with those of the product.

People skills tend to be relatively stable over time, so this pattern protects organizations against shifts in staff.

The variation protected against here is the variation in staff skills over time. On a small enough project, a few people may have multiple skills that enable them to mix user interface (UI) design with infrastructure design and domain design. Unhappily, their successors may not possess these diverse skills, which makes system evolution more difficult and costly.

On larger projects, many people are more likely to have single skills and specialties. If their code is intermingled, two expensive difficulties accrue: getting different people to learn to understand each other and to come to common decisions and resolving the same system evolution difficulty as faced on smaller projects.

Separating specialties into different subsystems lets the team focus on their special issues in their own special vocabulary, lets their successors see those issues in isolation, and makes the project easier to staff, since the staff do not need to be so multidisciplinary. Once the subsystems are identified, various forms of teaming may be used to develop them.

The pattern, of course, should be applied in moderation, for too many subsystems leads to complex, slow software. And too fine of an organizational structure is unwieldy and cumbersome.

Note this pattern's relationship to DOMAIN EXPERTISE IN ROLES (4.2.22). This pattern removes one degree of freedom in DIVERSE GROUPS (4.2.16).

Related subsystems may be connected, while still providing a degree of independence between teams by using STANDARDS LINKING LOCATIONS (5.2.12).

UPSIDE DOWN MATRIX MANAGEMENT (5.1.19) is one way of handling SUBSYSTEM BY SKILL.

Alistair Cockburn offers the following analysis of the relationship between HOLISTIC DIVERSITY (4.2.19) and SUBSYSTEM BY SKILL (4.2.23):

> HOLISTIC DIVERSITY is aimed at streamlining communication: For each function or set of functions to be delivered, create a small team ... evolve specialists in requirements gathering, UI design, technical design, ... Evaluate the team as a single unit. Arrange the team size and location so they can communicate directly. You will have to coordinate the teams to get the ... UI design, software architecture and so on consistent across teams.

> SUBSYSTEM BY SKILL is aimed at protecting the system against "variation in staff skills over time"— I thought of it primarily as a software design pattern, rather than a project management pattern, which is why I hadn't thought of them together. "Many people are more likely to have single skills and specialties ... Separate their specialties into different subsystems."

What happens if you put the two together? You get the team structuring I described in my book [Cockburn 1998, p. 88] for a 40-person project: function teams using HOLISTIC DIVERSITY, infrastructure teams, ARCHITECTURE TEAM, and technology teams. The UI gets its own subsystem, the domain model gets it own subsystem, the database gets its own subsystem ... and now you have to use HOLISTIC DIVERSITY to get all the parts put back together to make a working system. [Put] expertise from each specialty on each team (some team members bring more than one specialty with them). And you also have to run a UI group across function teams to get consistent UIs; a persistence and a domain group similarly to get consistency there, too. The software ends up partitioned by skill. So you work extra hard to see that the teams don't get similarly segregated. This is the stuff that my book covers, in its tiny way.

What happens if you don't put the two together? If you don't do SUBSYSTEM BY SKILL, then you get UI, domain, persistence, networking code all mixed together. Yuck, but that's well known. Why have we long separated these things? Because they change independently or because they capitalize on different specialties? or we have those specialties because they change independently or they change independently because we have those specialties?

I don't know and won't guess.

What if you don't do HOLISTIC DIVERSITY? Then you get a room full of UI designers, another room full of domain modelers, another room full of persistence designers / DB [database] designers, etc. I think we have all seen enough of this and its negative consequences. I am, by the way, currently in an organization separated this way, and [am] trying to get the people, who sit only steps apart, to talk to each other on microteams.

So I think we need both: a project management pattern and a software architecture pattern that work together [Cockburn 2000].

4.2.24   Moderate Truck Number

In an insurance company we studied, the project scheduled some of its release dates around the vacation times of a small number of key staff. While such planning is much better than constraining vacation times to the release schedules, it would have been better if the project had been less dependent on those employees. As should have been predicted, the release dates slipped and interfered with the vacation dates anyhow.

... you have built an organization around specialists whose background and training match the expertise required by the application and market, the DOMAIN EXPERTISE IN ROLES (4.2.22).

A project cannot become overly dependent on any small number of individuals. It's important to have specialization. No amount of general accomplishment can compensate for experience. And this experience is not embodied in any abstract concept of roles and is seldom found in any supporting document or knowledge base that a plug-compatible-interchangeable developer could leverage. Instead, the expertise is most often embodied in a living human being who can make choices.

Such human beings may make unpleasant choices, such as leaving the organization for another company. Or they may make silly choices, like walking out in front of a truck at a busy intersection, never to return to the project again.

And life may make choices for such individuals, such as giving them prospects for promotion. Sadly enough, there is a high correlation between individual's perceived expertise and the chances that a company will offer them promotion to optimize the chances for the Peter Principle to have its way. Or, another project within the organization may take them away.

It is a risk if your project depends too heavily on such individuals for their singular knowledge. You know you're in trouble if your project schedules release dates around their vacation times.

Yet, it's still important for individuals to possess areas of expertise in order to reduce the need for communication between individuals regarding decisions within a certain business area. That helps ensure that the right experience is brought to bear in decision making.

And, it's important to recognize that *everyone* brings some expertise to the table. If everyone were the same, there would be useless redundancy in the organization [see DIVERSE GROUPS (4.2.16) and HOLISTIC DIVERSITY (4.2.19)].

However, not everyone can know everything. Being a true expert in an area requires all of one's attention, and it is difficult to sustain multiple areas of expertise.

Define the *truck number* as the number of people in the organization who have unique *critical* domain expertise. You don't want the truck number to be large, because that means that the probability is large that the loss of any given team member would mean the loss of critical expertise. The risk would be too high. Yet, it's also impossible to make the truck number very small (and it's almost impossible to make it zero). Even if you could make it small, you probably wouldn't; if it were one, then everyone but the critical resource is intellectually redundant. In other words, by some rationale, all of the other members of the organization could turn into overpaid worker bees or software assembly-line workers.

Therefore:

Keep the truck number low, thus retaining a small number of key experts with unique knowledge. Build a culture of shared knowledge that increases the breadth of knowledge over time, particularly for knowledge that easily can be codified, taught, or otherwise conveyed.

How do you build such a culture? One way is to use DEVELOPING IN PAIRS (4.2.28). Another way is to make sure the experts rub shoulders with the mere mortals [use ARCHITECT ALSO IMPLEMENTS (5.2.10)]. Of course, you retain a nonzero truck number by keeping the architects from becoming mere mortals themselves [see ARCHITECT CONTROLS PRODUCT (5.2.3)].

Cross-training can be an effective technique for sharing knowledge. In particular, APPRENTICESHIP (4.2.4) is an effective form of cross-training. However, some of the deepest forms of knowledge and gut feeling cannot be conveyed from an expert to an apprentice.

A pattern language of the organization's key competencies can provide some relief for experts and can reduce the risk to the organization. Collect patterns from domain experts.

The goal is *not* to level the playing field. You still need DOMAIN EXPERTISE IN ROLES (4.2.22). It is too expensive (in time and talent) to guard against any possible staff loss by completely replicating talent. You want to implement enough cross-training to control the costs of recovery from losing a person. Trying to spread expertise too broadly will, in fact, just dilute the overall expertise by detracting from each expert's focus.

The Truck Number is a measure of the vulnerability of an organization. It's usually pretty easy to calculate it: Just ask yourself, "Which people in my project can we absolutely not do without?" It's likely that several names immediately come to mind. These people are the key architects, programmers, or perhaps even testers. And they are critical in part because they know things that others don't. So we try to get them to share that knowledge with the rest of the team.

Note that although we speak of the Truck Number as a number, it has a subjective qualitative aspect to it as well. In other words, not all experts are created equal. The loss of some experts may cause serious problems, but the loss of others may be absolutely devastating!

One of the authors once studied a small software company. While the company and its (single) product looked good, one particular employee seemed to be unusually dominant. If he were to leave, the company would be in serious jeopardy. Unfortunately, he left, and the company suffered greatly. The moral: Watch such individuals closely, and make sure they continually share their expertise.

Why doesn't DEVELOPING IN PAIRS (4.2.28) solve the problem completely? It certainly helps, but people are still individuals who possess different skills. A pair in which each member is good at something different is greater than the sum of the individuals.

As with any risk reduction activity, reducing the Truck Number is an exercise in trade-offs. You may find that duplicating the expertise of certain people just isn't cost—or time—effective. So you live with the risk. Maybe you try to reduce it in other ways, such as creating incentives for those people to stay on the team [e.g., see COMPENSATE SUCCESS (4.2.25)].

4.2.25   Compensate Success **

When I was in fourth grade (about 9 years old), we had a spelling test every Friday. Our teacher told us that if everyone got a perfect score on a spelling test, she would bring each of us a candy bar the following Monday. We were excited about the prospect, but as time went on it seemed that our class might never earn our candy bars. Some people just couldn't seem to spell. Jimmy was probably the worst speller of all. He typically missed about half of the words. There was no hope for us with him in the class.

But one week the words were particularly easy. In the practice test on Wednesday, everyone except Jimmy got all of the words right. And Jimmy missed only four words. The anticipation in the class was electric, and we all gave special help and encouragement to Jimmy. On Friday, when everyone got a perfect score, it was hard to tell whether we were more excited about the candy bar or about Jimmy's success.

... a group of developers is striving to meet tight schedules in a high-payoff market. It is important to reward individuals in a way that motivates them to do things that achieve business objectives that are in line with the value system of the enterprise.

❖   ❖   ❖

Successful projects remain successful by rewarding behaviors that lead to success.

Schedule motivations tend to be self-fulfilling, and a wide range of schedules may be perceived as equally applicable for a given task. Furthermore, pre-ordained schedules are poor motivators.

Some organizations count on altruism, but selfless, egoless teams are quaint, Victorian notions.

Companies often embark on make-or-break projects, and such projects should be managed differently from others.

You need to reward both teams and outstanding individuals. Yet, disparate rewards that motivate those who receive them may frustrate their peers.

You need both to reward solid workers and risk takers. However, from an economic perspective, you need to manage the risk of any investment in speculative work. And if speculative work fails and the contributors are rewarded according to performance, the organization will have a disincentive from embarking on future risk-taking projects.

Some contributions are difficult to quantify, such as those of the catalyst (see [De Marco Lister 1976]) who facilitates communication between team members and perhaps helps morale.

Therefore:

Establish lavish rewards for individuals who contribute to successful make-or-break projects. The entire team (social unit) should receive comparable rewards to avoid demotivating individuals who might assess their value by their salary relative to that of their peers. Extremely valuable team members might receive exceptional awards that are tied less strongly to team performance.

A celebration is a particularly effective reward [Zuckerman Hatala 1992].

As a result, you get an organization that focuses less on schedule [See SIZE THE SCHEDULE (4.1.2)] and more on customer satisfaction and systemic success.

In most enterprises, you do not want to reward risk-taking in a way that encourages people to take risks that don't serve the long-term viability of the enterprise. The reward should always be more focused on meeting the organization's goals than on the manner in which the goals are met. If the organization's job is to produce a product, then reward people for what they do in support of delivering the product. Sometimes this support involves an element of risk-taking, and to that degree risk-taking should be rewarded. However, you want to remove *obstacles* to risk-taking in order to allow people to take appropriate risks motivated by a desire to meet organizational objectives, rather than for the sake of having taken a risk. See more about this concept in SKUNKWORKS (4.2.14).

Similarly, most software development organizations shouldn't encourage people to seek crisis situations as opportunities to make the contributions that will receive the highest reward. Doing so almost guarantees that the project will become crisis driven. Some jobs are legitimately built around a hero culture, such as (real-world) fire fighters and their figurative namesakes inside software projects, but these jobs are the exception rather than the rule. Be sure to reward what the organization values, knowing that people will tend to do what they are rewarded to do.

Similarly, it can be problematic to reward those who work for the sake of the work ethic alone. Reward accomplishments more than hard work; there should be no prize for the most hours worked. Paul Bramble relates the following [Bramble 2003]:

> Working for stock options that could be expected to turn into $12 million was a horrible experience. And having peers with similar expectations only made it worse. It clouded their judgment and they stopped using DOMAIN EXPERTISE IN ROLES [4.2.22]. Instead, they started giving the more difficult assignments to the perceived "gung-ho" crowd rather than to the people most likely to be able to do them. ... Some of the fanatics were regularly working 80-hour weeks and used the reward system as leverage to exact punishment against those who tried to work reasonable hours and balance work and family life.

The liability of providing big rewards for meeting key corporate objectives is that people who take on those responsibilities can overextend themselves, leading to personal stress and potential risk to the project. Rewarding management staff can be particularly problematic since those staff can run the risk of developing a burnout culture in their subordinates to meet development objectives [see THE OPEN/CLOSED PRINCIPLE OF TEAMS (6.1.4)].

Some factors that lead to success are difficult to measure or even identify, so it's best to orient rewards around the organization's shared value system of what is important to achieve. Scoping the concern of "organization" in this context is key to the long-term success of the enterprise; in other words, a closed group can't sustain values that are inconsistent with those of the enclosing organization or the next higher level of management.

Success makes it possible to improve the work environment infrastructure, making it a more attractive place to work. This form of long-term compensation or of recognition of success is particularly important in team settings. In one organization, we used windfall funds to buy an interactive terminal, which in that era (about 1974) was a treat for the staff. On a broader scale, you can buy an espresso machine (for which Bell Labs' computer science Research department was famous), a coffee machine, or a watercooler—or build an entire culture of food. See THE WATERCOOLER (5.1.20).

Large rewards to some individuals may still demotivate their peers, but rewarding everyone on a team basis helps remove the "personal" aspect of this problem, helps to establish the mechanism as a motivator, and provides a "postmortem soother." On the other hand, see the discussion in THE ROLE OF MANAGEMENT (6.3.7) that puts individual contributions in a broader perspective. For example, are individual successes really just team success in misleading packaging?

The grounding for this pattern is empirical. There is a strong correlation between wildly successful software projects and a lucrative reward structure. Cases include QPW and cases cited at the Risk Derivatives Conference in New York on May 6, 1994 (see [Lawler 1981]). The place of reward mechanisms is well-established in the literature [Kilmann 1984].

At the PLoP review of this pattern, Dennis DeBruler noted that most contemporary organization cultures derive from the industrial complex of the 1800s, which was patterned after the only working model available at the time: military management. (One common model of military management is reward individually punish corporately, which leads to a fear of failing and to resentment towards those who fail.) He notes that most American reward mechanisms are geared more toward weeding out problems than toward encouraging solutions. A good working model is that of groups of doctors and lawyers, where managers are paid less than the employees [DeBruler 1996].

   Paul Bramble adds, "The trick is to be discerning—sometimes it's the quiet plodders who generate the success, and you have to be able to see past the self-promoting employees to see who really gets the work done" [Bramble 2003].

   See also Compensate Results [Beedle 1997].

4.2.26   Failed Project Wake *

The Trident project was the most exciting project I had ever worked on. We were a small team with an aggressive schedule, but we made good progress and were actually ahead of schedule. Then one day the company made a major business decision that meant that the Trident project was probably unnecessary. Sure enough, the project was canceled a few days later. We all agreed that it was probably the right decision, and we appreciated the speed with which it was made; nonetheless, the decision still hurt.

For a week, we walked around in a fog. We did nothing. Finally, we took the afternoon off and had a party at someone's home. We brought our families and played croquet in the backyard. After that, it was much easier to move on to the next project.

... projects fail for a variety of reasons. Many of these reasons are attributable to the team involved in the project; in fact, this pattern language is designed to help with many such problems. But software developers don't work in a vacuum. Many external factors contribute to the success or failure of any project. Changes in the market, for example, can doom a product before it ever gets out the door. The greatest, hardest-working team in the world still might have their project canceled in spite of their best efforts.

Canceling a project, even for the best external reasons, is particularly demoralizing to a team that has put its heart and soul into it.

It doesn't matter much that the team members fully understand the reasons behind the cancellation: Regardless, they still feel bad. They feel powerless, somewhat apathetic, and sometimes betrayed. At best, they will need some downtime, even if they have another project to jump into immediately. At worst, they may quit.

They may note that successful projects are rewarded, but it wasn't their fault that their project was canned. This feeling of inequity can be quite strong.

Therefore:

Hold a wake for the failed project (e.g., much like an Irish wake, a party for the dead).

Don't try to placate the team with false praise about the project's "success." They all know the project bombed.

Go ahead and make it a big party, that involves more than just cake and punch in the cafeteria. And make it a real party, not a project retrospective. There is a time and a place for retrospection, and this isn't it. ([Ackermann 2002] points out that it is possible to combine a party and a retrospective event, if you have a strong facilitator and if the main purpose of the gathering is to hold a wake.)

It's best to hold the wake offsite. Doing so helps people break from the old project and avoids even the appearance of a retrospective event.

It's even more helpful to hold the wake during working hours, perhaps one afternoon. Holding the wake during work hours sends a subtle "thank-you" message: everyone knows they don't get a bonus [see COMPENSATE SUCCESS (4.2.25)], but they appreciate some acknowledgment of their efforts.

Just like the death of a loved one, the death of a project causes a period of mourning. A wake helps people get through the stages of mourning.

It also serves as a bit of a catharsis. People will come out of it much more ready to succeed on the next project. It is particularly important for upper management to express explicit appreciation for the effort, especially when the failure is due to business decisions rather than to decisions made by the development team. Paul Bramble notes that such acknowledgment helps "calm people down and ... be less worried about their future at the company" [Bramble 2003].

4.2.27   Don't Interrupt an Interrupt

See section 4.1.26.

4.2.28 Developing in Pairs **

Randy and I work on a software tool together. Over the years that we have developed it, we have spent a lot of time at each other's desks. We often write code, debug, and test together. It is not uncommon for one of us to type, while the other one indicates what to type. Oftentimes, the one who is not typing will point out typographical or logic errors. Such feedback can be annoying, but it certainly reduces the cycles of compiling and debugging.

Nobody told us to work this way. We just found that it works well.

... a development organization is in place, and people have started to commit to work and are about to start building the work artifacts. Some of the work may be allocated on the basis of CODE OWNERSHIP (5.2.13). There is enough understanding about overall requirements to start work, though many requirements may have loose ends.

❖   ❖   ❖

Some people don't want to work alone, and working alone has great risks of blind-siding and producing misfits. Furthermore, you need to take into account people who don't want to work alone, and you must engage people who are working alone but probably shouldn't be.

People sometimes feel they can solve a problem only if they have help. Some problems cannot be solved by just one person, so people who are comfortable working alone should still work closely with someone else who at least provides another set of eyes to look over the work.

It takes extra resources to put people in work pairs in real time. In fact, one might argue that code walk-throughs and inspections and reviews provide sufficient compensation for these problems. But these reviews are usually analytical rather than opportunistic. Reviews set up an adversarial context where the critics don't have the same stake in the results as the programmers. Furthermore, reviews catch problems after the programmer has committed to the corresponding structures and algorithms and has expended a lot of effort in elaborating them, rather than catching these problems at the conceptual stage. And many of these decisions are too complex to arise in design reviews or simply can't be foreseen until the programmer grapples with implementation; nonetheless, these problems can be weighty enough to threaten the viability and long-term health of the code.

Only a limited number of people can sit in front of a keyboard and screen each other's efforts. Communication and coordination efforts increase nonlinearly with the number of people. So you can't always create a team that works together as a unit to contribute to an artifact in front of a single screen.

Therefore:

Pair compatible designers. Together, they can work together to produce more than the sum of the two individually.

There are two keys to making this effort successful. First, the individuals must be able to work well together, which means that pair assignments must not be made arbitrarily. In fact, because a pair is in reality a small team, SELF-SELECTING TEAM (4.2.11) must be applied. The chief consideration for creating a pair is that the two *want* to work together.

Second, the style of pair development must not be dictated; instead, it should be left up to the individuals. Simply put, there should not be a rule that no line of code can be written unless both people are at the keyboard. Instead, give the pair the assignment and let them figure out how to do the development. Note that this practice supports FEATURE ASSIGNMENT (5.2.14).

The pair needn't always comprise developers only. In BUILD PROTOTYPES (4.1.7) and in many other activities, one of the pair can be a customer, systems engineer, or technologist representing an area of risk being explored by the prototype. At Mediagenix, for example, a tester sometimes pairs with a developer; the tester tests the code, and the developer fixes bugs. This pairing makes it possible to circumvent the project's formal bug-reporting bureaucracy, thus reducing the time to a stable load [see also COUPLING DECREASES LATENCY (5.1.22)].

Overall, this process leads to a more effective implementation process. Contrary to simplistic reasoning, experience has shown that it may cost less overall to program in pairs than to have one coder work on code at a time. In an analogous study, it was recently found that it actually saves hospitals money if a pharmacist follow doctors on their rounds as they make prescriptions. The pharmacist's insights in correcting the doctor's errors (e.g., prescribing drugs that are incompatible with each other) saved more money (in additional health care costs) than the cost of the pharmacist. In addition, this pairing capitalized on the pharmacist's dead time between activities.

A pair of people is less likely to be blindsided than an individual developer. Also, such pairings help ensure that SOMEONE ALWAYS MAKES PROGRESS (4.1.20).

If enough people use DEVELOPING IN PAIRS, and if the pairs rotate occasionally, the emergent structure and emergent organizational behavior contribute to cross-training efforts, information sharing efforts, and trust.

Compare this pattern with GROUP VALIDATION (4.2.32) and RESPONSIBILITIES ENGAGE (5.1.14). One special case of DEVELOPING IN PAIRS occurs when one developer asks another developer (or other suitable expert) to perform a desk check of recently written code, which is much less costly and not less effective than traditional code inspections, code walk-throughs, and code reviews. Though probably less effective than the "canonical" form of DEVELOPING IN PAIRS, this pattern's worth has been validated empirically [Votta 1993].

There are other configurations that have many of the same dynamics as DEVELOPING IN PAIRS, but that do not involve the pairing of a dynamic duo. At Mediagenix, we found teams that "programmed with the projector," where the computer screen was projected onto a wall, and a team jointly commented on and guided the work as one person sat at the keyboard. At Bell Laboratories, Joe Davison, Ricky Spiece, and Martin Biernat worked on a team where one of them stood at the whiteboard and one of them sat at the terminal, "thinking out loud" and representing the customer. In this case, the code was written on the board and transcribed into Smalltalk while the third person performed a real-time code review.

And in what might be viewed as another slant on paired programming, Doug Lea used a variant of the clean-room methodology that employed a single programmer who takes on a role as programmer and then takes on a role as tester. Clean-room techniques separate these two roles to make sure the individual can focus exclusively on the task at hand. In the extreme application of the clean-room methodology, developers are not allowed to use the compiler to check their own code; instead, they must await such feedback from the tester. Doug mimicked this behavior by wearing two hats. In one sense, this process is as unlike popular pair programming as possible: Each "side" of Doug worked in isolation. But the interplay between the two perspectives is where the power lies: bringing multiple perspectives to bear on the same artifact with tight coupling of minds. Doug's mind provided the tight coupling.

See [Williams 2002].

4.2.29   Engage Quality Assurance **

FSA supervisor and farmer-client examining silage from a trench silo, Sheridan County, Kansas.

... you have a development organization mature enough that roles have been congealed and a customer has been engaged [ENGAGE CUSTOMERS (4.2.6)]. You need some filter between the two to both facilitate and regulate interactions between them.

Customer engagement is a key element of QA. Though developers may feel they get everything right, a good dose of customer reality helps bring the perspective that development of perfect software is impossible.

Too many organizations defer quality until "later" or equate QA with testing which occurs late in the development process. Yet, success depends on the production of high quality work, and early feedback is important to address fundamental quality problems.

It's important to perform testing, and most developers in fact perform their own testing. But individuals easily get blindsided by their own design thinking in terms of what needs to be tested. Further, they may use testing as their quality criterion. However, you can't test quality into a product; instead, you can only build a product and test its quality.

Therefore:

Make QA a central role. Couple it tightly with development as soon as development has something to test. Test plan development can proceed in parallel with coding, but developers are the ones who declare the system ready for testing.

QA was central to the development of Borland's QPW:

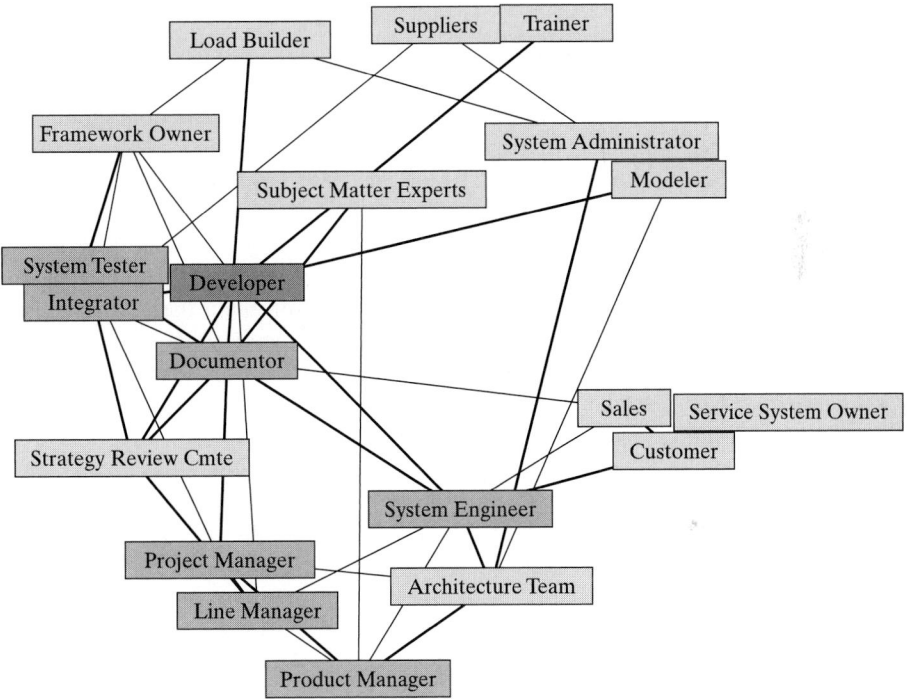

The QA organization should be outside the context of development; in other words, the planning and reporting of tests should not be accountable to the development organization. The development organization develops a sense of accountability for delivering a quality product, since their own view of their reputation is linked to the ability to minimize the bugs that "those people in QA" find.

QA should interact with marketing in order to understand the needs and challenges a system will face.

QA people have skills and experience that allow them to view customer needs from a perspective that may not be reflected in requirements or other articulations of needs. A good example is security companies that develop security software utilities for commercial applications. Their own probing of the operating system often uncovers security holes, and then they work with the vendor to fix the problems.

❖   ❖   ❖

Having engaged QA, the project is ready to approach the Customer. With QA and the Customer engaged, the QA process can be put in place (e.g., use cases can be gathered).

There are at least two reasons for making QA a separate organization from that holding Developers' allegiance. First, test development shouldn't be blindsided by the Developer perspective. If both the Developer and QA perform their own tests, testing becomes a double-blind experiment with the software as a subject. Second, QA should remain outside the domain of influence of the development organization in the interest of objectivity. This is an obvious pattern in QPW.

Indeed, ENGAGE QUALITY ASSURANCE requires a separate QA organization, which is in contrast to the ideals espoused in XP. XP advocates extensive unit testing, but in the words of Kent Beck, "documentation, design, formal review, separate QA; it's all a waste of our time" [Waters 2000]. This response may be a reaction to organizations that have a separate QA organization, but do not engage it. Such a setup is a recipe for disaster: You have the overhead of a separate organization without any of the benefits. In order for a separate QA organization to be effective, it must have frequent and positive interaction with development.

Note that QA should be engaged early in the project. By the time testing starts, it is too late to build the trust needed for QA to proceed smoothly, a problem that is clarified in GET INVOLVED EARLY (A.5.13) [Delano Rising 1998]. It is not just the developers' responsibility to engage the testers; instead, the testers must reach out to the developers as well (see DESIGNERS ARE OUR FRIENDS (A.5.10) [Delano 1998]).

See also APPLICATION DESIGN IS BOUNDED BY TEST DESIGN (4.2.30).

4.2.30   Application Design Is Bounded by Test Design *

An M4 tank tops the ridge on a test course. The tank was designed to meet all of the challenges of the test course, which should simulate all of the extremes of the field.

... a development organization has mechanisms to document and enforce the software architecture, and it has developers to write the code. You are planning how to engage your customer. A Testing role is being defined.

When do you design and implement test plans and scripts?
   Test development takes time and cannot be started just when the coding is done. One cannot have the mindset that, "we will know what to test once we have coded it."
   Scenarios are known when requirements are known, and many of these scenarios are known early in the process [see Scenarios Define Problem (4.2.8)].
   Test implementation teams need to know the details of message formats, interfaces, and other architectural properties in great detail (to support test scripts and test jigs). Both software developers and testers need to work closely together from the same "scripts"—the use cases that define customer needs.

Yet, external tests usually do not reflect an understanding of the internal software structure, so much test development can take place in parallel with design and implementation of the deliverable software. Implementation changes daily; as such, there should be no need for test designs to track ephemeral changes in software implementation.

Therefore:

Use-case-driven test design starts when the customer first agrees to use case requirements. Test design evolves along with software design, but only in response to changes in customer use cases; the source software, thus, is inaccessible to the tester. When development decides that architectural interfaces have stabilized, low-level test design and implementation can proceed.

Software designers can and should use test specifications as a major touchstone for requirements.

This pattern provides a context for Scenarios Define Problem (4.2.8) and complements Engage Quality Assurance (4.2.29). Once the expectations are established between the testers and developers in the context of customer expectations [perhaps through Firewalls (4.2.9) and Gatekeeper (4.2.10)] you can approach the customer to capture use cases.

Making the software accessible to testers causes them to see the developer's point of view rather than the customer's point of view and leads to the chance that they may test the wrong things or test at the wrong level of detail. Furthermore, the software will continue to evolve from requirements until the architecture gels, and there is no sense in causing test design to fishtail until interfaces settle down.

In short, test design kicks off at the end of the first major influx of requirements and touches base with design again when the architecture is stable.

4.2.31   **Mercenary Analyst**
See Section 4.1.24.

4.2.32   Group Validation *

Testing a homemade screen door for strength.

... an activity such as analysis, design, or implementation has been completed and is about to be assessed.

Product quality is crucial to the success of the enterprise. QA usually assesses the quality of the end product, performing only black-box validation and verification. Development groups may bring many insights on product problems and opportunities. Individuals, however, may not have the insight necessary to discover the bug plaguing the system (there may be issues with lack of objectivity).

Therefore:

Even before engaging QA, the development team—including the customer—can validate the design. Techniques such as CRC cards and group debugging help socialize and solve problems. Members of a validation team can also work with QA to fix root causes attributable to common classes of software faults.

The software shouldn't be the only focus of debugging and review. Recurring types of software bugs may point to systemic problems in the structure of the organization itself. For example, if the project is seeing a high rate of mismatches in interfaces between components, the integration may be taking place too quickly to allow all of the team members to keep in step with the current state of the architecture. The organization can write new patterns to solve these systemic problems [UPDATING THE PATTERNS (3.3)]. See [Fagan 1976].

One can create a culture where the quality of the system is constantly brought into focus before the whole team. Problems will be resolved sooner than if they are deferred to the "official" QA function, which typically interacts with the project at the boundaries of design and coding. The cost of this pattern is the time expended in group design/code debugging sessions.

The CRC design technique has been found to be a great team-building tool and an ideal way to socialize designs. Studies of projects inside AT&T have found group debugging sessions to be unusually productive. Bringing the customer into these sessions can be particularly helpful. The project must be careful to temper interactions between the customer and the developer, using the patterns mentioned later in this pattern.

There is an empirical research foundation for this pattern. An article in the Communications of the ACM (CACM) [CACM 1979] shows that team debugging contributes to team learning and effectiveness. A contrary position can be found in [Meyers 1978], though this study was limited to fault detection rates and did not evaluate the advantages of team learning.

There are times when reviews do not need not be a group effort; sometimes, all it takes is a little help from a friend. DEVELOPING IN PAIRS (4.2.28) is one example, and the kind of desk checks mentioned in [Votta 1993], where one person liberally marks up the work of another, also can be effective (Votta shows that this mode of review is almost as effective and much less costly than a meeting). The CREATOR-REVIEWER (A.5.8) pattern [Weir 1998] calls this person-to-person a "distribution review" as opposed to a "meeting review." Doug Lea once took this approach to an extreme, working on a one-person clean-room programming team where he played the roles both of programmer and reviewer, with no use of a compiler to validate the code between the steps (see DEVELOPING IN PAIRS). We imagine the psychological forces must have been both interesting and compelling.

STAND-UP MEETING (5.2.7) is an informal form of this pattern.

CHAPTER 5

Organization Construction Patterns

Once the design is done—the organization has been conceptualized and has been framed out—it's time to start putting it together. We hire people, fine-tune teams, and put processes in place. The patterns in this chapter are construction patterns: patterns that deal with day-to-day realities of building an organization.

There are two pattern languages here: one is about organizational style, and the other is about people and code. The ORGANIZATIONAL STYLE pattern language is about management style. Each manager will use different techniques to help an organization unfold.

The PEOPLE AND CODE pattern language talks about the day-to-day impact of CONWAY'S LAW (5.1.7). As the code takes shape, the organization structure should track it. There are architectural artifacts that themselves have achieved the stature of patterns and, by CONWAY'S LAW, we expect to find analogous structures in the organization. These are those organizational patterns, patterns that one allows to take shape piecemeal in the organization as the code itself changes. Of course, it can work the other way too. Thus, coding structures and interfaces can reflect business structures that are, in turn, reflected in the organization or in the geographical distribution of the development groups.

5.1 Organizational Style Pattern Language

The Pattern Language

Our organizational analyses have uncovered various styles of organization. Figure 5.1 shows organizational style patterns. As a result of our studies of these organizations, we have captured these patterns of roles and the communication links between them. Some styles work better than others in their respective contexts. There is no single right style, but different kinds of organizations suggest elements of style that are integral to their success.

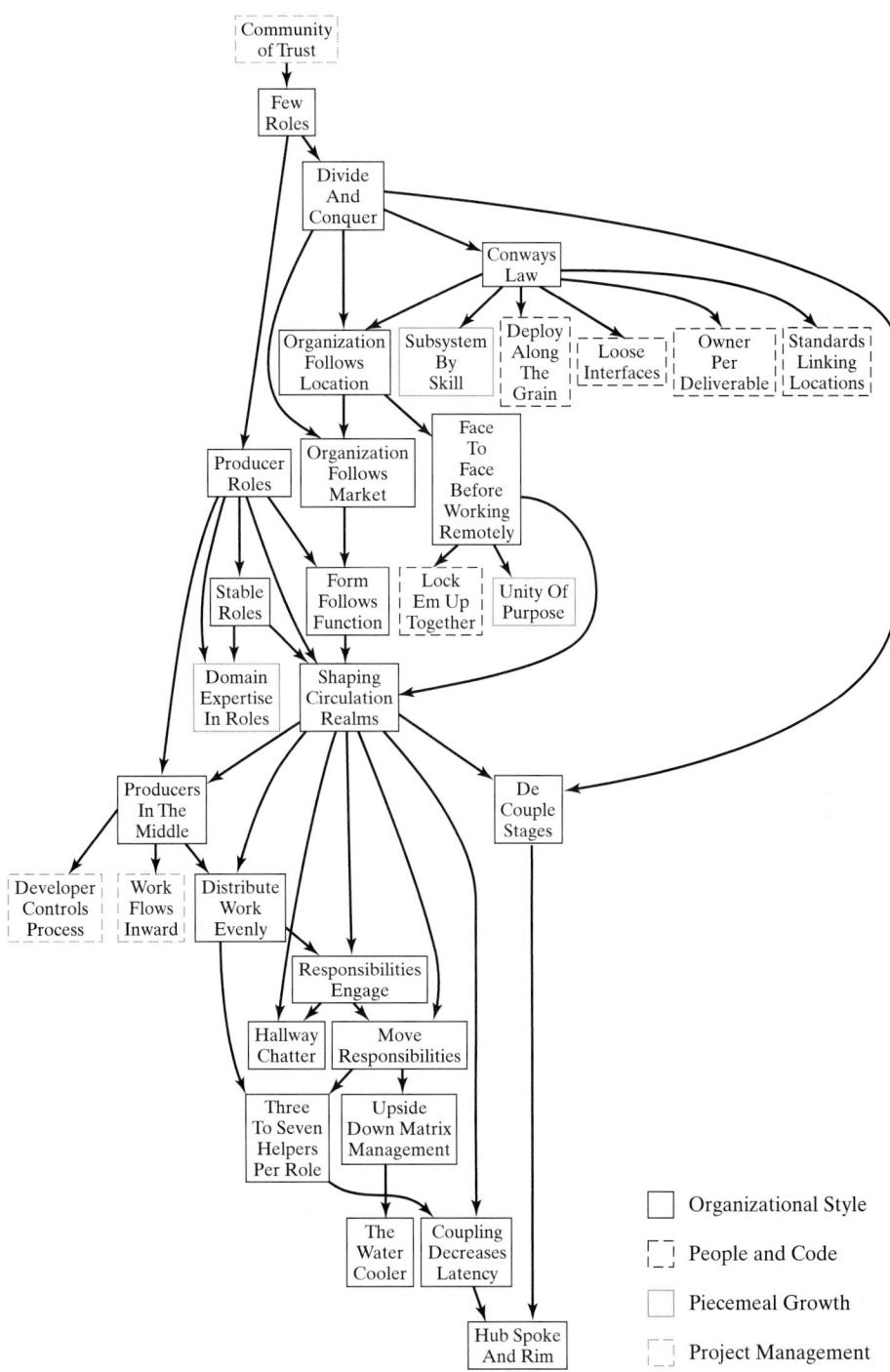

FIGURE 5.1

A Story about Organizational Style

One of the most fun projects I ever worked on was code-named Trident. We started out with about 10 people [see Size the Organization (4.2.2)], but we had Few Roles (5.1.2). Nearly all of the roles were Producer Roles (5.1.3). As a result, the producer roles were at the center of communication—they got the information they needed [Producers in the Middle (5.1.4)]. The roles remained stable throughout the life of the project [Stable Roles (5.1.5)].

We were making significant modifications to an existing product, so naturally our organization mirrored the architecture of the product [Conway's Law (5.1.7)]. We had a single market, but it was different from the market for the existing product, which was why we were formed as a separate organization in the first place [Organization Follows Market (5.1.9)].

The organization, small as it was, was split across two locations. We began with Face to Face Before Working Remotely (5.1.10) and then split the work along geographical lines [Organization Follows Location (5.1.8)]. One person agreed to a temporary move to the other location, which was a form of Shaping Circulation Realms (5.1.12), and helped Hallway Chatter (5.1.15).

There was no overloaded central role [Distribute Work Evenly (5.1.13)], which was helped by keeping Three to Seven Helpers Per Role (5.1.21). The smallness of the team allowed high coupling, which contributed to efficiency [Coupling Decreases Latency (5.1.22)].

Ultimately, shifts in the marketplace caused the project's demise. Fortunately, the decision was made quickly, and until that point the project was on or ahead of schedule.

5.1.1   Community of Trust

See section 4.1.1.

5.1.2   Few Roles **

Actors rehearsing a new play by Langston Hughes, Chicago, Illinois, 1942.

... as an organization establishes its identity, the roles that the members of the project assume begin to take shape. The roles emerge from project needs as well as from individual preferences. Project members fill these roles and pass information among themselves.

People on a project must communicate with each other in order for the project to make progress. Yet the overhead of this communication can hinder the very progress it should facilitate.

The number of possible communication paths among roles increases quadratically with respect to the number of roles. For example, 5 roles have 10 communication paths, but 10 roles have 45 paths. And 20 roles have 190 possible communication paths. It is clearly not possible for every role to communicate with every other role. Therefore, information often reaches roles indirectly through other roles. However, this process increases both latency (delay) and overhead.

Individuals may play several roles and receive information destined for one role that is useful for other roles that they embody. However, our experience in such cases is that there are enough different communication needs in the different roles that such overlap does not appreciably decrease the number of communication paths required. The source of information is sometimes as important as the information content itself.

Therefore:

Identify the roles in the organization. Try to keep the number of roles to about 16 or fewer. If necessary, try to reduce the number of roles by identifying the value of various roles and by consolidating or eliminating roles that add less value.

We have found that the healthiest and most productive organizations tend to have around 16–20 roles. Aiming for the lower number allows additional roles to emerge as needed.

The combinatorics of communication encourages few roles. Fewer roles means that communication becomes more efficient, both in resources consumed and in speed.

Roles tend to become stable in an organization over time, more so than processes and even personnel. Roles are a reflection of the culture and the values of the organization. Keeping the number of roles low makes it easier for new people to assimilate the organizational culture and become part of it.

Roles are not the same as people, for several people may play the same role. For example, most organizations have several people fill the Developer role. Conversely, one person may fill more than one role. For example, a person may be mainly a Developer, but may function part time as the Project Manager. Multiple roles per person is common in small teams, but is often seen in large organizations as well.

How do you determine an organization's roles? In particular, how do you know whether certain tasks are responsibilities of a role or whether those tasks form a new role? One can examine the collaborations that result from implementation of those tasks, and then one can see whether the tasks correspond to the role in question or have a different pattern of communication. In practice, though, it is simpler than that. Just ask the organization to identify its own roles. Every organization we have ever studied knew what its roles were. Organizational health seems to closely track the clarity with which project members can delineate roles.

Large organizations may find themselves with large numbers of roles. One can then approximate FEW ROLES (5.1.2) by applying DIVIDE AND CONQUER (5.1.6).

After you have identified the roles, it may not be obvious which roles can be combined or eliminated. Use PRODUCER ROLES (5.1.3) to characterize the roles.

As you keep the roles to a manageable number, communication saturation will stay high, and communication patterns will resemble RESPONSIBILITIES ENGAGE (5.1.14).

Note that this pattern is different from SIZE THE ORGANIZATION (4.2.2), which deals with the number of people on the project. FEW ROLES (5.1.2) is about the number of roles, regardless of the number of people.

This pattern is closely tied to PRODUCER ROLES (5.1.3). It also makes DISTRIBUTE WORK EVENLY (5.1.13) possible.

5.1.3   Producer Roles *

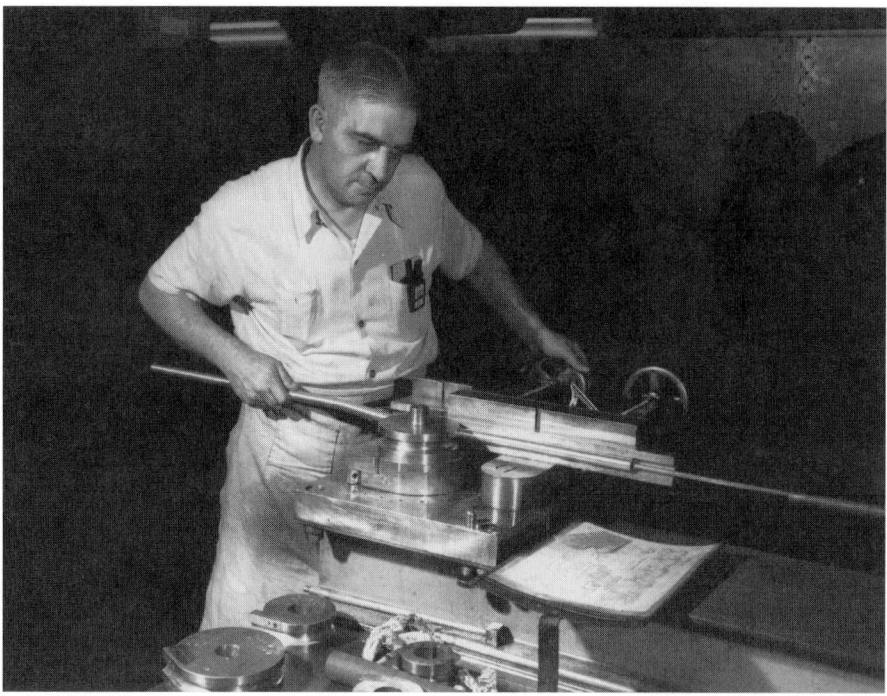

... once you have identified the roles in the organization, you are in a position to optimize the role structure, which usually involves reducing the number of roles, particularly for mature organizations.

The overhead and bureaucracy in the organization are excessive, as evidenced by the presence of too many roles. Yet, all of the roles seem important. It looks like there is no way to reduce the bureaucracy.

An organization needs some bureaucracy to keep projects running smoothly. There is much administrative work to be done, and programmers don't want to bother with it. But, left unchecked, bureaucracy tends to grow: new roles get created, and the communication overhead increases.

People tend to gravitate to those roles they are most comfortable with, which is healthy. However, some people need the recognition associated with titles (German: *Titelsucht*), and roles are obligingly created to fill that need. Such roles usually have no intrinsic value to the project.

Over time, the responsibilities of roles evolve. In some cases, the real benefit of a role drains off to other roles, leaving little more than a shell behind. In one organization, the chief responsibility of a particular role was "worry," which added no value to the project. But because of the history of the role, it is easy to simply assume that the role is important.

Therefore:

Identify each role as a producer, supporter, or deadbeat (i.e.) a role that adds no value to the project. Eliminate the deadbeats, and in some cases eliminate or consolidate some supporters. Nurture the producer roles, for they are the ones that pay the bills.

Producer roles are those roles that contribute directly to the end product; there is an obvious connection between their work and company revenue. The canonical producer role in software organizations is "Developer."

An organization has numerous support roles. These roles contribute to the effectiveness of the producer roles, but don't directly develop the products. Many support roles are vitally important, such as FIREWALLS (4.2.9), GATEKEEPER (4.2.10), and PATRON ROLE (4.2.15). Roles that provide computing support, for example, are also essential. But support roles are inherently higher in overhead than producer roles. There may, however, be opportunities to gain efficiency by combining support roles.

As with other types of roles, deadbeat roles can be identified by their responsibilities. They may do nothing more than receive information and pass it on without adding any value to it. Watch for other responsibilities that add no value to the project, such as the aforementioned "worry" responsibility. If a role truly adds no value to the project, it should be eliminated.

In some cases, a role that passes information adds value by doing so. For example, a person who passes information by "pushing" it to those who would normally not get the information may prevent project inconsistencies or may even detect such inconsistencies before they get out of hand [see WISE FOOL (4.2.21)]. Such an individual fills an important support role.

Although eliminating roles fosters greater organizational efficiency, it may also lead to bruised egos or even feelings of insecurity. In some cases, a role might be preserved and reshaped so that it can contribute more directly to the project. Refer to FORM FOLLOWS FUNCTION (5.1.11) and SHAPING CIRCULATION REALMS (5.1.12) for further help.

This pattern sets up PRODUCERS IN THE MIDDLE (5.1.4), and it is linked to DOMAIN EXPERTISE IN ROLES (4.2.22). See also FIREWALLS (4.2.9), GATEKEEPER (4.2.10), and PATRON ROLE (4.2.15).

5.1.4   Producers in the Middle **

... one of the first steps a project takes in self-understanding is the identification of roles and, in particular, the determination of which roles are the PRODUCER ROLES (5.1.3). But it is the information flow among the roles that helps get the work done.

In a project, not all roles hear everything. But much of the information communicated has important implications for the product.

Within any software project, many activities, roles, and individuals compete for attention. Project managers, for one, have a need to be at the center of everything. They need to have their finger on the pulse of the project and to know everything that is going on. That's their job. In a similar manner, perhaps to a lesser degree, other roles also need to be involved in the project.

However, all roles are not equal. Certain roles (Developer and a few others) contribute directly to the development of the product. Most other roles contribute indirectly to the product; as such, they (should) exist only to help the producers do their job. These producer roles need information in order to do their job.

Therefore:

The producer role(s) must be at the center or very near the center of the hive of communication. Make sure the producers are party to all (or nearly all) communication about the project.

The role at the center of the project must be a producer role; in fact, it should be the producer role (e.g., a Developer) that gets the most done. Consider the developer roles at the center of this healthy organization, an organization that develops financial trading software on tight schedules:

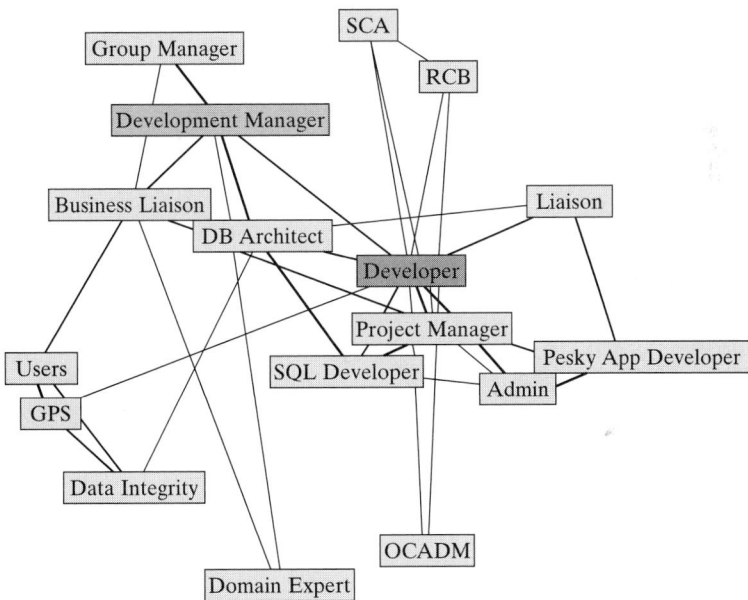

The role at the center shows the focus of the project. In most cases, it is a role like Developer or Coder. In a few rare cases, the most central role is a management role. In such cases, the project is focused not on developing the product, but rather on managing the development of the product.

If you find that your central role is not a producer, your project team needs to do some soul searching. Why isn't your focus on the product like it should be? What is getting in the way? For example, are you so preoccupied with something like ISO 9001 certification that you have lost your focus?

Note that this pattern can be taken to an extreme. If you have too many roles, and they all focus on the coder, for example, the coder will have to deal with so much communication that nothing will get done. As a result, this pattern must be applied together with Few Roles (5.1.2). See also Distribute Work Evenly (5.1.13).

❖   ❖   ❖

When this pattern is applied, the natural tendency is toward WORK FLOWS INWARD (4.1.18). Though developers will tend to get the information they need, they sometimes can get sidetracked by managers who are overly meddlesome. However, left alone, developers will naturally evolve first to this pattern and then to WORK FLOWS INWARD.

This pattern is closely related to DEVELOPER CONTROLS PROCESS (4.1.17). If the developer—a producer role—controls the process, that person is likely to be a hub of communication. In fact, allowing the developer to control the process is one way to help implement the use of this pattern.

5.1.5   **Stable Roles** *

No, not THAT kind of stable!

In our organizational studies, we ask teams to simulate their typical development experience. During one such exercise, the team described how they formed a task force to handle a crisis. I was struck that the team seemed to thrive on crisis, undoubtedly because crisis management was valued and rewarded. When I mentioned this observation during the debriefing, the architect said, "Yes, we run on crises like a car runs on gasoline."

... a team has been formed, and the PRODUCER ROLES (5.1.3) are in place. During the course of development, disruptions are common. The team's response to these distractions can have a long-term impact on the health of the organization.

If a team overreacts to disruptions, the team can become perpetually dysfunctional.

A well-functioning team is like a spring stretched over some distance. A disruption is like a wave that travels along the spring for a while, keeping things from working as they did before. The right response dampens the wave, and life returns to normal. But the wrong response tends to amplify the wave and keep it going. In organizations, the danger is twofold: (1) that the disruption interrupts the team more than it should and (2) that the team members begin to see the disruption response as the normal way of life.

Disruptions to teams come in many flavors. The most obvious ones are crises such as emergency bug fixes. However, team growth, changes in requirements, and reorganizations are also disruptions.

Each disruption requires action, which takes attention away from the task at hand. So, the challenge is to take the appropriate action while minimizing the attention it draws away from the main job. An important aspect of this challenge is rewards: an employee should be recognized for dealing adeptly with disruptions, particularly crises, but one must be careful not to value fire-fighting over fire prevention. People have been known to commit software development arson in order to become software firefighting heroes.

Therefore:

Whenever possible, keep people in roles for at least the duration of the project release. Avoid elevating transient tasks that deal with disruptions to the status of roles.

Obviously, in order for this strategy to work, the roles themselves must remain for the duration of the project.

The key is that as a disruption comes up, don't create a new role to handle it. Handling disruptions, particularly crises, has a certain status to it. If you allow a role to emerge, then the role institutionalizes the behavior, which tends to encourage the disruptions to happen. Instead, focus on nurturing the PRODUCER ROLES (5.1.3), this which can be done carefully using rewards [see COMPENSATE SUCCESS (4.2.25)].

Beyond typical crises, this pattern can also be used as the team composition changes. Such changes may be less dramatic than crises, but they are also often more devastating. Even team growth can cause serious disruption. So, as the team changes, keep the remaining people in the same roles as much as possible. Then, try to make necessary role changes during the natural breaks in the project, such as just after the project ships.

The impact of this action is manyfold. If you keep people in the same roles, the learning curve is obviously flattened and DOMAIN EXPERTISE IN ROLES (4.2.22) is maintained. If people's roles don't change when they must deal with a crisis, then they still retain their primary focus. Furthermore, the organization keeps its values focused on the long-term solutions and not on the short-term disruptions.

This advice may seem like simple common sense, and it is. But the trouble with common sense is that it is, well, so uncommon.

5.1.6   Divide and Conquer **

... the roles have been defined for a process and an organization, and their interactions are understood. The organization has grown to a point where it cannot easily manage itself. Perhaps there are too many people or, more seriously, too many roles, for the organization to hang together. The organization's decision process breaks apart, and progress bogs down for more and more decisions. Or the organization can foresee growth to a point where these problems arise.

For example, this organization has no apparent regular structure, and, though it is productive, it is not likely to evolve well:

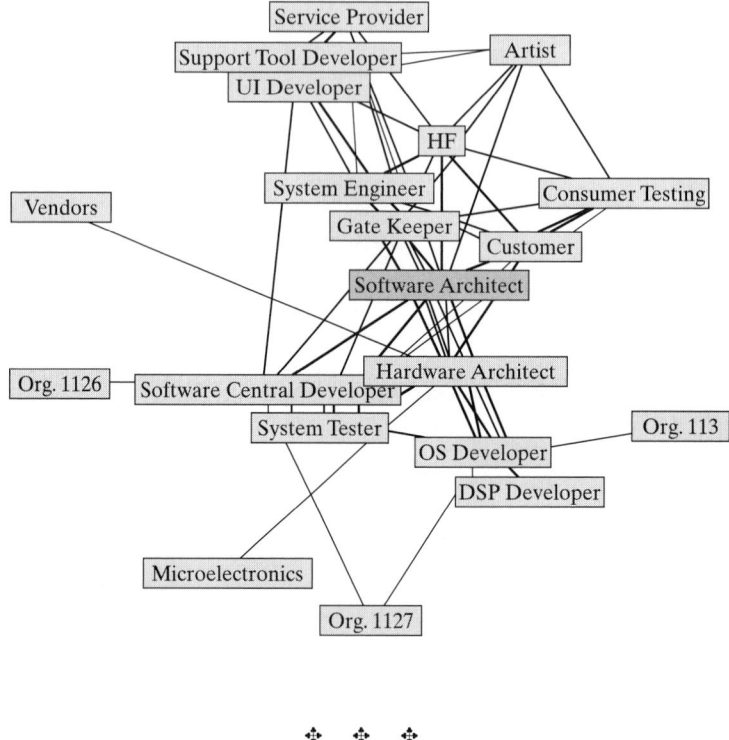

❖   ❖   ❖

Successful projects must learn to accommodate the growth that accompanies success and that outstrips team dynamics. If an organization is too large, it can't be managed. Incohesive organizations are confusing and dilute focus.

Even distribution of responsibility is good because it allows separation of concerns and divides up the workload. Regular structures, such as hierarchies, can easily be developed by adding more people, without destroying the spirit of the original structure. However, a regular hierarchical structure does not evenly distribute responsibility.

It is useful to have organizational boundaries that are somewhat lightweight.

Therefore:

Find clusters of roles that have strong mutual relationships, but that are loosely coupled to the rest of the organization. Form a separate organization and process around those roles. Make sure the organization has identifiable subdomains that can grow into departments in their own right as the project thrives and expands to serve a maintained market.

It is sometimes easiest to accomplish this task by identifying core roles that can form the root of suborganizations that precipitate from a larger organization. Let the suborganizations cluster around these roles.

You should apply this pattern between releases so as to minimize any turmoil that might confuse work in progress.

The organization shown below has no well-partitioned structures, but one can identify logical partitions within it (e.g., customer, developer and management):

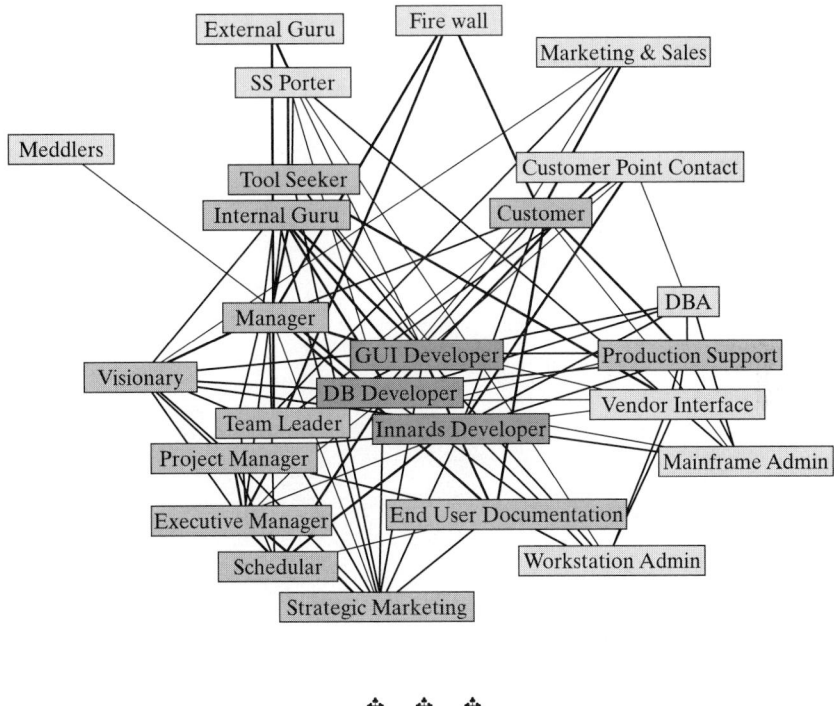

❖   ❖   ❖

This partitioning establishes an overall organizational framework as a basis for organizational growth. Each new suborganization is a largely independent entity to which the remaining patterns in this language can be independently applied. This pattern makes it possible to have FEW ROLES (5.1.2) in any given closure of interaction.

Implement this pattern using SACRIFICE ONE PERSON (4.1.22), ORGANIZATION FOLLOWS LOCATION (5.1.8), and ORGANIZATION FOLLOWS MARKET (5.1.9).

In the forces, note that each suborganization that arises from this pattern is fodder for most other patterns, since each subsystem is a system in itself. Also, to review an organizational structure that has been reverse engineered and redivided into new processes, see the picture for the pattern MOVE RESPONSIBILITIES (5.1.18).

The business structure is a key consideration in building an organizational structure. Much of the business structure becomes articulated in the architecture, so CONWAY'S LAW (5.1.7) is an important pattern that supports DIVIDE AND CONQUER.

If you can find no core roles around which sub-organizations might form, then the organization may not be partitionable. For example, it is difficult to grow a chief programmer team organization.

If you need to divide up work in *time* rather than across team structure, see GET ON WITH IT (4.1.3).

5.1.7   Conway's Law **

Construction of the Lincoln Memorial, 1916.

... an architect and a development team are in place. The architecture is fairly well-established.

If the parts of an organization (e.g., teams, departments, or subdivisions) do not closely reflect the essential parts of the product, or if the relationships between organizations do not reflect the relationships between product parts, then the project will be in trouble.

The system architecture shapes the communication paths in an organization. The de facto organizational structure shapes the formal organizational structure. The formal organizational structure, in turn, shapes the architecture. Early architectural formulations are only approximations and are unstable. However, there are major rhythms in the architecture that reflect areas of core business competency, and that level of concern is more closely tied to organizational structure than to the broader concerns of the whole architectural structure.

Therefore:

Make sure the organization is compatible with the product architecture. At this point in the language, it is more likely that the architecture should drive the organization than vice versa.

An organization will have periodic reviews of the architecture and potentially of project management strategies [see STAND-UP MEETING (5.2.7)]. At each of these meetings (if indeed they are separate) care should be taken to align the structure of the architecture with the structure of the organization by making piecemeal changes to one or the other.

The organization and product architecture will be aligned. It thus becomes easier for the pattern DEVELOPER CONTROLS PROCESS (4.1.17) to succeed.

One reason to let the architecture dominate more than organizational concerns is that the architecture is more often constrained by the problem, which ties into the core reasons for the existence of the enterprise [e.g., see ORGANIZATION FOLLOWS MARKET (5.1.9)]. However, political forces are also powerful and may even take precedence over core business needs; be wary that such situations often lead to serious organizational struggles.

The best structure in the long term is one derived from a three-way alignment of the main structures of the business (domain), the structure of the organization, and the structure of the software. One approach is to design the major software artifacts around domain analysis considerations and to align the organization with the architecture accordingly. This structure works best for greenfield projects and for small original design teams. Another approach is to design the organization around the business needs and to let the architecture follow the organization. This approach is more important in legacy organizations where a tradition of architecture closely held by the experts may suggest both organizations and architectures that don't follow more standard domain analyses.

Of course, all three of these structures must change over time to deal with evolution in the market, technology, and staff, though the fundamental assumptions about relationships between parts are unlikely to change frequently in a successful business. However, even less momentous changes must be dealt with and, more importantly, the project must take opportunities to leverage its growing understanding of the business, of the suitability of specific technologies to support the business, and of the organizational and system structures that can support the business. Much of this pattern language aims to maintain the project communication essential to the long-term alignment of these structures. Specific patterns like STAND-UP MEETING (5.2.7) should be viewed as opportunities not only to review the architecture, but also to review the organizational structure and business strategies as well.

Gerard Meszaros (formerly of Nortel) notes that the organization should be bound to the architecture only after the architecture has stabilized. If the architecture is bound to the organization too early, architectural drift will lead to interference between individuals' domains of control [Mezaros 1997]. On the other hand, Alistair Cockburn points out in SKILL MIX (A.5.28) [Cockburn 1996] that it is sometimes necessary (and advantageous) to separate subsystems according to the skills the team already possesses.

SUBSYSTEM BY SKILL (4.2.23) addresses finer team structure with regard to architectural considerations. DEPLOY ALONG THE GRAIN (5.2.8) or, more specifically, CODE OWNERSHIP (5.2.13), and OWNER PER DELIVERABLE (A.5.19) are CONWAY'S LAW in the small. Use STANDARDS LINKING LOCATIONS (5.2.12) to overcome the isolationism of CONWAY'S LAW.

This historical rationale is derived from Conway's timeless paper "How Do Committees Invent?" [Conway 1968].

5.1.8   Organization Follows Location **

Different parts of the country may have different cultures and architectural styles.

I was once involved in planning a large project that was to be split between two locations. My organization was located in a new building in Colorado with blue carpet. The other half of the project was in a building in New Jersey that had green carpet. When I presented our plan to my organization, I showed slides with different parts of the architecture colored blue or green, depending on where the development was to take place. The organization got the message immediately.

... a product must be developed in several different hallways, on different floors of a building, in different buildings, or at different locations. Multiple locations may be needed for political reasons, for the purpose of colocating development teams with remote markets, for reasons of standards or for the distribution of physical facilities (e.g., the separation between different trading centers or between a radio telescope site and a research university that uses its data), or even for economic or trade reasons that drive development to a different country.

There needs to be a degree of trust and camaraderie within an organization, since an organization is a decision-making body that must make and then buy into joint decisions. Allegiance to an organization falls strongly along the lines of geographic distribution.

It is important to assign tasks and roles insightfully across a geographically distributed workforce.

Communication patterns between project members follow geographic distribution. Coupling between pieces of software must be sustained by analogous coupling between the people maintaining that software. People often avoid communicating with people who work in other buildings, in other towns, or overseas. People in an organization usually work on related tasks, which suggests that they communicate frequently with each other.

Therefore:

The architectural partitioning should reflect the geographic partitioning, and vice versa. Architectural responsibilities should be assigned so decisions can be made (geographically) locally.

This pattern is a variant of CONWAY'S LAW (5.1.7). Since the organization *will* follow the architecture, you want the organization, architecture, and geography to line up. Geographical considerations are often the most severe, and since architecture can be a strong lever for organization, it is a good tool to use in bringing these three aspects into alignment.

One of the most significant characteristics of geographic differences is allegiance: People are naturally more loyal to local managers than to remote managers. Local loyalty is even more extreme if a remote location is part of a company as a result of a merger or acquisition. If work is performed at two locations and the work itself does not split cleanly, one of the two locations must be in charge, which naturally causes resentment on the part of the other location. Try to make the work assignments as autonomous as practical, in order to instill trust.

Suborganizations can be further split or organized by market or other criteria [see WORK FLOWS INWARD (4.1.18), ORGANIZATION FOLLOWS MARKET (5.1.9) and others]. You still need someone to break logjams when consensus can't be reached, perhaps using PATRON ROLE (4.2.15) or ARCHITECT CONTROLS PRODUCT (5.2.3). If the organization is modularized along geographic boundaries, but the architecture is not, then it will be impossible to apply ARCHITECT ALSO IMPLEMENTS (5.2.10). It's difficult for the architect at one location to oversee and contribute to the code at another.

Thomas Allen [Allen 1977] has found that social distance increases rapidly with physical separation [see also HOUSE CLUSTER ([Alexander 1977], ff. 197)]. We have noted frequent cases of international collaboration (usually overseas) that exhibit strong symptoms of this problem and that have had low prospects for success owing to such separation. This crucial pattern is often overlooked or dismissed out of consideration for political alliances or trends (e.g., outsourcing software development is very fashionable in management circles as of this writing). Peter Bürgi's studies of geographically distributed organizations in AT&T bore out the importance of this pattern.

We have seen few geographically distributed organizations that exhibit positive team dynamics. Of course there are exceptions, and there are rare occasions when this pattern does not apply. Steve Berczuk (then at MIT) notes: "communications need not be poor between remote sites" if the following are true:

1. The number of developers on a project, including all sites is small.

2. Most of the communication is done via something like email (wide distribution and asynchronous communication) in [one case] ... more people were in the loop than if the primary means of communication had been hallway chats.

3. The people involved have been together for *some* time so that they feel like they know each other [this can be as short as a kickoff meeting; see FACE TO FACE BEFORE WORKING REMOTELY (5.1.10)].

4. Folks aren't so burned out by "unnecessary" travel that they are willing and happy to travel when it is needed. In some situations [complete work split by location] is not possible because of the nature of the project, so we need a way to address the issue of remoteness [Berczuk 1994].

At times, the market demands geographic distribution (see ORGANIZATION FOLLOWS MARKET (5.1.9) and [Berczuk 1996]). In these cases, you need to use the pattern FACE TO FACE BEFORE WORKING REMOTELY (5.1.10).

As an organization grows, it may want to split geographically for a number of marketing and political reasons [DIVIDE AND CONQUER (5.1.6)]. The OTI corporation relates how it splits organizations geographically to keep reusable assets uncontaminated by each other.

Colocation of people within a building is probably more important to organizational effectiveness than allocation of offices as perks of seniority. Senior staff may have a need for larger or more secure offices than junior staff, but they do not necessarily need an office near the restroom or an office with a window.

See STANDARDS LINKING LOCATIONS (5.2.12) as a technique that supports this organizational structure.

5.1.9   Organization Follows Market *

Vegetable market, San Diego, California.

... the market comprises several customers with similar but conflicting needs. The project has adopted sound architectural principles and can organize its software according to market needs.

An identified role or organization needs to be accountable to each market segment.

For example, AT&T used to market both private branch exchanges (PBXs), which customers owned and administered onsite, and a feature called CENTREX, which ran on telephone company switches to offer PBX-like features to its customers. Different organizations marketed CENTREX and PBXs, which caused confusion about how best to serve the company's markets.

The development organization should track and meet the needs of each customer. Customers' needs are similar, and much of what they all need can be done in common. Different customers expect results according to different schedules.

Therefore:

In an organization designed to serve several distinct markets, it is important to reflect the market structure in the development organization. One frequently overlooked opportunity for a powerful pattern is the conscious design of a "core" organization that supports only commonalities across all market segments. Ralph Johnson calls this organization a *framework team*. It is important to put this organization in place up front.

Since CONWAY'S LAW (5.1.7) states that organization and architecture are isomorphic, the architecture must follow the market. In reality, if the organization is set up to follow the market, it is easier to have a clean architecture that follows market lines. The success of this pattern is necessary to the success of ARCHITECT ALSO IMPLEMENTS (5.2.10), since the architect's focus and intent are greatly driven by the market. ARCHITECT ALSO IMPLEMENTS should be seen as an audit, refinement, or fine-tuning of this pattern.

This pattern allows the organization to start forming around patterns like FORM FOLLOWS FUNCTION (5.1.11) in order to flesh out the structure at a finer level.

AT&T actually solved this problem in an extreme way—by spinning off its PBX organization as a separate company.

Most of the rationale is in the forces. Two of the major forces relate to individual customer schedules and to the posturing of the organization in order to respond quickly to customer requests. Two important aspects of domain analysis are broadening the architecture (e.g., by working at the base-class level) and ensuring that architectural evolution tracks the vendor understanding of customer needs. A single organization can't faithfully track multiple customer needs, so this organization allows different arms of the organization to track different markets independently.

5.1.10   Face to Face Before Working Remotely **

Camp Carson, Colorado. Colonel Wilfrid M. Nlunt, the commanding officer, shakes hands with Colonel Denetrius Xenos, military attache of the Greek ambassador to the United States. The two hold a face-to-face meeting before working remotely.

Designing a new aircraft is a big deal. A very big deal. It's a very complex, very expensive, and pretty risky process that requires the coordinated efforts of many different teams. When the Boeing Corporation began work on the new 777 airplane, it brought everyone on the project together for a kickoff meeting. Thousands of people gathered together to get the project off on the right foot. Fortunately, Boeing owns many large aircraft hangers, so it could accommodate a meeting of that size.

... market or personnel conditions sometimes require a project to be geographically distributed. In such cases, ORGANIZATION FOLLOWS LOCATION (5.1.8) is used to partition the work. But even when the work is partitioned in this manner, it is a challenge to actually implement the partitioning effectively. It may look good on paper, but real people will run into a host of difficulties as they work out the details.

The pull of local organizations is so strong that it can overwhelm the common architectural, marketing, and social aspects of a project.

Geographic distance makes communication harder. Different time zones create logistical difficulties for conversations. The cultural differences that often go hand in hand with long-distance cooperative work are sometimes staggering. The obvious problem is finding common communication times, but there are more subtle forces at work. One project was split between the United States and England. Conference calls took place in the morning in the United States, which was late afternoon in England. Consequently, the U.S. people were fresh, but their colleagues in England were winding down, ready to hit the local pub.

Difficulties in communication often weaken direct, effective communication paths, shunting communications to more indirect paths through the organization. Local leaders receive marching orders and pass them on to their colleagues, though they unintentionally add their own interpretation. Some may remember the children's game "gossip," where a message is whispered from one player to another until it bears no resemblance to the original message.

Although partitioning the project along geographic lines is necessary, it has the side effect of isolating one location from another. People must communicate using defined interfaces [see STANDARDS LINKING LOCATIONS (5.2.12)]; as a result, people who work together do not know each other. People naturally tend not to work as well with those they don't know. It's hard to work with someone who you only know through text in an email as a voice on the phone.

Therefore:

Begin a distributed project with a face-to-face meeting for everyone. This meeting should establish project unity, as well as give people a chance to get to know those they work with.

The meeting establishes unity by focusing on project goals, intended markets, competitors, and the project architecture. [It isn't necessary that the architecture be nailed down yet; in fact, future planning requirements can lead to LOCK 'EM UP TOGETHER (5.2.5).]

The social aspects of a meeting are vitally important. Betsy Hanes Perry notes, "It is vital to leave at least half of the on-site time as unscheduled time. This allows group members to have impromptu conversations with the people they're closely coupled to. If you don't provide time for these conversations, you will find that bathroom breaks stretch on forever, and that the visitors leave frustrated [Perry 1997]." Steve Berczuk adds, "At Kodak we once had a group meeting of everyone in the division, from every location. The agenda was packed so tightly that we never really got a chance to meet each other [Berczuk 1998]." These social interactions are one of the reasons that videoconferences are no substitute for a face-to-face meeting.

Every organization needs a place to call home. Hold the meeting outside of the office in a place that is memorable because of its uniqueness, beauty, great food, or other memorable qualities, so that the group can identify with that place and its good memories.

In a large project, the prospect of an initial face-to-face meeting may be daunting. But the Boeing company brought thousands of people together at the inception of the 777 project. Of course, they *do* own a few planes ...

The importance of this initial meeting should not be underestimated. For a distributed project, such a meeting may be the very best way to establish UNITY OF PURPOSE (4.2.12). Furthermore, the social aspects of people getting to know each other goes a long way toward resolving the tension between ORGANIZATION FOLLOWS LOCATION (5.1.8) and STANDARDS LINKING LOCATIONS (5.2.12). It sets up an environment where SHAPING CIRCULATION REALMS (5.1.12) can occur successfully.

An initial group meeting can easily be followed (often immediately) by a LOCK 'EM UP TOGETHER (5.2.5) architectural session.

It may not stop with a single meeting. You may find that regular "all hands" meetings are worth the transportation expenses.

5.1.11   Form Follows Function

... you know the key atomic process activities, but there is little specialization and few well-defined roles. People don't know where to turn for answers to questions.

A project must delineate well-defined roles to help identify and leverage expertise relevant to emerging problems.

Individual activities are too small and their sequencing relationships are too dynamic to be useful process building blocks.

You could build talent lists of the individuals in an organization and partition the work among them, but doing so makes the organization sensitive to personnel changes. Furthermore, it would be nice to sometimes be able to talk about the organizational structure at a higher level of abstraction.

You could delineate classic roles such as developer, and designer, and manager, but such organization provides only a partial solution. These roles don't apply to all organizations, and stereotypical roles can't generalize to a wide range of domains.

Activities often cluster together according to related artifacts or other domain relationships.

You want to match up specialization, expertise, and experience when staffing an organization.

Therefore:

Group closely related activities (i.e., those activities that are mutually coupled in their implementation, that manipulate the same artifacts, or that are semantically related to the same domain). Name the abstractions that result from the grouped activities, making them into roles. The associated activities become the responsibilities (job descriptions) of the roles. Roles, rather than activities, thus become the basic project building blocks.

For example, if a project depends heavily on a software library, some ownership [see CODE OWNERSHIP (5.2.13)] should be embodied in a role such as Librarian. The Librarian has responsibilities and social communication patterns distinct from those of a developer, making it a separate role. Other roles such as Vendor Coordinator, Rules Developer, or Computer Graphics Artist speak to the function of the organization and its product.

Other roles convey more subtle aspects of organizational function and structure. One organization featured the roles *Code Police* and *Agitator*, reflecting a lighthearted attitude towards what might otherwise be considered onerous functions.

This approach yields a partial definition of project roles. Some roles [e.g., MERCENARY ANALYST (4.1.24), developer, architect, and GATEKEEPER (4.2.10)] are canonical and are not derived from this pattern. Those roles, too, are in concert with this pattern, though at a more generic level.

The idea was used in a large project re-engineering effort that Jim Coplien worked with in March 1994.

Louis Sullivan is the architect credited with the primordial architectural pattern of this name ([Rybczynski 1989], p. 162).

This pattern interacts with other structural patterns such as ORGANIZATION FOLLOWS LOCATION (5.1.8), ORGANIZATION FOLLOWS MARKET (5.1.9), and ARCHITECT ALSO IMPLEMENTS (5.2.10). Also see ENGAGE CUSTOMERS (4.2.6).

An unnamed manager notes: "In my experience from Project Management Audits ... projects both leave out roles (e.g., no named architect) and define several people with the same role. The second is most problematic, since it causes staff confusion. But the missing role also occurs because projects have inexperienced managers. This is a big problem ... around System Engineering roles, or lack thereof."

5.1.12   Shaping Circulation Realms *

Square dancing—overt shaping of circulation realms.

... in the application of communication patterns, you need to reshape the social network of the organization to move roles closer to or further from the center, more roles closer to or further from the customer, balance load, or otherwise support some pattern of communication structure in the organization.

One cannot just expect communications to happen spontaneously; moreover, one cannot expect any particular configuration of communication to arise in an arbitrary social environment.

Proper communication structures between roles are key to organizational success. Communication can't be controlled from a single role; at least two roles must be involved. Further, communication patterns can't be dictated; some second-order force must be present to encourage them. Communication follows semantic coupling between responsibilities.

Therefore:

Create structures in the organization or in the work space that encourage the communication connections that support other patterns.

Give people titles that create a hierarchy or pecking order whose structure reflects the desired taxonomy. Give people job responsibilities that suggest the appropriate interactions between roles [see also MOVE RESPONSIBILITIES (5.1.18)].

Physically collocate people for whom you wish to have close communication coupling [this pattern partners with ORGANIZATION FOLLOWS LOCATION (5.1.8)].

Tell people what to do and with whom they should interact. People will usually try to respect your wishes if you ask them to do something reasonable that is within their purview and power.

❖   ❖   ❖

This pattern is a building block for other patterns in the language, including ORGANIZATION FOLLOWS MARKET (5.1.9), DEVELOPER CONTROLS PROCESS (4.1.17), DECOUPLE STAGES (5.1.16), ARCHITECT ALSO IMPLEMENTS (5.2.10), ENGAGE QUALITY ASSURANCE (4.2.29), ENGAGE CUSTOMERS (4.2.6), RESPONSIBILITIES ENGAGE (5.1.14), THE WATERCOOLER (5.1.20), HALLWAY CHATTER (5.1.15), SUBSYSTEM BY SKILL (4.2.23), and others. This pattern may also apply to circulation realms outside the project through patterns like FIREWALLS (4.2.9) and many others. The goal is to produce an organization with higher overall cohesion, with subparts that are as internally cohesive and externally decoupled as possible.

This pattern follows an Alexandrian pattern ([Alexander 1977], ff. 480) of the same name and has strong similarities to the rationales given in HOUSE CLUSTER ([Alexander 1977], ff. 197). An analogous rationale for organizational structures can be found in [Allen 1977]. In fact, the organizational structure may be homomorphic with the structure of the buildings and rooms in which the organization lives and works, so Alexander's pattern of the same name may be a crucial driving force behind this ostensibly organizational concern.

Note that MOVE RESPONSIBILITIES (5.1.18) is a closely related pattern.

See related notes in the rationale for GATEKEEPER (4.2.10).

5.1.13   Distribute Work Evenly *

A 20-mule team distributes work and communication evenly.

... an organization is working to organize itself in a way that makes the environment as enjoyable as possible and that makes the most effective use of human resources.

It is easy to depend on just a few people to carry most of the organization's burdens. Managers like to rely on a few key people in order to minimize the number of interfaces they need to manage. And some employees strive to do all they can out of a misplaced feeling of monumental responsibility. In fact, we find that PRODUCER ROLES (5.1.3) tend to have stronger communication networks than other support roles.

But if this uneven distribution of work continues, it becomes difficult for a heavily loaded role to sustain the communication networks necessary to the healthy functioning of the enterprise as a whole. Resentment might build among employees who don't feel like they are central to the action. And the central people may easily burn out.

Define the *communication intensity ratio* as the ratio of the number of communication paths of the busiest role to the average number of communication paths per role. Empirically, one finds that the organization has a problem—some unhealthiness—if this ratio becomes too large.

Therefore:

Try to keep the communication intensity ratio to two or less. (We have found that it isn't easy to get much below two.) The easiest way to keep this ratio low is to have Few Roles (5.1.2). It also helps to identify the Producer Roles (5.1.3) and eliminate any deadbeat roles. You can also identify all the communication paths of the most central role and see which are really necessary.

Some of this communication overhead isn't very subtle, and these cases are easy to identify. In many cases, you can eliminate redundant or misdirected communication using simple and direct methods without delving into the deep structure or principles of the organization.

Other situations require more finesse and generativity, building on other patterns in this pattern language.

If an organization becomes so out of balance that the work is concentrated in a few people, those people are likely to experience burnout. Such unevenness might also point to deeper problems in the organization. For example, the more lightly loaded people may not have the technical skills or the human interaction skills needed to be able to integrate into the larger team or organization. Personality differences can be addressed with human effectiveness training programs, (e.g., appreciating differences or giving effective presentations). Skill mismatches can be dealt with by reassigning people or by training.

An imbalance may also point to insecurity in the person or clique that tries to take on all the work. Such insecurity may manifest itself as lack of trust of others. Encounters between the insecure parties and the rest of the project team polarize the positions of each, and a form of schismogenesis may set in—the rise of factions in the organization [see The Open/Closed Principle of Teams (6.1.4)]. Insecure subgroups may withdraw from the rest of the team or even try to hijack the project by strong-arming people into doing their bidding. Such behaviors may be accompanied by some of the dynamics of burnout (e.g., shutting down communication with "outsiders"). Patterns like Gatekeeper (4.2.10), Wise Fool (4.2.21), and patron can help avoid the creation of unhealthy factions.

In any of these dysfunctional situations, it is the job of the manager to counsel the parties involved and to forcefully intervene. Correcting the problem is often an intricate and time-consuming process.

This pattern follows Producer Roles (5.1.3) and Producers in the Middle (5.1.4), which are prerequisites to Shaping Circulation Realms (5.1.12). This pattern itself is a refinement of Shaping Circulation Realms. Few Roles (5.1.2) makes this pattern happen.

This pattern can be implemented and elaborated by using Responsibilities Engage (5.1.14) and Three to Seven Helpers Per Role (5.1.21).

This figure shows communication intensity ratio data for some of our early research sub-jects. We find that successful organizations tend to be near the origin point on the graph.

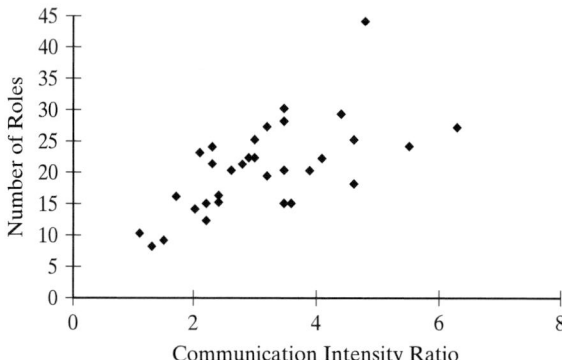

5.1.14 Responsibilities Engage

*The responsibilities of raising children encourage parents
to be actively engaged in their children's lives.*

... the organization has been established, and people have settled into their roles. Communication tends to be centralized.

If communication predominately flows through the center of the organization, two things happen: Communication takes too long, and the most central roles become overburdened with communication.

The most central roles in an organization have the most information about the project; thus, they are the most logical roles to handle transmitting and receiving information. However, they are the key producer roles in the organization as well, so time they spend communicating has a directly impact on their development productivity. This figure shows an overburdened central role of software developer:

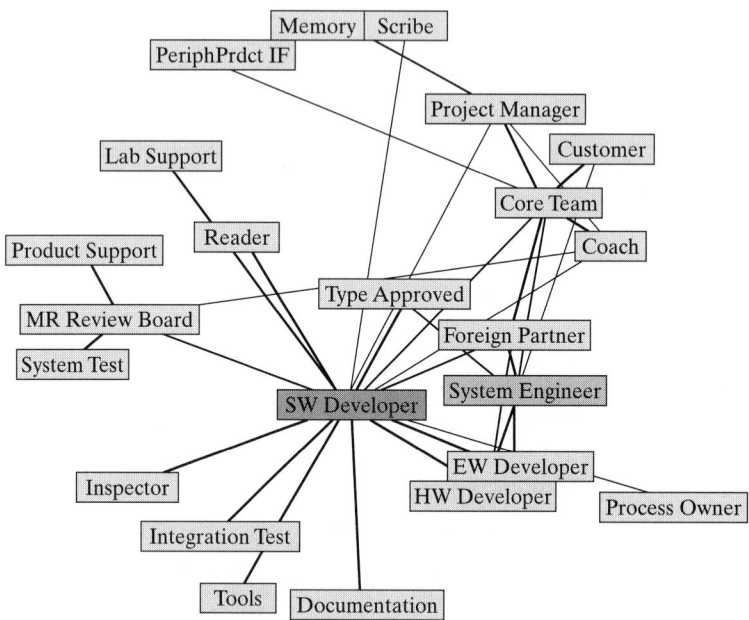

But there must be central coordination (which is a weak form of control) or some other acceptable point of control. Fully distributed control tends to lead to control breakdown. Coordination, on the other hand, improves accountability, efficiency, and camaraderie, as well as reduces decision time for changes in the business environment (e.g., requirements changes).

Therefore:

Shuffle responsibilities among roles in such a way that outer roles collaborate with roles other than the most central roles. The following interaction grid shows such a distribution of responsibilities and communications.

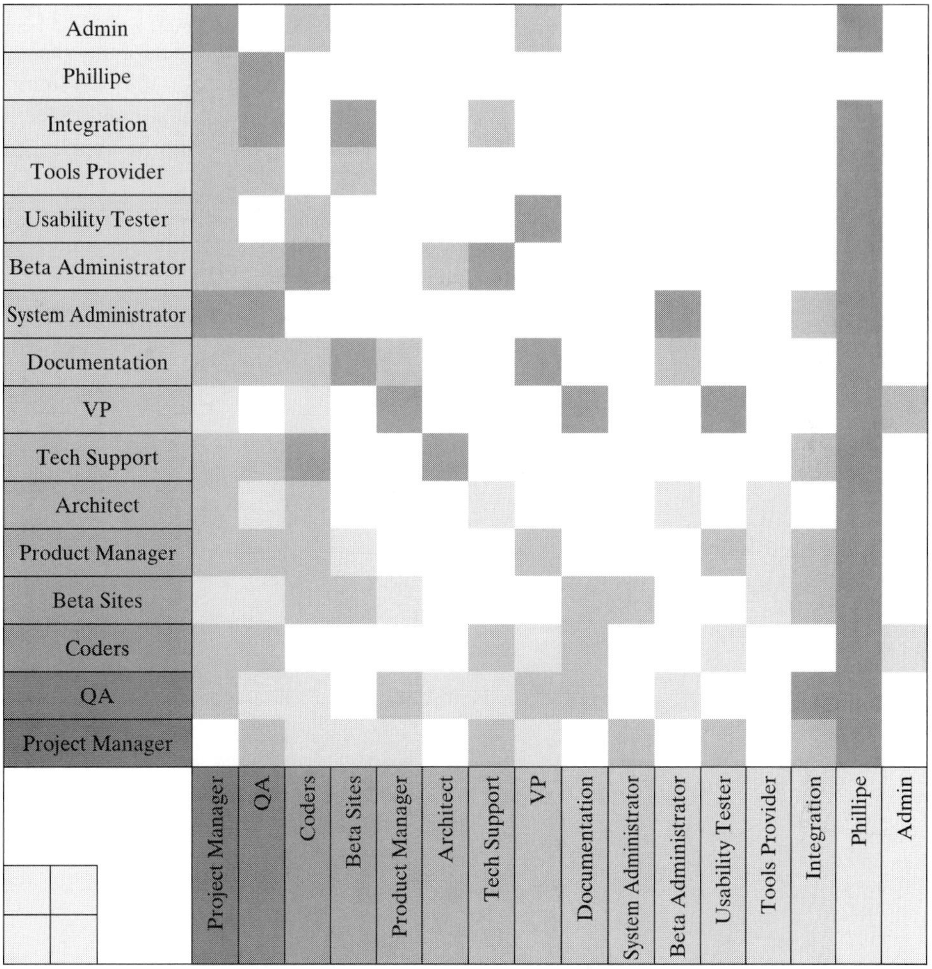

| Admin |
| Phillipe |
| Integration |
| Tools Provider |
| Usability Tester |
| Beta Administrator |
| System Administrator |
| Documentation |
| VP |
| Tech Support |
| Architect |
| Product Manager |
| Beta Sites |
| Coders |
| QA |
| Project Manager |

Columns (left to right): Project Manager, QA, Coders, Beta Sites, Product Manager, Architect, Tech Support, VP, Documentation, System Administrator, Beta Administrator, Usability Tester, Tools Provider, Integration, Phillipe, Admin

For example, a tester role may be isolated from the project. However, the tester needs to learn which areas of the project are especially troublesome so those areas can be tested especially rigorously. But this information is often not forthcoming. The tester could ask the key developers about the project "hot spots," but doing so would be inefficient and cause bottlenecks. Therefore, give the tester some project management responsibilities, thus allowing the tester to actively participate in status meetings and learn information relevant to testing through the project management responsibilities.

Note that in some cases, moving responsibilities will actually cause roles themselves to migrate and even merge which, in most cases, is actually a good thing.

This pattern infuses a level of distributed control with a central tendency, which lends overall direction and cohesion to an organization. It complements DIVIDE AND CONQUER (5.1.6), as both provide bonds within organizational clusters and provide links between subclusters [links that are less formal than a GATEKEEPER (4.2.10) role]. This pattern adds symmetry to DIVIDE AND CONQUER.

This pattern can stand on its own, but it is nicely complemented by the application of HALLWAY CHATTER (5.1.15).

Laurie Williams notes that DEVELOPING IN PAIRS (4.2.28) achieves some of the same effect. When she uses this pattern in a pedagogical setting, students learn to rely more on each other and less on the teacher for answers to common questions [Williams 2002].

5.1.15   Hallway Chatter *

One day a friend came into my office, depressed about her project. She was in a test group that was essentially shut off from the rest of the project. Her group didn't receive timely information about what was happening and didn't hear the latest project gossip. The only people they could talk to were each other. Following the anthropologist Bateson, we call this condition schismogenesis—the creation of schisms. My friend's situation was the most striking example of schismogenesis I had ever seen. She went on to other projects, so I didn't find out what ever happened with the organization. I suspect the problem wasn't fixed until the project was reorganized or until a quality crisis forced the project to work harder to involve the testers.

... the organization has been established, and people have settled into their roles. Unfortunately, the organizational structure has led to uneven communication among the team members, and some members do not feel they are a part of the team.

❖   ❖   ❖

If people are left out of the main communication flow, they become dissatisfied, complain to each other, and may even leave the project. And by the way, they can't do their jobs as well.

When people become disengaged from communication networks, they can feel alienated from the community. They sometimes commiserate with others in the same situation, forming alliances with people who are equally distant from the center of the community. This phenomenon, first observed by Bateson in the Sepik tribes in New Guinea, is called *schmismogenesis* [Bateson 1958].

The following interaction grid [see SOCIAL NETWORK THEORY FOUNDATIONS (7.5.2)] shows an organization exhibiting schismogenesis. One can see interactions along, but not on, the diagonal. These interactions are best defined as "comfort groups" that differentiate themselves according to their shared centrality (or relative lack thereof) with respect to the organizational structure. See THE OPEN/CLOSED PRINCIPLE OF TEAMS (6.1.4) for more information on schismogenesis.

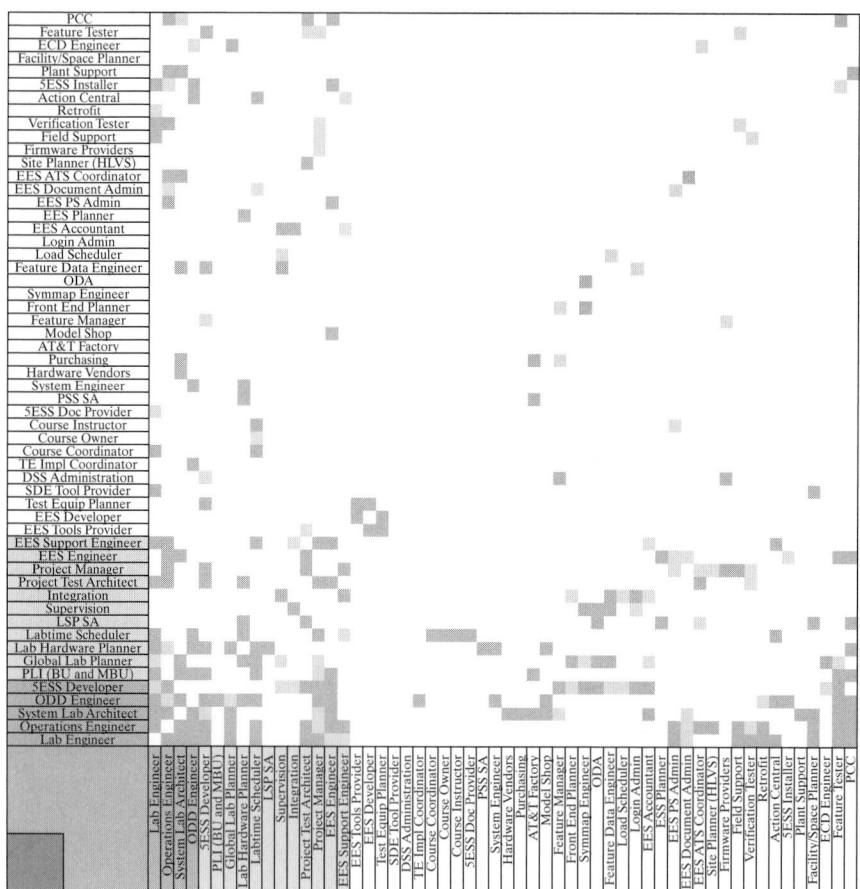

A certain amount of information is formally required for any given role to be fulfilled. But information alone is usually insufficient for optimal efficiency. We tend to do better when we have contextual information as well as essential information.

But the hard thing is knowing how to find that additional information, which can be elusive. For example, a project might be officially on schedule, but the developers are murmuring among themselves that development isn't going so well. While this information isn't concrete, it's obvious that something isn't quite right. This information is important if you are the tester waiting for delivery.

Therefore:

Move team members physically as close to each other as possible. Situate people with outer roles near the central roles.

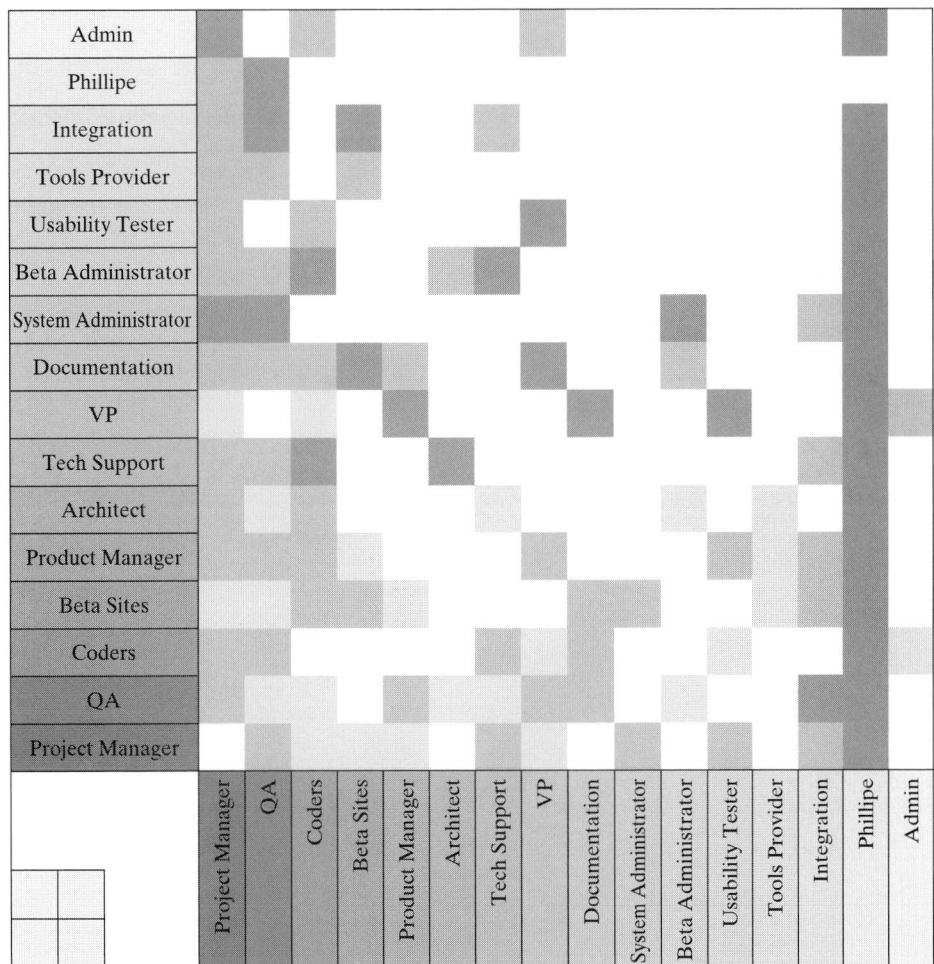

Thomas Allen [Allen 1977] gives guidelines for physical distance.

Of course, some projects, for various reasons, are split geographically. This distance can lead to exactly this problem unless CONWAY'S LAW (5.1.7) and ORGANIZATION FOLLOWS LOCATION (5.1.8) are applied.

Note that it is incorrect to apply this pattern to only a subset of an organization responsible for a project. If, for example, you cluster all of the developers together in a "developer's ghetto" and forget marketing or system test, you violate ENGAGE CUSTOMERS (4.2.6) and ENGAGE QUALITY

Assurance (4.2.29), as well as create rather than alleviate schismogenesis. In addition, communication with individuals outside the project is also important. Allen [Allen 1977] points out that high performers have significantly more communication outside the project than low performers. See The Watercooler (5.1.20) for additional ways to encourage communication, particularly outside the project.

The pattern complements Divide and Conquer (5.1.6), since both encourage symmetries within local groups and establish pathways between groups.

There are two complementary effects of using this pattern. First, the people in the outer roles feel like they are a part of the project, and their morale improves. They are less likely to gripe about the project with other outsiders because they are no longer outsiders. Second, they pick up more technical information through informal means, such as the chatter in the hallways, which allows them to do their jobs better. This secondary effect is the generative nature of this pattern: As communication improves, quality and time to market improve. As a result, the number of people needed for the project is reduced, which reduces communication overhead, which helps improve communication, and so on.

An organization consists of both roles and the people who fill those roles. Both roles and people must be considered. While most of the patterns in this language address one or the other, this pattern is unusual in that it bridges the two.

A Public Character (4.2.17) such as a Gatekeeper (4.2.10) or a Matron Role (4.2.18) can be a catalyst for Hallway Chatter.

5.1.16 Decouple Stages

... a design and an implementation process have been established for a well-understood domain. Well-understood, high-context domains have less need for patterns like BUILD PROTO-TYPES (4.1.7) and can actually proceed well according to a standard waterfall model.

Development stages should be independent to reduce coupling and to promote the autonomy of teams and developers. There is a tradition of decoupling architecture, design, and coding in a development process. While this tradition doesn't make sense for most software development projects—and is especially suspect for greenfield development—it sometimes makes sense in mature, high-context development projects. But there is still a trade-off: while independence creates opportunities for parallelism, it also hampers information flow.

Therefore:

For known and mature domains, serialize the steps. Handoffs between steps should take place via well-defined interfaces, which makes it possible to automate one or more of the steps or to create a pattern that lets inexpert staff carry out the steps.

The new organization allows for specialization in carrying out parts of the process, rather than emphasizing specialization in solving the customer problem.

This approach is "safe" only for well-understood domains, where the mapping from needs to implementation is straightforward. Well-understood domains are also good candidates for mechanization. For less mature domains, the process should build on the creativity of those involved at each stage of the process, and there should be more parallelism and interworking.

You can afford to implement mechanization in high-context, mature areas because the patterns of work are repeatable and rarely bring surprises. In other words, each stage can be carried out independently, which means less communication between stages and better efficiency. One can further raise the level of efficiency by building on specializations and domain knowledge pertinent to individual stages. Example domains include database administration (with steps such as database modeling, normalization, and query optimization), packaging, delivery and installation, and many administrative functions like bug tracking or the high-level business processes supporting field error report resolution.

Though interfaces between process steps help insulate the steps from each other, these interfaces should also be effective and useful. These interfaces shouldn't exist for their own sake, for the sake of empire building, or even for purpose of establishing formal organizational boundaries. They should encapsulate well-understood domains of control that facilitate handoffs between stages. If the interfaces increase cost and latency, they either have been implemented improperly or shouldn't be there at all.

This pattern leads into HUB, SPOKE, AND RIM (5.1.17).

5.1.17   Hub, Spoke, and Rim

... you have a design and implementation process in a well-understood domain, and you want to implement the principles of DECOUPLE STAGES (5.1.16). The organization is mature, and the process is well-understood. In fact, the process is fairly well optimized and has good partitioning in the spirit of DIVIDE AND CONQUER (5.1.6). Mature development organizations have well-defined development stages (e.g., such as requirements acquisition, design, and coding).

Some processes, especially highly detailed processes, can almost be automated, but still require a degree of human intervention and coordination.

For example, even if a process is mature enough to have well-delineated development phases, it may need additional mechanisms to integrate these stages and coordinate the interactions between them.

Process stages should be decoupled to reduce the communication associated with handoffs and promote independence between stages. Such independence creates opportunities for parallelism and increased throughput. Yet, independence generally hampers information flow.

Therefore:

Link each role to a central role that orchestrates serial process activities. The *hub* plays a simple coordination and management function to ensure all steps are completed successfully, while the work is done in the rim. The *rim* carries the handoff and its associated information between roles. The *spokes* link the rim to the central coordinating agent, the hub, providing lighter communication links than those that exist between the rim roles.

This organization, a front-end process for a large development project, exhibits a HUB, SPOKE, AND RIM pattern.

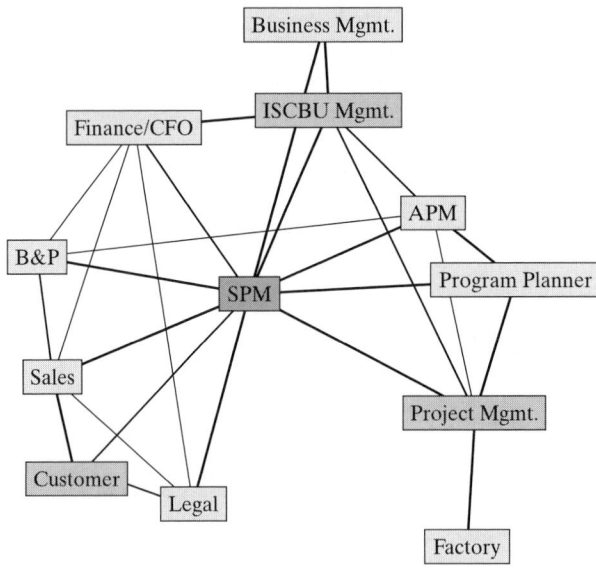

This highly responsive process supports sales and marketing activities.

The hub role should be encouraged to avoid micromanaging, particularly with respect to the mechanisms individual rim roles use in achieving their tasks. The hub role *should* scrutinize deadlines and schedules and should be in close enough contact with the rim roles to facilitate handoffs from role to role if necessary and to communicate the state changes to other parts of the project as necessary. In this sense, hub roles can also act as natural FIREWALLS (4.2.9) for the rim roles.

The rim roles still maintain a modicum of autonomy, and they can focus on their own domain-specific tasks. There need not be any essential *domain* coupling between the roles on the rim; coupling is needed only with respect to sequencing. The hub can coordinate that coupling and optimize it (e.g., juggle priorities, give different projects or customers different priorities) to meet project goals. The hub is a management role rather than a development role—a controller or sequencer. The hub role holds process activities together and ensures that progress ensues from state to state. Here, we want to ensure progress in the *process* [compare this pattern with the design pattern SOMEONE ALWAYS MAKES PROGRESS (4.1.20)]. HUB, SPOKE, AND RIM is an implementation pattern that achieves the intent of SOMEONE ALWAYS MAKES PROGRESS in a limited context.

Professor Aaron Gelman (Northwestern University) notes that in the contemporary airline market, the hub pattern contributes to congestion. Many airlines are acquiring small planes that can take small numbers of passengers directly between end destinations, acting as "hub busters" and relieving such congestion. The analogy points to concerns about overapplication of this pattern [Gelman 2000].

The organization must be wary of the central role becoming a bottleneck and address any such bottlenecks with other patterns [e.g., MOVE RESPONSIBILITIES (5.1.18)].

This configuration has higher latency than a highly coupled process, but it is likely to be able to support higher throughput [see COUPLING DECREASES LATENCY (5.1.22)]. However, it cannot easily support essentially creative processes that are common to design, coding, and testing. In the creative process of design, communication is more important than sequencing, since a repeatable sequence is unlikely to be found in such a creative process.

In a less mature domain, it is more appropriate to apply DEVELOPER CONTROLS PROCESS (4.1.17) as the alternative. *Most* domains, in fact, lack the maturity needed to apply HUB, SPOKE, AND RIM.

Parallelism can be reintroduced if the pipelined activities become a bottleneck.

5.1.18   Move Responsibilities *

Moving responsibilities among roles is a delicate balancing act.

... you want to change the communication patterns of the organization as a whole, not in a way that depends on a specific role, but in a way that optimizes the effectiveness of the communication of an entire organization.

Unscrutinized relationships between roles can lead to poor overall patterns of coupling in the greater organization.

In the spirit of CONWAY'S LAW (5.1.7), organizations tend to form around loci of communication; that is, the roles tend to communicate chiefly with each other, rather than with other (small) organizations in the larger enterprise. But some roles have substantial communication needs outside the organization and thus find themselves pulled in two different directions.

You want cohesive roles, and you want cohesive organizations. Decoupled organizations are more important than cohesive roles. And there may be fundamental trade-offs between coupling and cohesion. Moving an entire role from one process or organization to another doesn't reduce the overall coupling, but instead only moves the source. You could move a person from one organization to another to better balance responsibilities, but responsibilities don't always align with individuals. You could also replicate responsibilities across multiple roles or organizations to increase locality; however, doing so tends to confuse ownership and coordination and is not guaranteed to decrease the coupling.

Therefore:

Perform load balancing by moving responsibilities from the role that creates the most undesirable coupling to the roles coupled to it from other processes. The responsibilities should not be shifted arbitrarily; a chief programmer team organization is one good way to implement this pattern (in the context of developer role responsibilities).

❖   ❖   ❖

The new process may exhibit more highly decoupled groups. It is important to balance group cohesion with the decoupling, so this pattern must be applied with care. For example, the developer role is often the locus of a large fraction of project responsibilities, so the role appears overloaded. Arbitrarily shifting developer responsibilities to other roles, however, can introduce communication overhead. A chief programmer team approach to the solution helps balance these forces.

HALLWAY CHATTER (5.1.15) is an alternative load-balancing pattern, and RESPONSIBILITIES ENGAGE (5.1.14) can be seen as a refinement of this pattern that evens load. UPSIDE-DOWN MATRIX MANAGEMENT (5.1.19) is a refinement of this pattern that's particularly applicable across enterprise boundaries.

Most of the design rationale follows from the forces themselves.

This pattern is isomorphic to Mackenzie's model, which states that task interdependencies, together with the interdependencies of task resources and their characteristics, define project roles [Mackenzie 1986].

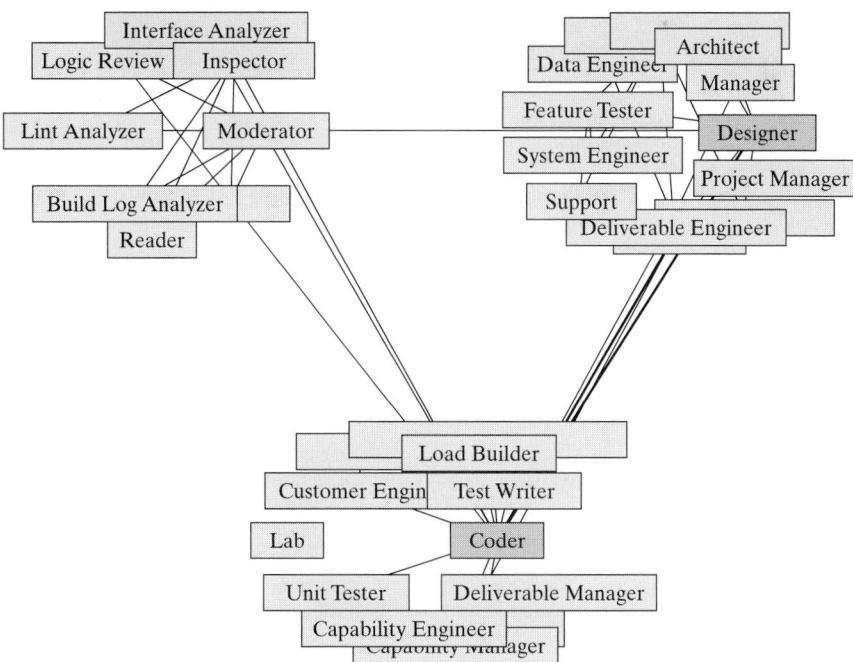

This organization can be improved by redistributing some of the responsibilities of the **Coder** role at the bottom center.

5.1.19   Upside-Down Matrix Management *

A rowing team has a single point of reporting and allegiance, embodied by the coxswain.

... you are assembling teams, and you tend to build teams and organizations within the framework of the indigenous corporate structure.

Sometimes it is difficult to reconcile a task or work function with the existing organization of the enterprise.

Assigning work to groups within your own organization may starve them from the resources or expertise that they need. While GATEKEEPER (4.2.10) and other roles can deal with this problem to a degree, sometimes the need is so great that no existing organizational structure seems to fit the need.

For example, you may not have staffing resources that fit a given profile of domain expertise, which makes it difficult to achieve DOMAIN EXPERTISE IN ROLES (4.2.22). Or, you may not be able to achieve scheduling goals with the staffing constraints of your organization. Or, the problem may require interdisciplinary solutions that don't fit your current structure (e.g., the logical and physical business architectures may not be aligned).

You could reorganize into a new set of disjoint groups that are a better fit for the problem, but there are always concerns that cut across other groups, so there is no guarantee that a useful disjoint partitioning scenario even exists.

Any team assignments you make may have long-term repercussions for the organization and the architecture [per CONWAY'S LAW (5.1.7)]. While some teams can be created to address intermittent problems, some of these "misfit" needs reflect bona fide long-term core competencies or business concerns; accordingly, an organization should nurture such work.

Therefore:

Form new groups from the right roles and people in a way that may cut across the current organizational structure. Temper legacy structures that owe to casuistic barriers (e.g., historical, political, or organizational boundaries). Challenge financial barriers that keep the dysfunctional partitionings in place by adjusting funding models.

These new structures can be often found in organizations other than your own. Consider creating these structures in the customer space, or partner with other internal organizations, external contractors, and suppliers to fill these organizational needs. However, beware of jumping to an outsourcing solution. Carefully create groups and teams around key areas of competency and concern, letting the partitioning fall across enterprise boundaries where it may. Temper this pattern with ORGANIZATION FOLLOWS LOCATION (5.1.8), whose forces are probably more powerful than those at work here.

Note the name of this pattern. In a matrix-management paradigm, individuals or groups are asked to report to two (or more) managers in an attempt to solve a problem. This pattern turns that notion on its head. Instead of multiple reporting roles, a separate team is formed so that the team members have a single point of reporting and allegiance.

❖   ❖   ❖

In his pattern WORK ALLOCATION (A.5.29), which is related to this one, Beedle reports use of this pattern between Navistar and Goodyear. Navistar has shifted some of its work back to its suppliers. Instead of managing its own warehouse inventory of tires to be installed on the trucks it manufactures, it delegates this task to Goodyear because the company has better inventory management methods. He also reports similar arrangements between Wal-Mart and its suppliers and between Ford and its suppliers [Beedle 2000].

THE WATERCOOLER (5.1.20) is similar to this pattern, but it works in the space of everyday social life rather than in institutional structures.

5.1.20   The Watercooler *

Boys cooling off around a fire hydrant, Chicago, Illinois, 1941. The cool water of the fire hydrant created a setting for social interaction among the boys.

When I transferred to the Forward Looking Work department at Bell Laboratories, I eventually found myself working for a manager who was a fanatic hobby runner. Each day, instead of taking lunch he would go for a 5-mile run outside, even in inclement weather. Several of his group members, not to mention several of his peer managers, were also runners. There was a culture of crossorganizational communication both in the locker room (a makeshift converted service corridor) and on the running trails that surrounded the site. I quickly learned that becoming a runner was a good way to communicate with the boss about topics that would be difficult to discuss in the office.

... your teams are starting to build identities. Team locality and identity lead to isolation and insularity in team dynamics.

Organizations need crossteam structures that guard against isolation.

In a large organization, individual teams build their identity around their team or their geographic location. In a large building, it is difficult to support frequent interaction across teams; as such, most "excuses" to visit other teams arise in the forms of meetings and other formalisms that don't support spontaneous communication. Distance, inconvenience, or xenophobia discourage informal interactions.

Yet people need to have social contact with each other. And, in fact, people want to "get out" now and then to see what life is like in other organizations.

Therefore:

Encourage social structures that are unrelated to workplace structures and that will likely cut across the formal partitioning of the organization.

The watercooler is the time-honored example of this pattern. One Allianz site in Vienna has a strong coffee culture that revolves around coffee machines on each floor of each wing of the building, where one can find small groups congregating all day, especially mid-morning and mid-afternoon. Another common (but dying) practice is the smoker's area. At a company in Houston, members of this group would gather at an outside terrace; in another company, they met secretly in the stairwell.

The Navision company in Copenhagen had a strong food culture: the company served breakfast and lunch. Breakfast, in particular, was a time of social connection, a relaxed beginning to the day. The company also had well-stocked refrigerators and pantries for snacks during the day, and much of this food was enjoyed in a group setting. Food is fun and a key element of any culture, but the main contribution to the communication network comes from the social structures built around food.

Corporate clubs, singing groups, running clubs, chess clubs, and a million other social structures can also help serve this social purpose. What can you do to encourage such structures? Give them a place to live: a coffee machine or a watercooler is a first step to allowing social dynamics to unfold. Make it special. People won't come by for coffee that is worse than the instant coffee they can make in their office. Investing in quality also has the added benefit of demonstrating a sense of caring within the organization.

Remember: location, location, location! You can't just plop a watercooler down in a hallway and expect people to congregate around it; instead, you must put it in a place where people can sit or stand comfortably for a time. You may wish to incorporate several of Alexander's patterns [Alexander 1977] as you lay it out. The research department in AT&T, where both authors worked for a time, had a room with comfortable furniture and a pleasant ambiance. As an added draw, it had a small library. On the other hand, one facility had a watercooler stuffed in a back storeroom of a lab that restricted access—it was no more than a place to get (or perhaps just store) cold water.

This pattern not only gives people a break during the day, but it also contributes to fundamental human needs and desires that lie in the deep foundations of any human culture. And it will contribute strongly to interteam communication, especially since most professional communication takes place outside formal channels [Grinter Herbsleb 2000].

One potential danger of this pattern is "cliquishness," a form of schismogenesis [see THE OPEN/CLOSED PRINCIPLE OF TEAMS (6.1.4)]. If the group is in any way exclusive, some people will feel left out; the locker room is one such example. A runners' club may (literally and figuratively) leave nonmembers (and even novice members) behind. Coffee clubs might not appeal to those who do not drink coffee. Problems of complementary schismogenesis can be solved by having a bounty of such crosscutting organizations, but that can also lead to symmetrical schismogenesis. A better solution, where feasible, is to broaden the base of the organization (e.g., the coffee corner can also offer tea and juice). However, a healthy environment should be able to sustain even highly specialized groups. In all cases, build on the local culture and its mores.

This pattern rounds out UPSIDE-DOWN MATRIX MANAGEMENT (5.1.19) by going outside the context of the business interests of the enterprise and building on potentially deeper social relationships and normative practices of the culture of the area, town, or other constituency. It complements and rounds out RESPONSIBILITIES ENGAGE (5.1.14) as an independent pattern.

This pattern is similar to HALLWAY CHATTER (5.1.15); in fact, both patterns work to improve informal communication. But notice the differences between the two. HALLWAY CHATTER physically moves people close together so that they will go to each others' offices or cubicles. That communication, while informal, is planned and tends to be more of a technical nature. On the other hand, THE WATERCOOLER enables chance meetings and nontechnical conversations. Both are necessary; as such, these patterns are complementary.

Combined with ENGAGE CUSTOMERS (4.2.6), where you seat your developers in the customer work space, THE WATERCOOLER can be a powerful way to uncover important requirements details. Beyer and Holtzblatt ([Beyer Holtzblatt 1998], p. 37) relate the following:

> Many of the important aspects of work are invisible, not because they are hidden, but just because it doesn't occur to anyone to pay attention to them. Intuition doesn't help make these aspects explicit:
>
> An entire project team hangs out in the hallway outside their offices every morning and chats over coffee and donuts. Does anyone on the team know this is a critical project coordination session?
>
> A worker in accounting calls a friend in order processing to gossip and mentions that a rush order is on its way. Does his manager know this informal communication is the only thing keeping the company's rush orders on time?

5.1.21   Three to Seven Helpers Per Role

Chef and helpers in the camp kitchen, Allegan project, Michigan, 1937.

... the organization basically has a functional social network. However, the organization shows overly strong centrality; individual roles are overloaded, while others are starved for communication.

❖   ❖   ❖

An effective organization has a well-balanced distribution of communication.

You don't want to overload specific roles with interrupts and meetings, which is a waste of resources. Manager roles often suffer from this problem, but so do roles staffed by domain experts. On the other hand, you must not starve other roles of human interaction, because doing so drives them to work ineffectively and results in lowered process efficiency. Underutilization relates to information starvation and poor coupling to other roles. Overutilization can be caused by having too many suitors, particularly in the case where productivity falls because of thrashing, context switching, or indecision.

Therefore:

Organize the enterprise so that each role has three to seven long-term stable relationships.

You can implement this organization by using MOVE RESPONSIBILITIES (5.1.18) and other ORGANIZATION CONSTRUCTION PATTERNS in this chapter. Most of this load balancing can build on intuitive and innovative shifting of work.

This pattern leads to a more balanced organization with better load sharing and fewer isolated roles. It helps DISTRIBUTE WORK EVENLY (5.1.13).

With a lot of focus and energy, it is possible to increase coupling and decrease latency, particularly for short periods of time [see COUPLING DECREASES LATENCY (5.1.22)].

For roles such as domain experts that become magnets for people, use a pattern like SACRIFICE ONE PERSON (4.1.22) or DAY CARE (4.1.23) to balance load.

Our empirical results from the organizations studied in the Pasteur project show that, on most projects, any given role can sustain at most seven long-term relationships. In extremely productive organizations, the number can be as high as nine. Particular needs might compel the process designer to stray outside these bounds so long as there is a suitable rationale.

The following histogram presents a distribution of collaborations per role for the roles in our early organizational analyses.

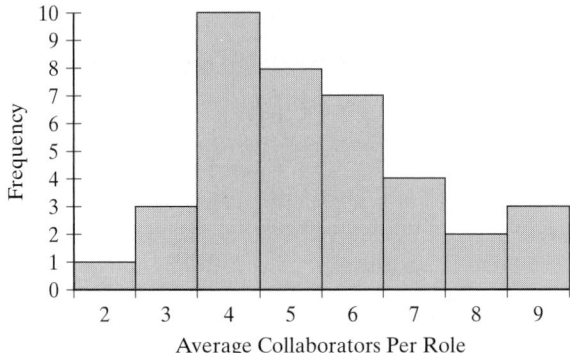

The highest number of organizations is able to support four collaborators per role. As the number of collaborators per role increases, we find that fewer and fewer organizations are able to sustain those levels. But about 75 percent of the organizations can sustain three to seven helpers per role.

Communication between roles is complete in an organization if every role communicates with every other role. As stated in DISTRIBUTE WORK EVENLY (5.1.13), the *communication intensity ratio* of an organization is the ratio of the number of communication paths of the busiest role to the average number of communication paths per role. For a given project size, Harrison has found this ratio to be lower in highly productive organizations than in average organizations [Harrison Coplien 1996].

5.1.22 Coupling Decreases Latency *

Northern Pacific freight train going over Bozeman Pass, Gallitan County, Montana.

... the organization supports a service process or, in some special cases, a small design/implementation process using an iterative or incremental approach. Responsiveness is important, but you note that development intervals are too long and market windows are not met.

The structure of an organization can artificially reduce the throughput and increase the latency of business processes. And in most business processes, speed (e.g., time to market and service responsiveness) is of the essence. An organizational structure that causes information to flow through many roles not only increases latency (delay), but can also cause loss of information fidelity. Like light, as information passes through many filters, it loses definition and accuracy.

Process stages should be independent to reduce coupling and thereby promote developer independence. Developers can be more effective the less their work is encumbered by communication. Furthermore, independence improves opportunities for parallelism, though it hampers information flow.

Therefore:

Open communication paths between roles to increase the overall coupling/role ratio, particularly between central process roles. Communication between roles can be shaped using patterns such as WORK FLOWS INWARD (4.1.18), which helps concentrate more communication at the core of the organization, and RESPONSIBILITIES ENGAGE (5.1.14), which deals with the issue more broadly. Both of these patterns can be helped more generally with MOVE RESPONSIBILITIES (5.1.18).

This pattern suggests either increasing the density of the communication network or finding the key communication paths that are important to market success and focusing on making them more effective (e.g., communications between marketing and engineering). The support organization shown below has a highly responsive process, which owes in part to its high degree of internal coupling.

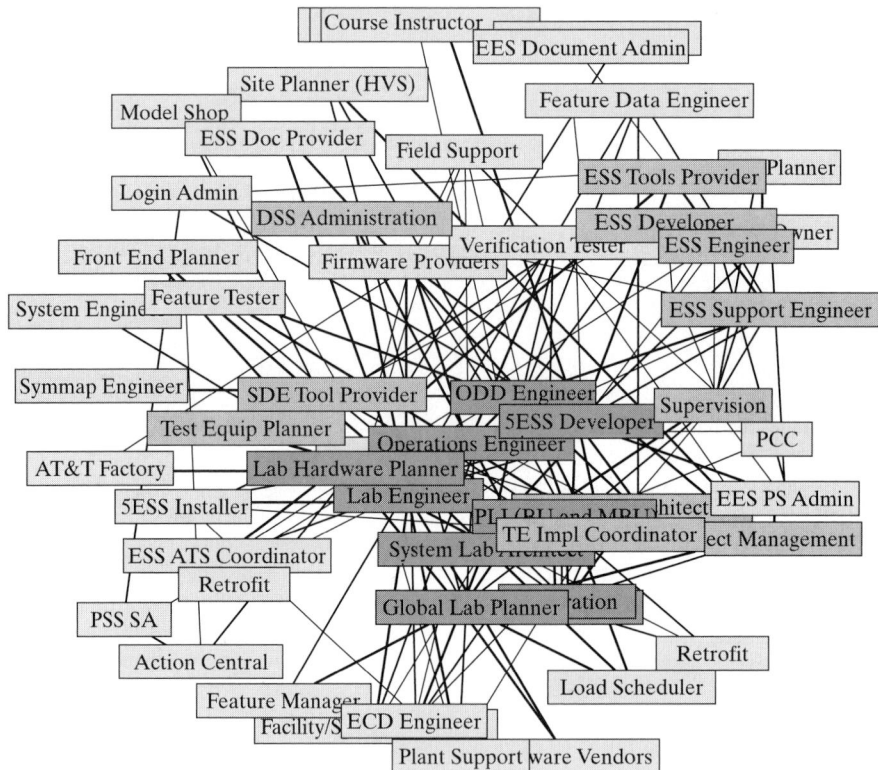

The second approach is more difficult because it's difficult in general to know which communication links are more important than others. Organizational introspection can help identify such links, however.

Coupling, of course, increases dependence between roles, which may not always be a good thing.

This pattern is somewhat related to INTERRUPTS UNJAM BLOCKING (4.1.25). Information flow in an organization can be compared with that of a batch processing system or a timesharing system. In the batch mode of communication, information is channeled through certain central roles in the organization (generally manager-type roles) and then is disseminated to the producer roles. In a timesharing mode of communication, interrupts drive the communication, thus decreasing communication latency, as information flows to the producer roles directly and in a timely manner.

Handoffs can increase latency. The number of "hops" between roles should be kept small for any given problem. Eliminating "pipeline" and "deadbeat" roles helps eliminate hops. One way to eliminate hops is to use HUB, SPOKE, AND RIM (5.1.17), where appropriate. In fact, that pattern logically progresses from this one. Occasional close coupling between developers and testers reduces administrative overhead, which also reduces latency.

5.1.23   Standards Linking Locations

See section 5.2.12.

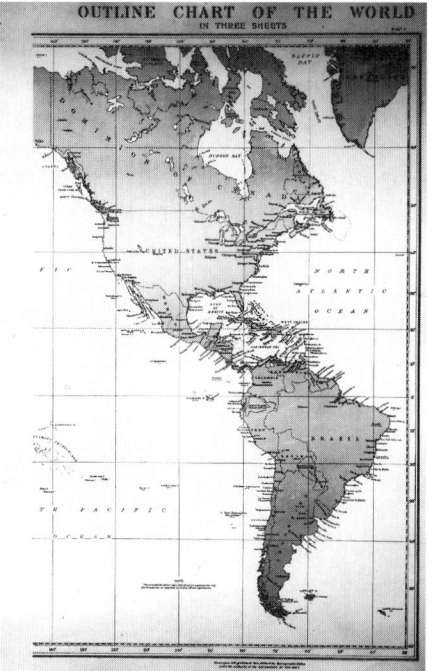

5.2 People and Code Pattern Language

The Pattern Language

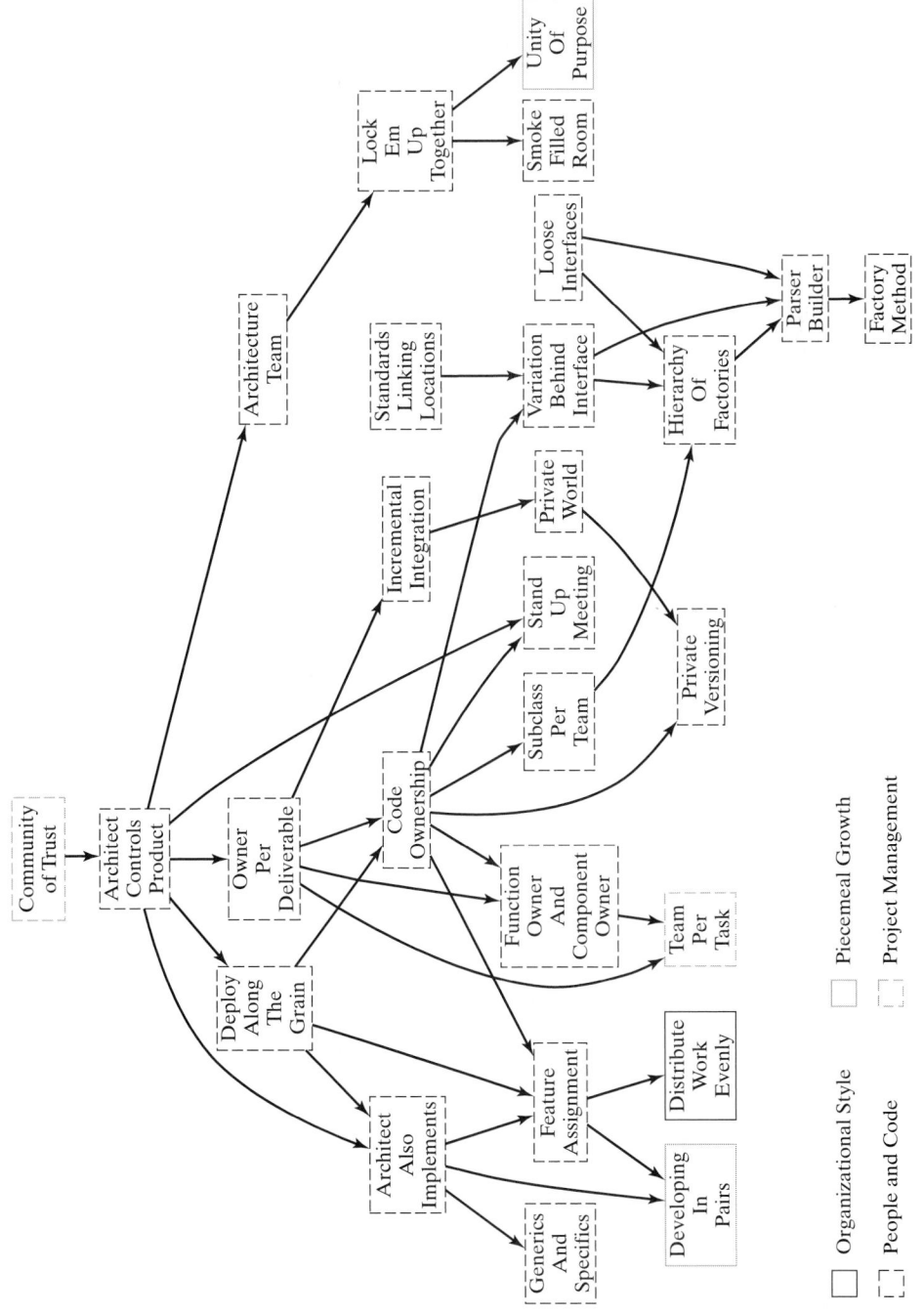

A Story about People and Code

"The system engineer wrote a set of requirements, and then left the project." These words, spoken by a team member, point to a project's inauspicious beginning. Yet, in spite of this initial setback, or perhaps in part *because* of it, the team came together in a remarkable way to complete the project on time. We learned much from analyzing this team.

Project development began with architecture design, but there was no single architect; instead there was an ARCHITECTURE TEAM (5.2.4). [A manager later commented that he could not identify a single architect because the entire team knew the architecture so well. See MODERATE TRUCK NUMBER (4.2.24)]. The team met numerous times to create the architecture, but made little progress until they isolated themselves [LOCK 'EM UP TOGETHER (5.2.5)]. By the time they had emerged, they had designed an architecture that guided them through the project [ARCHITECT CONTROLS PRODUCT (5.2.3)]. As importantly, they had a very high degree of UNITY OF PURPOSE (4.2.12). All of the architects practiced ARCHITECT ALSO IMPLEMENTS (5.2.10).

The project was geographically split, which created a natural organizational break. They recognized the need to apply CONWAY'S LAW (5.1.7) and ORGANIZATION FOLLOWS LOCATION (5.1.8). In practice, these patterns led to the application of CODE OWNERSHIP (5.2.13) and FEATURE ASSIGNMENT (5.2.14). They defined interfaces over time [LOOSE INTERFACES (5.2.17)], and while they hardened the interfaces, they allowed VARIATION BEHIND INTERFACE (5.2.15).

The project used a unique variation of DEVELOPING IN PAIRS (4.2.28). They performed group debugging! In fact, the entire team at one of the locations gathered around one person's computer to debug problems. Group debugging didn't turn out to be any less efficient than single-person debugging, and it had the benefits of maintaining a MODERATE TRUCK NUMBER (4.2.24) and of preserving the architectural integrity of the system. Interestingly, since the entire team was present, the group debugging sessions also served many of the purposes of the STAND-UP MEETING (5.2.7).

The team had some novices and used GENERICS AND SPECIFICS (5.2.11) to help make the novices productive.

At the end of the project, personnel from a partner company paid them a very high compliment: "We don't believe any other company could have pulled it off."

5.2.1 Community of Trust
See section 4.1.1.

5.2.2 Conway's Law
See section 5.1.7.

5.2.3   Architect Controls Product **

... an organization of developers needs strategic technical direction.

❖   ❖   ❖

Even though a product is designed by many individuals, a project must strive to give the product elegance and cohesiveness. One might achieve this end by centralizing control, but such control is viewed by most development teams as a draconian measure. One person can't do everything, and no single person has perfect foresight. However, the right information must flow through the right roles, and individual areas of competency and expertise must still be engaged.

Furthermore, there needs to be some level of architectural vision. While some domain expertise is distributed through the ranks of the development team [DOMAIN EXPERTISE IN ROLES (4.2.22)], the system view—and, in particular, the design principles that create a common culture for dialogue and construction—usually benefits from the conceptual integrity we associate with a single mind or small group.

Therefore:

Create an architect role as an embodiment of the principles that define an architectural style for the project and of the broad domain expertise that legitimizes such a style. The Architect role should advise and influence Developer roles and should communicate closely with them. The Architect doesn't dictate interfaces (except in cases where arbitration is necessary). Instead, the Architect builds consensus with individual developers, developer subteams, and, if necessary, with the entire development staff, commensurate with the architectural style. The Architect is the principal bridge builder between development team members.

The Architect should also be in close touch with Customers to ensure that the domain expertise is current, detailed, and relevant.

This pattern does for the architecture what the Patron Role (4.2.15) pattern does for the organization: It provides technical focus and a rallying point for both technical and market-related work.

The architect doesn't *control* the product in any dictatorial sense; instead, the architect provides inspirational guiding and leadership. We could have called this pattern "Architect Leads Product" or "Architect Guides Product," but all of these words have their own problematic connotations.

Resentment can build against a totalitarian architect, so patterns like Stand-Up Meeting (5.2.7) should be used to temper this one.

Intellectually large projects can build an Architecture Team (5.2.4).

We have no role called "Designer" because design is really the whole task. Managers fill a supporting role; empirically, they are rarely seen to control a process except during crises.

While the Architect controls the architectural direction, the Developer Controls Process (4.1.17), and there is still an Owner Per Deliverable (A.5.19). The Architect is a "chief Developer" [see Architect Also Implements (5.2.10)] or, as Alexander thinks of himself, a "master builder." The architect's responsibilities include understanding requirements, framing the major system structure, and guiding the long-term evolution of that structure. The Architect controls the product in the visualization process that accompanies the pattern Engage Quality Assurance (4.2.29).

Because Organization Follows Location (5.1.8) and because of Conway's Law (5.1.7), there should probably be an architect at each location. Architects can be the focus of local allegiance, which is one of the most powerful of cultural forces in geographically distributed development.

A more passive way of implementing this pattern is to have the Architect review everything. We have seen this process work on several projects. However, the "truck number" was in danger on most of these projects as a result [see Moderate Truck Number (4.2.24)]. Also, if there is a conscious plan for architect's to review everything, they—in their capacity as developers [see Architect Also Implements (5.2.10)]—may "swoop down" and fix things that are the responsibility of others [see Code Ownership (5.2.13)], which can be demoralizing to the original code author. The architect can review everything if that role still defers to the implementor for execution and even for the decision about making the change. See Stand-Up Meeting (5.2.7).

Architectural control must balance developer authority, and this role of being "keeper of the flame." Architects should tread neither on developers' feelings of code ownership nor on their ownership of the code development processes. Architects intervene in processes largely at the business level and should meddle in implementation processes only in exceptional circumstances.

"Les oeuvres d'un seul architect sont plus belles ... que ceux d'ont plusiers ont taché de faire." ("The works of a single architect are more beautiful than those that several have tried to achieve.")—Pascal, *Pensées*

5.2.4   Architecture Team *

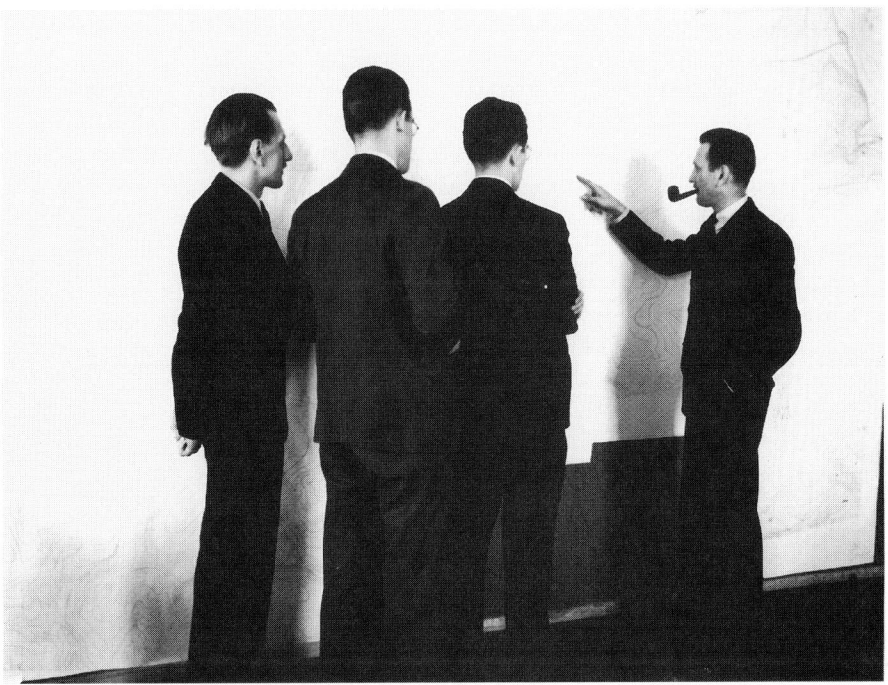

Architects and engineers studying plans for the Greenhills project, Ohio, 1936.

... you have defined a project direction, and now you need to come up with a structure for the system.

You need to create an architecture that is simple and cohesive, but that also accommodates a variety of constituencies.

Most systems are too large for a single mind to analyze and resolve. Not only is the system too complex for a single person, but the architecture must also accommodate multiple viewpoints to be successful. You can solve this dilemma with a team of architects who bring diverse views, but the collision of diverse views brings difficulties of its own.

A design by committee usually looks that way. Such a design tends to include everything, even the kitchen sink!

Committees are inherently less efficient than individuals [e.g., see SOLO VIRTUOSO (4.2.5)]. Yet, there is safety in numbers, and teamwork makes it possible to keep a MODERATE TRUCK NUMBER (4.2.24).

The entire organization will need to accept the architecture. The more people that are involved in the architecture, the better the chance of "selling" the results. But the more constituencies involved, the more difficult it is to come to an agreement in the first place.

Therefore:

Create a small team of "resonating minds" to define the initial architecture in such a way that the team covers the expected partitioning of the system. The key idea is that most or all of the team members should be assigned a piece of the system for which they have architectural responsibility. While it may be difficult to predict all of the architectural divisions, one can usually easily identify the areas of grossest partitioning beforehand. For example, it is probably easy to guess that a system might have a user interface, back-end storage, and Internet communication areas. The careful selection of the team thus is aimed at preventing the haphazard "designed by committee" look.

Other representatives may be needed to round out the team. Luke Hohmann points out the difference between the technical architecture and the marketing architecture, noting that the marketing viewpoint may be very valuable to this team. [Hohmann 1998]

The ARCHITECTURE TEAM's task is to create a high-level partitioning. Much architectural work remains to be completed at lower levels. Charles Weir designates the high-level architecture team as the "master," while "journeyman architects" take on the design of the smaller pieces. The MASTER-JOURNEYMAN (A.5.17) pattern also suggests typical partitioning of the core architecture, the architectural vision, interfaces, and specification control [Weir 1998].

❖   ❖   ❖

Legitimizing this activity as a team, with an organizational structure, lends support to the social interaction necessary to forming and sustaining the shared vision [see UNITY OF PURPOSE (4.2.12)].

The team should have a periodic STAND-UP MEETING (5.2.7) to maintain the architectural integrity of the system. Early in the project, these meetings can take place daily.

Note that an architecture team focuses on the *initial architecture*. The result should be a gross partitioning of the system, allowing members of the architecture team to design their own subsystems [see also CONWAY'S LAW (5.1.7)].

The best way to accomplish a shared architectural vision is probably through the use of LOCK 'EM UP TOGETHER (5.2.5).

HOLISTIC DIVERSITY (4.2.19) is a pattern that ties together multiple teams (e.g., infrastructure teams and other teams) that relate to individual domains and technologies. The ARCHITECTURE TEAM either may be such a team or may contribute to a crossdisciplinary team that goes beyond architectural issues into issues of business and implementation.

This pattern is a refinement of Harrison's DIVERSITY OF MEMBERSHIP pattern [Harrison 1996].

This pattern draws heavily on Gerard Meszaros's ARCHITECTURE DEFINITION TEAM (A.5.4). Meszaros further suggests that a separate ARCHITECTURE ORGANIZATION should *own* the architecture [Meszaros 1997]. Here, we propose that ownership and function be tied together. This pattern also arises in Alistair Cockburn's analysis of the interaction between HOLISTIC DIVERSITY (4.2.19) and SUBSYSTEM BY SKILL (4.2.23). See also ARCHITECT CONTROLS PRODUCT (5.2.3) and ARCHITECT ALSO IMPLEMENTS (5.2.10).

5.2.5 Lock 'em Up Together *

... you have an ARCHITECTURE TEAM (5.2.4) to pull together the initial structure of the project, and you need to get off top dead center and move toward production.

A team of diverse people must come up with a single, coherent architecture.

A product needs a single architecture that is self-contained and consistent. But programmers have a (strong) tendency to work separately. Each person's design bears that person's unique signature; as such, many people working on separate parts of an architecture will produce parts that do not necessarily work well together. Designs by committee usually look incohesive and inelegant. You can allow a single person to create the architecture, but then not everybody will understand it (and follow it). Further, you need to keep in mind the MODERATE TRUCK NUMBER (4.2.24).

Therefore:

Gather domain experts together in the same room to work out the architecture (or some other strategic issue). Every person must commit to total participation until the architecture is complete enough that a clear picture has emerged.

There are two keys to this pattern. First, everyone must be physically together, in the spirit of FACE TO FACE BEFORE WORKING REMOTELY (5.1.10). Togetherness is necessary to ensure good communication at this critical time. Teleconferences are not sufficient.

Second the architecture team must commit totally; the team members must be insulated from distractions and interrupts. In effect, a temporary organization is created for the architecture effort: Previous responsibilities are suspended, and existing collaborations are halted for a time.

Both of these keys are critical to providing a continuity of ideas so that the architecture can coalesce.

As with ARCHITECTURE TEAM (5.2.4), this work is focused only on creating an *initial architecture* that results in a gross partitioning of the system.

This pattern is superficially similar to FACE TO FACE BEFORE WORKING REMOTELY (5.1.10), but they are essentially different. The purpose of FACE TO FACE BEFORE WORKING REMOTELY is to establish roles, develop allegiances, and build teams. The purpose of LOCK 'EM UP TOGETHER is to hammer out technical issues. However, the two patterns might be applied at the same time.

This pattern works best when UNITY OF PURPOSE (4.2.12) is already in effect, although the LOCK 'EM UP TOGETHER pattern can help achieve UNITY OF PURPOSE.

Variants of LOCK 'EM UP TOGETHER can also bring teams together in other development phases. In Western Geco (a Schlumberger company), the development team sometimes spends days together in close quarters at the company's deployment site: a ship at sea. This experience inevitably helps team members to get to know each other better and leads both to team building in general and to the development of working relationships between the team and its end-user constituency on the boat.

This approach also works well for other combinations of constituencies: architects and coders, architects and users, marketing folks and customers, marketing folks and end users, and so forth. This approach is central to JAD ([Kendall 2002], p. 132). See also ARCHITECT ALSO IMPLEMENTS (5.2.10). PATRON ROLE (4.2.15) helps make this pattern happen.

SMOKE-FILLED ROOM (5.2.6) is a dark variant of this pattern.

5.2.6 **Smoke-Filled Room**

Alias: Brown Bar, Cabal

Smoking room, Paul Smith's Casino, Adirondack Mountains.

... as in Lock 'em Up Together (5.2.5), an enterprise comprises a diverse group of people with varying positions, and the enterprise is not sure how to proceed in making a big decision. This situation may be precipitated during the early stages of a new group or as a result of an externally imposed policy change.

An organization must make a timely decision about urgent strategic directions.

You would like everyone involved to have a say in the decision, and in particular, you would like all stakeholders to have a say in the decision.

However, in organizations where accountability does not naturally align with authority and responsibility, a consensus process is not favorably viewed. For example, if team members are not viewed as having the legal power, the positional authority, or even the experience to make a key business decision, their participation in a consensus process is viewed as that of a "loose canon on deck."

Furthermore, sometimes the need for expediency thwarts a consensus process or even a socialized accounting of the decision process. And, additional political forces can cause individuals or groups to want to keep secret the rationales for a given decision or to eliminate some people from the decision-making process because they may be affected by the decision in ways that power holders feel would weaken their objectivity.

Therefore:

Make the decision among power brokers as in the storied smoke-filled rooms stereotypically associated with tycoon businessmen. Publicize the decision, but either keep the rationale private or rationalize why selected stakeholders were prevented from being part of the process. However, note keeping the rationale private because of political concerns indicates significant problems in the culture.

This pattern is to be used sparingly in the right context to balance the right forces. Overuse of this pattern strains other patterns, such as ENGAGE CUSTOMERS (4.2.6), DOMAIN EXPERTISE IN ROLES (4.2.22), ENGAGE QUALITY ASSURANCE (4.2.29), ARCHITECT CONTROLS PRODUCT (5.2.3), etc.

Examples include most decisions about corporate takeovers, corporate mergers, and project cancellations, which are viewed more as business phenomena than as domain phenomena.

5.2.7   **Stand-Up Meeting** **

Alias: DAILY MEETING

... a project is in the early architecture stage, a period of high stress or a period of quick change. Or it might just be a period of high stakes, even though you don't expect things to change rapidly. Regardless, change must be dealt with responsively, as during the end game.

At times of fast change or high stress, it is essential that all members of the organization receive the same information.

When a project is changing quickly, information becomes outdated almost instantly. People must have the latest information, or they risk making obsolete or incorrect decisions. Early in a project, during the initial architecture design, decisions are made that have a lasting impact on the product. These decisions tend to be based on incomplete information, on assumptions that require validation. Because these architectural decisions tend to build on each other, an early incorrect assumption can cause significant long-term directional errors.

At times, change is dictated by stress or a crisis, and crisis management demands a quick response. But a quick response demands a coordinated effort, and things can go terribly wrong if people don't have the latest information. Architects as well as individual developers can develop tunnel vision, and low-level decisions can become just as important as more visible architectural decisions. Tom DeMarco has said that all things are "deeply intertwingled." In other words, interdependencies affect both the long-term integrity of the product functionality and structure, as well as the smooth day-to-day functioning of a team that has a shared vision.

Some organizations simply operate at a high change velocity, which requires very tight communication coupling to prevent ensuring chaos. The most productive organizations we have seen operate this way, although this sort of communication is not their only distinguishing characteristic.

Yet in all of these cases, because the need for communication is high, the communication overhead will also be high.

Therefore:

Hold short daily meetings with the entire team to exchange critical information, update status, and/or make assignments. The meetings should last no more than 15 minutes and generally should happen first thing in the morning.

The focus of the meetings is on the technical progress in the architecture and in the work plan. Obviously, these meetings work best with small teams comprising mostly developers and architects. If the project is too large for a single meeting, subteams may meet instead. The project is probably already partitioned appropriately. However, the STAND-UP MEETING is as much an opportunity to revisit the organizational structure as to revisit the system architecture [see CONWAY'S LAW (5.1.7)]. For this reason—and because resource reallocation is also a concern in these meetings—regular management presence at these meetings is also important.

Early in the project, these meetings may be held for the purpose of reviewing the architecture. Architectural decisions may be examined, tweaked, and rereviewed very quickly. If the architecture team is "sequestered" [LOCK 'EM UP TOGETHER (5.2.5)], the daily reviews can be used as a sanity check and as an opportunity to allow the team to come up for air. Or if the team prefers, the daily reviews can be used instead of LOCK 'EM UP TOGETHER. Near the end of the delivery cycle, these meetings can keep the team focused on the delivery, and they can help the project to shift assignments quickly to meet project needs. Near the beginning of a project, the code changes quickly; near the end, you may want to be able to shift assignments quickly as the product starts to move toward the shipping dock and out the door. Roles may also shift accordingly (e.g., developers become testers and connections with beta sites intensify).

Such meetings can be used to make other technical decisions as well. One team reported having meetings almost daily with human factors engineers and with a SURROGATE CUSTOMER (4.2.7) as part of an iterative approach to UI design.

❖   ❖   ❖

Other daily meetings are used for status and assignments. Beedle et al. describe these meetings as "SCRUM" meetings [Beedle 1999, pp. 644–649] used to report progress, make assignments, and replan if necessary:

> To control an empirical and unpredictable development process, meet with the
> team in a short daily meeting where participants say: (1) what they have done
> since the last meeting, (2) what roadblocks were encountered, and (3) what they
> will be doing until the next meeting [Rising 2000, p. 147].

SCRUM meetings mention technical issues as forces, but provide only project management solutions. A STAND-UP MEETING treats all of these issues as inseparable, but its first focus is on the most volatile element of change and on the project component closest to the largest numbers of technical staff: the artifact being delivered to the customer.

This pattern is reiterated almost exactly in XP [Beck 1999]. In the Borland QPW project [Coplien 1994b], the architecture team met in the morning to socialize problems from the previous day. The system was updated to reflect the meeting decisions, and implementation and testing continued for the remainder of the day in preparation for the next morning's meeting.

These meetings are similar to those held at the beginning of every shift in hospitals and police stations. Note, though, that in these cases there is an explicit handoff of work from one shift to the next. Theoretically, international software teams in different locations worldwide could take advantage of different time zones and work on a piece of software 24 hours a day. However, the authors are unaware of any such scenario that has actually worked [e.g., see ORGANIZATION FOLLOWS LOCATION (5.1.8)].

A short daily meeting is an efficient way of transmitting information to the entire team with minimum communication overhead. Such meetings help overcome some of the tunnel vision problems that can result from CODE OWNERSHIP (5.2.13).

Beyond the benefits of communication, these meetings have a salutary effect on morale. They are a slightly institutionalized form of HALLWAY CHATTER (5.1.15), while also being an informal form of GROUP VALIDATION (4.2.32) that helps maintain UNITY OF PURPOSE (4.2.12).

But there is a potential danger with such meetings. In some organizations, particularly where tight communication is not the norm, daily meetings are instituted in response to a crisis. While the meetings give morale a temporary lift, they are subject to—and contribute to—burnout. Conversely, one must be careful that the purpose of regular daily meetings is to exchange information and not to create an artificial crisis mentality in order to elevate performance. Such a purpose is not only unsustainable, it is a little bit dishonest.

When should the meeting take place? In California shops, where people can wander into work any time from 8:00 A.M. until noon, you want to schedule the meeting carefully.

Use a MERCENARY ANALYST (4.1.24) to make a record of the fast-paced decisions.

Ward Cunningham's EPISODES pattern language [Cunningham 1996] suggests that weekly personal interviews be held rather than full meetings. The pattern WORK QUEUE REPORT suggests "Collect status in regular personal interviews conducted at weekly intervals. Solicit days of remaining effort estimates using contrasts with Comparable Work." Cunningham presents the following example:

> *"I put two full days into the new tax calculations, and one day with Joe on his U/I."*
>
> *"How many uninterrupted days do you think you need to finish the calculations?"*
>
> *"Oh, say two. It's no different from the accruals."*
>
> *"And, working with Joe?"*
>
> *"Well, we didn't get to the real work. I had three down last week? Must still be three days."*

Cunningham then goes on to say:

> Use these estimates along with individual dilution factors (how many uninterrupted days of development does the individual have access to a week) to predict elapsed days to completion for each assigned deliverable. Compute and publish COMPLETION HEADROOM (4.1.10) from this data. Include a cover page with a few sentences explaining numbers that might have shifted in an interesting way.

This pattern is derived from the foregoing citations as well as from REVIEW THE ARCHITECTURE [Coplien 1995]. Luke Hohmann's input in particular is greatly appreciated.

5.2.8   Deploy along the Grain **

Alias: Deploy People along the Grain of the Domain, One Person/Many Hats

One person, many hats.

... in the past, the roles of analysis, design, and implementation have been split among different people.

❖   ❖   ❖

Some of the most powerful design insights come late in the design cycle, particularly during the phase we affectionately call *maintenance*. But traditional staffing profiles deploy the most skilled designers at the front end of the life cycle, leaving the later phases to maintenance engineers.

Valuable architectural insight tends to emerge late in the life cycle as a result of having addressed requirements from concrete, successive problems drawn from a given domain. It is at this late stage that a system can be refactored to consolidate design insight and to polish reusable artifacts. (More can be said on this topic, but that's another tale.)

Such insight can best be harvested if people are deployed along the grain of the domain and if a given individual has responsibility for a well-defined part of it. Organizational categories like Analyst, Designer, Coder, Maintainer, and Reuse Expert can cut across the grain and greatly increase organizational communication overhead and inertia. However, when responsibility for all of these functions for a given part of the system is vested in a single person, the communication overhead for the redesign of that part of the system can be largely "intracranial." In this one-person/many-hats strategy, a single individual can cope far more quickly with ongoing bidirectional tensions between top-down elegance and bottom-up detail than can a functionally partitioned organization. Such a person can develop a more comprehensive sense of the possibilities that the design space allows and exploit these possibilities to develop more genuinely durable artifacts.

A reusable application programming interface (API) or OO framework is, in many respects, a domain-specific language. As such, Wirth's classic admonition applies: Language design is better done by a single guiding intelligence than by a committee. [See the Pascal quote in ARCHITECT CONTROLS PRODUCT (5.2.3).]

Small teams deployed along the grain should be able to glean similar benefits. Team members would be responsible for distinct parts of their team's domain. Metafunctions like pure management and documentation might be factored in and assigned to additional individuals. Interpersonal communication would primarily be concerned with interface negotiation instead of focusing on approval of internal changes.

The key here is committing talented designers to a part of the system and keeping them there until late in the life cycle, when hindsight is available as a result of addressing a range of design issues.

This pattern, Alexander's architect/builder notions, and ARCHITECT ALSO IMPLEMENTS (5.2.10) all share some commonality. This sort of personnel deployment strategy is a de facto favorite in academic environments and in some small organizations, both of which often exhibit marked productivity advantages over traditional industrial organizations. If an organization really wants to develop truly reusable software, it will have to be willing to budget time and talent in such a way as to exploit appropriate insights at the point in the life cycle where they become available. But reuse isn't something that can itself easily be factored into its own department. The people who build and maintain systems in the first place have the best, most intimate knowledge of how to generalize it.

There is a certain amount of Alexandrian wiggle room with regard to how one knows where the grain is, especially at the onset of a project. Often, the grain of the domain something people settle into.

Therefore:

Deploy people along the grain of the domain. That is to say, give them dedicated, long-term responsibility for a manageable piece of the system, thereby enabling them to exploit opportunities to consolidate and improve the reusability of their parts of the system as experience accrues.

Frequently, a significant degree of *self-selection* is at work when this pattern is employed, thus making this pattern a variation on SELF-SELECTING TEAM (4.2.11). Managers should keep a watchful eye on emerging new roles as people spontaneously elect to fill them.

This pattern plays out in specializations such as OWNER PER DELIVERABLE (A.5.19) and, more specifically, CODE OWNERSHIP (5.2.13). It should be contrasted with the approach suggested by XP [Beck 1999] advocates, though the effective divisions of labor may not be as different as a simple comparison might suggest.

This pattern is constrained by the forces of CONWAY'S LAW (5.1.7) (or, perhaps this pattern is the embodiment of it). You also need to take people's skills into account, as stated in SKILL MIX (A.5.28) [Cockburn 1996] and SUBSYSTEM BY SKILL (4.2.23).

This pattern originally appeared as Brian Foote's DEPLOY PEOPLE ALONG THE GRAIN OF THE DOMAIN at PLoP 2000 [Foote 2000]. The material was drawn largely intact from a discussion of reuse teams that took place in early December 1993 in either comp.object or on an early incarnation of the patterns mailing list.

5.2.9 Subsystem by Skill

See section 4.2.23.

5.2.10   Architect Also Implements **

Architects of a housing development working onsite, 1942.

... an organization is being built to serve an identified market or markets. [ORGANIZATION FOLLOWS MARKET (5.1.9)]. Going forward, the project needs the necessary architectural breadth to cover its markets and to ensure smooth evolution, but it can't be blindsided by pragmatic engineering and implementation concerns. Furthermore, the project needs to carry through a singular architectural vision from conception to implementation if it is to have conceptual integrity.

A software project must broaden the scope of leadership without sacrificing depth and attention to pragmatics. Though developers are good at making individual design and implementation decisions, a project needs an overall guiding strategic technical direction. This direction usually comes from the architect. However, too many software architects limit their thinking and direction to abstractions, and abstraction is a disciplined form of ignorance. Too many projects fail to capture the "details" of performance, subtleties of APIs, and interworking of components—or, at best, they discover such problems late.

It's possible that this problem could be solved with totalitarian control if one had a perfect plan. But even if that were possible, totalitarian control is viewed by most development teams as excessive.

The right information must flow through the right roles. In particular, the developers must latch onto the strategic vision and carry responsibility for implementation. The architect, and to some degree the developers, must also understand the application needs and be able to portend the long-term structure of the system. But a more centralized locus of strategic direction should keep the project from floundering, make sure the necessary details are addressed, and track the emerging fit of all of the pieces into a whole. Sometimes, understanding how these pieces fit together requires a corresponding understanding of low-level details of component interaction, protocols, APIs, performance, or reliability concerns.

Therefore:

Beyond advising and communicating with Developers, Architects should also participate in implementation.

The Architect should be organizationally engaged with Developers and should write code. The Architect may implement along with a developer using DEVELOPING IN PAIRS (4.2.28).

If the architect implements, the development organization perceives buy-in from the guiding architects, and that perception can directly avail itself of architectural expertise. The architects also learn by seeing the first-hand results of their decisions and designs, thus giving them feedback on the development process.

The importance of making this pattern explicit arose recently in a project I worked with. The architecture team was being assembled across wide geographic boundaries with narrow communication bandwidth between them. Though general architectural responsibilities were identified and the roles were staffed, one group expected architects to also implement code, whereas the other did not.

One manager suggests that, on some projects, architects should focus only on the implementation of a common infrastructure; the implementation of noncore code should thus be left solely to the Developer role. This division of responsibilities may work on some projects; however, the architect must have a strong feel for the recurring application needs in order to build long-term robust frameworks. If architects work only on infrastructure concerns and lack an engaged appreciation of application needs, there will be a disconnect between the infrastructure (framework, middleware) and the application. Rybczynski notes the following:

> It would be convenient if architecture could be defined as any building designed by an architect. But who is an architect? Although the Academie Royale d'Architecture in Paris was founded in 1671, formal architectural schooling did not appear until the nineteenth century. The famous Ecole des Beaux-Arts was founded in 1816; the first English-language school, in London, in 1847; and the first North American university program, at MIT, was established in 1868. Despite the existence of professional schools, for a long time the relationship between schooling and practice remained ambiguous. It is still possible to become an architect without a university degree, and in some countries, such as Switzerland, trained architects have no legal monopoly over construction. This is hardly surprising. For centuries, the difference between master masons, journeymen builders, joiners, dilettantes, gifted amateurs, and architects has been ill defined. The great Renaissance buildings, for example, were designed by a variety of non-architects. Brunelleschi was trained as a goldsmith; Michelangeo as a

sculptor, Leonardo da Vinci as a painter, and Alberti as a lawyer; only Bramante, who was also a painter, had formally studied building. These men are termed architects because, among other things, they created architecture—a tautology that explains nothing [Rybczynski 1989, p. 9].

Marcus Vitruvius Pollio notes that

> ...[A]rchitects who have aimed at acquiring manual skill without scholarship have never been able to reach a position of authority to correspond to their pains, while those who relied only upon theories and scholarship were obviously hunting the shadow, not the substance. But those who have a thorough knowledge of both, like men armed at all points, have the sooner attained their object and carried authority with them [Vitruvius 1960] p. 5.

John Thomas [mail of 18 Mar 1997] writes,

> C. E. Walston and C. P. Felix did an extensive multiple regression study of software productivity ... As I recall, the proportion of architects who were also on the implementation team had a very large coefficient. It was a much more powerful variable, e.g., than use of a high level language or use of structured programming [Walston Felix 1977] pp. 54–73.

Though the architect should be able to understand the minutiae of development, it is not necessarily the architect's business to deal with such details day in and day out. The architect is the keeper of the flame, the owner of the principles that the project follows. These principles, in turn, shape structure. Much of the structure can come out of a consensus process guided by the architect; in fact, in practice, much of what architects do involves such high-level guidance [Coplien Devos 2000].

A related pattern is GURU DOES ALL (A.5.15) from the collection of Don Olson [Olson 1998, pp. 153–154], which states the following [Rising 2000, p. 130]:

> A newly formed team is given a project with a tight schedule, uncertain require-ments, uneven distribution of skills, and new technologies. Let the most skilled and knowledgeable developer drive the design and implement the critical pieces. This can be an antipattern.

The key element of this pattern is to give the critical pieces to the most skilled and knowl-edgeable practitioners [DOMAIN EXPERTISE IN ROLES (4.2.22)]. But this pattern also contains ele-ments of SOLO VIRTUOSO (4.2.5) and can be thought of as an interim application of SOLO VIRTUOSO in the context of a project that will mature out of the need for such a pattern. This pat-tern should be tempered with DAY CARE (4.1.23), PHASING IT IN (4.2.3), APPRENTICESHIP (4.2.4), and others to move toward more of a peer team over time. (DAY CARE, in fact, talks explicitly about problems with the belief that "a few experts could get the project done faster.") Putting too much of a burden on one developer can lead to early burnout [see THE OPEN/CLOSED PRINCIPLE OF TEAMS (6.1.4)]. Note also that it is sometimes difficult for a lead developer to give up SOLO VIR-TUOSO behavior on a given project once having filled that role, so this pattern should be applied with care.

5.2.11   Generics and Specifics

Erecting a framework.

... most projects, particularly early in the development cycle, have a mix of novices and experts. Of course, even the novices are expected to come up to speed quickly and contribute to the project.

Novices, even when mentored, tend to produce weak designs and to cut and paste code.

One does not acquire design prowess overnight; instead, such skill is the result of years of experience. Even expert designers look back on their early work and shudder at how bad it was. As with every other skill, one must practice design in order to attain proficiency.

But we need the novices. Few projects have the luxury of being staffed entirely by highly experienced people. And even if it were possible, would we really want to? Novices come in with fresh ideas, unencumbered by narrow viewpoints honed through years of experience. And, most importantly, they will eventually become the experts; a lack of novices now means a dearth of experts in a few years.

Like everyone else, novices do the best they can. They try to learn from what they see. Unfortunately, such imitation leads to cutting and pasting code, which becomes a maintenance nightmare. And when they lack guidance from existing code, their designs tend to be weak.

Therefore:

Separate problems into generic and specific parts. Use an expert, a framework designer, to design generic parts. Let the novice programmers design the specific parts.

GENERICS AND SPECIFICS is derived from SUBSYSTEM BY SKILL (4.2.23) and SUBCLASS PER TEAM (5.2.18). It is applicable to any technology that permits plug-in frameworks (e.g., object orientation).

A framework can provide a generic solution to a problem, which can be completed, extended, or tailored in the specific through subclassing. The generic solution, residing at the higher level of the class hierarchy, is considerably more difficult to design than any one specific solution. Once programmed, it is considerably quicker and easier to complete than the specific solutions would be to design.

Therefore, the experts can design a generic framework solution, and the novices can tailor it for a specific solution. This pattern fits well with the SUBCLASS PER TEAM (5.2.18) principle, since the expert will be optimizing the design from a slightly different vantage point than that of the novice.

Generics are used in most OO systems. In a UI system, generics were used for generic displays, search collection, transaction backout, and error handling. In the domain, generics were used for generic transaction, as well as error, persistence, and model behavior. In the infrastructure, they were used for error handling and the persistence mechanism. In each case, novices were able to use the generic/specific structure to accomplish their tasks in less time and to develop a more subtle architecture than that which they would have thought up on their own.

This pattern was originally written by Alistair Cockburn in SOCIAL ISSUES AND SOFTWARE ARCHITECTURE [Cockburn 1998].

5.2.12 Standards Linking Locations **

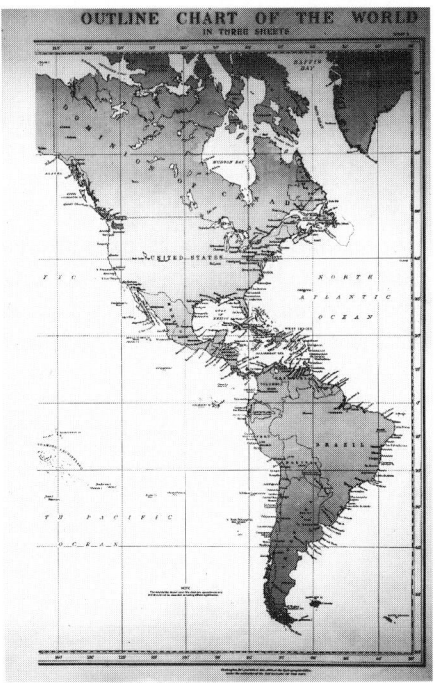

Standards in cartography allow people in different nations to use the same maps.

We once worked on a project building a wireless communications architecture. The project was spread across three states and two countries, though most of the work centered in two states. Each of those two locations built software for the locations' respective hardware boxes, and those boxes communicated closely with each other. Of course, there was a standard message protocol, but it wasn't articulated anywhere; instead, each location used its own C language structures to define its understanding of the messages. Each location emphasized the message fields in which it was most interested. In some cases, one location gave a field one name while another location gave it another name. It doesn't take much imagination to envision the confusion that ensued.

... a product must be developed in several different hallways, on different floors of a building, in different buildings, or at different locations. The code developed at these different locations must interact.

It is difficult for geographically distanced teams to find the opportunity or time to meet and interact. Yet the system must act as a system, and, as such, the parts must talk to each other. Common conventions must be used to enable the parts to talk to each other. The many parties could come to an agreement in a common meeting, but such a meeting would require too much master planning, would not sufficiently build on experience, and would not leave much room for correction and iteration.

Communication patterns between project members follow geographic distribution. Local groups should be as autonomous as possible. Coupling between pieces of software must be sustained by analogous coupling between the people maintaining that software. People tend to avoid communicating with people who work in other buildings, other towns, or overseas. People in an organization usually work on related tasks, which suggests that they communicate frequently with each other.

Therefore:

Use standards to express architectural concerns that cross geographic boundaries. This technique may extend to organizational boundaries, which can be as severe as distant geographic location. It might even extend to organizations separated only by one floor in a building. Small geographic distances can loom large if the building architecture doesn't support close interworking.

One of the good things about standards is that they are almost context-free. At the very least, they give the illusion of a shared context across organizations that otherwise can find little in common.

This pattern is a variant of CONWAY'S LAW (5.1.7). There is low cultural context between locations, so the interaction between locations is mediated at a technical level using the most vernacular approach: industry or corporate standards.

Local groups have a higher context and more effective communications. Use of standards within one location or within groups can actually reduce understanding, add overhead, and complicate communication.

Be sure to use FACE TO FACE BEFORE WORKING REMOTELY (5.1.10) to temper what can too easily become a sterile exchange of standards-based communications.

The problem described in this pattern might, in extreme cases, extend to work between adjacent cubicles. However, in that case, there may be nothing that can help, and such a technological solution certainly won't solve the underlying organizational or personality problems.

Example:

A project might use standards like Extensible Markup Language (XML) or the Reference Model for Open Distributed Processing (RM-ODP) to communicate between corporate subsidiaries working on a project. But to use a standard within just one of the subsidiaries would be counterproductive. For example, requiring *all* interobject communications to use Common Object Request Brokes Architecture (CORBA) would both complicate architectural understanding and put system performance in jeopardy.

Standards such as protocols and conventional data formats can provide a cultural context that lowers the need for communication between remote sites.

5.2.13 Code Ownership **

Pride in ownership is apparent in the well-kept grounds and immaculate condition of this building.

Paul Bramble relates the following: "Code Ownership: Boy, can you say that again. I have been in a place without code ownership. We had token code ownership in that we were generally held responsible for some products—and hence the code. But others could and would change the code to add new features provided that you weren't updating the code during a release cycle. Part of that was nice, as I would be busy doing other things, and didn't need the aggravation of figuring out the details necessary to implement their changes (which could be complex). But this positive effect was far less than the havoc these changes could wreak. While my general framework was only adequate (it could have been better), it became rather disjoint with several encapsulation and abstraction problems once other developers finished changing things— beyond repair, short of a major refactoring effort involving several people". [Bramble 2003]

... a project is underway, and mechanisms are in place to document and guide the software architect and to support coding and unit-development activities. The project is too large for one person to comprehend. No single developer can keep up with the changes being made across the system.

Something that is everybody's responsibility is really no one's responsibility.

You want multiple developers to be able to code concurrently.

Most design knowledge lives in the code, and navigating unfamiliar code to explore design issues takes time. Beyond that, changing unfamiliar code is dangerous, for one does not always know the impact of the changes.

Provisional changes never work.

Not everyone can know everything all of the time. Even the architect does not know the code well enough to be proficient in all aspects of the project [although an architect should understand some coding issues through ARCHITECT ALSO IMPLEMENTS (5.2.10)].

Therefore:

Each code module in the system is owned by a single Developer. Except in exceptional and explicit circumstances, code may be modified only by its owner. Anyone else who wants to make changes must approach the owner and get approval.

Note that ownership implies responsibility for the quality and architectural integrity of the module, which encourages the owner to gain a deep understanding of the module. An owner new to the module will need to learn the code in depth, usually quickly. Paul Taylor, in his pattern ARRANGING THE FURNITURE (A.5.1), suggests that new owners can gain familiarity and confidence by starting with cosmetic changes to the code [Taylor 1999]. (As the authors of this book, we followed a similar strategy in working with this manuscript!)

How large should a project be to use CODE OWNERSHIP? Gerhard Ackermann points out that it doesn't matter because code ownership is a principle of honoring another person's work [Ackermann 2002]. We have seen benefits in projects supported by as few as two persons. In such cases, ownership may not be formally conferred, but each person knows who owns what and consults with the other before changing the code [see also DEVELOPING IN PAIRS (4.2.28)].

This pattern is very similar to OWNER PER DELIVERABLE (A.5.19). There is, however, a subtle but significant difference between the two. Ownership of deliverables lasts for the duration of release, and its purpose is to provide accountability in project management. Ownership of code modules, on the other hand, lasts for the long term, ideally for the duration of the software. The goal, thus, is to maintain quality and architectural integrity and to improve speed by reducing discovery costs. This effort can be helped by the related pattern DEPLOY ALONG THE GRAIN (5.2.8).

Arguments against code ownership have been many, but empirical trends uphold its value. Typical concerns include the tendency toward tunnel vision, the implied risk of having only a single individual who understands a given piece of code in depth, and a breakdown of global knowledge. Other patterns temper these potential problems.

The pattern STAND-UP MEETING (5.2.7) helps keep Designers and Architects from developing tunnel vision that is often associated with strict application of CODE OWNERSHIP.

CODE OWNERSHIP can lead to bottlenecks, as all changes to a module must funnel through the owner. Furthermore, CODE OWNERSHIP can tend to pair critical information with individuals, violating MODERATE TRUCK NUMBER (4.2.24). Both of these issues can be counteracted by DEVELOPING IN PAIRS (4.2.28), as well as practices such as design reviews and code inspections. In addition, one can implement CODE OWNERSHIP with some flexibility to allow exceptions if needed to resolve bottlenecks (with the approval of the owner after the fact). Gerard Meszaros also notes that the owner may be a single person or a group with a designated "group head," which is especially helpful in large projects [Meszaros 1999]. (Note that ownership is not the same as "collective ownership," as advocated by some [Beck 1999]. Ownership by everybody is really ownership by nobody.)

Empirical support for this pattern is strong, although the most striking examples are the problems encountered when there is no CODE OWNERSHIP.

One of the authors remembers living a "nightmare" with a code module that nobody owned. Because everybody could—and did—refactor the code at will, the architecture changed constantly. Keeping up with changes that others made became a significant chore. Ironically, the project had a policy of code ownership, but nobody had taken on ownership of this module. At length, he volunteered to take ownership of the module, even though we were not part of the project it belonged to.

Lack of code ownership is a major contributor to discovery effort in large-scale software development today. Note that code ownership goes hand in hand with architecture: To have ownership, there must be interfaces. This pattern is a form of CONWAY'S LAW (5.1.7) in the small [see also ARCHITECT ALSO IMPLEMENTS (5.2.10)].

As a result of using this pattern, the architecture and organization will better reflect each other [CONWAY'S LAW (5.1.7)]. Related patterns include INTERRUPTS UNJAM BLOCKING (4.1.25), ORGANIZATION FOLLOWS MARKET (5.1.9), and ARCHITECT ALSO IMPLEMENTS (5.2.10).

Tim Born argues that there is a relationship between code ownership and encapsulation, in the sense that C++ protection keeps one person from accessing the implementation of another's abstraction [Born 1994].

One can tie this concept all the way back to the philosophy of law. In *L'Esprit des Lois*, Rousseau argues that law is property, and the lack of identifiable property leads to anarchy [Rousseau 1972].

It has been argued that code ownership should be applied only to reusable code. Such a constraint would be worthy of consideration if someone is able to come up with a good distinction between usable code and reusable code.

GERARD MESZAROS wrote a related pattern called ARTIFACT OWNERSHIP [Meszaros 1999].

People can abuse code ownership to protect their artifacts from inspection by colleagues or to take unilateral control of system-level issues whose changes fall into their domain. Temper these problems with COMMUNITY OF TRUST (4.1.1) and DEVELOPING IN PAIRS (4.2.28). FEATURE ASSIGNMENT (5.2.14) brings a review perspective that cuts across the code partitioning, which can help the code owner avoid tunnel vision.

5.2.14   Feature Assignment *

Day laborers waiting to be assigned work, Raymondville, Texas, 1939.

... in a multiperson project of medium size or larger, one gets to the point that the work must be partitioned among team members. The initial architecture is complete, but where do we go from here?

For every nontrivial project, it is impossible to partition the work cleanly.

You have to get the work done, and you need to get the new release out the door. Everyone needs to work on the project, yet, no matter how you slice the work, people will all tend to work on the same piece of code. The essential complexity of the problem (see [Brooks 1995]) means this lack of partitioning will happen in all but the most trivial developments.

The act of partitioning the problem through the architecture is mainly for people's benefit. Through CODE OWNERSHIP (5.2.13), we maintain the integrity of the architecture in order to attempt to maintain the comprehensibility of the problem. But to a greater or lesser extent, features cut across the architecture. So CODE OWNERSHIP is not the right model for developing the features.

Take the canonical example of an automatic teller. There are natural architectural entities such as the display subsystem, the input subsystem, and the communication layer, among others. Yet the feature "display account balance" cuts across all of these entities.

Therefore:

Assign features to people for development. Feature development has a finite duration and is, therefore, an assignment, not a role.

Feature assignment works together with CODE OWNERSHIP (5.2.13) to develop the product and maintain its architectural integrity. The developer of a feature will consult with the code owner about changes.

The owner of the code most affected by a particular feature is often the natural person to receive that feature assignment, although someone else could receive the assignment instead.

Features may be assigned to more than one person, or, better still, developers may choose to work together to develop them [see DEVELOPING IN PAIRS (4.2.28)].

There is some danger that the combination of FEATURE ASSIGNMENT and CODE OWNERSHIP (5.2.13) will tend to encourage excessive management bureaucracy, but such bureaucracy doesn't need to be the case. Features are a natural unit of project tracking, and CODE OWNERSHIP (5.2.13) need not add anything substantial to the project overhead.

The temporary nature of FEATURE ASSIGNMENT and the role nature of CODE OWNERSHIP (5.2.13) together strike a balance between maintaining architectural integrity and getting the work done. Together, they complete DEPLOY ALONG THE GRAIN (5.2.8).

Note that some project methodologies advocate making assignments every day, delegating chunks of work that can be completed in a single day. If the project is small and the work can be appropriately partitioned, this approach may work well. FEATURE ASSIGNMENT, however, is broader. It encompasses this approach, but it can also be applied to large complex projects and to those where work is so complex that it cannot be broken into such small chunks.

5.2.15   Variation Behind Interface **

These houses are identical on the outside, but you can be sure that the interior decoration varies.

... the architecture has been established, and CODE OWNERSHIP (5.2.13) has been put in place. Features have been assigned. Now the easy part is over.

Once you start developing software, you find that things change. And these changes can affect not only your software, but also software written by others.

In a typical scenario, you are working on a feature, and you need to change a certain file. Unfortunately, someone else needs the same file to work on a different feature. Good configuration management and workspace tools can use file locking to prevent one of you from undoing the other's work, but there is still a problem with merging both of your modifications. Or, perhaps you just wait for the other person to finish with the file before you start your work.

In another scenario, you are working on a feature, and you call a function that someone else is working on. When you build against the official base, you find that the function has changed, and you need to change the way in which you call that function.

On the flip side, you are working on a function that others call. When you build against the official base, you find that your changes cause build errors in other peoples' code whenever your function is called.

These problems illustrate the technical problems that arise when multiple people work on a software project.

Even worse, you may be waiting for someone to check in code so you can make your own changes to it. When you are able to check out the image for editing, you find out that some things you would like to use have been added and some things you need have been deleted, both in the same unit of editing. Tools and technology alone cannot solve this fundamental dilemma.

Therefore:

Create interfaces around predicted points of variation.

Note that this pattern requires one to predict or, at the very least, make educated guesses about what will change and what will remain constant. This commonality and variability analysis, or domain analysis, is described in various places such as [Weiss 1999] and [Coplien 1999].

In spite of our best efforts at analysis, it will be necessary to change the interfaces on occasion, which can have an impact on others. To minimize the impact, use NAMED STABLE BASES (4.1.4) to manage these changes.

This pattern really involves nothing more or less than information hiding, as originally described by Parnas [Parnas 1978]. Here, the motivation for hiding information is to insulate others from expected changes. This pattern also underlies Alan Kay's work in OO programming [Kay 1997].

This pattern forms the basis for SHEARING LAYERS (A.5.26) [Foote Yoder 2000], which states that you should factor your system so that the artifacts that change at similar rates remain together. One difference is that SHEARING LAYERS is often applied at the system level, whereas this pattern is applied at the module level.

So what does this pattern have to do with creating effective software development teams? Quite a bit, actually. Of course, a project is partitioned among team members who depend on each other's software; therefore, the connection points of the software—the interfaces—must change as seldom as possible. Otherwise, people find themselves spending much time rewriting parts of code that once worked. And, people begin to get testy with each other. The way to minimize interface changes is to hide variations behind the interfaces.

However, don't get too carried away. Too many interfaces cause the system to slow down.

Designers sometimes try to anticipate all variations. However, extra interfaces slow down and complicate the software. Often, anticipated situations never happen, so some interfaces serve no useful purpose. The trick in good design is to correctly anticipate the changes or to weigh the cost of the interface against the cost of the change.

HIERARCHY OF FACTORIES (5.2.19) and PARSER BUILDER (5.2.20) provide examples of this approach.

This pattern first appeared in [Cockburn 1996] as Protected Variations, and appeared in a refined version in SOCIAL ISSUES AND SOFTWARE ARCHITECTURE, published in [Cockburn 1998].

5.2.16   Private Versioning **

"Solitude," an isolated outhouse on the property of Frank Weeks, Willston, North Dakota, 1937.
A place for anyone's private version ...

... a developer should have a way to checkpoint changes without making these changes available to the development team at large. We want to implement Code Ownership (5.2.13) but subsystems never work entirely in isolation.

Periodic integration of a developer's work with that of other members of the development team is important for ensuring stability.

Checkpointing only after completing major changes can make it difficult to back out of one phase of a change. Using the revision control area to manage such changes can lead to changes being "published" before they are ready for integration. Also, publishing intermediate changes can lead to a deceptive number of revisions listed in the software configuration management (SCM) system. It is necessary to be able to save intermediate steps in a change in case a coding step results in an error. This capability is particularly important when the following criteria are met:

- The mechanism for specifying that a version is ready for integration is primitive, and another developer has access to a version as soon as it is checked in.

- There is a desire to keep the revision history database "uncluttered" by logging only significant changes.

Therefore:

Developers should be provided with a mechanism for checkpointing changes at a granularity that they are comfortable with. This mechanism can be provided for by a local revision control area. As a result, only stable code sets are checked into the project repository.

Add a private repository to the developer work space so that a developer can save intermediate versions before checking them in to the repository. The private repository can use the same mechanisms as the project repository [i.e., the revision control system (RCS)], or it can simply be a means of maintaining copies of intermediate files.

The key point is to provide a way for a developer to use revision control to save changes in increments that make sense to them, thus eliminating the risk that the changes will be made available to others before the developer decides to publish a consistent and correct version. Some SCM tools support this capability without the need to set up a physically separate repository area.

It is important to make sure that developers who use PRIVATE VERSIONING remember to migrate changes to the shared version control system at reasonable intervals.

The revision control mechanism could also provide a means for restricting access to checked-in versions that are not yet ready for use by others and for filtering log messages to eliminate trivial changes.

Note that PRIVATE VERSIONING works together with VARIATION BEHIND INTERFACE (5.2.15) to help prevent developers from stepping on each others' toes, though the patterns accomplish this goal in very different ways. Code owners [CODE OWNERSHIP (5.2.13)] can work together to perform coordinated development and testing of private features before they are released to the project as a whole.

This pattern is derived from the pattern with the same name in [Berczuk Appleton 2002].

5.2.17   Loose Interfaces **

Cattle exiting through a "loose interface."

... sometimes architecture and organization are aligned in a particular way [CONWAY'S LAW (5.1.7)] because of geographical and organizational constraints.

To avoid development bottlenecks, we need to be able to limit the effect that one team's work will have on another.

When many teams are proceeding at a reasonable pace to help develop a system, it is important for interfaces between systems to remain somewhat flexible. This flexibility is particularly important in a situation where teams of developers are geographically distributed [ORGANIZATION FOLLOWS LOCATION (5.1.8)] and where rapid turnaround time for design and development is important. As an example, consider a project that is trying to build a prototype for an early customer demonstration to support a tender for a bid.

Communication is difficult. When requirements are changing and the teams are located in a variety of places, then poor communication often results. These communication difficulties can stall a project and can be particularly problematic when an organization does not have an architectural center, such as that described by ARCHITECT CONTROLS PRODUCT (5.2.3).

This pattern is particularly applicable in a research, pilot, or new technology application where teams are small, requirements are changing, and the potential for gridlock is great if dependencies are too high. There is typically an *administrative* or organizational center of the architecture, but this center does not always have the capability to design a complete system.

Therefore:

Limit the number of explicit, static interfaces. Define large-grained interfaces that allow developers to code against interfaces defined early, but that do not overly constrain functionality. Use LOOSE INTERFACES like HIERARCHY OF FACTORIES (5.2.19), and PARSER BUILDER (5.2.20) to achieve this goal.

Decoupling interfaces in this way will also facilitate EARLY AND REGULAR DELIVERY (A.5.11) by making it easier to build incremental systems. It can also make it easier to set up an environment where DEVELOPER CONTROLS PROCESS (4.1.17) by defining independent features at a small enough scale that they can be controlled by a developer or group. The end result is that as long as the components meet interface, quality, and other requirements, teams in different organizational units can implement these components using any micro-process that suits them.

Take care that the empire which supports the interfaces doesn't itself become a dominating focus that can drain project energy or create accidental coupling across the project. Brokers and other large communication frameworks have this danger. Keep the interfaces simple and in concert with business needs.

SUBSYSTEM BY SKILL (4.2.23) addresses a similar situation, where the driving force is the skill set of the various teams.

This pattern is derived from the pattern with the same name in [Berczuk Appleton 2002].

5.2.18 Subclass Per Team

A small team of students with a common interest in photography.

... dividing up work among different teams is less straightforward than it looks. It is simply impossible to partition the work perfectly; as a result, one team's work will always overlap that of another.

Subsystem teams have differing interests and design points.

When two teams work on the same class definition, they may be optimizing different maintenance and performance characteristics. Besides being in conflict as to the way in which they perform optimization, they will also lose track of which parts of the module are used by whom [see OWNER PER DELIVERABLE (A.5.19)].

Therefore:

Where two subsystems collide in one class, factor the code into separate classes that align with the interest of two or more development teams. Each class can be owned by its respective team [OWNER PER DELIVERABLE (A.5.19)], and the classes can be combined with inheritance and design patterns to integrate functionality.

OO programming provides the class hierarchy, which is a particularly nice way to split a class along lines of separate interests. It is appropriate that different interests reside in different places [VARIATION BEHIND INTERFACE (5.2.15)], since a change to one team's module should not damage the other teams' modules). If inheritance is not available (in non-OO development), it sometimes can be mimicked using call delegation.

Various design patterns can be used to support flexible and convenient combination of such classes; in particular, see the TEMPLATE METHOD in [Gamma 1995].

An example of a mixing of team interests is at the root domain class, which is where the domain team puts its generic behavior and where the persistence team puts generic transaction behavior. Ideally, the two are independent. Further, by job description and expertise, the domain class person is different from the persistence mechanism person. The teams will be making changes to their interfaces and implementations concurrently, and they have different interests and different ideas as to what is best. Introducing layers of subclassing allows the groups to hone their designs with minimal impact on each other. HIERARCHY OF FACTORIES (5.2.19) [Berczuk 1996] illustrates a specialization of this pattern for the case where the application is a creational system and where different subsystems control the format of different types of products. PARSER BUILDER (5.2.20) is an example of a pattern that provides a single base class interface to variant implementations in derived classes.

Beware of overapplying this pattern: Excessive levels of inheritance make the system harder to understand and potentially slower.

The principle would make a wonderful, universal argument-mediation technique, except that the addition of a new level of subclassing for every disagreement would produce a system that is difficult to understand.

This pattern was originally written by Alistair Cockburn in SOCIAL ISSUES AND SOFTWARE ARCHITECTURE, published in [Cockburn 1998].

5.2.19   Hierarchy of Factories
Alias: COMPOSITE FACTORY

Making cheese in a small rural cheese factory.

Cheeses in a larger cheese factory.

... once we decide that using a PARSER BUILDER (5.2.20) is the right way to create objects, we need to partition the details of how to construct objects of various classes into the various groups responsible for this construction; in other words, we need to have LOOSE INTERFACES (5.2.17). We want to complete FORM FOLLOWS FUNCTION (5.1.11) or ORGANIZATION FOLLOWS LOCATION (5.1.8). On a lower level, we want to implement DEVELOPER CONTROLS PROCESS (4.1.17) for a system that creates objects of various types.

❖   ❖   ❖

In a distributed work group, it is important to divide responsibilities for creational systems as cleanly as possible and to reduce coupling.

Sometimes the secrets of classifying elements in a data stream are divided between various groups. The reasons for this partitioning can involve company politics or a strong desire to reduce coupling because the knowledge of the telemetry formats is distributed. We need a way to partition the responsibilities for classifying the telemetry packets, while also maintaining a centralized client interface and keeping VARIATION BEHIND INTERFACE (5.2.15).

In a telemetry application, various instruments can generate telemetry, which is then fed into one stream. The instruments are developed by different teams (e.g., at different institutions), and these teams have control over the format of the telemetry that they generate (after taking some standard headers into account).

We want a way to isolate the details for identifying each team's objects, while at the same time allowing the objects to be identified and created in a single application. The scheme that we develop should be layered so that the main factory needs to know only of the existence of a class of objects and thus does not need to know the depth of the hierarchy below that class. Packets created from the hierarchy are processed in a generic way, perhaps by using virtual functions.

One way to address the classification problem is to put all of the classification/dispatch logic into a single PARSER BUILDER (5.2.20) (combining the INTERPRETER [Gamma 1995] pattern with a BUILDER pattern [Gamma 1995])—perhaps by using a big switch statement—and to rely on communications between groups to ensure that the details make it into the master code through some communications method. This method is error prone and is subject to delays. We could also divide the processing into a number of factories and have the client call each in turn. However, this method violates our requirement of transparency, and the client needs to know when a new class of object is added.

It would be useful to have a way to allow the client interface to emulate a single factory, but hide the details of the construction hierarchy.

The following list summarizes the forces:

- There is a division of responsibilities [ORGANIZATION FOLLOWS LOCATION (5.1.8)].
- There is a need for a central interface for parsing data streams and building objects.
- There is a need to add objects to the construction hierarchy in a manner transparent to clients.
- There is a capability (or a requirement) to process entities by virtual functions.
- Each class of object can know about its immediate derived classes.

Therefore:

Use a hierarchy of factories, each of which understands the criteria for making a packet of its type and knows about the immediate subtypes. The client invokes the `make` method with the base class factory instance. That factory checks to see that, based on some attributes, there is indeed an object of class `Packet` in the stream. The factory then passes the data stream to the factories of each of its immediate subclasses, which in turn check the appropriate data fields in the manner of the PARSER BUILDER (5.2.20) pattern.

The SINGLETON pattern [Gamma 1995] can be used to access the factories for the derived classes, or the members of the hierarchy can be registered with the master factory at run time.

While this pattern violates encapsulation to some extent by requiring a base class to know about its immediate subclasses, it can be made acceptable by agreeing on generic interface classes (say, one per team) and allowing each team free reign to subclass these interface classes. Also, this requirement is not terribly limiting in this application, since the top level operations team knows about the basic instrument team interfaces and since the number of instrument teams is fixed by contract when the project begins.

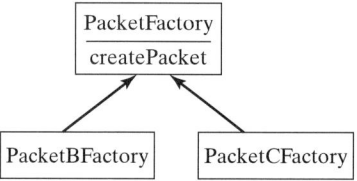

Hierarchy of Factories

An example implementation in C++ is

```
//Base class factory method
Packet* PacketFactory::make(Stream* dataStream){
Packet* pkt=0;
if(isAPacket(dataStream)) {
    if(! pkt = APacket::factory()->make(dataStream))
      if(!pkt = BPacket::factory()->make(dataStream)) {
            pkt = new Packet(dataStream);
      }
    return pkt;
}
```

The result of applying this pattern is that each class needs to know only (1) the criteria for what constitutes a member of that class in terms of elements in the data stream and (2) the immediate subclasses.

It is possible to use a *registration* mechanism to inform the base class of what the subclasses are rather than hard coding the relationship. [This pattern is not yet written, but it would specify a mechanism for notifying a base class factory that a derived class factory has been created. The basic idea would be similar to the View/Model connection in a Model/View/Controller mechanism, but it would also address issues of uniqueness (i.e., only one instance of each derived class can notify a base class) and guaranteed notification. Thus, the construction of any object/factory of the derived classes would generate a registration event automatically].

It is also possible to implement this pattern using containment rather than inheritance.

This pattern is also useful for isolating the definition of packets for which a single team is responsible. The information can thus be encapsulated, making it easier to work on a project with large or widely distributed teams.

This pattern is similar to the BUILDER [Gamma 1995] pattern in that it has a hierarchy of factories. It is different in that the data stream defines what is made rather than the application explicitly specifying what objects to construct by making arguments to the factory.

This pattern is also similar to CHAIN OF RESPONSIBILITY [Gamma 1995]. This pattern specializes CHAIN OF RESPONSIBILITY for a creational system, using the different *handlers* to facilitate separation of design responsibilities.

This pattern helps us realize ORGANIZATION FOLLOWS LOCATION (5.1.8) and CODE OWNERSHIP (5.2.13). This pattern implements SUBCLASS PER TEAM (5.2.18) for a creational system.

This pattern is derived from the pattern with the same name in [Berczuk Appleton 2002].

5.2.20   Parser Builder *

*Decoding a message at the message center, which was established by the Signal Corps during a
field problem, Fort Riley, Kansas. (Parsing is a form of decoding.)*

... many systems need to read data from a stream and classify elements on the stream as
objects. Many times, the knowledge of how to interpret a stream is possessed by a different group
than the knowledge of how to use that stream, making LOOSE INTERFACES (5.2.17) advantageous.

We want to interpret a given data stream, classifying the elements into the appropriate
class of object. The data stream contains tags that can be used to identify the raw data, and we
want to convert the stream into object form so we can process the data.

We need a way to create arbitrary objects based on tokens in the data stream.

For example, consider the problem of reading in raw UNIX files and classifying them into
types of files based on their "magic number," as in the tags in the /etc/magic file. You could
create the appropriate subclass of File and then invoke its virtual edit() method by bringing
up the appropriate editor.

In a telemetry processing system, each telemetry packet has identifying information in
its header. The telemetry processing system design requires that an object, once created, knows
how to process itself [i.e., we will not use a dispatch table or a switch on type in order to satisfy the terms of the ORGANIZATION FOLLOWS LOCATION (5.1.8) pattern]. At the lowest level,
objects will be created using a FACTORY METHOD [Gamma 1995]. Each class of packets will be

processed differently; some will assemble themselves into larger units, while others will issue messages. The hierarchy for a spacecraft has two subclasses of `Packet`: `APacket` and `BPacket`:

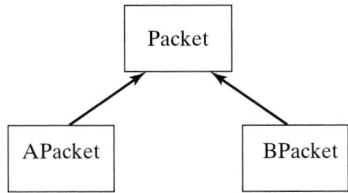

Sample Packet Hierarchy

We want each `Packet`, once created, to process itself by using a virtual method, `process()`. If we pass a data stream into a factory, we want to return a pointer to a `Packet` that has the appropriate type. The following list summarizes the forces:

- There is a need to interpret a raw data stream.
- There is a generic way to process the packets once they are returned from the factory.
- The raw data contain tags that can be used for classification.

Therefore:

Use a Parser Builder that reads the identifying information from the header of the packet and creates an object of the appropriate type, removing only one object's worth of data from the stream.

An example of a client interface in C++ is

```
while (!dataStream.empty()) {
    PacketFactory f;
    Packet* p = f.make(dataStream);
    if(p) p->process();
}
```

This pattern is a variant of Abstract Factory [Gamma 1995], but the object to be created is defined in the data stream rather than by the client. Hierarchy of Factories (5.2.19) and Parser Builder can be used to implement Loose Interfaces (5.2.17) by providing a means of separating clients from producers of data (assuming that data producers also define the factories).

OTHER USES:

In some object-persistence mechanisms, objects are assigned class IDs that are placed in the storage stream. These IDs are restored first to allow the system to decide what class object to make from the restored stream.

Parser Builder is used in the pattern Query Objects [Brown Whitenack 1999] to convert Structured Query Language (SQL) statements to QUERY objects. (Query Objects address the problem of handling the generation and execution of SQL statements in an OO way when a relational database is being used to store objects.) [Riehl 1999] discusses similar issues, using specifications to build objects on a desktop.

The distinction between this pattern, BUILDER [Gamma 1995] and FACTORY METHOD [Gamma 1995] is that in this pattern the factory reads from a stream and the client does not know which type of object will be returned. For text interpretation, PARSER BUILDER can be a front end to the INTERPRETER [Gamma 1995] pattern.

This pattern was derived from a pattern with the same name in [Berczuk Appleton 2002].

5.2.21   Incremental Integration

See section 4.1.5.

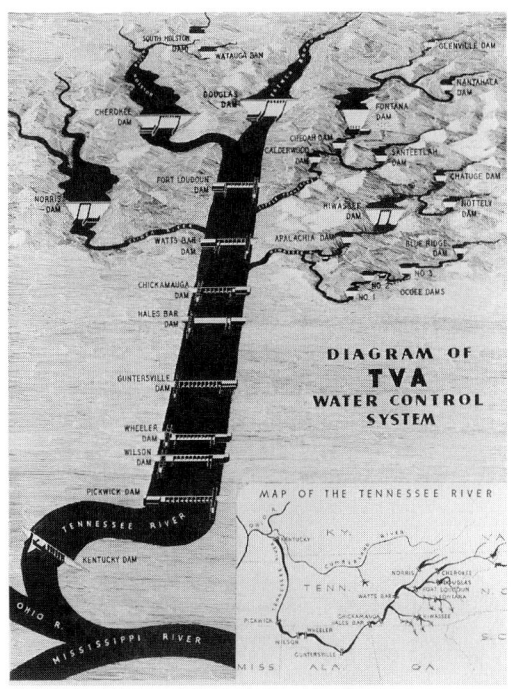

5.2.22   Private World

See section 4.1.6.

5.2.23   Named Stable Bases

See section 4.1.4.

PART III

Foundations and History

Anthropology can't claim to be the oldest profession (or even the second oldest), but people have been thinking about the structure of human organizations for thousands of years. Many of the ancient texts on organizational structure deal with military organizations, and most of them are rooted in hierarchy.

In the next two chapters, we investigate principles behind organizational structure. These chapters will give you a deeper appreciation of how organizations work and of how organizational change happens. The first chapter, ORGANIZATIONAL PRINCIPLES, gives some practical insights that will help you use these patterns more effectively. The second chapter, ANTHROPOLOGICAL FOUNDATIONS, looks at the ties between our work, which uses patterns and CRC cards, and the classic techniques and models of anthropology.

CHAPTER 6

Organizational Principles

This chapter offers practical advice that will make it easier to apply the patterns. You need to know when an organization is ready to try out patterns, and, once it is ready, you need to know how to apply the patterns. You also need to know what to do when a pattern doesn't seem to be working. This isn't an academic exercise: The future of your organization is on the line. Success often lies in the details. Here, we offer some insight on the most important contextual factors that contribute to the long-term success of the patterns themselves.

6.1 Priming the Organization for Change

All patterns build on the ability to reflect on the state of the world and to take reasonable steps toward repair and change. The organizational patterns described in this book probably feature this property more strongly than any software design patterns, and perhaps even more than Alexander's patterns of urban design, because the structure undergoing evolution is a human structure, the structure of an organization. An organization must have reached a certain baseline of organizational health in order to apply these patterns, and a large fraction of the organizations out there are not yet ready. How do you know whether you're ready to use these patterns? And if you're not yet there, how do you get there?

If you're not ready to deal courageously with your shortcomings and to embrace organizational change, then you need to work on building enough mutual trust and respect to lay a foundation for introspection and dialogue. Without trust and respect, there cannot be deep enough communication to go beyond discussion about process (which often involves blaming problems on the role or person responsible for a given step of the process) to discussion about structure and ultimately about principles. Structure is about relationships. The principles that generate these structures and relationships relate directly to the organizational value propositions and what they portend for trust between roles and individuals. See BEYOND PROCESS TO STRUCTURE AND VALUES (7.2).

Increasing trust and respect means engaging people who are not currently in dialogue. To engage them, you need to persuade them to become involved in something they currently aren't involved in. Block [Block 1983] defines politics as the attempt to have influence over that which one cannot control directly. Accordingly, this problem is fundamentally political in nature.

This problem can be attacked in two major ways. The first approach involves organizational team-building exercises, changes in reward mechanisms to encourage risk taking, or changes in management. The second approach assumes that such a core already exists somewhere *within* the structure of the larger organization and uses that core as the target for the patterns with hope that the health can spread to neighboring organizations.

Yet, before any positive change can happen, the organization must be ready to change. In our studies, we have seen organizations in various states of readiness for change. Let's explore the most common conditions that prime an organization for change.

6.1.1   Dissonance Precedes Resolution

In the timeless play *Fiddler on the Roof*, Tevye comments about his daughter and son-in-law in Siberia, noting that "They're so happy, they don't know how miserable they are." In the same vein, many organizations are not sufficiently self-aware to realize the problems they have. More commonly, though, some individuals in the organization are aware of the shortcomings in the organization. They may or may not know exactly what the problems are, but they do know that something is wrong. Unless enough key people in the organization acknowledge the organization's problems, however, things are unlikely to change.

In some cases, such as was true in our intervention at ParcPlace systems, the problems are already apparent. Other organizations, however, need prodding to face up to their problems. TEAM BUILDING (6.1.5) exercises can help people confront their problems by creating a crisis in the organization. The dissonance of a crisis is often a prerequisite for large-scale cultural change. In Virginia Satir's model of organizational change, such a stimulus is called a *foreign element* [Satir 1991]. It takes a foreign element to get an organization off of top dead-center.

One organization we studied was mired in cumbersome processes and overly focused on management. It was clear to us (and to the developers) that most of the troops chafed under their development processes, but the manager roles did not see the problem. The team-building exercise made the managers see things as the developers saw them, thus revealing the reality of the situation. This exercise resulted in serious introspection among the managers. It wasn't clear whether they were ready to change their organization, but the exercise did provide a golden opportunity for them to do so.

While we don't advocate that organizations should look for trouble, dissonances that present themselves may lead to opportunities for improvement. Dissonances that are vague, such as feelings that something somewhere isn't right, invite introspection exercises that can help sharpen the focus of pattern application.

6.1.2   Team Burnout

One of the biggest problems with teams is burnout. Organizations experiencing burnout may be particularly ready to change: They are looking for relief from *any* source. Yet the path to organizational improvement of team burnout is fraught with danger: The very conditions that make the team open to change may also sabotage such change. Let's explore the concept of *burnout* in more detail and consider some patterns that might be applied in cases of team burnout.

6.1.2.1   The Psychology of Burnout

Sometimes, ill feelings can pervade an entire group or team, and the resulting negative dynamics can often be laid at the feet of first- and second-level managers. If a team as a whole or the team's manager feels threatened, the team is in danger of succumbing to two near-term counter-measures that often go hand in hand: work harder and hunker down. Hard work, overtime, and shortened schedules are a common reaction to a wide spectrum of threats. A team will close in on itself in the interest of completely shutting off distractions that could sap its time and energy or that could in any way detract from a focused effort to maintain control. Such a response, an overapplication of the pattern FIREWALLS (4.2.9), can put the team at odds with influences that it should be heeding. The situation can lead to a spiral of increased desperation, harder work, and more overtime. These are the dynamics of burnout.

An organization that is burning out can't learn. In fact, such an organization doesn't take the time to learn; instead, all of its time is focused on the deliverable. It may even make stupid mistakes by failing to step back and see the big picture. This is why patterns like COMPLETION HEADROOM (4.1.10) and RECOMMITMENT MEETING (4.1.12) are crucial to a healthy organization. They keep the organization *open* to other individuals and teams—teams they depend on, and teams that depend on them.

A group in burnout often tries to take charge of everything it can because its members need the comfort of feeling they are in control. They may overstep their domain of authority and claim ownership for parts of the system outside their usual domain. A dysfunctional services group may rewrite parts of the operating system because they feel they can't trust the operating system people to do it right or to do it fast enough. In these scenarios, no one wins.

A worrisome sociological configuration arises in cases of extreme burnout. One strong team member—often, but not always, a manager or lead technical person—takes charge, usually by creating a culture of fear, intimidation, co-option, or coercion. The resulting configuration, fed by the controlling individual, discourages social discourse, openness, and interactions out-side the group. As a result, the group turns inward for all of its needs. In the most extreme cases of burnout, people spend much of their lives at the office, and team-centeredness extends beyond professional relationships to personal relationships. People start deriving their *personal* identity from work and from the team. Work relationships thus displace family relationships. The organi-zation becomes ingrown, and incest becomes a good metaphor for what happens to the organiza-tional family. The health of the organization and its individuals deteriorates, and there often is no turning back. Family and personal lives suffer. Eric Fogelin, a developer on the first release of Microsoft's Windows NT, had the following experience, as described by G. Pascal Zachary [Zachary 1994]:

> In the final push for the July release, ... [he] worked every day during the month of June, some days as long as twenty hours. He took most of his meals at Microsoft; the cafeterias on campus served breakfast and lunch, and a special meal was prepared for those working late on NT in building Two. Since he lived on an island about ninety minutes away, requiring a ferry ride to and from work, Fogelin never went home for thirty days during the height of the push. He slept on a cheap green cot he'd bought. It was nothing more than a piece of canvas stretched over a narrow metal frame. By day it stood upright near his desk, a sturdy reminder of the forfeiture of creature comforts for the soul of a computer program.

There is a small body of fascinating literature on this phenomenon. In particular, see the analyses by Bill White ([White 1997] and [White 1986]).

You've probably heard the term "get a life." People who work in healthy organizations have a life. They have outside interests, and their identity doesn't draw solely from their workplace or the work they produce. A healthy work environment—one that can sustain its employees, learn, and grow—gives people the time and freedom to pursue this individuation.

6.1.2.2   Crisis Management and Burnout

Ask a software professional about burnout, and crisis management or "death march" projects often come to mind. Some projects are poorly managed, and differing expectations between the customer and provider can lead to obvious burnout.

However, some organizations manage by crisis. It is exactly this mentality that Deming railed against. His arguments, instead, focus on driving fear from an organization and taking the power of crisis away [Deming 1986]. Some popular methods today, such as XP, offer this fear of fear as one of their prime drivers. But if one looks deeper, one can find a more complex form of crisis management.

A protracted crisis mentality creates burnout, even in the absence of a real crisis. For example, daily status meetings can be a hallmark of organizations in crisis. Thus, if the organization adopts a policy of daily status meetings, it perpetuates the crisis mode or even creates a crisis mode, which can incent people to work harder. Even when not at work, the people will have work on their minds so they can be prepared for the next day's status meeting. Other aspects of XP—such as the inability to work alone and the need to always have your thought processes open to a pair programmer—help sustain the crisis mentality.

Our studies have shown that crises strengthen management roles. In crises, managers tend to move toward the center of the organization, displacing the domain expert roles that carry the organization through everyday business. [A social network diagram depiction of this phenomenon is shown in STABILITY AND CRISIS MANAGEMENT (6.1.3)].

6.1.3   Stability and Crisis Management

Stewart Brandt [Brandt 1995] describes "sheer layers" of change in a building that evolve at different rates. The foundation changes rarely, and the plumbing and wiring also seldom change. The wallpaper and paint change quite a bit more frequently, and the interior decor is almost always in flux. Each one of these layers is part of the system we call a building. A crisis is a change that happens at a deep enough level that it goes beyond routine experience and touches the structure of the building (or organization), but it is also a shallow enough change that it doesn't stop the organization dead in its tracks. Furniture that has been moved wouldn't be construed as a crisis, whereas a leak in the plumbing would.

A crisis is almost always a surprise, an unforeseen glitch in the stability of the organization. A crisis upsets stability, and it does so precipitously. (We sometimes talk of the "software development crisis," but something that has gone on for 30 years can hardly be called a crisis!)

In the same sense that you want to build a new organization on the stable core inside the existing organization, you also want to keep the environment stable while you are making change. You don't want to be constantly changing the foundations. If the environment is noisy, and if the organization exhibits arbitrary behaviors, then you can never know whether a given change resulted in an improvement or made things worse (or neither!). This fundamental principle of organizational change is one of the deepest principles of Deming's approaches to organization management [Deming 1986], and one finds it at the foundations of ISO process-improvement methods.

The pattern approach to organizational improvement is attentive to the stable parts of an organization and attempts to detach itself from noisy, day-to-day variations. Part of this stability comes from attentiveness to the deep structure that ties to values and relationships; these tend to change less frequently than practices, policies, and processes. Part of this stability comes from role normalization.

Crises can and will arise, and some of the patterns [e.g., Sacrifice One Person (4.1.22) and Day Care (4.1.23)] specifically address contexts with a crisis component. However, these crises are small relative to the overall organizational structure and to the goals of the enterprise. Most of the patterns instead strive to head off crises; most of the scheduling patterns [e.g., Completion Headroom (4.1.10)] are of this nature, as are some of the structural patterns [Firewalls (4.2.9) and Engage Customers (4.2.6)].

Software development, like mountain climbing, is an inherently risky undertaking. In the software world, there are two types of risks: The risk that you won't reach your goal (the summit) and the risk that your product is a flop in the marketplace. These are risks we must take; in fact, we enjoy taking these risks! On the other hand, though, there are also risks that the whole undertaking will go to ground because we didn't plan for the weather or, more significantly, because the team doesn't function well in the face of unforeseen difficulty (e.g., see [Krakauer 1997]). These are the true risks we must avoid.

There is no pattern—or pattern language—for risk management. Risk averseness is an *emergent* property of healthy organizations. As in Alexander, there are no patterns for building a safe house; instead, safety is an *emergent* property of houses built around concepts of appropriately joined spaces that draw on a human context. We have provided this one section on crisis management in the book to address this popular concern and to draw out the principles we believe address that concern. Most of the solutions to so-called crisis management are distributed through these patterns:

- Compensate Success (4.2.25) describes the problem of rewarding people who excel under crisis situations.

- The Open/Closed Principle of Teams (6.1.4) describes the danger of making crisis management a way of life. (In some cultures, everything is treated as a crisis, making it impossible to identify the true crises.)

- The same section describes the psychology of burnout, which is closely tied to crisis-management styles.

- Stand-Up Meeting (5.2.7) takes a current crisis as its context.

- Team Per Task (4.1.21) is one way of isolating crises.

There are some things to be aware of in crisis situations. First, during a crisis an organization contracts and management influence increases. Consider the sociogram of a regression testing organization shown in Figure 6.1, which shows the relationships between roles under "normal" operations (connections between roles have been removed for clarity).

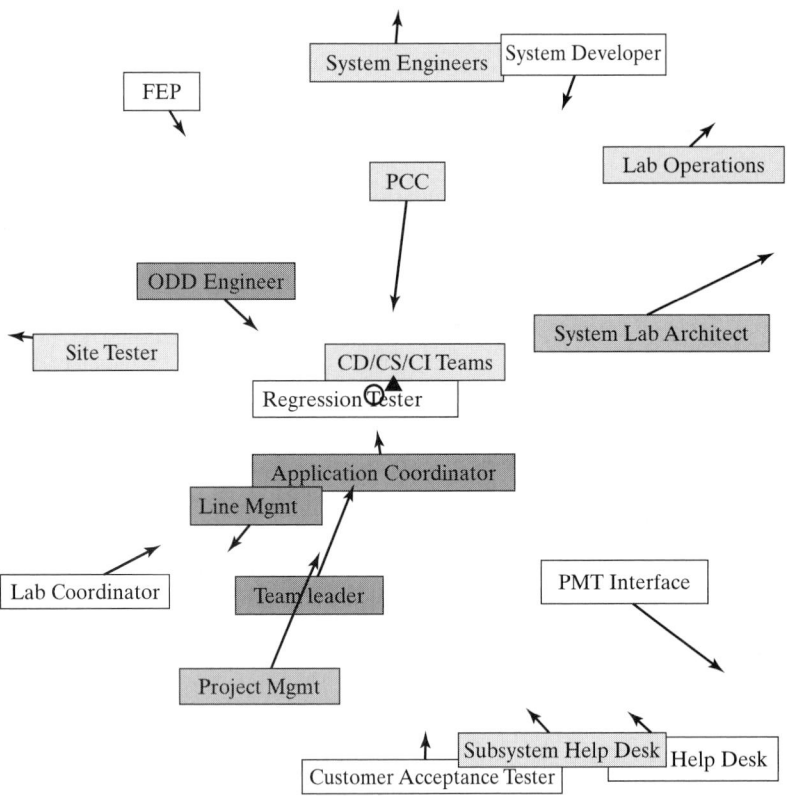

FIGURE 6.1 Relationship Between Roles under Normal Operations

The arrows depict how the roles are displaced in the social network diagram when the organization goes into crisis mode. Note that local control roles take over [Project Management, the Program Change Committee (PCC), Team Leader], while technical roles (like the Lab Architect) and even Line Management get out of the way. In fact, the process gurus [the Process Management Team (PMT)] are among the first to go! Coupling between roles skyrockets under stress, and the organization's "diameter" sharply decreases. This is a typical pattern that offers great expediency *as long as it does not become the norm for day-to-day business*. Note that one way to keep an organization stable is through a STAND-UP MEETING (5.2.7), where managers get frequent status from everyone. That pattern highlights the dangers of allowing ongoing daily meetings to perpetuate the crisis mentality. Such meetings are fine for redressing short-term crises, but prolonged recurrence of very frequent status meetings can create a crisis mentality. Every developer can relate to this problem.

In addition, crisis situations lead to suspension of the normal organization, which is replaced by an artificial, temporary organization. For example, a "firefighting" team might be organized to deal with a sudden serious quality problem in the software. Note, however, that firefighting can easily become a way of life: Firefighting teams usually get special rewards, which makes fire-fighting a desirable activity. Before long, the team is lurching from one crisis to another. Instead, you want to isolate firefighting activities [see TEAM PER TASK (4.1.21)].

Finally, crises can be a good thing. We don't believe that organizations should normally *seek* crises, but they also should not be so risk averse that crises create undue fear. Crises create opportunities for learning; a postmortem of a crisis can sow seeds of great organizational learning. A crisis in a healthy organization provides an "opportunity" for a retrospective [Kerth 2001].

Furthermore, crises create opportunities for large-scale culture changes. A perceived (and probably real) crisis at ParcPlace Systems precipitated a focused introspection and postmortem exercise that led to organizational renewal [Gabriel 1996].

In summary, crises can and will happen, and they can provide opportunities for learning. The learning should drive the organization to a better sense of order and stability, but not to the point where other changes can't surprise the organization into learning again!

6.1.4   The Open/Closed Principle of Teams

Change is disruptive, yet most people adapt to new situations extremely well. However, change is more disruptive to teams than to individuals, because there is an additive effect of the disruption to the individual members of the team. When change violates the open/closed principle of teams, the team may be ready to apply these patterns to achieve positive change.

Or not. Read on.

Bertrand Meyer teaches an *open/closed principle* of OO design [Meyer 2000] that combines two ideas:

- A class should be closed so that other classes don't come to be preoccupied with or otherwise depend on its internals.

- A class should be open to extension by inheritance so it can evolve into a new entity with both a new structure and behavior.

Team evolution also follows this principle. If a team does not have final say over its membership [SELF-SELECTING TEAM (4.2.11)], focus [TEAM PER TASK (4.1.21)], and direction, resentment will build, and the team will lose its sense of identity. Teams, of course, must sometimes negotiate with other individuals and organizations and sometimes must compromise, but as a rule teams should conduct their own business.

As a result, CONWAY'S LAW (5.1.7) is a key pattern in two of the pattern languages in this book. Teams and groups are built around domains of specialization and expertise, and teams are staffed with the people who can serve that discipline [DOMAIN EXPERTISE IN ROLES (4.2.22)]. Meddling from the outside only detracts from the team's focus.

So a team enjoys some autonomy in reaching a healthy steady state. But what about dealing with growth and dysfunction? And how about dealing with change? The outside world (e.g., the market and technology) is always changing! The team must remain open to external communication.

We can talk about this openness at two levels. As the software evolves, the architecture inevitably evolves, and the teams must align their software to track architectural creep. (Actually, each team's software *causes* the collective architectural creep, but from the perspective of any single team it appears as though the rest of the world is responsible for these changes.) So, though the team is *closed* to meddling with the invariants related to its core competencies, it must be *open* to changes in interactions with other parts of the system. Such architectural changes may change the organization's communication network.

For example, let's say that you're working on a telephone switching system, and your company is incorporating a new integrated circuit to accommodate market demand for a new protocol. The expertise about that chip resides in the heads of some people somewhere, and if you are going to develop software that interfaces with that chip, you're going to need to talk to those people. Conway's Law (5.1.7) runs rampant in dynamic projects.

This simple example is based on software change. Organizational change, however, can be much more subtle. Technological change (e.g., adding the new integrated circuit) doesn't seem all that frightening to most people. Organizational change, on the other hand, can seem like a strong threat. People can feel that their power base is threatened if they are made to report to a new manager. People can feel their job security is challenged if a new person is hired into the same area of specialty.

6.1.4.1   Empowerment

Sometimes the best laid plans of mice and men go astray. In complex systems such as human organizations, cause and effect can be quite separated from each other in time and space. Peter Senge makes the following observations [Senge 1990, p. 63]:

> A fundamental characteristic of complex human systems ... [is that] "cause" and "effect" are not close in time and space. By "effects," I mean the obvious symptoms that indicate that there are problems—drug abuse, unemployment, starving children, falling orders, and sagging profits. By "cause" I mean the interaction of the underlying system that is most responsible for generating the symptoms, and which, if recognized, could lead to changes producing lasting improvement. Why is this a problem? Because most of us assume they are—most of us assume, most of the time, that cause and effect are close in time and space.

Introducing an *empowerment* program is intended to increase the energy level, to remove constraints that will free people to do what the enterprise needs to have done, and to give people a sense of control over their destiny.

Think about this concept from the perspective of the open/closed principle. Empowerment increases the degree of closedness of a team. Giving a team autonomy might cause the team to weaken its interactions with important stakeholders and with sources of information and constraints that are important to the successful operation of the team. Empowerment might be particularly effective in diluting information exchanges with roles that exercise control in general and with management in particular. In theory, empowerment might create problems with respect to the open/closed principle. Unfortunately, we find these problems are very real in practice. We have seen such results in some of our organizational studies, and research from Rutgers also concludes that communication issues are a general outcome of empowerment programs [Yates 1995].

Empowerment is an attempt to achieve an effect (increasing individual leverage) by directly attacking its cause (the "distractions" of coupling and communication that "get in the way of work"). However, the solution cuts off the very nurturing that may have propelled the team to its level of performance in the first place. Empowerment, thus, is a possible contributor to burnout.

6.1.4.2   Schismogenesis

We have also seen a lighter though almost equally destructive form of this phenomenon, which we describe as *schismogenesis*. The term dates back to Gregory Bateson's [Bateson 1958] work with tribes along the Sepik River in New Guinea in 1936. *Symmetrical schismogenesis* occurs when two factions each rise in power (or in fear or distrust of each other) and form cliques or splinter groups that tend to focus inward rather than resolve issues in dialogue with each other. This phenomenon is also a natural outgrowth of efforts to merge separate companies, which can be difficult since disparate groups already exist with different values and cultures. The merger, engendering fears of job cuts, sows fear and distrust just at the time the organizations need to learn to work with each other.

Complementary schismogenesis occurs when a stronger side is compelled to actions by its fear of being taken down by a weaker side. We have seen this phenomenon in organizations experiencing the stress of an impending downsizing program, where the core members of the organization become disconnected from the support arms of the organization. It also occurs in mature organizations, where power structures have become entrenched. Complementary schismogenesis is the main reason for the patterns Responsibilities Engage (5.1.14) and Hallway Chatter (5.1.15), which are derived from an earlier pattern named Buffalo Mountain whose purpose was in part to address schismogenesis. The pattern The Watercooler (5.1.20) can also help reduce tensions between constituencies by creating a "place" for new social structures that are allowed to violate institutional structures. The Hallway Chatter pattern gives an example of an organization exhibiting schismogenesis.

It may be obvious at this point, but organizations suffering from serious issues related to empowerment and schismogenesis are not candidates for use of the patterns in this book. Application of the patterns requires open dialogue and interaction. It also requires focus and a *healthy* sense of team pride [see Unity of Purpose (4.2.12)]. This issue, of course, is not black and white. The balance between an open and a closed organization is somewhat subjective. It is also true that burnout is a spectrum. For example, organizations sometimes need people to put in long periods of hard work. But to go more than a month with consistent 60-hour weeks is a real danger sign. Even if the organization is not suffering from burnout, individual effectiveness and efficiency wear down very quickly after a lengthy death march.

Many of the patterns in this book address this issue in an attempt to keep the organization vibrant and healthy *so that it can adapt to change.* A closed organization has difficulty changing effectively. Look at the Public Character (4.2.17), who helps information flow efficiently, or the Gatekeeper (4.2.10), who explicitly breaks down barriers around the organization and helps balance the Firewalls (4.2.9) pattern. Hallway Chatter (5.1.15) reflects an informal social infrastructure of both technical and friendly exchanges in the workplace. Even Developing in Pairs (4.2.28) can be a useful pattern for the exchange of ideas and information across groups if the pairing is done across team and organizational boundaries. And, of course, it's important to keep in contact with the people who pay the bills by using patterns like Engage Customers (4.2.6).

6.1.5 Team Building

There is an aspect of team building in every organizational intervention we've done. After all, the goal of an organizational study is to analyze the communication in the organization, for such communication is the foundation of team dynamics. Team building can have the unanticipated and beneficial side effect of pointing out the necessity of change. Hidden wounds come to the surface, where they can receive the treatment they need.

As described in How the Patterns Came to Us (Chapter 2), role-playing is a staple of our research technique. We bring the organization together in one room where they role-play one of their processes that needs attention (e.g., the design-coding process, the testing process, the acquisition process, the analysis process, or the field support process).

One of our goals is to put the team members into the psychological roles they play on a day-to-day basis. In a large group, this activity helps the group as a whole see itself in action and see the patterns of interaction that emerge. Reflecting on these patterns, these communication structures within the group, is the main foundation of organizational growth and renewal.

In addition, the formal role-play can sometimes be the key to more powerful modes of introspection or to processes that are more suitable to the organization's culture or comfort zones. At Allianz, we did some initial role-play exercises with two of the development teams. Those exercises prompted a bit more dialogue and interest in organizational issues, but they themselves did not initiate major changes in ways of doing business. However, those initial studies led to follow-up work to explore the application of DEVELOPING IN PAIRS (4.2.28) and other ideas from XP [Beck 1999] under the leadership of Thomas Tik of Allianz, Jim Coplien, and Laurie Williams of North Carolina State University. We decided to hold an offsite meeting with the engineering teams. There, we created an environment for open, constructive criticism of management, and we left open a lot of unstructured time for discussion. In addition, we spent time teaching the teams about DEVELOPING IN PAIRS. These activities led to some important management insights. Later, we were able to draw from this experience to leverage change at the next higher level of management, which broke a logjam that opened the floodgates of dialogue at the next level. Organizational improvement followed as a result.

Similarly, at ParcPlace Systems [Gabriel 1996] we held a team role-play exercise. The vice president of engineering, Richard Gabriel, had already started creating history timelines and developing other forums that built on the team's frustration with its current state and on its desire to return to the environment of its glory days. The role-play was a watershed event to the extent that it underscored much of the dysfunction in the organization at that time and provided external corroboration of the current state of affairs. It also provided a forum where the team members could start thinking about patterns and talking about their dysfunction in terms of patterns. While the role-play exercise was only a fraction of the overall introspection effort, it was one of the main introspective events that involved the *entire* team, and it offered foundations to support ongoing dialogue and organizational renewal. Yes, they even used some of the patterns in the process of turning the organization around. But more importantly, they wrote their *own* organizational patterns and took charge of their destiny. This sense of ownership and control, along with the creation and implementation of a tangible body of patterns was the centerpiece of the organizational turnaround.

Techniques such as organizational role-play can help develop the models and shared perspectives that form the seeds of the dialogue that strengthens a team. A *retrospective* [Kerth 2001] is a powerful team-building tool that yields both explicit and implicit benefits (e.g., the aforementioned role-playing exercise is a form of retrospective). Most importantly, retrospectives help build a foundation for trust between the members of an organization. Seeing themselves in relationship to others helps people establish models of expected behaviors. These models either open communication paths or show where communication paths have broken down because of mistrust, environmental factors, temperament mismatches, and other factors. Team dialogue can identify environmental and other factors, as well as actually strengthen the most important factor: trust. The patterns in this book can offer a rallying point for the team and can offer a shared vocabulary for talking about the team's problems and potential solutions. But many other team-building techniques can be equally effective.

6.1.6 Building on the Solid Core

An awareness of the need for change does not mean that the organization is ready for change. The team (not just the individuals who make up the team) must be willing to change. Many teams are lucky enough to have a solid core of people, which tends to make change easier. The team members thus have a shared sense of security and are less worried about the impact of change.

In the case of both ParcPlace Systems and Allianz, we found a solid core of people to start working with. Establishing a core group is almost always preferred to doing team building for its own sake, because the structures are already in place to support the communication and dialogue necessary to discuss *improvements* to communication and dialogue!

In the case of ParcPlace Systems, the engineering group was drawn together by a common sense of disappointment and by a desire to have a feeling of control. From this perspective, it wasn't an ideal organization for the application of organizational patterns. But on the other hand, desperation can drive out fear. We visited the organization, held a role-playing exercise, and provided an initial round of evaluations. Afterwards, we left them with the knowledge that they were indeed in very bad shape. Coming to grips with that fact perhaps gave the group courage to do things it otherwise wouldn't have done.

In the case of Allianz, the engineering group was one of several groups that had difficulty integrating their processes into the work environment. There was strong support for organizational work in second-level management and to some degree in third-level management, while first-level management (team leaders) were more focused on technical solutions than on organizational solutions. But the support for organizational work was stronger in engineering than in the other organizations. This concern for human issues was evident in the engineering work environment. For example, a high degree of camaraderie and interworking could be found within the engineering team—and with their colleagues in the other teams. Further, their concerns about organizational health related more to the interactions between teams than to the dynamics within their own teams, since they had already reflected on these intrateam dynamics and had reached a point of satisfaction with their own operation.

The adoption of patterns in the small cohesive teams gave those teams tools for dealing with other organizations in the enterprise. These patterns gave those teams a firmer foundation for establishing congruent, productive relationships with the other organizations, showing them how to stop relying on the more contentious and sometimes (openly or subversively) combative behaviors of the past. Reinforced ideas involving integrity and well-reasoned behavior became more difficult to subdue than in the past, which, in turn, caused behavior changes and even doubts in the other organizations. The growth experienced by one organization led to the eventual spread of the culture change to those organizations as well.

The key in both cases was to start with the healthiest team—in terms of its ability to introspect and learn—and to nurture it.

6.2 Piecemeal Growth

Once your organization is primed for change, where do you go from there? How do you start applying the patterns?

The answer is simple: Pick a pattern to start with and then begin applying the patterns one at a time. We will go into more detail shortly, but first a warning: Do not attempt to apply all of these patterns at once! Do not sit down with the pattern book in one hand and your organizational plan in the other and attempt to redesign your whole organization. These patterns must be applied in a piecemeal fashion. In fact, the only way an organization can change effectively is if it grows and matures organically.

A style of organizational design that believes in formalism, repeatability, and control is typified by ISO 9001 compliance programs. Perhaps Osterweil's (now quite out of vogue) process programming proposal [Sutton Lerner Osterweil 1997] is the epitome of this school of organizational design. Such approaches suggest that if we get everything right up front, everything else will run smoothly.

Unfortunately, it is impossible to foresee all of the complexities that beset even the healthiest organizations. Human behavior is extremely difficult to predict because it emerges from thousands of considerations and inputs, each weighted differently, that feed the decision processes behind organizational evolution. Unpredictable human behavior makes it difficult to plan organizational structure. Changes in economic conditions and markets, the employment roll, the law, and even the national mood can upset organizational design.

Some organizational structures change slowly and can provide stable foundations for the evolution of an organizational design. These structures come not from predictions about the future, but instead from an analysis of the past. Such structures can be formalized using techniques such as domain analysis, and in this case one can make an analogy between domain analysis and patterns, especially those patterns included in PROJECT MANAGEMENT PATTERN LANGUAGE (4.1).

But most of the time, successful organizational growth takes place in a piecemeal fashion, in real time. One of the pattern chapters, PIECEMEAL GROWTH PATTERN LANGUAGE (4.2), contains patterns about how an organization grows and develops—gradually. Note, however, that although you apply the patterns one at a time, they do not operate in isolation from one another. In a process of piecemeal growth, you must consider the eventual application of *all* of the patterns.

In a piecemeal-growth environment, the focus is on ongoing *repair* rather than on forecasting and anticipation. In fact, all design is in some respect an act of ongoing repair: We employ feedback derived from the emerging design to modulate the direction of the design from that point on. It is even better when one is dealing with receiving feedback from a live system, rather than working in the abstract with only a design. Nature works the same way. Organizations, and their evolution, seem to follow the laws of nature more than the laws of modular design in any field with human-created artifacts. And nature works in the now, with feedback, employing repair.

The piecemeal growth philosophy comes from Alexander's vision of how patterns should be used and pervades his work. The six-step process described in THE FUNDAMENTAL PROCESS (6.2.1) is derived from his yet unpublished work *The Nature of Order.* (The first three volumes have been published so far [Alexander 2003].) But piecemeal growth also surfaces frequently as a key management strategy. One of the main principles of organizational change in AT&T organizations in the 1980s was that one shouldn't try to change more than three things at once. Culture can change, but at its core it loves stability.

More broadly, the pattern philosophy of piecemeal growth is a broadening of the popular notion (particularly during the late 1980s) of *organizational learning.* Of several excellent books on organizational learning, our favorite is *Becoming a Learning Organization: Beyond the Learning Curve* by Joop Swieringa and Andre Wierdsma [Swieringa Wierdsma 1992]. There are strong parallels between the organizational learning field and patterns. For example, each believes in building on a small number of principles that generate rich emergent behavior; as a result, complex systems of rules don't work [Swieringa Wierdsma 1992, p. 9].

A pattern-based piecemeal-growth repair process is robust for two major reasons. First, we don't do random things at random times. The patterns encode wisdom born of experience and follow sequences that have repeatedly worked in the past. Second, the patterns build structures that themselves offer a degree of resiliency under change. DOMAIN EXPERTISE IN ROLES (4.2.22) and FUNCTION OWNER AND COMPONENT OWNER are good examples of patterns that help an organization ride through common changes. If one organized around expertise related to a given product, the organizational structure would be sensitive to changes in the market. The market can be fickle and tends to change much more rapidly than the expertise associated with a given domain. FUNCTION OWNER AND COMPONENT OWNER honors the tradition of giving focus to the marketable item; after all, that's where the money is. At the same time, it guards the long-term stable structure of the system, its underlying knowledge, and the organization that sustains it by *also* according ownership on the basis of components. DOMAIN EXPERTISE IN ROLES helps the organization build foundations around core competencies rather than around current market (or management) fads. The organizational patterns encode this robustness and experience.

The PROJECT MANAGEMENT PATTERN LANGUAGE (4.1) can provide the principles and structures to get you started. It offers many long-term stable domain structures related to organizational structure in general and software development organizational structure in particular. Rough forms of these patterns will fall in place early in the formation of a new organization, and these patterns can be fine-tuned over months or maybe even years. While DEVELOPMENT EPISODE (4.1.15) can be an almost methodological construct, one that can be implemented almost overnight, patterns like WORK FLOWS INWARD (4.1.18) have more emergent results that come about over time. And even the seemingly simpler patterns like DEVELOPMENT EPISODE initiate cultural changes that will breed discomfort and take some getting used to. Each pattern is a small foreign—even upsetting—element in its own right [see DISSONANCE PRECEDES RESOLUTION (6.1.1)]. Still, the PROJECT MANAGEMENT PATTERN LANGUAGE provides a good "starter set" of patterns for *most* organizations. But your mileage will vary, and you should *defer to your instinct and insight.*

That foundation in place, you can slowly make improvements by applying one, or maybe two, patterns at a time. Fundamental to the nature of patterns is that each can be applied in its own right without undue consideration of other patterns. Each pattern encapsulates a set of forces, or trade-offs [see WHAT ARE PATTERN LANGUAGES? (1.2)], that are as independent as possible from the forces in other patterns. Ideally, each can be applied in isolation. Ideally, there is no backtracking.

There are, of course, limits to this idealistic approach. An organization is a system, and a system view can keep you from being blindsided. There is no formula or recipe for combining pattern applications; indeed, your deeper insight will tell you the proper mix. As authors of this book, we trust you to shepherd your organization and build on that insight. We provide some hints in the form of patterns and some insights on how organizations tend to work well, and we trust that this guidance will serve as inspiration for you. This book is not a textual medicine cabinet, and patterns are not magic remedies for curing ills [see ORGANIZATIONAL PATTERNS ARE INSPIRATION RATHER THAN PRESCRIPTION (6.3.2)].

6.2.1   The Fundamental Process

There is a rhythm to the application of patterns, and people tend to underestimate the *process* that makes patterns work. That process involves piecemeal growth. One follows a *sequence* through the pattern language to increase wholeness, one pattern at a time. How, basically, does this process work? Here is a synopsis of the process, derived from [Alexander 2003]:

1. Consider your organization as a whole, get a feeling for how the entire enterprise (e.g., the development group or the department) is working, and try to pinpoint its "weak spots." Maybe you have recently applied another pattern, which left you in a new *context*. What forces are unresolved in that context, either from incompleteness in the pattern you just applied or from other forces in the system that have now become visible or taken on a higher priority?

2. Focus on what can be done to increase organizational wholeness. "Wholeness" here reflects your personal and corporate values. Are you striving for profitability? If so, what are the weaknesses in your organization related to profitability? And, is profitability *really* your main concern right now, or is morale affecting productivity, which is in turn affecting profitability? Dig deeper. Read about the patterns—and particularly about their forces—to help resolve these questions. Reflection is key: It is important to focus on *recurring* issues and to avoid reacting to immediate concerns or to concerns that bear a high priority at the moment.

3. Find a place where the application of a new pattern—the creation of a new role, the addition of a new group, the restructuring of a process—will achieve your goal. Will any of the patterns help you? Do *you* know of other techniques that will help, regardless whether they bear the pattern banner? (We don't get paid by how many of our patterns you use; our satisfaction comes from helping organizations succeed!) Don't get stuck in pattern tunnel vision. And, be sure to take good notes—today's odd heuristic might be tomorrow's pattern, and we want you to record your ideas.

4. Apply that pattern or technique *locally*: Think locally, and act locally [Gabriel 2000]. *But* apply the pattern in a way that might also increase the wholeness at the next level in the organizational structure or in the next larger context or scope.

5. Strive for balance. Most of the patterns here are communication patterns. Communication is rarely a one-party phenomenon; instead, it tends to affect at least two loci. When you apply most of these patterns, then, there will be some kind of local symmetry. Be attentive to that symmetry and attend to both sides of the communication, structure, or other facet of the pattern.

6. Reflect on the implementation of the pattern Does it feel right? Does it work? Filter the feedback from the organization, keeping in mind that people will generally resist change. Are structure and behavior trending in a direction that increases organizational wholeness? **If not, back out.** It is much better to back out at this local level, with respect to the application of a single pattern, than to forge blindly ahead and do more damage. Eventually, a good pattern will lead you to a new context—and to a new set of forces to balance and of problems to address.

This process iterates after the pattern has had time to gain acceptance in the culture. Results might take days, or they might take months. Again, use your judgment.

Piecemeal growth is guided by *sequences*. A pattern language is a graph, and there are almost innumerable useful paths through it. There are two cues you can use to know which pattern to apply next. First, look at the structure of the pattern language. The individual patterns indicate which patterns should come next as refinements and progressive steps, and the pattern language graphs can also be a guide. Second, use the sequences that other organizations have followed as guides. CASE STUDIES (PART IV) examines the paths followed by several organizations on their rough road to success. These stories can offer powerful insights into business choices, and we offer them to you for that reason. Read them through and look for things that hit home.

6.2.2 When Do I Apply These Patterns?

If you are familiar with design patterns in software architecture, then you probably feel that the time to apply a pattern is obvious: when a problem arises during design or implementation. That said, when do you apply organizational patterns?

Remember that the *system* you are building is more of a human organization than a software artifact. Change upsets organizations. Good change comes from a process of consensus, and it takes time and focus to develop consensus. Project retrospectives [Kerth 2001] are an opportune time to consider the new application of organizational patterns to the organization. Retrospectives are an opportunity to consider the organization as a whole and to find the pressure points of change that will give rise to the right kinds of emergent structure and behavior. Making changes during a consciously planned retrospective helps avoid the need to make decisions in the heat of battle and helps lead the team to changes that are more systemic and less reactionary in nature.

It is better to introduce organizational patterns between development cycles rather than in the middle of a cycle. Pattern implementation may coincide with a project delivery, a change in technology, or perhaps an externally imposed change in organizational structure. Remember to make piecemeal and local changes.

The patterns in PEOPLE AND CODE PATTERN LANGUAGE (5.2) might be applied as problems arise during development cycles. These patterns are a hybrid between organizational patterns and software design patterns.

6.2.3 Writing Your Own Patterns

Each organization has its own patterns of effective communication and development. There are many different kinds of software development organizations, and an organization that develops embedded software is likely to be quite different than one that develops in-house interactive tools. Each of these organizations is typified by its patterns.

The patterns in this book are neither universal individually nor complete as a set. Each organization can augment this book's patterns with its own patterns. Again, retrospectives provide an opportunity to capture good patterns and add them to the repertoire of good organizational practices.

See the story of the resurrection of the ParcPlace Systems team in [Gabriel 1996] for an example of a team that rebuilt itself around a pattern-writing effort.

6.2.4 Master Planning and the Theory of Constraints

One contemporary management fad is presented in Goldratt's *Critical Chain* [Goldratt 1997] and *Theory of Constraints* [Goldratt 1999], which has both some similarities to and some stark differences from the aforementioned process. It is similar in that the focus at any given time is local and is situated at a particular juncture of problems. But the pattern approach differs from Goldratt's approach in that there is a broader theory and structure guiding the process, a structure based not only on action/reaction but also on encoded experience. Goldratt's techniques are more applicable to industrial and inventory processes that are less tainted by human emotion and dynamics. The pattern process is more suitable to organizations, which have a life of their own.

The greatest danger is to try to take control, to attempt to foresee *exactly* how patterns will work together, and to plan now in a way that anticipates how you will plan in 6 months' time. The world is more complex than that [see PEOPLE ARE LESS PREDICTABLE THAN CODE (6.3.6)]. An organization is an ever-evolving structure, and organizational process improvement happens in the present. It pays to know history, and one shouldn't ignore the market and technological trends coming over the horizon; however, planning structure based on predictions of human behavior is usually a mistake. This concept is difficult for most managers to grasp because it requires a "letting go." Let go. Think locally and act locally, and trust your instinct and experience, as well as the experience encoded in the sequences of the pattern language.

6.2.5   Communication and Organizational Learning

We mentioned that organizational learning is a key property of effective organizations. Many of the patterns in this book concern effective communication in an organization. But communication can't have a long-term impact unless group learning occurs. Such learning requires introspection. So, the second main component of long-term viable teams is that they take time to introspect. This concept, of course, builds on good communication skills and leads to UNITY OF PURPOSE (4.2.12), which is one of the core properties of any effective team.

6.3 Some General Rules

We wish organizational science were, in fact, a science, but it's not. Organizational improvement is an art that requires craftsmanship in building the right structures, as well as a fine human touch. And it requires innovations, some of which have come to us in dealing with organizations over time.

In this section, we offer some brief, general rules for how to apply the patterns. Most of these rules have come from our experience during the past 10 years, but others come from more general principles of patterns.

6.3.1   Make Love, Not War

The great Chinese generals observed that they who achieve their goals without fighting are the most victorious. There are fewer victories and winners in wartime than in peacetime. Most people are well-intentioned, given reasonable hope of a secure future, and are driven by seeing their needs met. The art of negotiation is to bring as many peoples' needs, and then desires, into alignment as possible.

Sometimes circumstances make it impossible to avoid fundamental conflict. If the enterprise is cutting staff, it is rare that any amount of negotiation will be able to save everyone's jobs and positions in the company. In these situations, people are driven by needs that are lower on the Maslow hierarchy [Maslow 1987] and will act in ways that others may find less professional or civilized. These situations call for particularly strong leadership and tough decisions. These situations also call for constructive action: Inaction is sometimes worse than either going to war or avoiding war. The worst thing that can happen is for people to sit around and plan their investment strategies for survival and life after the organization goes bankrupt; it is important for leadership to stay energetically focused on solving the problem. The goal of this leadership and of these decisions is to facilitate dialogue among people who are concerned about their joint welfare all at the *same* level of the Maslow hierarchy of needs. If one can build on health at the lower levels of the hierarchy and carry on this dialogue at the higher levels, so much the better.

Having achieved that level of stability, the process of inclusion and dialogue can start. This process needn't always be genteel and highbrow. For example, perhaps everyone is worried about the company going bankrupt within a few months or about the parent company firing all of its employees. Desperation is the mother of invention—or it can be, under leadership that can rally such a group to introspection and dialogue. But success comes from dealing constructively with the problem rather than from making war on a shared enemy.

6.3.2   Organizational Patterns Are Inspiration Rather Than Prescription

The first thing to remember is that these organizational patterns, like all patterns, are not meant to be applied blindly or wholesale. The patterns are synthesized from many diverse experiences, and your situation will surely be different than those we have observed. Therefore, the patterns are intended to serve as inspiration, rather than as a blueprint to be followed exactly.

Most of us tend to be solution oriented, and we naturally focus on the solutions in patterns. Yet the *problem* in a pattern is as important as the solution. The insights we gain about the problem—captured most often in the forces—can be just as helpful as the solution itself. In many cases, the solution becomes clear once we understand the problem thoroughly.

As you read the patterns, look for problems that are similar to problems that you now have or that you once had. But don't look for exact matches, because they won't exist. You unleash the power in the patterns when you learn to adapt them to your own situations.

6.3.3   It Depends on Your Role in Your Organization

As you read these patterns, it will soon be apparent that you lack the power or the authority to implement many of them. For example, few of us are in a position to COMPENSATE SUCCESS (4.2.25), simply because we don't hold the purse strings of the organization. Frankly, many of these patterns have management overtones, and nonmanagers are relatively powerless to apply them. Furthermore, many of the "nonmanagement" patterns apply to specialized roles; ARCHITECT ALSO IMPLEMENTS (5.2.10), for example, applies to only a few roles.

You can address this reality in one of two ways. You can become angry and frustrated. You can even identify yourself with Dilbert and begin to see your manager as the pointy-haired boss.

There is a much better way to react, though. Instead of focusing on what you can't change, focus on the patterns that may apply to you. That set of patterns varies depending on your role. For example, you might find it useful to ENGAGE CUSTOMERS (4.2.6) or ENGAGE QUALITY ASSURANCE (4.2.29). Perhaps you see yourself as a GATEKEEPER (4.2.10) or a MATRON ROLE (4.2.18). It may be worthwhile to strive to become so good at what you do that you eventually become a LEGEND ROLE (4.2.20).

In reality, we will react both ways because we're human. The trick is to try to let go of the things we can't change or to at least use them as filtering mechanisms when we consider taking a position in a new organization.

6.3.4   It Depends on the Context of the Organization

Obviously, every organization is different. Therefore, every organization will use these patterns somewhat differently. For a given organization at a given time, certain patterns may be very important, others may be only somewhat useful, and still others may not apply at all. So, how do you use these patterns to best advantage?

Note that every pattern has a context that defines the boundaries of usefulness for that pattern. The context generally shows up at the beginning of the pattern description, although some context is buried in the exposition of the problem. It is often difficult to separate the context and the problem, so you should read them both carefully to determine how they fit in your particular organization. Note that the context of an organization changes over time. In particular, consider the following questions:

- How large is your organization? In addition, how large and complex is the software you are working on? Several of these patterns apply best to large or small organizations.
- How mature is your organization? How long have people worked together? In mature organizations, the roles tend to be well understood. New organizations will find the patterns of piecemeal growth of the organization more useful.
- How mature is the software under development? This maturity level is different from the maturity of the organization. Hub, Spoke, and Rim (5.1.17), for example, is more appropriate for mature software.
- What is the culture of the organization? Sometimes, the organization's culture makes it easier—or harder—to apply certain patterns.

6.3.5 Organizational Patterns Are Used by Groups Rather Than by Individuals

There are many things we can do as individuals to become more effective in our organizational environment. We can improve our knowledge through study and practice, and we can improve the way we do things. We might, for example, follow Watts Humphrey's personal software process [Humphrey 1995]. But applying organizational patterns is not something we do alone.

Some patterns, however, are oriented toward individuals. The Gatekeeper (4.2.10) and Matron Role (4.2.18) patterns, for example, describe single-person roles. Yet, on closer examination, these roles are useful because of how they interact with others. They thus cease to exist in isolation. Even a Solo Virtuoso (4.2.5) is set up and managed by another person. Furthermore, a critical key to the power of patterns is that they establish a shared high-context vocabulary intended for use by groups.

So the question becomes not only how to disseminate knowledge of the patterns throughout the organization, but also how to get people to use them. While nothing replaces old-fashioned evangelism, we can offer a few specific suggestions.

One approach is to spread the word pseudosubversively. Dick Gabriel, for example, left copies of the patterns by the printer so that people could read about them. You can also call out the patterns as you see them (or see their need) in your organization. People will become curious about Conway's Law (5.1.7) and ask questions.

The most effective way we have seen to introduce these patterns is through organizational studies. Such studies not only provide a natural forum for introducing the patterns, but they also expose the need for them. We heartily recommend this experience.

6.3.6 People Are Less Predictable Than Code

Perhaps the biggest challenge of organizations is that they are made up of people. And people are not as well behaved as computers! Although we may not like to admit it, computers do pretty much what we tell them to. People, on the other hand, don't necessarily do what we want or even what we expect.

The results of applying organizational patterns, therefore, are going to be inherently less predictable than the result of applying OO design patterns, for example. Imagine that your organization uses the RESPONSIBILITIES ENGAGE (5.1.14) pattern to help communication. But what happens if two people involved simply don't like each other? Personalities play a large part in organizations.

Organizational patterns have everything to do with the culture of the organization. Remember that applying these patterns requires, in many instances, changes to the organization's culture. Because culture is deeply ingrained in organizations, these changes can be difficult and sometimes even painful to implement.

6.3.7 The Role of Management

Managers are in a unique and paradoxical position with respect to organizational effectiveness. On the one hand, they have little or no direct impact on the product being developed. Manager roles are support roles rather than PRODUCER ROLES (5.1.3). The only way managers can contribute value to the corporation is through the efforts of the producers they manage. Management is limited to changing policies and organizational structures in order to influence the behaviors of individuals and groups. Managers are particularly powerless.

Furthermore, it may be the case that great managers are the product of the great organizations they head as much as organizations are the product of their own talents. Kroeber [see PATTERNS IN ANTHROPOLOGY (7.1)] talks about the role of genius in culture. We think of Aristotle and Plato as exemplifying the greatness of Greek philosophy, and we think of them as having *produced* that philosophy ([Kroeber 1948], p. 145). But it is more likely that the culture produced the philosophers and that the philosophers articulated the latent structures and concepts that the culture was primed to deliver. Aristotle and Plato are, therefore, remembered as great leaders, while the masses fade into collective obscurity.

Along similar lines of reasoning, Kroeber argues that great inventions such as the telescope, logarithms, calculus, photography, and the telephone are products of their respective cultures and not of the individuals usually associated with them. As evidence, he notes that each of these landmark achievements were made by at least two discoverers *in the same era* (in most all cases by individuals whose efforts were unknown to each other). The telescope was independently invented by Jansen, Lippershey, and Metius in 1608; logarithms, by Napier in 1614 and Burgi in 1620; calculus, by Newton in 1671 and Leibnitz in 1676; photography, by Daguerre and Niepce and by Talbot, both in 1839; and the telephone, by Bell and Gray, both in 1876. He lists about 20 other such historical coincidences ([Kroeber 1948], p. 149).

By similar reasoning, great corporate managers—and even great line management supervisors—might be as much a product of the culture of their groups and corporations as the groups and corporations are products of their excellence. The patterns and the culture lead an organization to excellence; the manager is the figurehead, mouthpiece, or icon that serves as the catalyst for progress made towards achieving excellence. [This same reasoning has sobering repercussions for common American interpretations of COMPENSATE SUCCESS (4.2.25).]

Therefore, we feel that the best thing a manager can do is to lead a culture where it wants to go. This role wields a great deal of power in shaping the organization and in helping both individuals and the organization work effectively. Managers can instill vision, sponsor the organization, and protect the organization from distractions. These contributions may be indirect, but they can also be sizable.

Many of our patterns are best applied by managers, which should come as no surprise since the creation, care, and feeding of organizations tends to be responsibilities of management. Even those patterns applied by individual developers are usually influenced in some way by nearby manager roles.

Managers can apply some of our patterns by themselves or even *to* themselves. For example, managers should protect developers from distractions by becoming Firewalls (4.2.9). They might be advocates of the group and even serve in a Patron Role (4.2.15) capacity. They can mold roles in their organization with Team Per Task (4.1.21), Size the Organization (4.2.2), and Owner per Deliverable (A.5.19). To a certain extent, they may be able to effectively Compensate Success (4.2.25), although some reward policies are dictated from stratospheric levels in the corporation.

Note that most of these activities can be viewed as keeping the organization in its own element and focusing on what makes that organization good, rather than as activities that attempt to bring good or guidance to the organization. This rule of thumb is a guiding principle in all of these patterns. A corollary for managers is that a great manager probably cannot save a dysfunctional culture, but a poor manager might be able to keep an otherwise viable culture from thriving. We view these patterns as tools that help the manager guide the organization in finding its way, at the system level, partly by steering the manager away from practices that might stunt organizational growth.

Managers can nurture critical roles that are outside of their own sphere, such as Public Character (4.2.17), Matron Role (4.2.18), Legend Role (4.2.20), and Wise Fool (4.2.21). They cannot force these or other patterns to be adopted by the team, but they might encourage their use. Often, a team is primed to make a change and just needs a light to show them the way. Further, one might argue that if the desire to make major changes isn't already in the soul of the organization, those changes can't happen regardless of managerial intent. Dick Gabriel made copies of the patterns in this book and left them by the printer. He encouraged the team to pick them up and read them, and they did so. Then the team applied the patterns themselves; Dick didn't forcefeed the patterns to the group (and he probably wouldn't have been successful had he tried).

It is important for managers to realize the limitations of their influence. They exercise their influence when appropriate, but they don't try to do more than is possible. We might remember the example of Oscar Hammerstein, who collaborated with Richard Rodgers on many Broadway musicals. When a friend once asked Hammerstein what it was like to work with Rodgers, he said, "I just hand him a lyric and jump out of the way" [Linkletter 1968].

An internal AT&T management publication once featured a cartoon with a manager standing at the podium of an orchestra. The manager, clearly having been called to do something above his station and outside his experience, has opened the score to find the words "Wave the baton until the music stops, and turn around and bow."

CHAPTER 7

Anthropological Foundations

Most organizations, including software development organizations, have cultures and styles they can call their own. Yet we can talk about software cultures that map onto technologies or industry segments and that cross organizational, corporate, and national boundaries, and we dare to even speak of a "software development culture" at the highest level.

Too often, computer people use their own tools—processes, tasks, and functions—to describe the structure and practices of their organizations. Since we followed cultural leanings in writing this book, we thought it would be a good idea to build on insights and foundations from anthropology, the formal world of the study of culture.

Certainly, much more work can be done in this area, and some anthropologists are pursuing the study of such organizations (e.g., [Brajkovich 1994]). Broad cultural findings might be turned into relevant insights. For example, we find that most of the patterns we have discovered have a strong element of *polychronic culture* in them, meaning that the cultures value personal relationships over objects and value broad social networks over punctuality. This concept seems paradoxical in a world of introverted engineers working toward deadlines and schedules. The contrast, in fact, is striking. Anthropological tools can highlight and perhaps explain these contrasts in ways that prior models cannot (and should not).

We look at a few interesting aspects of culture and anthropological foundations in the next few sections. We also look at closely related patterns in other contemporary pattern languages. These sections are supplementary to understanding and applying the patterns, but they offer an interesting historical context.

7.1 Patterns in Anthropology

Most software designers ascribe the origins of the contemporary pattern discipline to the building architect Christopher Alexander, whose works (e.g., [Alexander 1977] and [Alexander

1979]) are often cited as the inspiration for software patterns. However, patterns have broader and much older roots than Alexander's work, finding expression in mathematics and the natural sciences. Some of the most interesting work (and certainly the most relevant work to our interests here) is the research on anthropological patterns by early anthropologists like A. L. Kroeber [Kroeber 1948].

Kroeber writes the following:

> Patterns are those arrangements or systems of internal relationship which give to any culture its coherence or plan, and keep it from being a mere accumulation of random bits. They are therefore of primary importance ([Kroeber 1948], p. 119).

He talks about several levels of patterns. *Universal patterns* are those that fit a general culture scheme (i.e., that more or less fit all human cultures). *Systemic patterns* talk about broader, more normative groupings around collections of beliefs, behaviors, alphabets, or economics. Of systemic patterns, Kroeber writes:

> A second kind of pattern consists of a system or complex of cultural material that has proved its utility as a system and therefore tends to cohere and persist as a unit; it is modifiable only with difficulty as to its underlying plan. Any one such systemic pattern is limited primarily to one aspect of culture, such as subsistence, religion, or economics; but it is not limited areally, or to one particular culture; it can be diffused cross-culturally, from one people to another . . . What distinguishes these systemic patterns of culture—or well-patterned systems, as they might also be called—is a specific interrelation of their component parts, a nexus that holds them together strongly, and tends to preserve the basic plan ... As a result of the persistence of these systemic patterns, their significance becomes most evident on a historical view ([Kroeber 1948], pp. 120–121).

This description is, of course, reminiscent of pattern languages, which are descriptions of systems, or "wholes," that grow piecemeal from tightly knit patterns. In this book, each systemic pattern is part of a pattern language, of a greater whole. It is the whole and the interweaving of individual patterns that correspond to culture—not just a loose collection of individual patterns.

Our everyday vernacular use of the word "culture" most closely corresponds to what Kroeber calls *total culture patterns* that give a culture its identity and to *styles* that reflect further localization and specialization. Total culture patterns might be what distinguish C++ developers from Smalltalk developers—not only from the perspective of language, but also from consideration of the normative behaviors, beliefs, and practices that relate to the languages and to the environments of these languages and their associated technologies. Kroeber talks in particular of how style changes over time (e.g., clothing styles).

Patterns also figure strongly in isolated examples of more contemporary organizational literature. Senge talks about *patterns of organization* in Chapter 6 of [Senge 1990]. There are other examples in more obscure literature as well. Our point here is that patterns are not just about software or even building architecture; instead, they have deeper and perhaps even more suitable roots in the human sciences. We have followed this approach in this book. Our goal is not just to capture ideas in the form of patterns, but to apply the systems principles of the human sciences to express the structure and practices of a culture that we have studied and experienced firsthand—software development organizations.

7.2 Beyond Process to Structure and Values

A good organization doesn't just focus on process, at least not in the sense that the term is used in ISO 9000 series organizational work. Process emerges from *structure*, and structure emerges from values.

Swieringa and Wierdsma are systems thinkers who describe organizations as organisms that exhibit certain behaviors, driven by principles, insights, and rules, with the goal of producing certain results [Swieringa Wierdsma 1992]. *Organizational learning* is a change in behavior. There are three kinds of learning: single-loop, double-loop, and triple-loop.

In single-loop learning, collective learning causes the rules to change ([Swieringa Wierdsma 1992], p. 37). Swieringa and Wierdsma note that "[m]any of the measures applied in industry to improve quality, service and customer relationships take place at the level of single loop learning." But they note that such changes have only a surface effect: "No significant changes take place in the strategy, the structure, the culture or the systems of the organization." It is a question of changing the *how*, but hardly ever changing the *why*. There is hope for improvement, largely as a result of doing more of the same, but doing it better.

In double-loop learning, the focus is on *learning at the level of insight*. Now the focus moves to *why,* to a desire to increase knowledge and understanding rather than to a simple desire to "improve." This learning is called *renewal learning* since it relates to a renewal of insights in the organization.

Finally, triple-loop learning is about the organization's *identity*, which is called *organizational development*. This strategy helps organizations answer the following questions: What kind of business do we want to be? What are our values and principles?

All of these types of learning can be beneficial. The deeper one delves into the learning process, the longer it takes (single-loop learning can take place over days: double-loop, over months; and triple-loop, over years). Whereas single-loop learning is about process and reaction, the other levels deal with the structure of the organization and with learning how to learn.

Learning is a process, and one must, in fact, learn how to learn. The patterns in this book are learning tools, and moving from pattern to pattern is a learning experience. Most of the patterns tend to involve double-loop learning. At the core of this learning process is the fundamental process of PIECEMEAL GROWTH (6.2). This focus on organizational learning distinguishes organizational patterns from other organizations such as XP [Beck 1999], which, though rooted in principles, imposes those principles from without instead of from within the organization. Further, XP offers no process for "learning" one's way to success, supposing instead that the incorporation of all of the principles and practices (in some unspecified order over some unspecified amount of time) can lead to success. Patterns put the organization and its members, as well as their collective talents, insights, and intelligence, at the center of the learning process.

7.2.1 The Shortcomings of Process

Many traditional approaches to software productivity have focused on *processes*, on what steps are taken and how they are executed. Indeed, the implication is that if the process is followed, then the software will be of high quality and will be developed efficiently. Let's examine this premise in more detail.

If following the process produces high quality software, then what is the cause of failures in the software? It must be that the process is not being followed or that the process is deficient somewhere. The process must have missed something. If you think this idea is far-fetched, think again. One of the authors once attended a briefing session for an upcoming ISO 9001 audit. The leader stated that everyone should remember that the person was not being audited, but rather the process and compliance with that process were being audited. This statement was intended to reassure people, and it probably did provide comfort—temporarily. For, after all, if processes can be tweaked to handle every eventuality, then developers stand in grave danger of being replaced by programming robots.

But we all know that software developers are in no danger of being replaced by robots, because software design is a highly creative activity done by intelligent people. As a result, process becomes much less relevant. In fact, highly intelligent people have been known to ignore or subvert the official process when it does not apply to them. Every organization has two processes: the official process and the one actually followed. One of the authors once interviewed a group of key developers from several different projects. Although they all used processes that called for design documents and design reviews to precede coding, each one admitted to completing the code first and then writing and reviewing the design document— "so we can check off the design review box." They had found that for them, design documents were not relevant; as such, it was easier to write the documents once the design was instantiated in the code.

7.2.2   Structure

So, if process has little impact on organizational effectiveness, then what does? It turns out that the structure of the organization is more stable over time and thus provides a better indicator of effectiveness. Herein lies the break between single-loop learning and higher-order feedback loops. One reason for this break is that the structure of an organization reflects its values, and values drive the organization. Some examples illustrate this idea.

Prior to the breakup of AT&T in 1984, the Bell System was a monopoly, and one of its core values was to provide telephone service to everyone all of the time and at a reasonable cost. This philosophy led to groups dedicated to producing extremely high-availability hardware and software. On the other hand, because cost and speed were nonissues for a monopoly, organizations became bloated and were not structured to facilitate speed.

In 1993, Borland was in the midst of developing QPW. Risk taking, hard work, and human relationships were important company principles, even to the point that employees played jazz with Philippe Kahn, the president. Not surprisingly, the QPW team showed some of the tightest communication coupling we have ever seen.

Organizations that have a strong commitment to customers' satisfaction often have customer, surrogate customer, product support, and customer service roles that are tightly coupled to the rest of the organization. A thread that runs through all of our patterns (and that is fundamental to the principles of the pattern languages presented here) is the focus on *product*. Neither the development processes nor the internal documentation are delivered to the customer. The customer does not pay for elaborate project plans or architecture documents, or, if they do, it is probably a sign that something is more deeply wrong than such measures can ever address. These patterns don't focus on the development of a process, nor do they advocate the creation of a process organization. Instead, the patterns strive to manage the resources that go into internal documentation. The focus is always on product. A product has strong structural elements, and that structure reflects itself in the organization. We believe that aligning these structural elements through good communication practices offers the key to effective development.

7.2.3   Values: The Human Element

Heeding the communication problem implies attentiveness to human issues. While individuals sometimes stand out in history for their accomplishments, most great things are done in groups, teams, and societies that are guided by cultural or social norms. To the degree that the group has a common vision or UNITY OF PURPOSE (4.2.12), the organization can come together to do great things. Perhaps the deepest hallmark of a great organization is its ability to engage in triple-loop learning, working as one mind, to some purpose. Perhaps the second deepest hallmark is the devotion and care with which the organization pursues this vision, including its dedication to learning and improvement.

Once in a great while, great minds think alike. But for the rest of us, it takes communication to align minds, motives, and methods in order to build an effective team. Communication is a complex human activity filled with social context, psychological complexity, and emotion. So, building a *communication* structure that in turn supports the building of a *product* is also a complex activity that requires a cultural setting conducive to effective communication. There is no guarantee that any set of guidelines can produce such an environment. However, these patterns can provide one foundation for an effective communication environment by defining a development culture suited to the needs of software development and taken from projects attentive to human needs. They also provide structures that can contribute to an organization's ability to reduce time to market, solve the right problem, and meet other customer expectations. Shared patterns can contribute to a high(er) context culture, a shared vocabulary and shared culture, rather than a mechanical or bureaucratic environment full of rules that are either inhuman or arbitrary.

The focus explicitly is *not* on process. Process is a good tool in mature domains with predictable steps. In other domains, it's not clear what good process portends for product quality. A *flexible* process can contribute to good communication in a domain that must deal with change. But one can't just install a process; instead, a process must emerge from the structures of communication and production beneath it. And the structures, in turn, are held in place by the values of the organization. Thus, the values of an organization are the foundation of not only *what* is done, but also *how* it is done.

Some organizations' values are rooted in making money. If such values are pervasive, the organization may have strong links to marketing or sales roles. Customer roles are likely to be present, but they are less central than they are in customer-satisfaction-oriented organizations.

Many organizations that we see value management highly. Manager roles show up in the middle of organizational diagrams, sometimes even trumping the critical producer roles such as Developer. When we probe, we often find that people are rewarded more for management than for development.

It shouldn't be surprising that most of our patterns have a strong, although not obvious, impact on the values of the organization. These patterns go beyond superficial processes to get at the heart of an organization. Yet changes at this level do not come easily. It may take years, or perhaps even a crisis, to shake the foundation of the organization—its value system.

7.3 Roles and Communication

All the world's a stage, and all the men and women merely players: They have their exits and their entrances; And one man in his time plays many parts, His acts being seven ages.

— *As You Like It, Act 2, Scene 7*

Within every organization, every person plays one or more roles. We have found that the roles people play are very significant: they are an important indicator of what *really* happens in the organization.

Why are roles so significant?

First, the roles define *what* is done in the organization. This concept is more important, and lasting, than *how* things are done, which is captured in the organization's processes. Defining *what* is done helps shape the organization's identity. It also illuminates the organization's values.

Second, people identify with roles. You may hear someone say, "I'm a developer," or "I'm a tester." People occasionally may change roles, but there is generally a great deal of stability among roles. People often carry roles from project to project; in that sense, roles are more stable than the projects themselves. Through these roles, people use their creativity to develop software.

Third, communication flows among roles; thus, information is linked to roles. Information flow is one of the biggest factors in an organization's success—or failure.

We have learned much about organizations by examining their roles and the communication among those roles. The presence or absence of certain roles tells a lot about the project. Occasionally, we notice that a role is missing, which may indicate that the organization does not see that role as important. For example, a few organizations have not included "customer" as a role. As a result, one wonders how responsive such organizations are to customer problems. Other organizations have no Architect role, and they probably feel that software architecture is unimportant.

The amount and pathways of communication among roles is significant. A Developer role should be well connected to other roles, but a Manager role that is too well connected may indicate an overly meddlesome manager. A System Test role that has few connections to the rest of the project may spell trouble. It could even indicate that the development organization does not see the value of rigorous system testing, which leads to even bigger trouble.

Communication among roles can lead to the formation of groups. Sometimes these groups optimize opportunities for productive communication, but other times these groups are tantamount to social cliques. Such cliques can be very damaging to the organization in a number of ways. We can differentiate between groups and cliques by examining the particular roles involved in the communication groups.

Many of the patterns in the patterns chapters describe the characteristics of roles. Some of the patterns describe communication among roles. Each of these patterns can be vital to the success of an organization.

7.4 Social Network Analysis

Once we identified the roles, we elaborated the relationships between roles using a group role-play exercise based on CRC cards [Beck 1991]. We then built organizational models based on these data, drawing heavily on social network theory and social network analysis. Social network theory was first developed by Moreno [Moreno 1934] to build models of the structure of interacting groups of people. We sought patterns across the models of numerous organizations, and these patterns formed the basis for the material in this book.

We presented an overview of the social network analysis techniques earlier in the book [HOW THE PATTERNS CAME TO US (CHAPTER 2)]. In the following sections, starting with DISTILLING THE PATTERNS (7.5), we describe our research methodology in more detail.

7.5 Distilling the Patterns

When we set out to write this book, we were determined to make a pattern language, not just a list of patterns. We did so for the following reasons:

- An organization is a system. Most organization problems are system problems. Pattern languages are about systems, and individual patterns don't rise to the system level.
- Patterns *need* each other. No pattern stands alone; instead, each pattern must be tailored by smaller patterns. A pattern language is a structure that guides the reader through the patterns.
- A pattern language implies choice. Users of a pattern language can choose patterns that fit their needs and can skip others. They can also tailor patterns to their needs with confidence.

7.5.1 CRC Cards and Roles

Sociometric modeling can be based on several varieties of network relationship data. These differences correspond to properties of formal graphs in graph theory. The relationships between roles can be labeled (e.g., with a number that indicates the strength of the interaction) or unlabeled, directed or undirected, and so forth. During the CRC interview, we collected only dichotomous network data: In other words, a relationship either exists between two roles or it doesn't. We take care to capture directed lines to support studies of information flow. A directed line is called an *arc*, and a graph of arcs is called a *digraph*. Participants annotate the arcs at the end of the interview, giving them strengths so they become valued arcs.

CRC cards had some unanticipated benefits as well. They can be used as part of a therapy session of sorts that helps an organization introspect about itself in real time. Our CRC sessions usually served as mirrors in which organizations could see themselves in a new light. As such, the data gathering technique itself played out the sociodrama and laid the seeds of group therapy.

CRC cards also have some drawbacks involving groupthink, consistency, and granularity. Perhaps the most serious problem is the opportunity for groupthink, the tendency for a group to fall into modes of social conformity [Janis 1971]. Most of the organizations we visited had a diverse collection of strong personalities who avoided many of the problems of self-censorship found in organizations dominated by groupthink. We avoided meeting with "mindguards," those who protect the power holders in the organization from painful truths. We specifically asked the subject organizations not to send process professionals from their organization, since those individuals usually perform a policing function and frown on departures from stipulated practice. Most groups viewed the exercise as an opportunity to help their self-improvement efforts and didn't seem to be blinded by illusions of invulnerability. We observed rationalization-based groupthink in some groups that participated in these studies because they perceived an allied group—such as the organization that created or managed their development process—as an "enemy." While we feel these factors would have affected our results if we had been explicitly looking for process compliance, we don't feel that they affected our models of role relationships within these organizations. For more on the concept of groupthink, see [Janis 1971].

The second problem with CRC cards is consistency. Each group has its own culture that colors the meaning of common role names. For example, is it fair to compare the "Developer" role in a start-up company with the role of the same name in a legacy organization? Is there a commonly understood meaning for "role" itself? Furthermore, different organizations produce different products that solve problems of widely varying difficulty. Is it fair to compare otherwise similar teams if one produces aerospace software and the other produces biomedical engineering control software? Such problems plague most software studies. Not surprisingly, the number of control variables is large.

Granularity is another issue. A complete understanding of process incorporates roles, actors, artifacts, and other dimensions. Here, we are focusing on roles. It is difficult to define roles formally (we "define" them in terms of their responsibilities). A given person may play several roles, and a given role may be played by more than one person. For example, one person might be both a Developer and a Tester, and, of course, several people may adopt the Developer role. The Pasteur tools [see Social Network Theory Foundations (7.5.2)] have an option to combine selected roles, which helps us to evaluate some actor-to-role mappings. The general problems of granularity and mapping remain research issues.

7.5.2   Social Network Theory Foundations

For those of you interested in the social network theory foundations and the techniques for analyzing the data, we provide a short summary here.

We collected the CRC data in a database and created an environment called Pasteur [Cain Coplien 1993] to analyze the data. The data were stored as a digraph representing a social network. Each node in the graph corresponds to an organizational role as characterized by a CRC card. Each arc in the graph corresponds to a collaboration between roles, starting with the role that initiates a collaboration and terminating with the "helping" role of the collaboration. Subjects in the organizational studies assign a weighting value to each arc to express how dependent one role is on the other with respect to the corresponding interaction.

Pasteur supports a variety of network-data visualization techniques. These visualization techniques rely on graphical placement algorithms, each of which accentuates different organizational characteristics. We most often used a natural force-based placement technique that employs a simple relaxation algorithm, which is described as follows:

1. All nodes are assigned random coordinates on a segment of a plane.

2. A repelling force is set up between all pairs of nodes, following an inverse square law.

3. Arcs exert an attracting force between the nodes they connect; the stronger the interaction between a pair of nodes, the stronger the force.

4. The graph reaches a stable state when all of the nodes migrate to positions where their forces balance.

(The parallels to the use of the term "forces" in pattern parlance here is striking and, though unintentional, is certainly no coincidence.)

There are other fine points of the algorithm that avoid anomalous "cornering" of nodes that suffer an unfortunate initial placement. This algorithm creates a spatial representation of an organization's interaction graph in two-dimensional space (so far, we have not resorted to multidimensional scaling). Pasteur supports other placement algorithms as well, such as two-dimensional hierarchies (created by a topological sort that employs heuristic cycle-breaking techniques) and automatic graph partitioning around selected "seed" roles. This framework accommodates customized rendering techniques for individual experiments using a rich programming environment based on the experimental languages GIL and Romana-I [Burrows 1986].

Pasteur displays the graph on either an interactive graphical display or a color printer. Nodes are color-coded according to their intensity of interaction with neighboring nodes, relative to the organization as a whole. The graphical interface allows researchers to directly interact with the model. A user can interactively remove nodes or arcs, create annotations, merge graphs, or invoke any placement algorithm. While analytical techniques can be applied to sociometric data to discover cliques, cutsets, cutpoints, and the like, visual techniques offer the researcher quick intuitive insights into many facets of organizational structure at once. Social psychologists use a pictorial social network called a *sociogram*, a network analysis technique developed by Moreno in the 1930s [Moreno 1934]. Like our visualizations, sociograms graphically depict network data. Figure 7.1 shows a sociogram as used in the social sciences.

Sociograms lack the spatial cues of the visualized placement algorithms. The placement techniques amplify the sociogram data, presenting it in a format where patterns can be directly observed by the organizational analyst. We call these diagrams *amplified sociograms* for that reason. As shown in Figure 7.2, Pasteur social network visualizations depict interactions as simple lines rather than as directed arcs, focusing on the coupling between roles rather than on the flow of information.

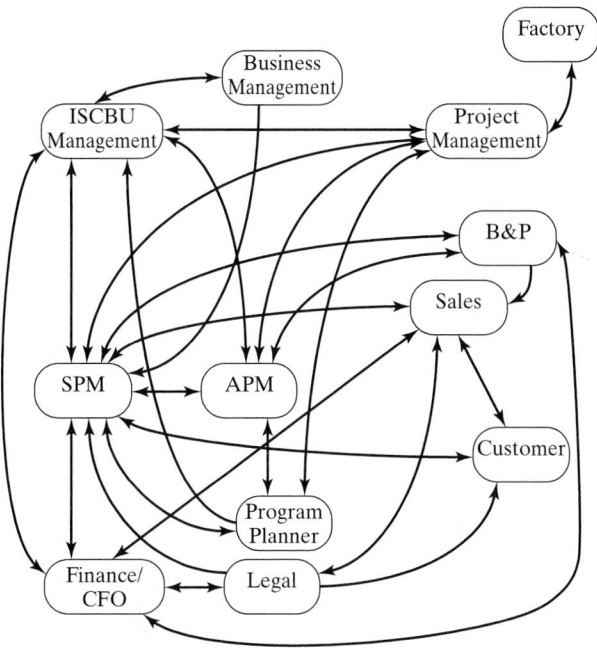

FIGURE 7.1 Sociogram for an Organization

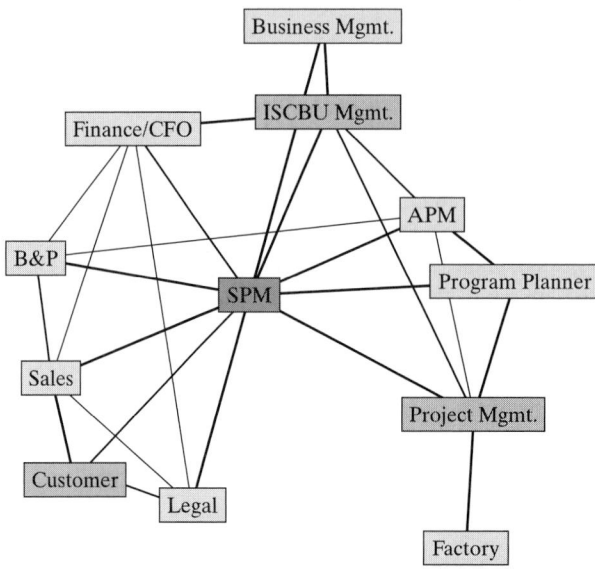

FIGURE 7.2 Pasteur Social Network Diagram for an Organization

Few human interactions are truly directed; instead, they usually involve dialogue or meetings. The Pasteur diagrams emphasize this aspect of organizational structure. Whether the interactions are directed or not, they provide a good depiction of the major highways of interaction between roles. One powerful way to interpret sociograms is as *workflow diagrams*. Workflow models have been around for a long time as ways of studying a wide variety of processes. Workflow has recently resurfaced in the contextual design discipline, as exemplified in the book *Contextual Design* by Beyer and Holtzblatt ([Beyer Holtzblatt 1998], p. 92). Their workflow models are strikingly similar to the sociograms that we used. Their models are, in fact, based on several of the same principles and concepts that underlie our work: individuals (which become roles in their "consolidated models"), responsibilities of the role, and flow (which is the equivalent of our helping relationships). To these concepts they add five more: groups, artifacts, communication topics, places, and breakdowns. Our models took these aspects into account only informally. We recommend *Contextual Design* to practitioners seeking a more extensive taxonomy of flow model properties than our roles and responsibilities alone provide. Workflow considers the same structures we examine in social network analysis. It is perhaps not a coincidence that *Contextual Design* claims that "[w]ork flow is the rich *pattern* [emphasis ours] of work as it shuttles between people, the interweaving of jobs and job responsibilities that gets the work done" (Beyer Holtzblatt 1998, p. 91).

We also employ interaction grids, a technique inspired by the work of Church and Helfman at AT&T Bell Laboratories [Church Helfman 1992]. Each of these diagrams is reminiscent of the structure of a sociomatrix, a square matrix whose columns are the roles that initiate collaborations and whose rows are the roles receiving the collaborations. Figure 7.3 shows a simple sociomatrix for the same organization as depicted in the preceding sociogram. Figure 7.4 shows the corresponding interaction grid from the Pasteur tools.

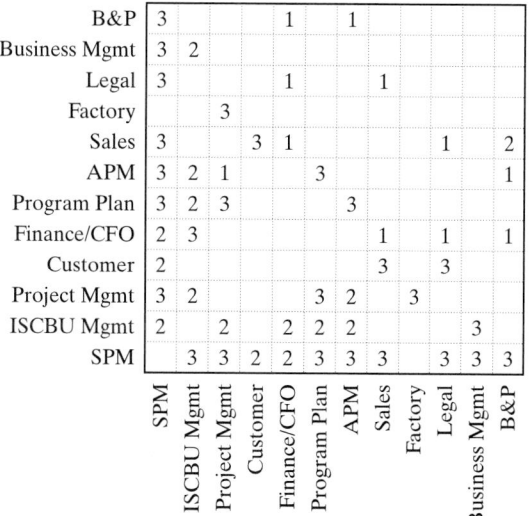

	SPM	ISCBU Mgmt	Project Mgmt	Customer	Finance/CFO	Program Plan	APM	Sales	Factory	Legal	Business Mgmt	B&P
B&P	3				1		1					
Business Mgmt	3	2										
Legal	3				1					1		
Factory			3									
Sales	3			3	1					1		2
APM	3	2	1			3						1
Program Plan	3	2	3				3					
Finance/CFO	2	3						1		1		1
Customer	2							3		3		
Project Mgmt	3	2				3	2		3			
ISCBU Mgmt	2		2		2	2	2			3		
SPM		3	3	2	2	3	3	3		3	3	3

FIGURE 7.3 Sociomatrix for an Organization

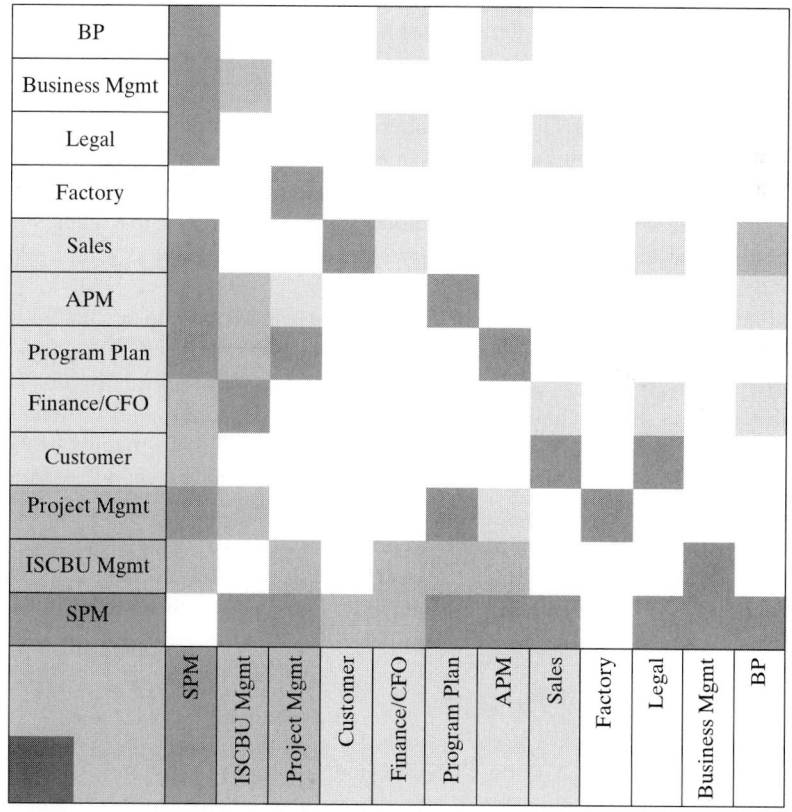

FIGURE 7.4 Pasteur Interaction Grid for an Organization

The sociomatrix—and hence the interaction grid—has information that is isomorphic to that in the social network diagram. The sociomatrix and interaction grid communicate patterns of directed interactions, something that is present but difficult to read in sociograms and that is missing entirely in the force-based network visualizations. Shading in the interaction grids makes it easier to recognize patterns than the numbers of the sociomatrix allow. The ordinate axis of the interaction grid enumerates roles that initiate interactions; the coordinate axis enumerates (the same) roles as they are the targets of interactions.

Visualizations are an intuitive presentation of more formal underlying concepts. We can analytically measure the centrality of an organization using several formal definitions. The centrality of the organization is often given as a number: Let's say, 5.76. Which do you find more clear and convincing: the number or the picture? Instead of explaining sociometric vocabulary to team members (particularly to managers), we appeal to their intuition and imagination with these organizational portraits.

These visualizations also support the second phase of introspection by the subject organizations: They provide data that help the organization face and understand its problems. The location of key roles in the diagram usually confirms the development team's expectations or helps team members explain exceptional or problematic behavior. For example, one organization immediately noticed the remoteness of its architectural role in the social network diagram, and gained insight that this remoteness was one of the reasons for the lack of product focus in the organization. A crucial point here is that an individual sociogram or interaction grid alone doesn't pinpoint organizational problems; instead, it is a mirror in which team members can see themselves better and thereby better understand their problems.

We collected pictures into a catalogue and categorized them. Following Gamma's [Gamma 1992] studies of recurring, reused patterns of code in software systems, we wanted to find the recurring patterns of communication in software organizations. One goal of the study was to collect and catalog typical recurring patterns from a wide spectrum of organizations (i.e., to investigate the social anthropology of software development). Such studies would form an empirical basis for models of contemporary software development as it really happens, as opposed to ideal models built from first principles.

We were particularly interested in finding the patterns peculiar to successful, productive organizations in order to investigate whether any organizational "shapes" correlated to productivity or success. We quantified "successful" or "productive" only informally or through very coarse-grained metrics. For example, like everyone else we used thousands of noncommentary lines of code (KSLOC) per staff month as raw productivity data, but we thought of these data in terms of metrics like $\log_{10}$(KSLOC)/staff month. We also took note of remarkably short development intervals. Patterns did emerge over time, and these patterns are the bulk of what we present to you in this book. At about the same time, we started extracting sociometric parameters from the sociograms. These parameters include standard sociometric data such as graph density and graph centrality. Some of these data correlated well to productive organizations, and some of the data are interesting in their own right.

7.5.3 Scatterplots and Patterns

Many of the patterns in this book came from insights offered by a tool called **dot**, a public domain tool authored by AT&T Labs. We used scatterplots to find patterns in the data. For example, we could plot the communication intensity ratio against the number of roles in the corresponding organization, against the number of communication links, against other sociometric quantities—against just about anything and everything. We created dozens of these plots for many data sets and then looked at them to find patterns. Some scatterplots showed a roughly linear correlation, as in the plot of the number of roles as a function of communication intensity ratio that is shown in Figure 7.5. Other plots showed polynomial trends, and many others showed linear trends.

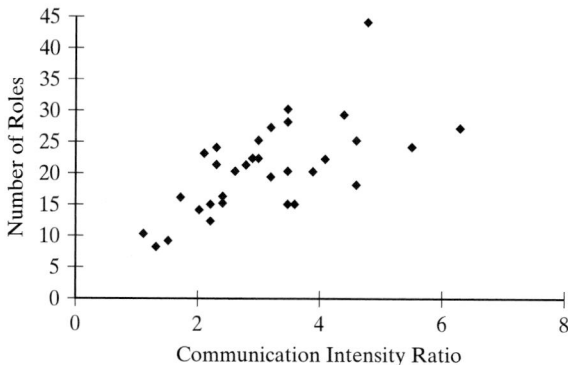

FIGURE 7.5 Scatterplot for several organizations from early in the Pasteur project

PART IV

Case Studies

The patterns in this book were drawn from empirical studies of about 100 organizations in dozens of companies in several countries around the world. This chapter looks at two actual case studies of organizations we have worked with in order to provide real-world examples of how the patterns can be applied.

The first organization is Borland QPW. Much has already been published in the literature about this study; however, we include the same information here for convenience and completeness.

The second organization is a project in Lucent Technologies called SNAP. It is probably the second most productive organization we have studied.

Yes, these case studies are old in terms of Internet years. But they nonetheless reflect a culture that uses timeless practices. We believe that today's organizations, a few years later, would demonstrate no major departures from the practices of these organizations if they were operating at the same levels of effectiveness. Furthermore, the distance of time allows us to reflect on these organizations and their practices in the context of history, rather than in the heat of the moment. The conclusions and finding bear out such considerations. Last, we have continued to find similar configurations and practices in the few high-productivity organizations we have worked with in the years closer to the publication of this book, and we find that most organizations that follow these Agile practices also enjoy a level of success far above average.

CHAPTER 8

Borland Quattro Pro
for Windows

Adapted from an article written by Jim Coplien and Jon Erickson that appeared in Dr. Dobb's Journal of Software Tools [Coplien Erickson 1994].

8.1 Introduction to the QPW Case Study

> Jim — Thanks again for speaking at BIC international [Borland Conference] '93. I'm also glad you could stop by Borland and experience what we call Borland Software Craftsmanship. We are a young company, started by a Frenchman, with young bright and excited developers. In my 8 years at Borland I have been in the center of it all and can't imagine another place to be. — David Intersimone, Director of Developer Relations, Borland.

In 1993, Borland invited me to speak at the fourth annual Borland International Conference in San Diego, California, and to visit the company's location in Scotts Valley, California. I made arrangements with David Intersimone, Borland's Director of Developer Relations, to speak at the conference in exchange for access to one of the company's development organizations. Interviews with such development organizations have helped the process community better understand the high-level characteristics of software development organizations. We can use this understanding to help projects assess their development methods against those used in other development cultures. I was enthusiastically received and graciously hosted, which was a harbinger of other positive signs of the Borland culture that I would observe that day. I was treated to insights into one the most stunning development efforts I have ever had the pleasure to study.

In this chapter, I relate what I learned while meeting with the development team for Borland's QPW 1.0 on May 20, 1993, in Scotts Valley. I feel there is much to be learned about their process, technology, and organization that we can apply to projects across the industry, including large projects and perhaps even embedded and real-time system developments such as those at

AT&T. This chapter is distilled and updated from a paper published in *Dr. Dobb's Journal of Software Tools* in 1994 [Coplien Erickson 1994]—before the organizational patterns were even published!

It is important to understand that this discussion is a retrospective on the development of the software for the initial offering of QPW. There was little or no embedded base, and the project didn't face the constraints one finds in the legacy code projects common in large, traditional telecommunication projects. Even so, the phenomenal productivity of this group and the factors contributing to that productivity are thought-provoking. Most organizations should be able to take a page from Borland's book as a basis for their own process improvement efforts.

This chapter starts with a high-level description of the project and describes the personalities involved in the development effort. Analyses of the data derived using our process analysis technique follow in the next section. Subsequent sections of the chapter describe aspects of the QPW development that stood out as contributing to its success.

8.2 Origins and Description of QPW

Borland launched development for QPW as a natural follow-up to the company's DOS spreadsheet offering. QPW offers spreadsheet and database functionality in the spirit of most spreadsheet products on the market today. The team I interviewed created QPW 1.0, the so-called base generic development for the product. Figure 8.1 shows a high-level business flow of the Borland QPW development effort.

The initial development was to be heavily loaded with features. The project goal was to produce a product with the maturity and feature richness of a third- or fourth-release product. The team felt they had achieved that goal when the product shipped.

Like most Borland products, QPW is designed to be a self-contained deliverable that is compatible with other members of a product family. Its human interface is consistent with other Borland products, and its database interfaces allow it to interwork with other Borland products. Borland views itself as a vendor of individual business solution components, from which customers can select combinations to meet their needs. The total code volume of all Borland products, expressed as original source lines, is huge: tens, if not hundreds, of millions of lines of code (my estimate). Products are largely independent of each other, yet they share a common infrastructure and look and feel (and, conjecturally, the code providing this functionality).

QPW had a small core team—four people—who interacted closely over 2 years to produce the bulk of the product [ARCHITECTURE TEAM (5.2.4) and ARCHITECT ALSO IMPLEMENTS (5.2.10)]. Prototyping was heavily used, and two major prototypes were built and discarded (the first in C; the second, called "pre-Crystal," in C++). Four core developers defined an architecture, built early prototypes and the foundation code for the product, and participated in implementation through the product's delivery. Additional programmers joined the team after about 6 months of intense effort by the core of four. This experience was one of our initial substantiations for the pattern BUILD PROTOTYPES (4.1.7). These prototypes drove architectural decisions that were discussed in frequent (almost daily) project meetings [STAND-UP MEETING (5.2.7)]. Based on that feedback, the team made architecture and implementation changes and reintegrated and tested before the next meeting—usually the next day. This cycle closely approximates the patterns involved in PROGRAMMING EPISODES (4.1.19) and, in a broader sense, DEVELOPMENT EPISODE (4.1.15). A million lines of code were written over a period of 31 months by about eight people (that's about 1,000 lines of code per person per week). And that doesn't include the code in the prototypes.

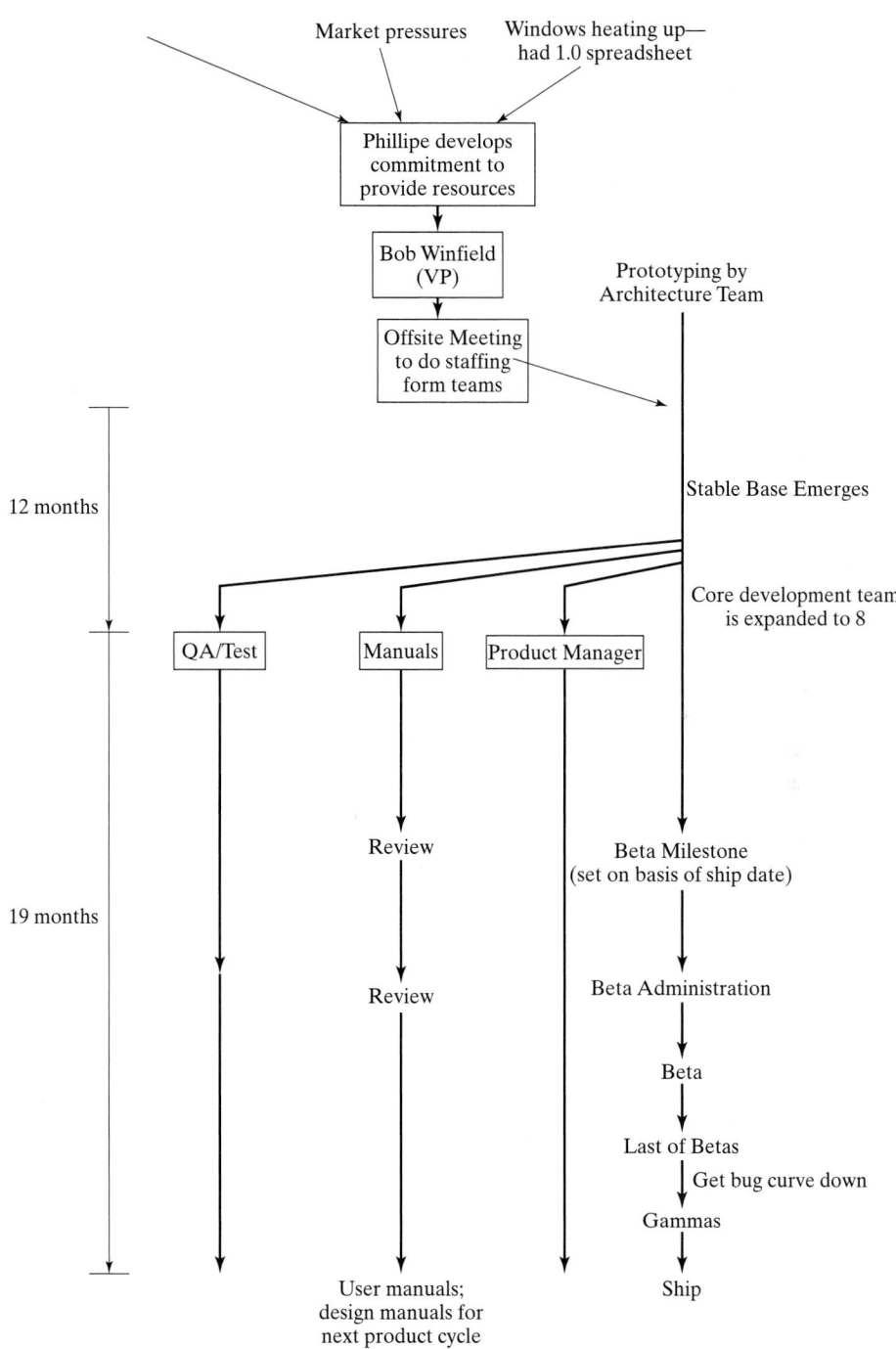

FIGURE 8.1 High-Level Business Flow of the Borland QPW Development effort

The methodology was iterative. Except for the architectural dialogue, the core developers worked independently. Early code can be viewed as a series of prototypes that led to architectural decisions and that drove the overall structure of the final system. This concept supports not only BUILD PROTOTYPES (4.1.7), but also patterns outside the language like Cockburn's EARLY AND REGULAR DELIVERY (A.5.11) [Cockburn 1996].

The programming language was C++. The final implementation stages of QPW stressed their C++ compiler—which was being developed in parallel with QPW—to its limits. There was uncharacteristically tight coupling between the QPW group and the language group. QPW was one of the largest and earliest projects to stress their C++ compiler release. Cooperation between the two groups allowed each to contribute to the quality efforts of the other.

After the product took shape (after about a year), additional roles were engaged in development activities. QA, testers, and others were at last allowed to see and exercise copies of the code that had been kept under wraps during early development. These roles had been staffed earlier, but they had engaged in development only when the developers felt they had something worth testing. This QA and test structure gave us foundations for patterns such as ENGAGE QUALITY ASSURANCE (4.2.29) and APPLICATION DESIGN IS BOUNDED BY TEST DESIGN (4.2.30).

While the QA organization conducted its own testing, an active beta program uncovered bugs as only real users can. The use of such a program is a luxury that tool purveyors enjoy to a greater extent than most telecommunications companies (and that they in turn enjoy to a greater extent than some contractors in, say, the aerospace industry). Beta programs are a form of ENGAGE CUSTOMERS (4.2.6), and they are specifically a form of SURROGATE CUSTOMER (4.2.7). Beta customers are "surrogates" because they are not paying customers and aren't really in a position to *expect* any level of performance or quality.

The QPW product entered the market to high acclaim. *PC Sources* said, "Borland International Inc's Quattro Pro for Windows spreadsheet software package makes better use of the Windows graphical user interface (GUI) than any other spreadsheet package to date" [O'Malley 1993]. *PC User* called QPW "the world's best spreadsheet software" [Whitehorn 1992]. As *Computer Shopper* noted, "Borland International Inc's Quattro Pro for Windows spreadsheet software outperforms the standing champion of Windows spreadsheet management, Microsoft Corp's Excel 4.0" [Bonner 1992]. *INFO WORLD* [Walkenbach 1992], *PC Magazine* [Stinson 1992], and many others also offered positive reviews, the kind of which dominated the press perspective on the product. I found other reviews that show a little less enthusiasm for the product, but I uncovered no reviews that found the product lacking in key areas.

The team members I interviewed included the following individuals:

- Charlie Anderson—Borland's Director of Applications and one of the QPW architects; he is the experienced and thoughtful "spiritual leader" of the group.

- Weikuo Liaw—a renowned expert on spreadsheet engines and one of the QPW architects; he is a highly revered developer, almost to the point of inspiring awe, but he is rather shy and among the most introverted of the group.

- Murray Low—one of the QPW architects; he is an energetic, daring, bright, and witty engineer who worked on the QPW/UI side.

- David Intersimone—Borland's Director of Developer Relations; he arranged for me to have access to the QPW development team, though he was not part of the QPW development effort.

- Dan Horn—A member of the developer relations team; he helped put me in touch with the Borland people while I was at the conference to make final arrangements.

From almost any perspective (except gender) we found this team represented diverse kinds and levels of experience, ages, ethnicities, and areas of domain expertise. [See DIVERSE GROUPS (4.2.16) and HOLISTIC DIVERSITY (4.2.19)]. In particular, the team had a very strong sense of DOMAIN EXPERTISE IN ROLES (4.2.22).

8.3 Analysis of QPW Data

We most frequently use a *natural force-based* network analysis to analyze organization data collected in the Pasteur database. This analysis produces an *adjacency diagram*. In these diagrams, a default repelling force is established between each pair of roles. There is also an attracting force between pairs of roles that are coupled to each other by collaboration or mutual interest; a stable placement occurs when these forces balance. Figure 8.2 shows the picture that results by applying this analysis to QPW.

Each rectangle represents a role. Each role's shading is proportional to its degree of coupling to the rest of the organization as a whole. Roles are connected with lines that indicate the strength of interaction between the respective roles. Thick lines indicate strong interaction; medium lines indicate moderate interaction; and thin lines indicate the weakest interaction. Roles are grouped so that the ones that interact most closely with each other are closest to each other on the diagram, while those with the least mutual coupling are the furthest from each other in the diagram.

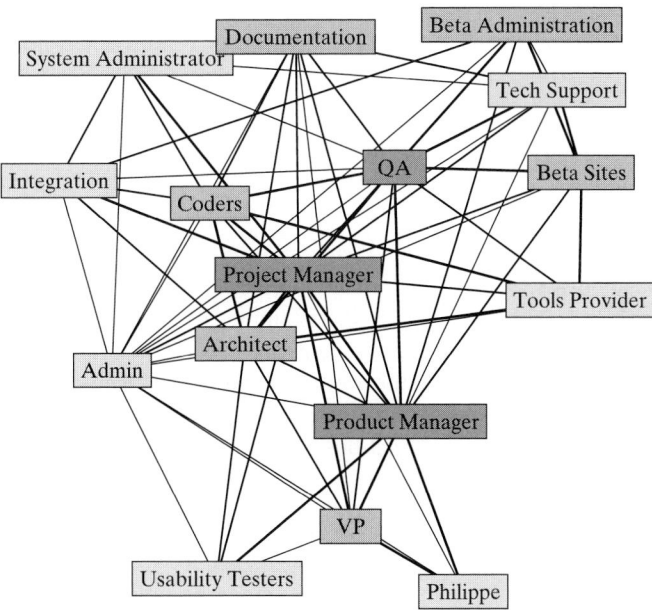

FIGURE 8.2 Adjacency Diagram for the QPW Project

Several elements in these pictures set them apart from most other organizational process models we've made. Here is a summary of those properties:

- *The QPW process has a higher communication saturation than 89 percent of the other processes we've looked at.* The adjacency diagram shows that all roles have at least two strong connections to the organization as a whole. The project's interaction grid is dense. The coupling per role is in the highest 7 percent of all processes we have looked at. This is a small, intensely interactive organization. We find patterns like FEW ROLES (5.1.2), and PRODUCER ROLES (5.1.3), THREE TO SEVEN HELPERS PER ROLE (5.1.21), and COUPLING DECREASES LATENCY (5.1.22) in this structure.

- *The QPW process has a more even distribution of effort across roles than most other processes we've looked at.* The roles in the adjacency diagram are shaded according to their intensity of interaction with the rest of the organization. In the QPW process, Project Manager and QA have light shading; Coders is a little less so; Architect, Product Manager, and Beta Sites are "third-magnitude stars"; and Tech Support, Documentation, and VP still show some illumination. Most "traditional" processes we've studied show a much higher concentration of interaction near the center of the process; that is, roles are more loosely coupled to each other. QPW's process may be more tightly coupled because the QPW project was self-contained, because it was small, or because it was an intense, high-energy development effort. Here, we see the patterns FEW ROLES (5.1.2), and DISTRIBUTE WORK EVENLY (5.1.13).

- *Project Manager and Product Manager are tightly coupled, central roles in the process.* These managerial roles were filled by individuals who were also key technical contributors to the project (they wrote real code), which played a significant part in their acceptance and success as process hubs.

- *A Product Manager* role was employed only after a year of development.

- *Quality Assurance is a tightly coupled and central role.* Many organizations consider QA to be an external function that is outside of their organization and process. At Borland, QA becomes a way of life after developers have converged on a good design and a stable user interface. For QPW, QA entered the picture about 12 months into development. [see ENGAGE QUALITY ASSURANCE (4.2.29)].

- *The CEO (Philippe Kahn) figures strongly in the organization.* In a company of thousands of employees, it is unusual to find the CEO as tightly coupled to development as Kahn was to QPW. It is instructive to examine the responsibilities associated with Philippe Kahn's role: to ensure that the product is commensurate with the current market environment; to ensure that the product market coordination occurs in a timely and cost-effective manner; to determine pricing and product positioning; to shape public perceptions and handle public relations for the product prior to and after shipment; to determine cosmetic changes that need to be made to ensure consistency among all Borland products and to call out certain features (i.e., ensure that usability testing is performed); and to play jazz to avoid press questioning on ship dates. Kahn's role is a combination of FIREWALLS (4.2.9), PATRON ROLE (4.2.15), and LEGEND ROLE (4.2.20) (Kahn was an icon of 1980s software culture).

- *The overall interaction grid pattern is uncharacteristic of that found in other processes.* Interaction grids show patterns of interactions in an organization, and they are particularly useful when the organization is large or when its interactions are dense. We most often use an interaction grid when roles are ordered on both axes by their degree of coupling to the organization as a whole. The most integral roles are placed near the origin. Most other processes exhibit a characteristic pattern of points along the axes, with lower point density and lower intensity for increasing distances from either axis. In QPW, however, there is a general reduction of density and intensity as one moves toward the northeast quadrant of the interaction grid. The northwest and southeast quadrants of the QPW grid remain more dense than we've seen in other processes, thus demonstrating a combination of DISTRIBUTE WORK EVENLY (5.1.13) and RESPONSIBILITIES ENGAGE (5.1.14). Figure 8.3 shows the QPW interaction grid.

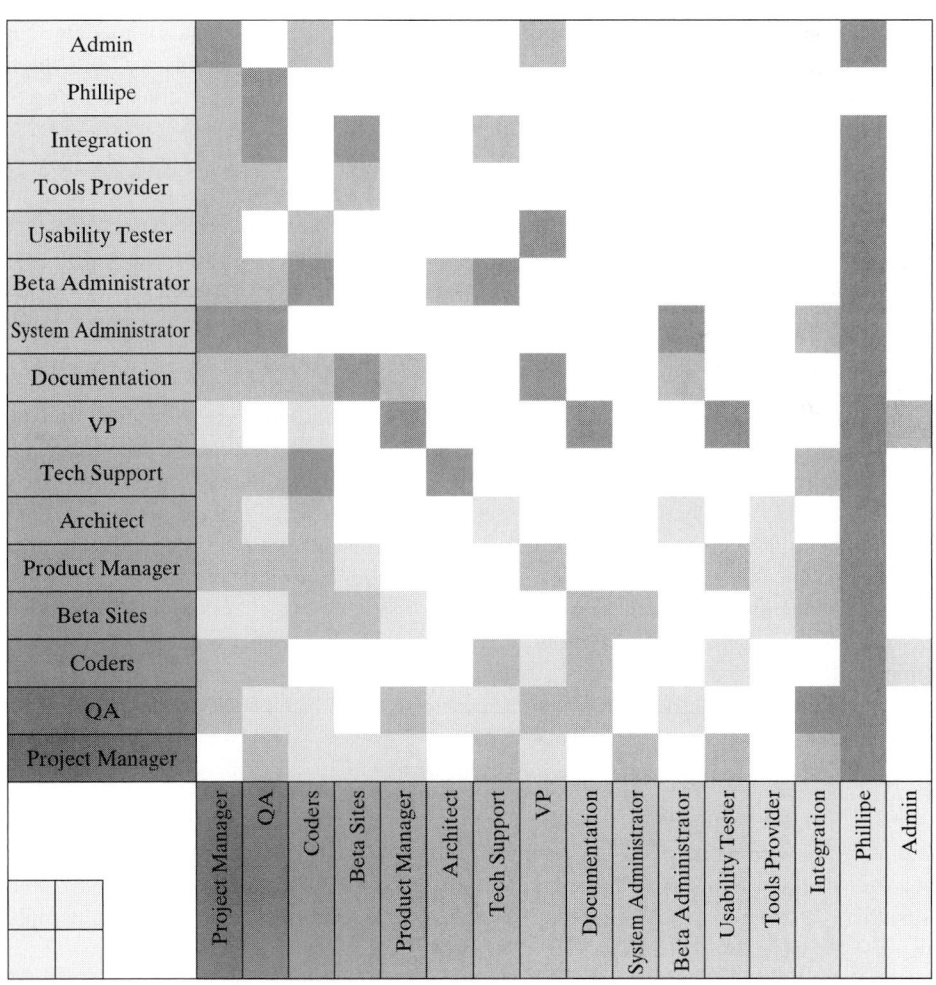

FIGURE 8.3 QPW Interaction Grid

Between 30 and 50 percent the processes we've studied exhibit a pattern called *schismo-genesis* [Bateson 1958] [see also THE OPEN/CLOSED PRINCIPLE OF TEAMS (6.1.4)]. To summarize, schismogenesis is a term from classic anthropological literature that describes a tendency for societies to stratify into sociological "comfort zones." This phenomenon appears in interaction grids as a clustering of points around the diagonal. For organizations where this phenomenon is present, the effect is particularly pronounced in the northeast quadrant of the interaction grid. The clustering of points in this quadrant indicates that organizations contain splinter groups.

The QPW process is characteristically "antischismogenetic." That is, there is *blank space* around the diagonal of the interaction grid, particularly in the northeast quadrant. While we have seen graphs with random scatterings of points, the QPW graph is the first where the points seem to avoid the diagonal and yet fill out the rest of the graph.

8.4 Personal Excellence and Integrity

The initial QPW development team comprised highly productive professionals who viewed each other with the highest respect. While in some cases words like "highly productive" and "highest respect" may ring hollow, these words seem appropriately applied to the QPW team and their development efforts.

The QPW development team had mature membership by industry standards. "We have professionals, not hired guns," noted one member of the development team. People are brought into the team for their recognized expertise in domains of central importance to the project, such as spreadsheet engines, graphics, databases, and so forth. No one is viewed as a warm body, a general engineer, or an interchangeable employee; instead, each person brings special talents to the effort [see DOMAIN EXPERTISE IN ROLES (4.2.22)]. Implicit here is that developers were trusted to conduct their business: DEVELOPER CONTROLS PROCESS (4.1.17).

The trust level among the team members was so high that developers felt code reviews were unnecessary. But while reviews were rare, group buy-in and trust were still considered important. Each project member *personally* signed off on a set of project delivery media before those media were released to the next stage (e.g., beta testing, or to the "street"). Both CODE OWNERSHIP (5.2.13) and OWNER PER DELIVERABLE (A.5.19) were valued on the project, partly because of the high degree of specialization and partly because of a high degree of personal pride in craftsmanship. Personal evaluation of the software, as well as informal dialogue, built the confidence necessary for such a sign-off.

There is a complex and highly nonlinear relationship between project productivity, programmer skill, and project organization. Thus there will always be debate about how much of QPW's phenomenal productivity is owed to its culture, to its choice of staff, and to other factors.

8.5 Do One Thing and Do It Well

The phrase "Do one thing and do it well" is an admonition from C language expert Brian Kernighan about how to write good functions. The phrase has also been used more recently in Arthur Riel's heuristic that each class should manage one key abstraction [Riel 1996]. Analogous advice is starting to appear for classes in OO systems, and the same advice might apply to the people who write those classes.

QPW was organized along lines of domain specialization. Domains important to QPW were dependency registration software, human interfaces, databases, and a few others. An individual was identified to lead each of those domains.

In each of their domains, team members focused on doing what they were good at. They excelled at sharing their domain expertise in architecture meetings. They knew the right abstractions and how to implement those abstractions. They brought C++, DOS, or Windows proficiency to the project or quickly developed that proficiency (as a result of their related domain experience).

Equally important, these individuals were not expected to take responsibility for domains that were not related to their specialization. Instead of working *in* these domains, they worked *with* these domains. One good example involves documentation. Developers were supported by a documentation organization that develops internal and external documentation. The time spent by developers in conveying information to the documentation organization was far less than the time it would take for them to commit that information to writing, put the information into an acceptable format, and have the work edited for linguistic elegance.

By contrast, we knew that most of our AT&T developers wrote their own memos. It's not clear whether this deeply rooted cultural behavior owes to our history, our organizational boundaries, the nature of our business, or our reward mechanisms. Developers thus spent much time (roughly 13 percent of total development time) creating and refining memos at AT&T [Votta Staudenmayer 1993]. At Borland, that job was deferred to people who were expert at it.

8.6 A Piecemeal Architecture Process

QPW development was highly iterative. To understand the nature of the iteration, one must understand its ramifications for architecture and implementation. One must also understand the culture by which changes were approved and the manner in which decisions were made. This discussion takes us into the realm of project meetings, always a topic of interest in a large development organization.

The core architecture team met daily to hammer out C++ class interfaces, to discuss overall algorithms and approaches, and to develop the basic underlying mechanisms on which the system would be built. These daily meetings each lasted several hours. From what I heard, the project involved more meetings than anything else. Everyone's external interfaces were globally visible and globally discussed. The product structure was built on the domain expertise brought to the table by domain experts, but it was socialized and tempered by the needs of the product as a whole.

In spite of the project's intense meeting-oriented development culture, class implementations were fleshed out in private. Individuals were trusted to do a good job of implementing the product; after all, project members were acknowledged experts in their domains. Code reviews were rare. The trust and respect engendered by this domain expertise made it possible to focus meetings on system-level issues.

There are three project principles worth noting about the QPW organization's communication architecture:

1. *Meetings are not a bad thing.* We all cringe at the thought of a project centered on a meeting that carries over from one day to the next throughout early development. But our fear of meetings likely comes more from our memories of the *ineffectiveness* of our meetings, not from their *frequency*. At the First International Workshop on Software Process, I polled several process luminaries with the following question: If I am among the most mature software organizations in the world (Capability Maturity Model (CMM) Level 5 [Humphrey 1992]), how much of my time do I spend in meetings?

Responses from Vic Basilli, Watts Humphrey, and Barry Boehm ranged from 30–50 percent. Project communication, a shared vision, and meetings are important and productive if meetings are properly conducted.

2. *Development takes place on two levels: architecture and implementation.* There is an architectural thread and a development thread. Both are ongoing, and they interact with each other strongly. New implementations suggest architectural changes, which are discussed at the daily meetings. Architectural changes usually require radical changes to the implementation. The implementors' ability to quickly reflect those changes in their implementation is key to turning around architectural changes quickly. This capability is due in large part to ARCHITECT ALSO IMPLEMENTS (5.2.10). Here, the outstanding productivity of the project members comes into play; their incredible productivity supports iterative development. There may also be a third development thread—product management and marketing—that goes beyond the scope of this inquiry.

3. *The development interaction style is a good match for the implementation technology the group has selected.* OO development leads to abstractions whose identity and structure are largely consistent across analysis, design, and implementation. Classes hide implementations and localized design decisions, though their external interfaces are globally visible. Mapping C++ classes and people close together makes it possible for developers to reason about the implementation offline, away from the meetings that deal with interface issues.

Notice this idea is contrary to the commonly presumed model that the object paradigm makes it possible for an individual to own a class, interface and all, with a minimum of interaction with other class owners in the organization. It should be emphasized that classes are good at hiding implementation and detailed structure (e.g., in derived classes), but they are not good at reducing the ripple effect of interface changes. In fact, because interactions in OO systems form an intricate graph and because interactions in structured procedural systems usually form a tree, the ripple effect of interface changes in an OO system can be worse than in a block-structured procedural design.

The following question is frequently posed to organizations that use iterative techniques: "How do you mark progress or perform scheduling?" For QPW, the answer has two parts. First, they relied on experience sizing similar jobs and found their overall estimates to be satisfactory. Second, they kept multiple sets of books internal to Borland to achieve different goals. The hardest of the dates was owned by (and not divulged by) the parts of Borland that manage the financial books. A "real" street date was needed so the company could provide planning and resource support to the development effort. But internal scheduling provided incentive, focus, and pressure for development to move ahead. Project management and corporate executives presented deadlines to the development teams to avoid telegraphing the business view of the schedule, presenting a more compressed schedule for development than the business case allowed for. This approach is reflected in the SIZE THE SCHEDULE (4.1.2) pattern.

8.7 Personality and Development

Thomas Allen at MIT has noted the correlation between effective communication skills and prospects for advancement and success in technical organizations [Allen 1977]. He uses the term *gatekeepers* to describe individuals who exhibit extraordinary communications skills and exercise those skills outside their line organization [see GATEKEEPER (4.2.10)]. These individuals "control"—or, more accurately, facilitate—the flow of information between the development organization and scholastic and competitive sources.

One might expect the team of developers on the highly successful QPW project to follow this model. My observations of the QPW team were brief, but I was left with the impression that their personalities and communication skills did not align with this model. "Nerds" would characterize them more accurately. However, individuals were able to communicate intensely with each other as a group using stereotypical male-style communication dynamics. Only David Intersimone—an outsider—took on the role of posing pointed questions to the group (probably to make sure certain ideas were clear to me).

While it is unclear exactly what their communication behavior would portend for success in a more structured setting, their technical prowess has earned them the highest esteem at Borland. Perhaps one needs to call Allen's models into question, at least regarding their application to small, inbred developments (most of the organizations Allen studied were large government or military contract projects).

One might consider evolutions of the AT&T development culture where such technical expertise could be a better harbinger of advancement. Different AT&T organizations have emphasized different professional qualities at different times as criteria for supervisory promotion. These criteria include technical ability, coordination and interworking skills, administrative skills, and so forth. In our current business environment, the common perception is that technical skills don't dominate considerations for reward or advancement to the same extent that they did in the heyday of academia in the 1960s and 1970s. However, these skills are clearly the key to success in the Borland value system.

8.8 No Wine Before Its Time

The QPW project team used iteration from early in its development cycle through the latest stages of development, increasing the stability of their software and decreasing iteration over time. This iteration took place in what might be described as a traditional corporate context. From its outset, QPW was a strategic, visible product in the company, which meant that all development areas were primed for its deployment, including QA, documentation, and product management.

Though these areas were staffed from the outset, they were denied access to the details of the product until it had "conceptually congealed" about a year into its development. As a result, the architects/developers had room to change the functionality, interface, and methodology of the project before interfacing it with the corporate culture and ultimately with the "street."

8.9 Create Rather Than Conform

Even though Microsoft's Excel may have been a significant market motivator for the launch of the QPW program, QPW developers paid it little heed during the design of their code and human interfaces. Functionality and interface were derived from first principles (project members were strongly conversant in spreadsheet issues) and from consideration for compatibility with other Borland interfaces.

One major distinction between QPW and most of the work done on large telecommunications projects we studied at AT&T is that QPW wasn't conforming to documented customer requirements. Instead, they simply knew what needed to be done. They owe this understanding to their DOMAIN EXPERTISE IN ROLES (4.2.22) and to their ability to act as a special kind of SURROGATE CUSTOMER (4.2.7).

8.10 California Gold Rush?

One cannot ignore the motivating power of bonuses that are on the same order of magnitude as annual compensation. While much of corporate America is turning more and more to "egalitarian" compensation structures, other companies strive to tangibly tie financial rewards to the market success that results from the fruits of an individual's labor. The stereotype may actually be true that bonuses and rewards for jobs well done are higher at companies west of the Rockies than elsewhere. While I did not explore this with the Borland crowd, one might imagine that this west coast bonus structure extended to the QPW culture. The prospects for such rewards may make it easier for individuals to justify the energy and commitment they must devote to a high-intensity development effort for it to succeed.

See additional thoughts about rewards and compensation in COMPENSATE SUCCESS (4.2.25).

8.11 Introspection by the Team

Can an organization without an explicit, established process enjoy the same process benefits as an organization that has full process certification? Though there may be a tendency for certified organizations to experience stronger process benefits than organizations lacking any formal concern for process, this Borland project had many of the hallmarks of a mature development organization.

Borland was not subject to the ISO 9000 series process standards, had no concept of its SEI CMM rating, and was not conversant with the software development process lingo being used increasingly in large software organizations. It was a rare event for someone interested in process to visit the company. Before going through the CRC card exercise, QPW developers viewed my presence as a process guru with everything from intrigued interest, to curiosity, to suspicious doubt. By the time the exercise ended, those involved were able to identify some parts of their value system and culture with what we call process. (By the way, the doubters went away saying, "You know, I think you've got something here.")

So even though the organization had no codified system of process, it was keenly aware of what it does, how it did it, and what worked. It viewed software development as something fundamentally driven by special cases (at least for initial generic development), and repeatability was not an important part of their value system. Members of the organization were nonetheless able to articulate in great detail aspects of their process that demonstrated to my satisfaction that they shared a single model, perhaps based on development rules, of how development should be done.

Many organizations we have interviewed have a weak or confused notion of their roles, the responsibilities of those roles, and the manner in which those roles interact. Most AT&T organizations that have a weak notion of process are those that have not gone through an ISO audit, yet developers' notions of their roles even in some ISO-certified organizations are fuzzy at best. Other organizations that do not have any conscious process culture are nonetheless able to articulate their process in explicit terms, at a level of abstraction that transcends technology, tools, or methodology [UNITY OF PURPOSE (4.2.12)]. In our other studies, we found that this consistency correlated to organizational health.

Borland's QPW development was one such organization. When I asked what their development roles were (after providing a short definition of what I meant by role), the answers were immediate and intuitive, reflecting a single model of the organization shared by its members. Team members easily listed their roles. Few roles were added during the role-playing exercise, and only one role was substantially redefined. The organization knew itself well and was conscious of how people interacted with each other at an abstract level.

In his book, Gerry Weinberg suggests that there is a paradigm shift between level 2 and level 3 of the SEI CMM [Weinberg 1991]. He believes that organizations at levels 1 and 2 need strong (managerial) direction, while organizations at level 3 and above are self-directing. Borland clearly appeared to be in this latter category—though it may not register a level 3 rating according to commonly accepted criteria.

Charlie Anderson entertained us with a thoughtful monologue on how the project felt about itself and its accomplishments. "We are satisfied by doing real work," he noted as he thought about how the project dovetailed daily architectural meetings with implementation efforts. They learned how to improve the structure of their product and how to improve their process as they went through development. "Software is like a plant that grows," he mused. You can't predict its exact shape or how big it will grow; in fact, you can control its growth only to a limited degree. In the same vein, he stated that "There are no rules for this kind of thing—it's never been done before." In retrospect, though, he notes that there are a few things that every project should have. At the top of his list: every project should have a good documentation department. This idea sounded intriguing to me (as it wouldn't have been first on my list), but I didn't get a chance to follow up on the topic with him [see Do ONE THING AND DO IT WELL (8.5)]. This documentation role, of course, is MERCENARY ANALYST (4.1.24), and, as we'll discuss, it is arguably a strong foundation for Borland's success.

8.12 Process and Quality

One widely held stereotype of companies that build PC products (or of California-based companies) is that they hire "hackers" and that their software is unreadable spaghetti. Meeting with this group destroyed that stereotype for me. Their constant attention to architectural issues [ARCHITECT CONTROLS PRODUCT (5.2.3) and CONWAY'S LAW (5.17)], their efforts to build an evolvable structure, and their care to document the system well both externally and internally [see MERCENARY ANALYST (4.1.24)], are all hallmarks of the highest professionalism. Those attitudes, coupled with the phenomenal *general-purpose* programming talents of the staff and the high level of *domain-specific* expertise [DOMAIN EXPERTISE IN ROLES (4.2.22)], defined the kind of quality value system necessary to implement an effective and productive process. There were few gratuitous shortcuts and few novice errors. From what I saw, these people produced *very* high quality code.

If there was any disappointment on the project, it was in their inability to reduce the bug curve in the project end game as fast as they wanted to. They noted that the shapes of software development bug curves were well known, so there was hope of predicting how long it would take to ferret out an acceptable fraction of the remaining errors. However, the boundary conditions for the curve weren't known at the outset, so it was difficult to predict the exact shape of the curve until experience with bug discovery and resolution was developed. Inability to predict the exact shape of this curve resulted in a modest schedule slip [SIZE THE SCHEDULE (4.1.2) and DEVELOPMENT EPISODE (4.1.15)].

Other questions about the project can be answered only over time. The process described here was for initial product development. Can a similar process be used for ongoing maintenance? Probably not, though vestiges of the original process will certainly live on. How will maintenance affect productivity? Can dual-line development continue to support architectural change with rapid alignment of the corresponding implementation? The initial experience was positive. In fact, the first maintenance release earned a *PC Magazine* Editor's Choice award [PCMag 1994]. The editors were astounded by the amount of functionality that had been added so quickly. Nonetheless, maintenance questions will become increasingly important to Borland, for we already recognize that such questions are crucial in telecommunications systems with long service lifetimes.

8.13 Concluding Thoughts about QPW

Many other patterns were developed out of our understanding of the QPW project. The project got a start even while the compiler was not finished, which is an example of GET ON WITH IT (4.1.3). NAMED STABLE BASES (4.1.4) reflects the project's daily builds in order to incrementally add functionality. For the QPW team, WORK FLOWS INWARD (4.1.18), particularly during testing: information came in from beta users through the help desk to the development team. The team was strongly supported by management and other support functions during the earlier periods as well. SACRIFICE ONE PERSON (4.1.22) occurred in many instances, the most graphic of which involved Philippe Kahn's interactions with the press and market. He also acted as one of many FIREWALLS (4.2.9) and assumed a PATRON ROLE (4.2.15) in this capacity.

This SELF-SELECTING TEAM (4.2.11) had a strong UNITY OF PURPOSE (4.2.12). Small and isolated, the group operated much as a SKUNKWORKS (4.2.14); however, it had a much shorter-term strategic focus.

The team had a very low "truck number" [see MODERATE TRUCK NUMBER (4.2.24)], however, because of the high specialization. But their very strong commitment to the project and good communications suggest that there may have been more cross-fertilization than we could see. While architects (and other roles) maintained their specialization, they also maintained an uncharacteristically high level of communication among themselves. This balance is rare in organizations, and we have found it only in the strongest, most "hyperproductive" organizations. We originally captured this structure in a pattern called BUFFALO MOUNTAIN [Coplien 1995] that was later split into RESPONSIBILITIES ENGAGE (5.1.14) and HALLWAY CHATTER (5.1.15). Communication was the glue that held this organization together.

Can we capture the architecture of the Borland development organization and process and expect phenomenal results if we apply it to large development projects such as those that we have at AT&T? Probably not. However, Borland's staggering productivity offers a target to shoot for, and some aspects of its management policies and process guidelines may serve small- to medium-sized developments well. To the extent that large jobs can be partitioned into small ones, the Borland approach may also be suitable for individual parts of large developments.

Borland develops products for a domain and market that, today, has little overlap with the traditional telecommunications market. As large software development organizations move into new markets—such as software development environment platforms and soft human interfaces—the techniques used at Borland will become increasingly difficult to dismiss out of hand as irrelevant for large system development.

The software industry has long embraced rationales that dismiss the productivity of stereotypical "Silicon Valley" cultures. We tended to think of PC development efforts of that era as small and simple. We say they have limited markets and don't need to evolve. Borland defies these stereotypes. The QPW product needed to move into a market supported by Windows, Windows NT, Pink, and possibly others such as Macintosh and maybe even UNIX. It will need to interface with a host of different windowing systems and hardware technologies. It is not a small project, even by AT&T's standards (it is larger than the first release of the 1982 flagship AT&T local switching product). Borland was able to coax 1 million lines of production code from about eight people in 31 months. Perhaps a PC-based development environment and a PC-based deployment platform make developers more effective, and perhaps QPW doesn't have the same fault-tolerance requirements one finds in large telecommunications systems. But those considerations alone don't seem to account for figures that are orders of magnitude above industry norms.

Software maintenance is critically important to today's large, complex software developments. One suspects that the same will be true for QPW, since it offers new features, runs on new platforms, and adapts itself to new operating systems and windowing environments in the marketplace. One might guess that foreseeing such evolution is one reason for Borland to have chosen OO development techniques and C++ as the basis for the development effort.

The Borland process operates at an extreme point in our continuum of development organizations. A set of extreme data points can be of use to us in our process research by helping to bound the models we make. We hope the Borland model will provide data that will help us calibrate our process models and help us better correlate properties of other models we study.

A great big thanks to Carol Johnson at Borland for taking care of most of the local arrangements. I'm indebted to Ruby Chu at AT&T for chasing down QPW product reviews. A special thanks to Doug McIlroy and Peter Weinberger for their critical comments.

A Hyperproductive Telecommunications Development Team

This chapter is distilled from a paper prepared in the spring of 1994 shortly after Jim Coplien studied the team in question.

The exact identity of the team is withheld for two reasons. One reason relates to the propriety of information about the product at the time the study was done. Second, the team *asked* not to be identified. They were concerned at the time that if they were identified as having built a better mousetrap, then the world might beat a path to their door asking them for process advice. They didn't want to be in the process business; they didn't want to be distracted from doing what they enjoyed doing. But though we have omitted the external name of the product, we've included many particulars of data that we hope will make the group more tangible and that will answer questions about the viability of the group's approaches.

The report, as originally written, follows.

I had the pleasure of meeting with the entire development team for a small network platform being built by a Network Systems organization within AT&T Bell Laboratories on February 17, 1994. This project is among the most interesting I have studied, and the organization has some of the best team dynamics of any I have observed anywhere. The people find their work challenging, stimulating, and rewarding. Likewise, this organization is productive, with 200 KSLOC to their credit at the hands of six developers over 15 months. (That interval includes conceptualization and design, and the code count does not include a similar number of lines purchased externally or reused from existing internal projects.)

Many of the tenets, practices, and characteristics of this project are eerily reminiscent of Borland's QPW team, the most highly productive organization I have studied [Coplien 1994] (see Chapter 8). The project is unique in many of its own ways, too—unique, perhaps, in the sense that the experience could not be easily reproduced elsewhere. Nonetheless, this project provides another data point in our study of hyperprogramming (very productive) organizations (for a current total of two such data points). We noted that the two organizations resemble each other in many ways, ways that perhaps portend high productivity and quality of work life. These factors are worth exploring.

Might their development process be related to all of these factors? Contemporary management thinking holds *process* to be a dominant factor in quality and productivity. The project's process and organization are indeed the source of their power, but the process is off the beaten path. Our research was attracted to the organization because of its emphasis on parallelism, which, taken almost to extremes, produced astounding results.

9.1 The Culture

This organization has been around in one form or another for about 15 years. They have a long history of prototyping and building small systems. About 4 years ago, the organization started working on trials in order to prove their product concepts. Development started in earnest about 2 years ago. The development team currently has about eight people. Most (all but two at the debriefing) have families. The group is demographically diverse.

The project has an excellent history of meeting seemingly impossible delivery dates, owing to much hard work. The team typically works 50- to 60-hour weeks, with some working 60- to 70-hour weeks over a 5-month spurt. The team is egalitarian in the sense that everybody writes code, but it is nonegalitarian in that everybody brings their own realm of expertise to the table (which is an important factor we explore later in [CODE OWNERSHIP AND PROGRAMMING ANTHROPOMORPHISM (9.4.2)]).

People perform much of their own risk management. As the meeting got started, Peter told how he was going to add line splitting to the architecture, which was going to make more work for Pat. Pat was playfully unhappy about the change, but it was a design change the team had decided some time ago that it wanted. The project had been granted a 1-month extension in its schedule, and Peter had taken the initiative to redesign part of the system that had been causing them to use resources inefficiently.

Parallelism is key to the organization's success. The organization got its start when it was presented with an ambitious scenario: Conceptualize and deliver a system prototype in 4 to 5 months. Almost coincidentally, the requirements, testing, and design all converged on the same date. It worked, and these elements converged faster than anyone had imagined possible. The small team size, the excellence in systems engineering, and the lack of dogmatism among team members were major factors in the success of the prototype. The organization became more introspective about their concurrent engineering approach to development and turned it into a way of life for themselves. The technique that made the prototype successful was carried into the development of the product itself. It is this way of life that I had come to study.

And the introspection isn't complete. There is still a feeling that part of what makes them successful is purely instinctive. Peter even worried that I might cause process understanding to surface into their consciousness, which could affect the way they worked by establishing a new introspection framework and potentially damage the delicate and almost magical balance that had propelled them to success. While there is a slight chance that the Heisenberg phenomenon could take them in that direction, there is an equal or greater probability that such a discussion could open their eyes to possibilities for improvements.

The programming language is C, and the development environment is UNIX. (Note that they use neither OO approaches nor C++, staples that have become stereotypically associated with high productivity and best current practices.) The product has performed well in the field.

Three installations have been running for 7 months, with only three unplanned outages to their credit totaling less than 8 hours (better than 99.94 percent uptime). The total number of faults found in the field has been about 25, out of which 20 have been addressed at this writing.

The organization's culture, self-image, and process have a rich human element that precipitates from the small team environment. These issues merit their own section later in this chapter.

9.2 The Development Process

Figure 9.1 shows a structured flowchart of the process, called a role-activity diagram (RAD). The diagram misses many of the interesting interactions between people who enact the Developer role. It also misses the richness of interaction between the Ambassador and his 50 or so contacts external to the project. The Ambassador, like Allen's gatekeeper [Allen 1977], handles most of the external project technical interfaces.

Parallelism can be seen throughout. Design might start before system engineering. Requirements continue to change and accumulate after coding has started and sometimes even after performance verification.

9.3 The Pasteur Analysis of the Process

I analyzed the interview data using the Pasteur organizational analysis tools [Cain Coplien 1993]. Figure 9.2 shows the adjacency diagram, or force-based communication network diagram, for the development organization. The graph has two communication "hubs" at the Developer and Ambassador roles, respectively. We generate coupling metrics from the same model used to build the adjacency diagram. Coupling per role is 41 percent, about at the median, but far above the mode and mean for all of processes we have studied. It is about half the value of 89 percent for QPW.

There is an amazingly even distribution of work across the project. The Mad Artichoke, Ambassador, Manager, and Service Development roles all share the same degree of coupling to the process as a whole. Hacker, Domain Experts, Service Management, Product Management and Performance Verification are slightly less coupled. As we have found in most organizations, the Developer role, more than any other single role, is tightly coupled to the process as a whole.

It is rare that we find a small organization with an architect, and it is rarer still that the architect occupies a central position. In this network platform development, the Mad Artichoke (architect) role is more coupled to the process as a whole than is any role except Developer, which links every role in the communications model (again, reminiscent of QPW). Much of the communication burden that normally falls on the developer's shoulders is taken on by the Ambassador, which is a secondary hub in the organization structure. This role fits Allen's description of the "gatekeeper" role exactly (again, reminiscent of QPW).

The centrality of the Architect is reminiscent of QPW. In QPW, QA was more central than we find in this organization.

Figure 9.3 shows the interaction grid for the project. The picture is curiously asymmetric. The large blank space at the top occurs because roles outside the process are not approached to do work; instead, they supply work, constraints, and input to the project. That anomaly aside, communication patterns are distributed evenly across the organization. Such an even spread of connectivity is rare in the processes we have studied, but it was a characteristic of the Borland QPW organization.

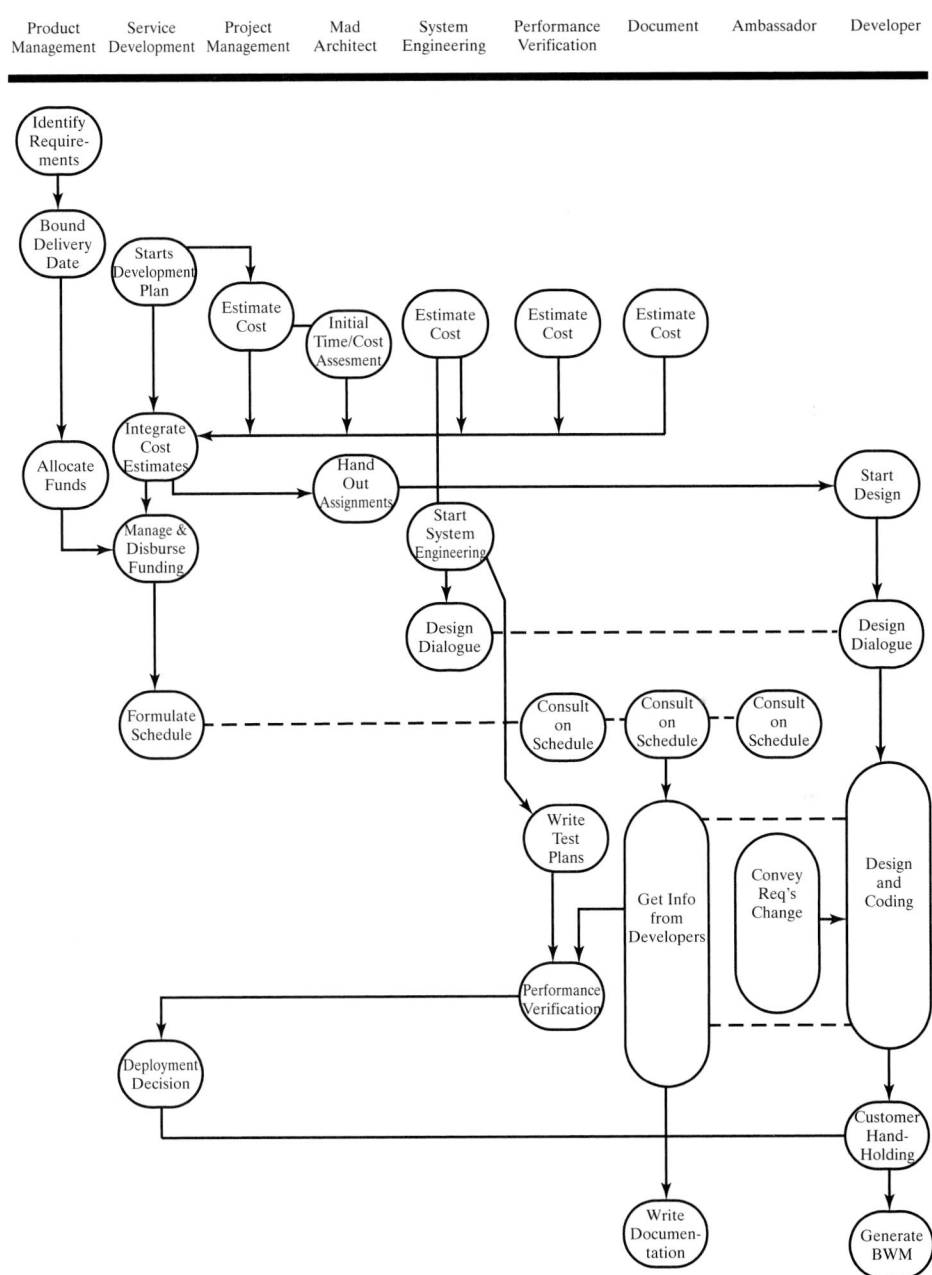

FIGURE 9.1 Role-Activity Diagram of the Process

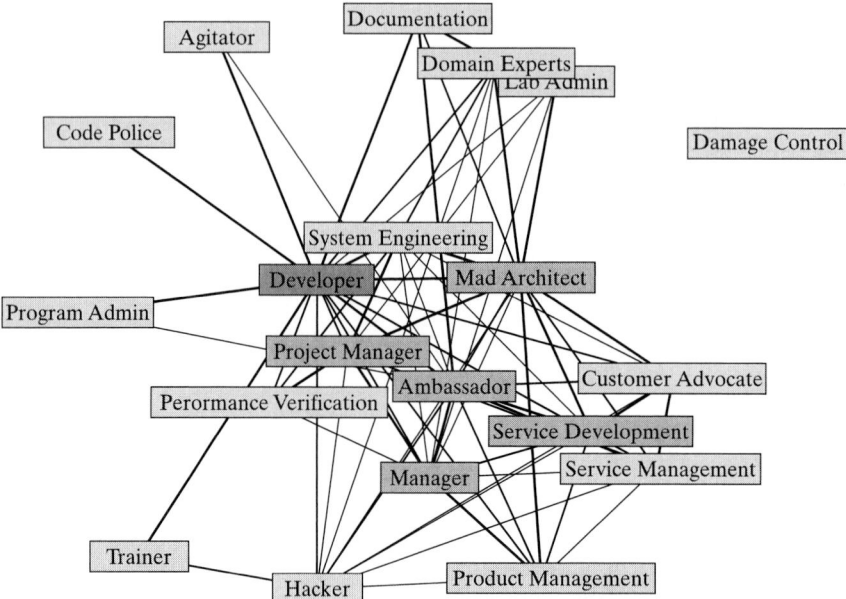

FIGURE 9.2 Adjacency Diagram (Natural Force-Based Placement)

9.4 The Human Side

The process and culture have a richly human side, which shows up in how the group talks about itself, as well as in its organization and process. We explore three aspects of the human issue here: the manner in which people issues are integrated into the process, the anthropomorphizing of code, and management practices.

9.4.1   Engineering People Issues into the Process

The "high-touch" flourish in this "high-tech" environment became clear from the outset [Naisbitt 1984]. People invented outrageous role names to describe themselves: Mad Artichoke for the architect, Agitator, Code Police, and Damage Control.

The "person-ality" of the project goes deeper. Consider the perceived responsibilities of the Agitator role:

- Keep the team from getting too comfortable.
- Trigger discussions.
- Say things nobody wants to say.

"Say things nobody wants to say"? Many conservative development organization cultures cut off painful avenues of progress by making many topics of conversation taboo. In this organization, everything is open to criticism by anyone. As Steve Bauman (then a director at Bell Laboratories) once said, the environment is not "warm and fuzzy"; instead, it is "open and productive." This behavior can be found in patterns like PUBLIC CHARACTER (4.2.17) and WISE FOOL (4.2.21). The Damage Control role has the following responsibility: "Repair interorganizational and interpersonal damage."

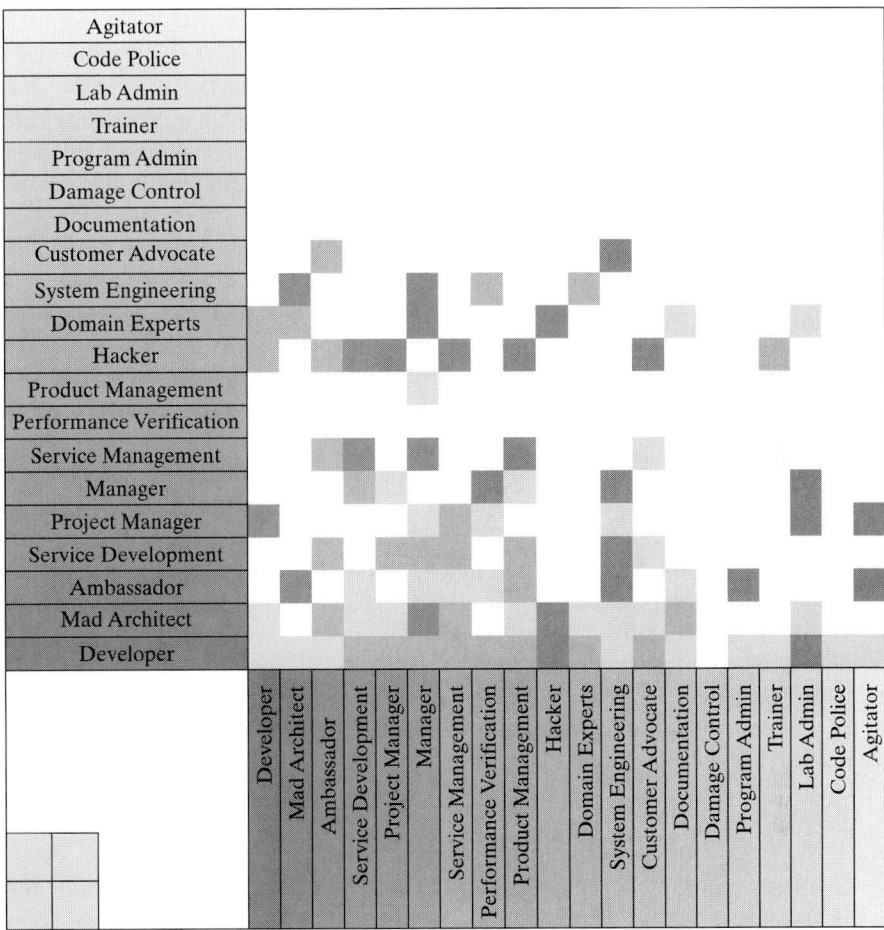

FIGURE 9.3 Interaction Grid

First-level managers play a less authoritarian role in the process than in a typical corporate development setting. Most of their role involves providing support and tracking project status, but "twisting arms" of people outside the team is also among their responsibilities. They see their job as ensuring that the team has the best people possible, that they have the resources and time necessary to do a good job, and that outside interference and roadblocks are kept out of the developers' way. They also fill the Damage Control role.

9.4.2   Code Ownership and Programming Anthropomorphism

The project has strong code ownership that transcends release cycles. Everybody knows what everybody else is working on. Nobody changes anyone else's code, except in an emergency. If one programmer finds a bug in another's code, the person who finds the bug asks the owner to make the change.

Code ownership creates an interesting project mentality that is difficult to codify, but which might be summed up in a wry comment from one developer: "We don't use ECMS or Sablime [source management tools], so we need code ownership." Code ownership makes job responsibilities visible in the culture, rather than burying them in a tool.

Code ownership goes so deep that the project team has anthropomorphized their software. Software anthropomorphizing is something taught in some analysis techniques, including the popular CRC technique for OO analysis, [Beck 1991] but this project takes this technique to an unparalleled extreme. During scenario walkthroughs, you don't hear them saying, "the X module sends this message to the Y module"; instead, they make some sort of statement like, "A message comes in from Dara and goes over to Roman." "Now, Peter kills Pat" describes a signal sent between processes. One can go by the lab at night and hear a programmer scream, "Oh, Peter! Why did you do this?" as Peter's code reaches out and creates some system atrocity that makes the tester's life difficult. The code is strongly identified with the individual who owns it.

Responsibility is a deep underlying value in this project. Ownership exists for its own sake, but if you own something and you make a change, you have responsibility for that change. Code ownership and the associated culture raise everybody's awareness, expectation, and assurance that such responsibility will be carried forward. It seems more powerful than having a tool to track down a change to an accountable individual; in fact, there is a mindset that transcends the need for such version-management tools in a small project. This makes site support and first office application (FOA) activities easier. Thus, when a problem is found in the field, it is usually clear who needs to be brought in to fix it.

Will the project need version management as it grows? Possibly, but the market is constrained enough that multifeaturism may not become a serious problem. If releases can be coordinated for all sites (it is believed that the market can bear 11 systems), then versioning may never be needed.

9.4.3   Growing a Garden

After the group session, I stopped by to debrief the department head on my findings. She briefly described her management philosophy, which she likened to gardening. Her main job, however, is to "keep the pests away." That, she said, is what a good project manager does. Curiously enough, the role we ended up calling "project manager" we were initially going to call "smoke screen," because it distanced the development community from surrounding organizations.

On the way out, I ran into a manager from another project who, in an unrelated context, talked about "controlling the people who sit in the bleachers and throw rocks." Insulation appears to be an important and successful management strategy in this culture.

9.4.4   Rewarding Excellence

Traditional rewards like money and promotions are in short supply; nonetheless, intrinsic motivators can be equally direct and even more effective. People *enjoy* their work here. Their talents are appreciated, and the people are respected as individuals. The people are *trusted*: they are given much latitude and much responsibility, and they are trusted to talk directly to customers. The issue of trust was also central to the Borland QPW team.

Their department head had this to say:

> [M]uch of the reward is intangible ... not something I as a manager give, but something I allow them to achieve. I give lots of personal attention to them and try to create a fun, creative environment with challenging assignments. I try to

personalize the whole set of interactions so that everyone thinks they are doing this to better ourselves and better our chances of getting more challenging, fun, creative work.

This approach is reminiscent of the "getting one's ticket punched" concept described in *Soul of a New Machine*, [Kidder 1981], a mentality common to Silicon Valley companies as well. The close coupling between influential management (in this case, a widely respected department head) and their staff members is also reminiscent of the Borland environment.

9.5 The Small Team Spirit

As was true for Borland's QPW, this product is developed by a small team. Small teams can achieve results that would be impossible in a traditional organization. Such teams make anthropomorphism feasible. They give everyone a feeling of connectedness. They smooth communication and, in fact, enable communication dynamics that may lie at the heart of concurrent engineering.

"I think I'm going to need this soon," Bryan yells down the hall to Dave about changes to a module that must be coordinated with Bryan's fixes. It's midmorning, and Bryan knows that before the morning is over he'll need Dave's module so he can test his own work. Further, Dave knows that unless he stops what *he's* doing and turns to the module Bryan has asked for, Bryan will become blocked. Dave drops what he's doing and moves to finish up the work he needs to do to support Bryan. At about 2:00, Dave yells down the hall, "Here it is." Bryan is now in shape to test after only a short delay, and Dave goes back to what he's doing, without ever having been idle.

An exceptional instance? Not exactly. In the interest of minimizing wait states, interrupt mode—also known as the INTERRUPTS UNJAM BLOCKING (4.1.25) pattern—becomes the modus operandi of the whole group. Wait states can add substantially to product interval. The microparallelism of this process alleviates much of the blocking one finds in large projects. Just as in processor scheduling, interrupts reduce the latency to service a request. If the context-switch overhead is low enough, the throughput for an interrupt-driven development will be about the same as for any other approach. It takes close-knit communications to make it work.

How do these communications take place? I asked if they held periodic team meetings. "Not if we can help it," was the reply. Team members have a small number of three- or four-person meetings during the day. Yelling up and down the hallway is *de rigueur*. These meetings are unlike those at Borland, where much more of the dialogue seems to have taken place at a round table under the banner of architecture. But the underlying principle—close-knit communication—is the same.

This approach leads to an unconventional view of time and schedule. Most software development projects are *monochronic societies*: They believe time adds up algebraically. This organization seems to be more *polychronic*: with parallelism and task shuffling, time becomes fluid and can be manipulated. The interrupt-driven nature can be somewhat nerve racking, and carrying on in parallel with people outside the team (e.g., in front-end and back-end processes) can be uncomfortable. But the resulting productivity gains are high.

9.6 Process Improvement Opportunities

Code ownership can be maintained in the long term only if there is a solid high-level architecture with clear, explicit interfaces. This project should work to make their architecture more explicit and to better formalize the interfaces. These tasks will become increasingly important as development moves from initial product formulation to ongoing evolution.

Right now, there is no clearly identified role in this project that is responsible for conducting arms-length black-box testing for faults. They are aware of this problem and are addressing it.

Bell Laboratories modular building construction may not be the most conducive to the interactions that seem to nourish this team. Alternative architectures and room configurations might support the necessary interworking while also maintaining the sense of "space" and privacy that has long been a valued aspect of the Bell Labs culture.

9.7 Thoughts and Conclusions

On a person-by-person basis, this organization is one of the most productive organizations we've studied. Such high productivity usually comes not only from good development and management practices, but also from a high commitment of time and energy from its developers. Such behavior should be encouraged through the reward system and through recognition, as it was at Borland.

The small-team dynamics of this organization have been the dominant factor in its prodigious success: The high degree of parallelism, the interrupt-driven development, and the use of concurrent engineering are all related to the team size. Other similarities to Borland QPW include the high degree of trust between members of the project, the tight coupling with respected and influential management, the centrality of the architecture function, tight code ownership and software anthropomorphism, and the even distribution of communication across all roles in the organization. These latter factors characterize a *true team*. Such distinguishing characteristics of organization and process should be carefully considered as key factors that differentiate highly productive organizations from most contemporary software development efforts and the mature practices they use.

PART V
Appendices

APPENDIX A
Summary Patlets

A *patlet* is a short summary of the problem and solution for a pattern. Patlets are often used as an aid to discovering patterns in order to solve a particular problem at hand. Here, we use the patlets as a way to index patterns you are looking for.

A.1 Project Management Patlets

The patlets in Figure A.1 point to patterns for initial organizational design. You can find the patterns in the section PROJECT MANAGEMENT PATTERN LANGUAGE (4.1).

Community of Trust (4.1.1):

If you are building any human organization, *Then:* you must have a foundation of trust and respect for effective communication at levels deep enough to sustain growth.

Size the Schedule (4.1.2):

If the schedule is too long, developers become complacent, *but* if it is too short, they become overtaxed; *Therefore:* reward people when they meet the schedule, and keep two sets of books.

Get on With It (4.1.3):

If you have enough information to get started on parts of a project, *Then:* don't wait until you have a complete schedule before you start to work.

Named Stable Bases (4.1.4):

If you want to balance stability with progress, *Then:* have a hierarchy of named stable bases that people can work against.

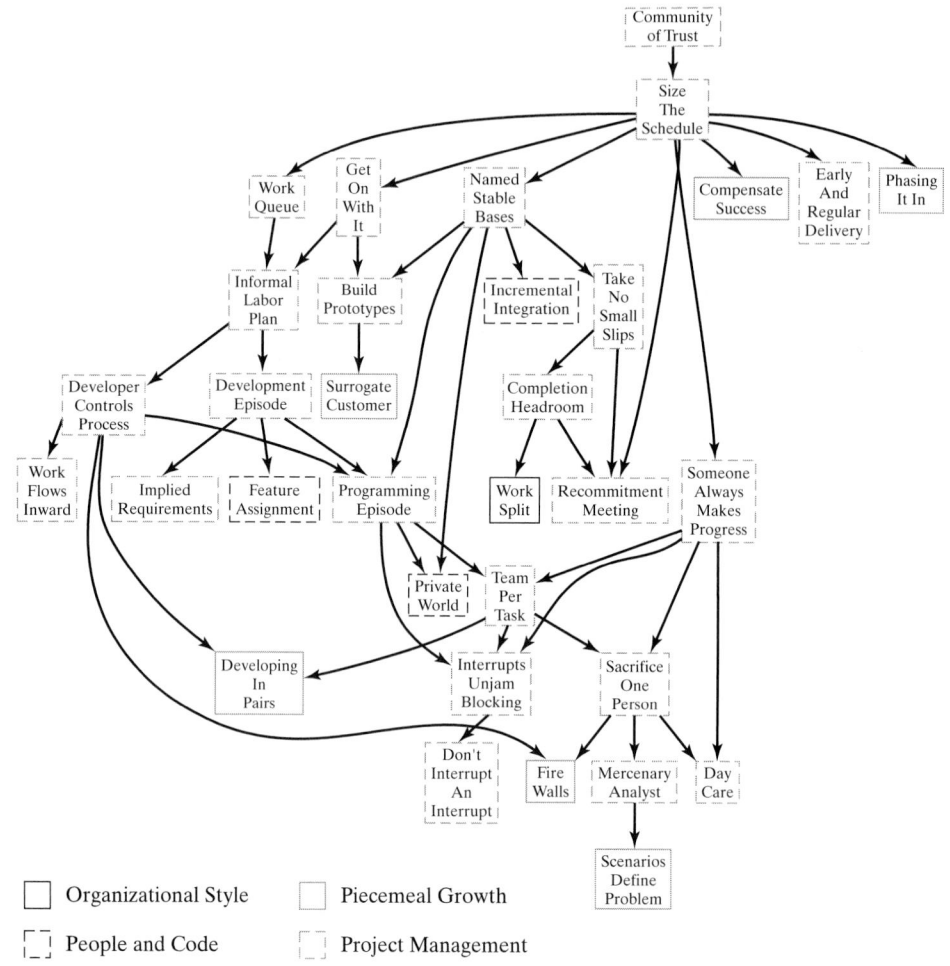

FIGURE A.1 Patterns from the Project Management Pattern Language

Incremental Integration (4.1.5):

If you want developers to be able to test changes before publishing them, *Then:* allow developers to build the entire product code independently to allow testing with the very latest base (not with the latest NAMED STABLE BASE).

Private World (4.1.6):

If you want to isolate developers from the effects of changes, *Then:* allow developers to have private work spaces that contain the entire build environment.

Build Prototypes (4.1.7):

If early requirements are difficult to validate without testing, *Then:* build a prototype whose purpose is to help clarify requirements and assess risk.

Take No Small Slips (4.1.9):

If you are getting behind schedule and you need additional time resources, *Then:* take one large planned slip instead of creating project instability and low team morale with small, unanticipated slips.

Completion Headroom (4.1.10):

If work is progressing against a set of hard dates, *Then:* make sure there is COMPLETION HEADROOM between the completion dates of the largest task and the hard delivery dates.

Work Split (4.1.11):

If people are escalating their problems, *Then:* split work into urgent and deferred components and make sure that less than half of development work focuses on the urgent component.

Recommitment Meeting (4.1.12):

If the schedule can't be met with simple adjustments to the work queue and staffing, *Then:* assemble developers and interested managers to recommit to a new strategy based on doing the minimal amount of work to reach a satisfactory conclusion.

Work Queue (4.1.13):

If deliverables are ill-defined, you need to allow time for everything to be done. *Therefore,* produce a schedule with less output than you have input. Use the list of IMPLIED REQUIREMENTS (4.1.16) (really just names) as a starting point and situate them into a likely implementation order, favoring the more urgent or higher-priority items.

Informal Labor Plan (4.1.14):

If development needs are fluid, *Then,* instead of master planning, let them negotiate among themselves to develop short-term plans.

Development Episode (4.1.15):

If we overemphasize the skills of individual contributors, work suffers. *Therefore,* approach all development as a group activity as if no one had anything else to do.

Implied Requirements (4.1.16):

If you need a way to nail down the functionality that needs to be covered, *Then:* make a list of functional areas and domains instead of breaking down functionality into traditional requirements.

Developer Controls Process (4.1.17):

If you need to orchestrate the activities of a given location or feature, *Then:* put the Developer role in control of the succession of activities.

Work Flows Inward (4.1.18):

If you want information to flow to the producing roles in an organization, *Then:* put the Developer at the center and see that information flows *toward* the center, not *from* the center.

Programming Episode (4.1.19):

If you need to split up work across time, *Then:* do the work in discrete episodes that combine to create concrete deliverables.

Someone Always Makes Progress (4.1.20):

If distractions constantly interrupt your team's progress, *Then:* whatever happens, ensure someone keeps moving toward your primary goal.

Team Per Task (4.1.21):

If a big diversion hits your team, *Then:* let a subteam handle the diversion so the main team can keep going.

Sacrifice One Person (4.1.22):

If a smaller diversion hits your team, *Then:* assign just one person to resolve it.

Day Care (4.1.23):

If your experts are spending all of their time mentoring novices, *Then:* put one expert in charge of all the novices and let the other experts develop the system.

Mercenary Analyst (4.1.24):

If you want to keep documentation from being a critical path roadblock for developers, *Then:* hire a MERCENARY ANALYST to write the bulk of the documentation.

Interrupts Unjam Blocking (4.1.25):

If you need to schedule urgent development activities according to some reasonable priority scheme, *Then:* use an interrupt scheme to keep individual problems from blocking the entire project.

Don't Interrupt an Interrupt (4.1.26):

If a new urgent need arises while you're already in the middle of handling an interrupt to keep the project from getting stuck, *Then:* continue handling the current issue before moving on to the new one.

A.2 Piecemeal Growth Patlets

These patlets summarize patterns for the growth of an organization once it is up and running. You can find the patterns in the section PIECEMEAL GROWTH PATTERN LANGUAGE (4.2).

Size the Organization (4.2.2):

If an organization is too large, communications break down, and *if* it is too small, it can't achieve its goals or easily overcome the difficulties of adding more people. *Therefore,* start projects with a critical mass of about 10 people.

Phasing It In (4.2.3):

If you can't always get the experts you need, *Then:* grow new experts from new hires.

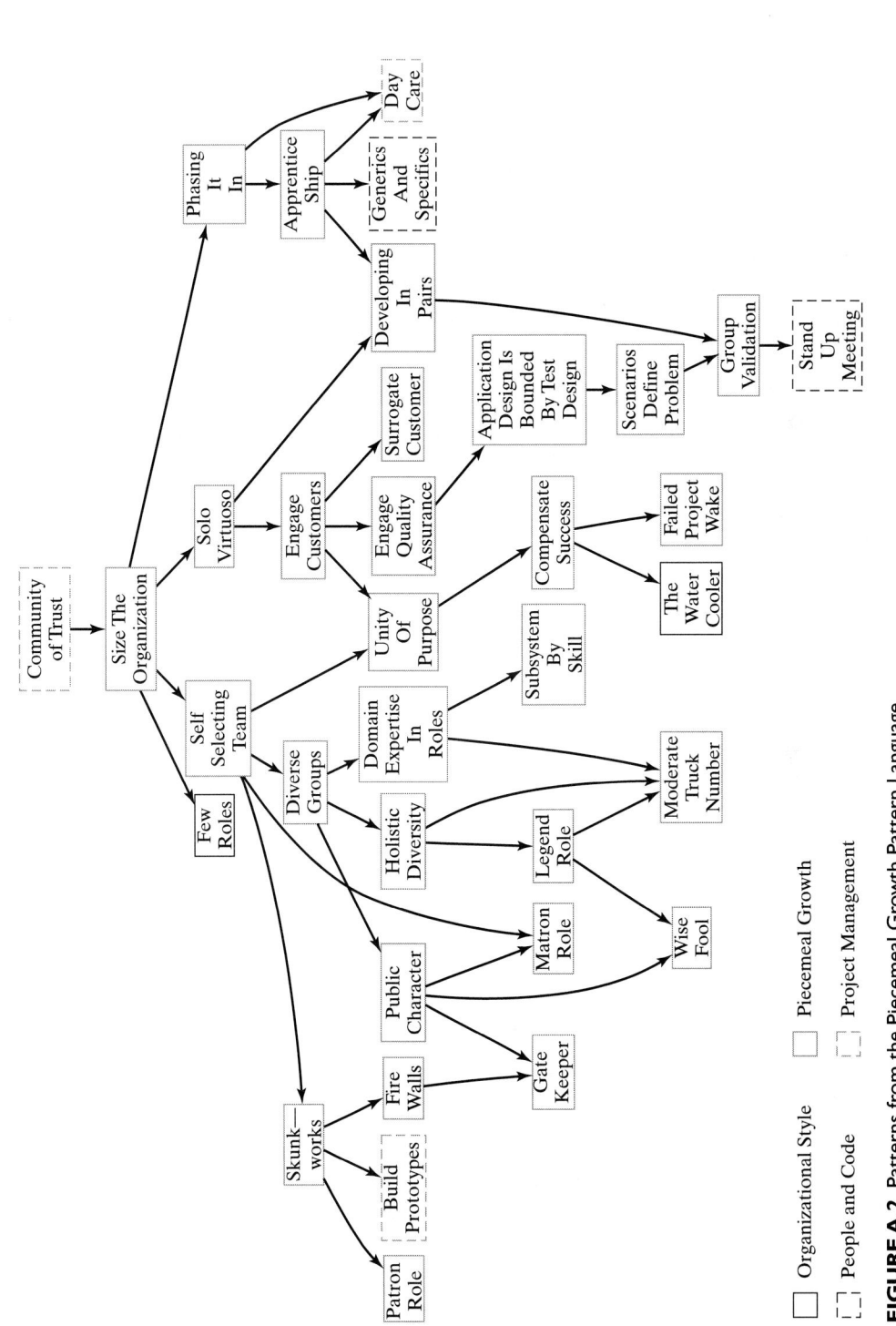

FIGURE A.2 Patterns from the Piecemeal Growth Pattern Language

Legend:

☐ Organizational Style   ☐ Piecemeal Growth

⌐⌐ People and Code   ⌐⌐ Project Management

Apprenticeship (4.2.4):

If you have difficulty retaining expertise, *Then:* grow expertise internally from existing employees or even new hires.

Solo Virtuoso (4.2.5):

If a project is intellectually small, then overstaffing it is a waste of time and money. *Therefore,* staff small projects with SOLO VIRTUOSOS.

Engage Customers (4.2.6):

If you want to manage an incremental process that accommodates customer input, and if you want the customer to feel loved, *Then:* ENGAGE CUSTOMERS after QA and project management are prepared to serve them.

Surrogate Customer (4.2.7):

If you need answers from your customer, but no customer is available to answer your questions, *Then:* create a SURROGATE CUSTOMER role in your organization.

Scenarios Define Problem (4.2.8):

If you want a good characterization of customer needs, *Then:* use scenarios to define the problem.

Firewalls (4.2.9):

If you want to keep your developers from being interrupted by extraneous influences and special interest groups, *Then:* impose a FIREWALL, such as a manager, to "keep the pests away."

Gatekeeper (4.2.10):

If you need to keep from being inbred, *Then:* use a GATEKEEPER role to tie development to other projects, research, and the outside world.

Self-Selecting Team (4.2.11):

If you appoint people to a team, the people don't come together as a team. People who share similar outside interests make the best team members. *Therefore,* teams should be largely self-selecting, performing limited screening of candidates based on their track record and outside interests.

Unity of Purpose (4.2.12):

If a team is beginning to work together, *Then:* make sure all members agree on the purpose of the team.

Team Pride (4.2.13):

If a team needs to perform above and beyond the call of duty, *Then:* instill a well-grounded sense of elitism in its members.

Skunkworks (4.2.14):

If a project innovates too much, then it increases its risk. Yet, there is a place for innovation. *Therefore,* give innovation organizational space and time.

Patron Role (4.2.15):

If you need to insulate Developers so Developer Controls Process (4.1.17) and support organizational inertia at a strategic level, *Then:* identify a Patron accessible to the project who can champion the cause of the project.

Diverse Groups (4.2.16):

If everyone has similar views, you have a good team, *but* too much normalization within a team leaves important problem areas unaddressed. *Therefore,* assemble a diverse team based on different experiences, cultures, and genders.

Public Character (4.2.17):

If you need a catalyst to bring people together, *Then:* recognize some roles as Public Characters.

Matron Role (4.2.18):

If your team needs ongoing care and feeding, *Then:* include a Matron Role on the team who will naturally take care of the team's social needs.

Holistic Diversity (4.2.19):

Development of a subsystem requires many skills, but people specialize. *Therefore,* create a single team from multiple specialties.

Legend Role (4.2.20):

If a key person will leave the organization soon, *Then:* train a replacement for that person and have the replacement assume a role named after the key person.

Wise Fool (4.2.21):

If critical issues do not get aired easily, *Then:* nurture a Wise Fool to say the things nobody else dares say.

Domain Expertise in Roles (4.2.22):

If you need to staff all roles, it's difficult to determine how to match people to roles in order to optimize communication. *Therefore,* match people to roles based on domain expertise, and emphasize that people play those roles in the organization.

Subsystem by Skill (4.2.23):

If you need to organize subsystems for the long haul, *Then:* divide them up by skills.

Moderate Truck Number (4.2.24):

If you can't eliminate having a single point of failure in allocating expertise to roles, *Then:* spread that expertise around as far as possible, but not more so.

Compensate Success (4.2.25):

If enterprises are to succeed, they must reward the behaviors that lead to success; however, these behaviors are varied, and success is difficult to measure. *Therefore,* establish a spectrum of reward mechanisms for both teams and individuals.

Failed Project Wake (4.2.26):

If people have put their hearts and souls into a project, that subsequently is canceled, *Then:* celebrate the project's demise and hold a "wake" for it.

Developing in Pairs (4.2.28):

If you want to improve the effectiveness of individual developers, *Then:* have people develop in pairs.

Engage Quality Assurance (4.2.29):

If developers can't be counted on to test beyond what they already anticipate going wrong, *Then:* engage QA as an important function.

Application Design Is Bounded by Test Design (4.2.30):

If you want to organize the interworking between test developers and software developers, *Then:* organize the process so APPLICATION DESIGN IS BOUNDED BY TEST DESIGN.

Group Validation (4.2.32):

If you want to avoid being blindsided in QA, *Then:* validate the system by using the patterns ENGAGE CUSTOMERS (4.2.6) and DEVELOPING IN PAIRS (4.2.28).

A.3 Organizational Style Patlets

Good design lends a sense of style to anything we build. Each great organization has its own style, and these patterns help to shape that style. Different organizational styles fit different needs, so these patterns provide a good foundation for tailoring an organization to your business and market. The patterns can be found in the section ORGANIZATIONAL STYLE PATTERN LANGUAGE (5.1).

Few Roles (5.1.2):

If your organization has high communication overhead and latency, *Then:* identify the roles in the organization and reduce the number of roles to 16 or fewer.

Producer Roles (5.1.3):

If your organization has too many roles, but does not know which to eliminate, *Then:* identify roles as Producers, Supporters, or Deadbeats. Eliminate the Deadbeats and combine some of the Supporters.

Producers in the Middle (5.1.4):

If your developers are somewhat lost, *Then:* make sure the producer roles are at the center of all communication.

Stable Roles (5.1.5):

If you have to deal with project disruptions, *Then:* keep people in their primary roles and deal with disruptions as temporary tasks.

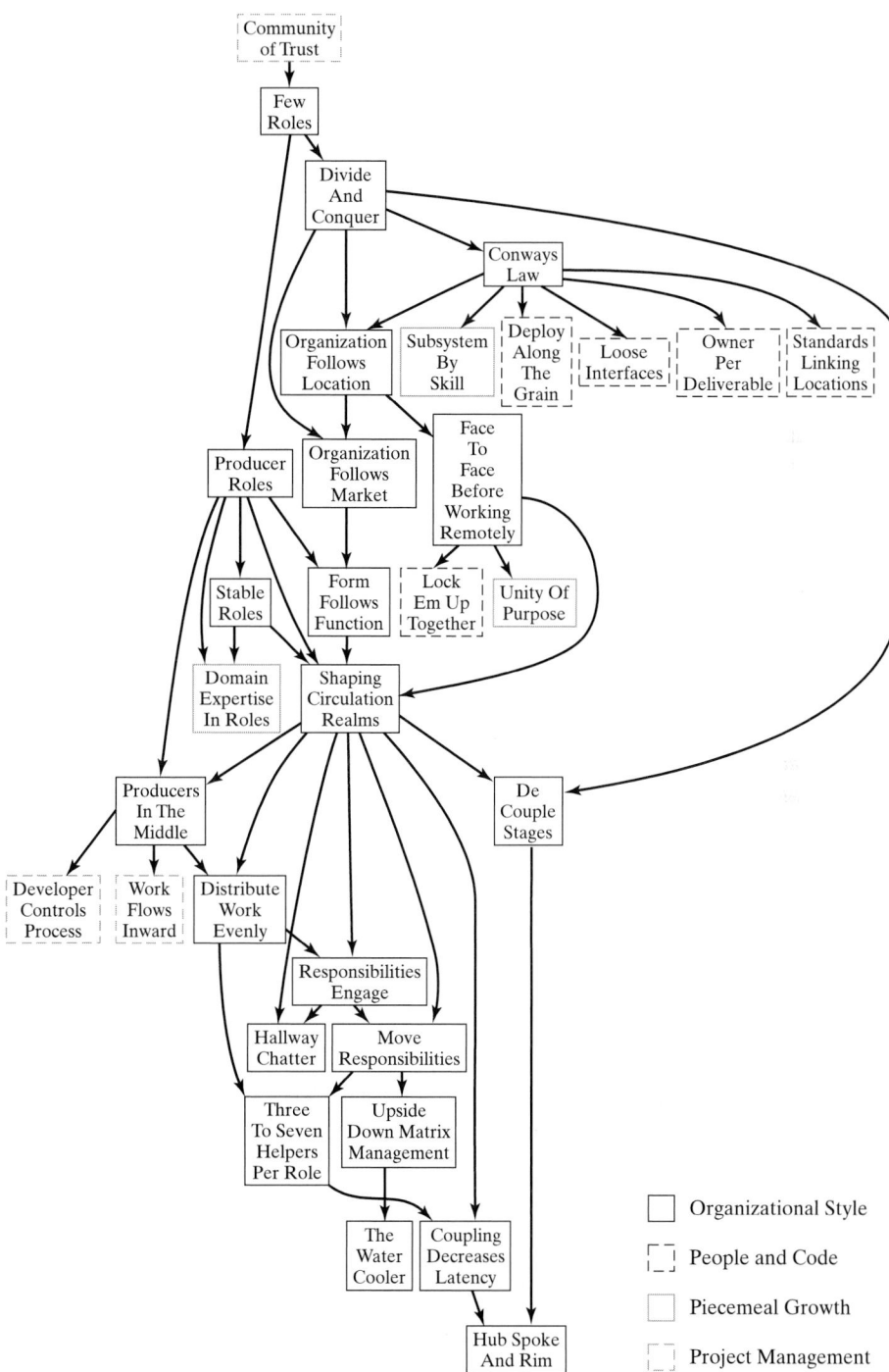

FIGURE A.3 Patterns from the Organizational Style Pattern Language

Divide and Conquer (5.1.6):

If an organization is getting too large for communications to be effective any more, *Then:* try partitioning it along lines of mutual interest and coupling, thus forming separate organizations and processes.

Conway's Law (5.1.7):

If organizational-structuring concerns are torn between geography, expertise, politics, and other factors, *Then:* align the primary organizational structure with the structure of the business domains, thus making it the structure that will be reflected in the product architecture.

Organization Follows Location (5.1.8):

If you need to distribute work geographically, communications suffer, *but* you can limit the damage if work is partitionable. *Therefore,* organize work so that groups of people that work together are at the same location.

Organization Follows Market (5.1.9):

If there is no clear organizational accountability to a market, *Then:* make some organization accountable for each market to ensure that the market's needs will be met.

Face to Face Before Working Remotely (5.1.10):

If a project is divided geographically, *Then:* begin the project by inviting everyone to a meeting at a single place.

Form Follows Function (5.1.11):

If there is little specialization and if people don't know where to turn for answers to technical questions, *Then:* create domains of expertise called *roles* that cluster around artifacts or specialization.

Shaping Circulation Realms (5.1.12):

If you need mechanisms to facilitate the communication structures necessary for good group formation, *Then:* create an environment that encourages effective interactions.

Distribute Work Evenly (5.1.13):

If you want to optimize team effectiveness and productivity, *Then:* alleviate overload on specific groups and individuals in your organization by DISTRIBUTING WORK EVENLY.

Responsibilities Engage (5.1.14):

If central roles are overloaded, but you don't want to take them out of the communication loop, *Then:* intensify communication among noncentral roles to lighten the load on the central roles.

Hallway Chatter (5.1.15):

If developers tend to huddle around the organizational core or *if* supporting roles are inadequately engaged with each other, *Then:* rearrange responsibilities in a way that encourages less isolation and more interworking among roles and people.

Decouple Stages (5.1.16):

If development stages overlap so heavily that they cause rework, and phases can be separated to increase parallelism, *Then:* serialize process steps and establish well-defined handoffs between steps.

Hub, Spoke, and Rim (5.1.17):

If you want to DECOUPLE STAGES (5.1.16) in a high-context development process, *Then:* orchestrate the process with a hub role and minimize coupling between other roles by using a hub-spoke-and-rim geometry.

Move Responsibilities (5.1.18):

If you want to change coupling between roles (particularly if you want to decouple roles), *Then:* MOVE RESPONSIBILITIES from one role to another.

Upside-Down Matrix Management (5.1.19):

If the right skills and resources don't seem to be applied to a particular aspect of the work, *Then:* go beyond corporate structures to leverage teams in other organizations (e.g., customers, partners, or other internal organizations).

The Watercooler (5.1.20):

If you need more communication between institutionalized organizations, *Then:* leave space for everyday human activities that can provide more complete and informal communication.

Three to Seven Helpers Per Role (5.1.21):

If you want to even out communication, *Then:* at least try to limit communication to THREE TO SEVEN HELPERS PER ROLE and pull up the outliers to the same level of engagement.

Coupling Decreases Latency (5.1.22):

If you need a high throughput development process, *Then:* increase coupling between roles to decrease latency.

A.4 People and Code Patlets

People and code are the two most important components of a software development organization. Customers wouldn't exist without code to sell to them, and code wouldn't exist without people. People write code, and the structure of code, in turn, affects how people organize. These patlets point to patterns that help an organization align the people and code structures properly. The patterns themselves can be found in the section PEOPLE AND CODE PATTERN LANGUAGE (5.2).

Architect Controls Product (5.2.3):

If a project has a long life, *Then:* assign the architect to carry the vision forward and serve as the long-term keeper of architectural style.

Architecture Team (5.2.4):

If you are building a system that is too large or complex to be thoroughly understood by a single individual, *Then:* build a team that has both the responsibility and the power to create the initial architecture.

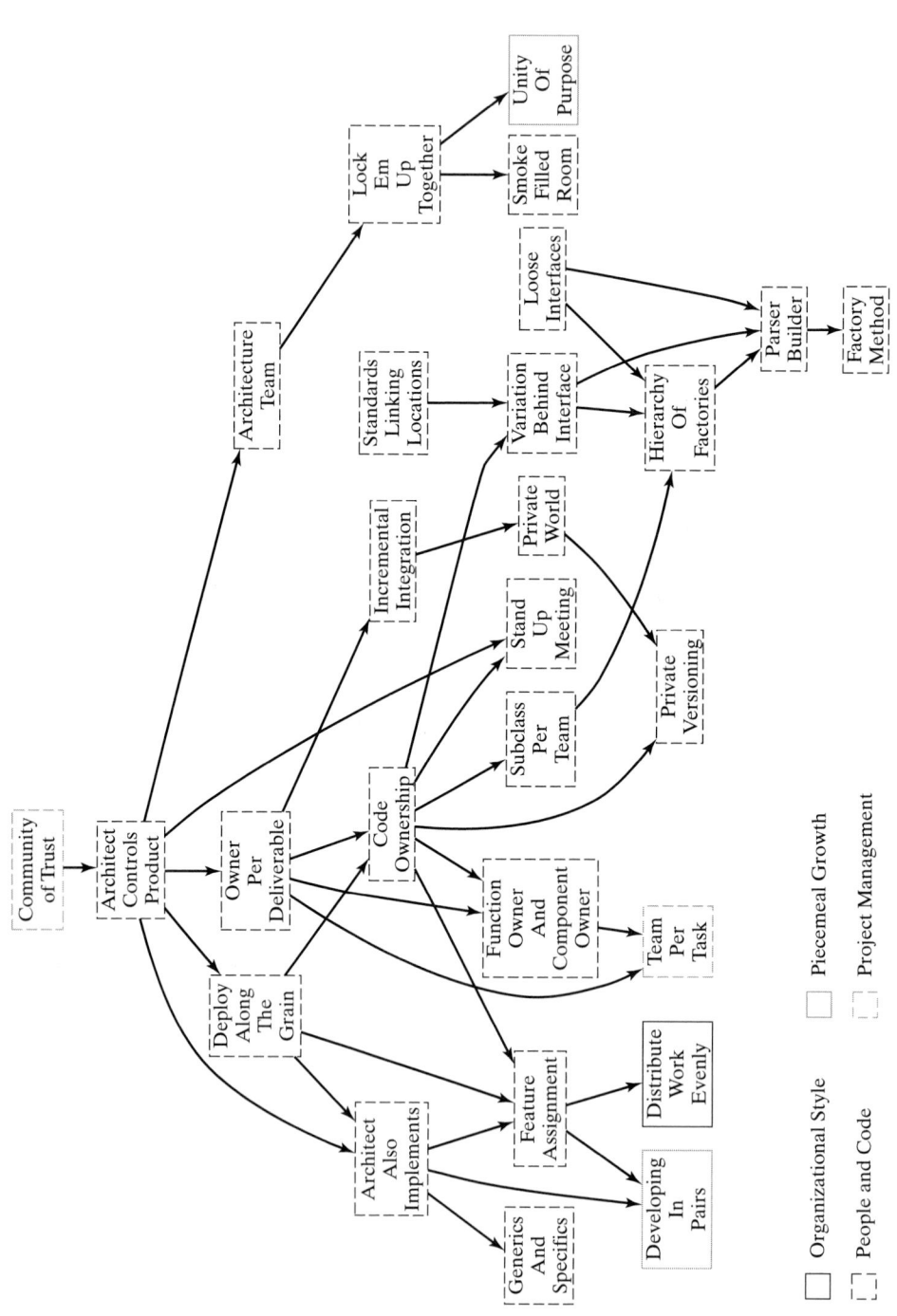

FIGURE A.4 Patterns from the People and Code Pattern Language

Lock 'Em Up Together (5.2.5):

If your team is struggling to come up with an architecture, *Then:* sequester them together physically for several days so they can work uninterrupted.

Smoke-Filled Room (5.2.6):

If you need to make a decision quickly and there are reasons to exclude others, *Then:* make the decision covertly so that the rationale remains private, even though the decision will be publicized.

Stand-Up Meeting (5.2.7):

If there are pockets of misinformation or *if* people are out of the loop, *Then:* hold short daily meetings to socialize emerging developments.

Deploy Along the Grain (5.2.8):

If reuse is suffering from fragmentation of responsibilities for an artifact, *Then:* give people dedicated, long-term responsibility for a piece of the system.

Architect Also Implements (5.2.10):

If an architect is in an ivory tower, he or she is out of touch with reality; yet someone needs to reconcile the high-level overview with practice. *Therefore,* ensure that the architect is materially involved in day-to-day implementation.

Generics and Specifics (5.2.11):

If you have many new people, *Then:* assign the experienced people to work on generic parts of the project and give specific assignments to the new people.

Standards Linking Locations (5.2.12):

If development is separated geographically, *Then:* use standards to link parts of the architecture that cross geographic boundaries.

Code Ownership (5.2.13):

If you need responsibility for code and want to build on DOMAIN EXPERTISE IN ROLES (4.2.22), *Then:* give various individuals responsibility for the overall quality of the code.

Feature Assignment (5.2.14):

If you are trying to partition work in a large project, *Then:* assign features to people.

Variation Behind Interface (5.2.15):

If more than one person is developing software, then changes affect not only the code, but people as well. *Therefore,* create interfaces around predicted points of variation.

Private Versioning (5.2.16):

If you want to enable incremental changes without publishing those changes, *Then:* set up a mechanism that allows developers to version code without checking it in to a public repository.

Loose Interfaces (5.2.17):

If you need to develop systems rapidly in an environment where communication is less than optimal, *Then:* limit the number of explicit, static interfaces. Instead, use loose interfaces like callbacks.

Subclass Per Team (5.2.18):

If subsystem teams have different design points, *Then:* where two subsystems collide in one class, assign those subsystems to different layers of the class hierarchy.

Hierarchy of Factories (5.2.19):

If you have a creational system that creates different products specified by different groups, *Then:* set up factories in a hierarchical arrangement, where each factory knows only about one level below it.

Parser Builder (5.2.20):

If you need to create objects based on type information in an input stream, *Then:* use a parser builder that reads type information from the stream and builds the appropriate objects based on this information.

A.5 Patlets from Other Pattern Languages

This book has been a team effort, incorporating pattern material from many sources including works by Alistair Cockburn, Ward Cunningham, Steve Berczuk, Brian Foote and others. Sometimes we have included patterns almost intact, and in other cases we have updated or edited the patterns to fit into the format or the context of the pattern languages in this book. For example, many of Alistair Cockburn's patterns have essentially the same content here as they do in their original publication, but here they have been radically reformatted from their original form for the sake of consistency.

Some patterns, while still relevant to the topic of organizational structure, didn't quite fit in with the pattern languages here, perhaps because they describe process instead of structure, because they are idioms sensitive to particular situations, because they are off topic, or because they are proto-patterns awaiting broad substantiation. Nonetheless, we still refer to some of those patterns, and we commend them to you as great reading.

In this section, we provide patlets for those patterns that didn't make it into the book. These patlets often do not follow the patlet style we used earlier in this chapter. Some of the patlets come verbatim from Linda Rising's *Pattern Almanac* [Rising 2000], which is a great source of other organizational pattern reference material.

A.5.1 Arranging the Furniture

Your established team is entering a transition period where members are replaced by newcomers who must quickly come to grips with large and complex software modules. People are territorial and need to mark their intellectual territory to establish a feeling of ownership. Newcomers should move in by cosmetically arranging code. This must be a background, incremental task and should not be used as an excuse to trash the backyard. ([Rising 2000], p. 27). Complete pattern in [Taylor 1999], pp. 632–635. Referenced in CODE OWNERSHIP (5.2.13).

A.5.2   Ad-Hoc Corrections

It's difficult to keep documents up to date. Keep a master hard copy of the design accessible to the entire team. Anyone who updates the design must make corrections in the margin, delete sections that no longer apply, or write a description of the change. Ultimately, one team member should update on-line copies to reflect the corrections ([Rising 2000], p. 119). Complete pattern in [Weir 1998]. Referenced in MERCENARY ANALYST (4.1.24).

A.5.3   All at Once

If your downstream implementation teams are ready to get started even though requirements aren't ready, *Then* let them go ahead and make progress based on their instinct and on the information at hand [Cockburn 2003]. Referenced in GET ON WITH IT (4.1.3).

A.5.4   Architecture Definition Team

You don't want the architecture to become convoluted, so create a small team of resonating minds charged with the job of defining the initial architecture [Meszaros 1997]. Referenced in ARCHITECTURE TEAM (5.2.4).

A.5.5   Balanced Team

Using teams of like-minded individuals to develop use cases can result in a set of limited, narrowly ranged use cases that do not satisfy everyone's needs. *Therefore*: staff the team with people from different specialties to champion the interests of the stakeholders in the development process. Make sure the team contains both developers and end users. From [Bramble 2002], p. 39. Referenced in DIVERSE GROUPS (4.2.16).

A.5.6   Business Process Model

If you need to understand requirements and business needs beyond the use cases, *Then:*

Understand first the network of agents and commitments that make up the business. Specify the conversations that take place at an appropriate level of abstraction, so that they are stereotypes for actual stories. Get people to tell these stories. Ensure that you produce both 'before' and 'after' business process models. Eliminate conversations that do not correspond to business objectives (or discover the missed objective). Ensure every objective is supported by a conversation ([Graham 2003], p. 59). Referenced in WORK SPLIT (4.1.11).

A.5.7   Clear the Fog

You don't know the issues well enough to put together a sound plan, so deliver something. This will tell you the real issues ([Rising 2000], p. 168). Complete pattern in [Cockburn 1998]. Referenced in BUILD PROTOTYPES (4.1.7) and in the patlet MICROCOSM (A.5.18).

A.5.8   Creator-Reviewer

People make mistakes. It's difficult to see problems and errors in your own work. When one or two designers are producing a design, there is a strong likelihood of undetected errors. Have each designer produce a draft or a complete design. Each of one or more reviewers receives a copy and provides feedback ([Rising 2000], p. 119). Complete pattern in [Weir 1998]. Referenced in GROUP VALIDATION (4.2.32).

A.5.9   Demo Prep

This pattern language is a "preparation for customer demonstrations" ([Rising 2000], p. 46). The pattern language comprises the following seven patterns: ELEMENT IDENTIFICATION, CATALYTIC SCENARIOS, MUTABLE CODE, PROTOTYPING LANGUAGES, LIGHTWEIGHT USER INTERFACES, JUDICIOUS FIREWORKS, and ARCHIVE SCENARIOS. From [Coram 1996]. Referenced in BUILD PROTOTYPES (4.1.7) and SCENARIOS DEFINE PROBLEM (4.2.8).

A.5.10   Designers Are Our Friends

How should testers work with designers? Build rapport with designers. Approach designers with the attitude that the system has problems that require cooperation to resolve. Designers and testers have a common goal. Use GET INVOLVED EARLY (A.5.13) and DOCUMENT THE PROBLEM ([Rising 2000], p. 126). Complete pattern in [Delano 1998]. Referenced in ENGAGE QUALITY ASSURANCE (4.2.29) and in the patlet GET INVOLVED EARLY.

A.5.11   Early and Regular Delivery

You don't know what problems you will encounter during development, so deliver something early. Discover what you don't know you don't know. Deliver regularly and improve each time. CLEAR THE FOG (A.5.7) is the general expression of this strategy ([Rising 2000], p. 168). Complete pattern in [Cockburn 1998]. Referenced in BUILD PROTOTYPES (4.1.7), SIZE THE SCHEDULE (4.1.2), LOOSE INTERFACES (5.2.17), and in the full text of the patlet CLEAR THE FOG.

A.5.12   Establish the Business Objectives

People tend to overemphasize use cases as the final authority on requirements at the expense of other considerations and particularly of business needs. Therefore:

Hold a workshop involving as many stakeholders as possible. Make sure that potential users are represented by marketing personnel or the results of focus groups, surveys, etc. Find a good facilitator. Agree on a mission statement. Find measures for each objective. Agree on a numerical rank ordering of the priorities ([Graham 2003], p. 54). Referenced in WORK SPLIT (4.1.11).

A.5.13   Get Involved Early

You're a system tester working on a large software project. To maximize support from the design community, establish a working relationship with the designers early in the project. For example, learn the system and the features along with the designers or attend reviews of requirements and design documentation. Invite designers to reviews or test plans. Use DESIGNERS ARE OUR FRIENDS (A.5.10). Don't wait until you need to interact with a designer; by that time it's too late. Trust must be built over time ([Rising 2000], p. 126). Original pattern in [Delano 1998]. Referenced in the patlet DESIGNERS ARE OUR FRIENDS and in ENGAGE QUALITY ASSURANCE (4.2.29).

A.5.14   Gradual Stiffening

The requirements and use cases may evolve during the lifetime of the project. How do you respond to such developments? Should you adhere strictly to the original plan? If not, what is fixed and what should be allowed to vary?

Therefore: A web site development project should start with loose design but clear business objectives, defined use cases and types and a sound project plan.

Allow the site structure to stiffen the design only as the site unfolds and only completely towards the end of the project ([Graham 2003], p. 77). Referenced in WORK SPLIT (4.1.11).

A.5.15   Guru Does All

A newly formed team is given a project with a tight schedule, uncertain requirements, uneven distribution of skills, and new technologies. Let the most skilled and knowledgeable developer drive the design and implement the critical pieces ([Rising 2000], p. 130). Complete pattern in [Olson 1998], pp. 153–154. Referenced in ARCHITECT ALSO IMPLEMENTS (5.2.10).

A.5.16   Market Walkthrough

When PRODUCT INITIATIVE (A.5.22) has been followed, hold a walkthrough of program and product concepts with both the development and business sides of an organization. When this pattern has been followed, use IMPLIED REQUIREMENTS (4.1.16) ([Rising 2000], p. 52). Complete pattern in [Cunningham 1996], p. 375. Referenced in IMPLIED REQUIREMENTS and in the patlet PRODUCT INITIATIVE.

A.5.17   Master Journeyman

You need to partition the design work for a large system. There must be a chief architect or small team to provide design integrity. Yet in a large development project, it might be possible for this core team to do all the design work. The core team should provide an overview of the system architecture and divide the system into independent components. Journeymen architects then design the components and act as chief architects for the components. ([Rising 2000], p. 118). Complete pattern in [Weir 1998]. Referenced in ARCHITECTURE TEAM (5.2.4).

A.5.18   Microcosm

You have to create a plan but have never done this sort of project, so run an 8- to 12-week instrumented pilot to get productivity and throughput data for your plan. CLEAR THE FOG (A.5.7) is the general expression of this strategy ([Rising 2000], p. 168). Complete pattern in [Cockburn 1998]. Referenced in BUILD PROTOTYPES (4.1.7).

A.5.19   Owner per Deliverable

Be sure every deliverable has one and only one owner. This general strategy is used with specializations [TEAM PER TASK (4.1.21) DAY CARE (4.1.23), and FUNCTION OWNER AND COMPONENT OWNER]. ([Rising 2000], p. 169). Complete pattern in ([Cockburn 1998], pp. 220–221). This patlet is widely referenced in many patterns, but it is key to TEAM PER TASK, CODE OWNERSHIP (5.2.13), FUNCTION OWNER AND COMPONENT OWNER, and SUBCLASS PER TEAM (5.2.18).

A.5.20   Participating Audience

You cannot satisfy stakeholders' needs without their input and feedback. *Therefore,* actively involve your customers and internal stakeholders in the use-case

development process when possible. From [Bramble 2002], p. 35. Referenced in
ENGAGE CUSTOMERS (4.2.6).

A.5.21   Peacemaker

A PEACEMAKER is a placeholder in an organization who tries to calm and hold
things together until a leader can be found or a reorganization is complete. The
peacemaker should be someone who is well liked but who is not necessarily
technically proficient. Usually this individual has many years with the company,
knows the political ropes, and can buy time for a team as well as the team's
management. Usually PEACEMAKER follows SACRIFICIAL LAMB and precedes CULT
OF PERSONALITY or GURU DOES ALL (A.5.15). ([Rising 2000], p. 131). Complete
pattern in [Olson 1998], p. 168. Referenced in MATRON ROLE (4.2.18). In this
book, SACRIFICE ONE PERSON (4.1.22) is an alias for SACRIFICIAL LAMB.

A.5.22   Product Initiative

When a wish list of features and functions is created for a product, clearly define
an initiative for product improvement and be sure everyone understands the initiative. When this pattern has been followed, use MARKET WALKTHROUGH
(A.5.16) ([Rising 2000], p. 52). Complete pattern in [Cunningham 1996], pp.
374–375. Referenced in IMPLIED REQUIREMENTS (4.1.16) and in the patlet MARKET
WALKTHROUGH.

A.5.23   Prototypes

To avoid the risk of commiting to production decisions prematurely and to avoid the problems of
long-term maintainability of code, work with customers to initially build LOW-FIDELITY PROTO-
TYPES using paper widgets, drawings, paper stickies, and index cards. If the skill and tools are
present, build HIGH-FIDELITY PROTOTYPES. From [Whitenack 1995], p. 288. Referenced in BUILD
PROTOTYPES (4.1.7).

A.5.24   Query Objects

You're using REPORT OBJECTS and need to create queries for reports at run-time.
Create objects that represent queries. Define operations on these objects and a
method to return query results ([Rising 2000], p. 41). Complete pattern in [Brant
Yoder 1999]. Historically from [Brown Whitenack 1999]. Referenced by PARSER
BUILDER (5.2.20).

A.5.25   Shared Clear Vision

The lack of a clear vision about a system can lead to indecision and contrary opinions among the
stakeholders and can quickly paralyze the project. *Therefore:* prepare a statement of purpose for
the system that clearly describes the objectives of the system and that supports the mission of the
organization. Freely distribute it to everyone involved in the project. From [Bramble 2002], p.
80. Referenced in UNITY OF PURPOSE (4.2.12).

A.5.26   Shearing Layers

Software systems cannot stand still, but different components change at different rates. Factor the system so that components that change at similar rates are
together ([Rising 2000], p. 21). Complete pattern in [Foote Yoder 2000]. Referenced by VARIATION BEHIND INTERFACE (5.2.15).

A.5.27   Small Writing Team

Using too many people to write a use case is inefficient, and the compromise made to align the many different points of view may result in a less-than-satisfactory system. *Therefore,* restrict the number of people refining any one work product to just two or three people. From [Bramble 2002], p. 31. Referenced in SIZE THE ORGANIZATION (4.2.2).

A.5.28   Skill Mix

> When team membership is likely to change, separate subsystems by staff skill requirements. This allows specialists to work in their area of expertise and enables successors to see the results of these special abilities in isolation ([Rising 2000], p. 135). Complete pattern in [Cockburn 1996]. Referenced in CONWAY'S LAW (5.1.7) and DEPLOY ALONG THE GRAIN (5.2.8).

A.5.29   Work Allocation

Work is not always assigned to right place, done at the right time, or assigned to the correct people. Accordingly, beyond the historical, organizational, financial, or political barriers and allocate work to produce the most effective outcome. From [Beedle 2000]. Referenced in UPSIDE-DOWN MATRIX MANAGEMENT (5.1.19).

A.5.30   Work Group

> When you've completed a work queue that (a) describes product initiative-related work, (b) is ordered by priority, and (c) shifts up as completed work is removed from the top, then allocate roughly two month's work from the top of the work queue. Be sure the team assigned to this work is committed to work together to complete the assignment ([Rising 2000], p. 52). Complete pattern in [Cunningham 1996], p. 377–378.

APPENDIX B

Bibliography

[Ackermann 2002] Ackermann, Gerhard. Personal Communication, 2002.

[Alexander 1977] Alexander, Christopher, Sara Ishikawa, and Murray Silverstein, with Max Jacobson, Ingrid Fiksdahl-King, and Shlomo Angel. *A Pattern Language: Towns, Buildings, Construction.* New York: Oxford University Press, 1977.

[Alexander 1979] Alexander, Christopher. *The Timeless Way of Building.* New York: Oxford University Press, 1979.

[Alexander 2003] Alexander, Christopher. *The Phenomenon of Life: An Essay on the Art of Building and the Nature of the Universe,* The Nature of Order Series, Book 1. Berkeley, CA: Center for Environmental Structure, 2003.

[Allen 1977] Allen, Thomas. *Managing the Flow of Technology: Technology Transfer and the Dissemination of Technological Information within the R&D Organization.* Cambridge, MA: The MIT Press, 1977.

[Ambler 1999] Ambler, Scott. *Process Patterns: Building Large-Scale Systems Using Object Technology.* New York: Cambridge University Press, 1998.

[AmHeritage 1982] *The American Heritage Dictionary College Dictionary, 2d ed.* Boston: Houghton Mifflin Company, 1982.

[Appleton 2001] Appleton, Brad. Personal communication, 2001.

[Barshefsky 1992] Barshefsky, A. "On the Road to Software Automation." *Proceedings of the XIV International Switching Symposium.* Yokohama, Japan, 1992.

[Bateson 1958] Bateson, Gregory. *Naven, a Survey of the Problems Suggested by a Composite Picture of the Culture of a New Guinea Tribe Drawn from Three Points of View,* 2d ed.

Stanford, CA: Stanford University Press, 1958. (First published in Cambridge, UK and NY: Cambridge University Press, 1936.)

[Beck 1991] Beck, Kent. "Think Like an Object." *UNIX Review* September 1991: 41.

[Beck 1999] Beck, Kent. *Extreme Programming Explained: Embrace Change.* Reading, MA: Addison-Wesley, 2000.

[Beedle 1997] Beedle, Michael. *BPR Pattern Language*, 1998. Located on the Internet at *http://www.easycomp.org/cgi-bin/OrgPatterns?BPRPatternLanguage.* (Accessed on February 22, 2004.)

[Beedle 1999] Beedle, Michael, Martine Devos, Yonat Sharon, Ken Schwaber, Jeff Sutherland. "SCRUM: A Pattern Language for Hyperproductive Software Development." In *Pattern Languages of Program Design 4*, edited by Neil Harrison, Brian Foote, and Hans Rohnert, Chapter 28, 637–651, Reading, MA: Addison-Wesley, 2000.

[Beedle 2000] Beedle, Michael. "Work Allocation," in *BPR Pattern Language*, November 9, 2000. Located on the Internet at *http://www.easycomp.org/cgi-bin/OrgPatterns?WorkAllocationPattern.* (Accessed on February 22, 2004.)

[Berczuk 1994] Berczuk, Stephen. Personal Communication, August 1994.

[Berczuk 1996] Berczuk, Stephen. "Organizational Multiplexing: Patterns for Processing Satellite Telemetry with Distributed Teams." In *Pattern Languages of Program Design 2*, edited by John M. Vlissides, James O. Coplien, Norman L. Kerth, James Coplien, and Norman Kerth. Reading, MA: Addison-Wesley, 1995: 193–206.

[Berczuk 1998] Berczuk, Stephen. Personal Communication, 1998.

[Berczuk Appleton 2002] Berczuk, Steve, and Brad Appleton. *Software Configuration Management Patterns: Effective Teamwork, Practical Integration.* Reading, MA: Addison-Wesley, 2002.

[Beyer Holtzblatt 1998] Beyer, Hugh, and Karen Holtzblatt. *Contextual Design.* San Francisco: Morgan Kauffman, 1998.

[Block 1983] Block, R. *Politics of Projects.* New York: Yourdon Press, 1983.

[Boehm 1976] Boehm, B. W. "Software Engineering." *IEEE Transactions on Computers* 25(12), 1976: 1226–1241.

[Boehm 1981] Boehm, Barry W. *Software Engineering Economics.* Englewood Cliffs, NJ: Prentice-Hall, 1981.

[Bonner 1992] Bonner, Paul. "Quattro Pro for Windows." *Computer Shopper 12*(11), November 1992: 605.

[Born 1994] Born, Tim. Personal communication, 1994.

[Brajkovich 1994] Brajkovich, Leo F. "Sources of Social Structure in a Start-Up Organization: Work Networks, Work activities, and Job Status." *Social Networks 16* (August), 1994: 191–212.

[Bramble 2002] Bramble, Paul, Alistair Cockburn, Andy Pols, and Steve Adolph. *Patterns for Effective Use Cases.* Reading, MA: Addison-Wesley, 2002.

[Bramble 2003] Bramble, Paul. Personal communication, 2003.

[Brandt 1995] Brandt, Stewart. *How Buildings Learn: What Happens after They're Built.* New York: Penguin, 1995.

[Brant Yoder 1999] Brant, John, and Joseph Yoder. "Creating Reports with Query Objects." In *Pattern Languages of Program Design 4*, edited by Neil Harrison, Brian Foote, and Hans Rohnert, p. 378. Reading, MA: Addison-Wesley, 1999. (Also on the Internet at *http:// www.joeyoder.com/papers/patterns/Reports/reports.pdf*. Accessed on February 18, 2004.)

[Brooks 1995] Brooks, Frederick P., Jr. *The Mythical Man-Month: Essays on Software Engineering* (20th anniversary edition), 2d ed. Reading, MA: Addison-Wesley, 1995.

[Brown Whitenack 1999] Brown, Kyle, and Bruce Whitenack. "Crossing Chasms: A Pattern Language for Object–RDBMS Integration." In *Pattern Languages of Program Design 2*, edited by John M. Vlissides, James O. Coplien, and Norman L. Kerth. Reading, MA: Addison-Wesley, 1995: 227–238.

[Burrows 1986] Burrows, T. A., D. Brown, and P. M. Zislis: "GOS: A Tool Providing Support for Graphical Human-Machine Interfaces." *Proceedings of the 1986 International Zurich Seminar on Digital Communications.* Zurich, Switzerland, 1986.

[Cain Coplien 1993] Cain, B. G., and J. O. Coplien. "A Role-Based Empirical Process Modeling Environment." *Proceedings of the Second International Conference on the Software Process*, Berlin, Germany, February 25–6, 1993.

[Chisholm 1994] Paul Chisholm. Personal Communication, June 1994.

[Christianson 1997] Christianson, Clayton M. *The Innovator's Dilemma.* Cambridge: MA: Harvard Business School Press, 1997.

[Church Helfman 1993] Church, K. W., and J. I. Helfman. "A Program for Exploring Self-Similarity in Millions of Lines of Text and Code." *Journal of Computational and Graphical Statistics* 2(2), 1993: 153–174.

[Cockburn 1996] Cockburn, Alistair. Prioritizing Forces in Software Design. In *Pattern Languages of Program Design 2*, edited by John M. Vlissides, James O. Coplien, and Norman L. Kerth. Reading, MA: Addison-Wesley, 1995: 319–334.

[Cockburn 1998] Cockburn, Alistair. *Surviving Object-Oriented Projects: A Manager's Guide.* Reading, MA: Addison-Wesley, 1998.

[Cockburn 1999] Cockburn, Alistair. *High Discipline Methodology.* Located on the Internet at *http://c2.com/cgi/wiki?HighDisciplineMethodology.* (Accessed on March 7, 2004.)

[Cockburn 2000] Cockburn, Alistair. *Writing Effective Use Cases*, The Crystal Collection for Software Professionals. Reading, MA: Addison-Wesley, 2000.

[Cockburn 2003] Cockburn, Alistair. "All At Once," in *The Risk Management Catalog.* Located on the Internet at *http://members.aol.com/acockburn/ riskcata/allatonc.htm.* (Accessed on September 3, 2003 and February 22, 2004.)

[Constantine Lockwood 1999] Constantine, Larry L., and Lucy A. D. Lockwood. *Software for Use: A Practical Guide to the Models and Methods of Usage-Centered Design.* Reading, MA: Addison-Wesley, 1999.

[Conway 1968] Conway, Melvin E. "How Do Committees Invent?" *Datamation 14*(4), April 1968, pp. 28–31.

[Coplien 1993] Coplien, J. O, Suzana Hutz, and Brent Marykuca. "Iterative development/OO: The bottom line." In Jerry L. Archibald, ed., *OOPS Messenger 4*(2), April 1993: 101—108.

[Coplien 1994] Coplien, James O. "Borland Software Craftsmanship: A New Look at Process, Quality and Productivity." *Proceedings of the Fifth Borland International Conference*, Orlando, Florida, June 1994.

[Coplien Erickson 1994] Coplien, James O., and Jon Erickson. "Examining the Software Development Process." *Dr. Dobb's Journal of Software Tools 19*(11), October, 1994: 88–95.

[Coplien 1995] Coplien, James O. "A Development Process Generative Pattern Language." In *Pattern Languages of Program Design*, edited by James Coplien and Doug Schmidt. Reading, MA: Addison-Wesley, 1995, 183–237.

[Coplien 1999] Coplien, James O. *Multi-Paradigm Design for C++*. Reading, MA: Addison-Wesley, 1999.

[Coplien 2000] Coplien, James O. "C++ Idioms," in *Pattern Languages of Program Design 4*, edited by Neil Harrison, Brian Foote, and Hans Rohnert, Reading, MA: Addison-Wesley, 2000, Chapter 29, pp. 167–198.

[Coplien Devos 2000] Coplien, James, and Martine Devos. "Architecture as Metaphor." *Proceedings of the World Multiconference on Systemics, Cybernetics and Informatics*, Orlando, Florida, Institute of Informatics and Systemics, pp. 737–742, July 24, 2000.

[Coram 1996] Coram, Todd. "Demo Prep: A Pattern Language for the Preparation of Software Demonstrations." In *Pattern Languages of Program Design 2*, edited by John M. Vlissides, James O. Coplien, and Norman L. Kerth. Reading, MA: Addison-Wesley, 1995: 407–416.

[Csikszentmihalyi 1990] Csikszentmihalyi, M. *Flow: The Psychology of Optimal Experience*. New York: Harper Perennial, 1990.

[Cunningham 1996] Cunningham, Ward. "Episodes: A Pattern Language of Competitive Development." In *Pattern Languages of Program Design 2*, edited by John M. Vlissides, James O. Coplien, and Norman L. Kerth. Reading, MA: Addison-Wesley, 1995: 371–388.

[Daley 1977] Daley, E. "Management of Software Development." *IEEE Transactions on Software Engineering 3*(3): 229–242.

[DeBruler 1994] DeBruler, Dennis. Personal communication, 1994.

[Delano Rising 1998] Delano, David E., and Linda Rising. "Patterns for System Testing." In *Pattern Languages of Program Design 3*, edited by Robert Martin, Dirk Riehle, and Frank Buschmann. Reading, MA: Addison-Wesley, 1998: 503–525.

[DeMarco 1993] Panel speech, Objex conference, Boston, Massachusetts, October 18–22, 1993.

[DeMarco Boehm 1986] De Marco, T., and B. W. Boehm. *Controlling Software Projects: Management, Measurement and Estimation.* New York: Yourdon Press, 1986.

[DeMarco Lister 1976] De Marco, T., and Tom Lister. *Peopleware: Productive Projects and Teams*. New York: Dorset House, 1976.

[Deming 1986] Deming, W. Edward. *Out of the Crisis*. Cambridge, MA: MIT Center for Advanced Engineering Study, 1986.

[Dikel 2001] Dikel, David M., David Kane, and James R. Wilson. *Software Architecture: Organizational Principles and Patterns*. Upper Saddle River, NJ: Prentice Hall PTR, 2001.

[Fagan 1976] Fagan, M., "Design and Code Inspections to Reduce Errors in Program Development." *IBM Systems Journal 15*(3), 1976: 182–211.

[Floyd 1992] Floyd, Christiane, Reinhard Budde, and Heinz Züllighoven and Reinhard Keil-Slawik (Editors). *Software Development and Reality Construction*. Berlin: Springer-Verlag, 1992.

[Foote 2000] Foote, Brian. "Deploy People along the Grain of the Domain." Located on the Internet at *http://www.laputan.org/patterns/grain.html*. (Accessed on March 7, 2004.)

[Foote Yoder 2000] Foote, Brian, and Joseph Yoder "Big Ball of Mud." In *Pattern Languages of Program Design 4*, edited by Neil Harrison, Brian Foote, and Hans Rohnert. Reading, MA: Addison-Wesley, 2000: 653–692.

[Fraser 1994a] Fraser, Steven, Kent Beck, Grady Booch, Derek Coleman, James Coplien, Richard Helm, and Kenneth Rubin. "How Do Teams Shape Objects? How Do Objects Shape Teams?" Position Papers, in *OOPSLA 1994 Proceedings 29*(10), October 1994: 468–473.

[Fraser 1994b] Fraser, Steven, Kent Beck, Grady Booch, Derek Coleman, James Coplien, Richard Helm, and Kenneth Rubin. "How Do Teams Shape Objects? How Do Objects Shape Teams?" Panel Report, in *OOPS Messenger (Addendum to the Proceedings of OOPSLA 94) 5*(20), October 1994: 63–67.

[Gabriel 1994] Gabriel, Richard P. "Productivity: Is There a Silver Bullet?" *Journal of Object-Oriented Programming 7*(1), March/April 1994: 89–92.

[Gabriel 1995] Gabriel, Richard. Electronic mail of May 8, 1995.

[Gabriel 1996] Gabriel, Richard P. *Patterns of Software: Tales from the Software Community*. New York: Oxford University Press, 1996.

[Gabriel 2000] Gabriel, Richard P., and Ron Goldman. *Mob Software: The Erotic Life of Code*. Redwood City, CA: Dreamsongs Press, 2000. (Also on the Internet at *http://www.dreamsongs.com/MobSoftware.html*. Accessed on February 22, 2004.)

[Gamma 1992] Gamma, Erich. *Object-Oriented Software Development Based on ET++: Design Patterns, Class Library, Tools*. Berlin: Springer-Verlag, 1992.

[Gamma 1995] Gamma, Erich, Richard Helm, Ralph Johnson, and John Vlissides. *Design Patterns: Elements of Reusable Object-Oriented Software*. Reading, MA: Addison-Wesley, 1995.

[Gladwell 2000] Gladwell, Malcom. *The Tipping Point: How Little Things Can Make a Big Difference*. Boston: Little Brown & Company, 2000.

[Goffman 1959] Goffman, E. *The Presentation of Self in Everyday Life*. Garden City, NY: Doubleday, 1959.

[Goldberg Rubin 1995] Goldberg, Adele, and Kenneth Rubin. *Succeeding with Objects: Decision Frameworks for Project Management*. Reading, MA: Addison-Wesley, 1995.

[Goldman 1975] Goldman, William. *The Princess Bride: S. Morgenstern's Classic Tale of True Love and High Adventure* (25th anniversary edition). New York: Ballantine Books, 2000.

[Goldratt 1997] Goldratt, Eliyahu M. *Critical Chain*. Great Barrington, MA: North River Press, 1997.

[Goldratt 1999] Goldratt, Eliyahu M. *Theory of Constraints*. Great Barrington, MA: North River Press, 1999.

[Goldratt Cox 1986] Goldratt, E., and J. Cox. *The Goal*. Great Barrington, MA: North River Press, 1986.

[Graham 1991] Graham, Ian. "Specification in Expert Systems and Conventional IT Projects." *Computing and Control Engineering Journal 2*(2), 1991: 82–89.

[Graham 2003] Graham, Ian. *A Pattern Language for Web Usability*. Reading, MA: Addison-Wesley, 2003.

[Grant Sackman 1966] Grant, E., and H. Sackman. *An Exploratory Investigation of Programmer Performance under On-Line and Off-Line Conditions*, Report SP-2581, Santa Monica, CA: System Development Corporation, September 1966. (Also in *Communications of the ACM 11*(11), January 1968: 3–11.)

[Grinter Herbsleb 2000] Herbsleb, J. D., and R. E. Grinter. "Architectures, Coordination, and Distance: Conway's Law and Beyond." *IEEE Software 16*(5), Sept/Oct 1999: 63–70.

[Harrison 1996] Harrison, Neil B. "Organizational Patterns for Teams." In *Pattern Languages of Program Design 2*, edited by John M. Vlissides, James O. Coplien, Norman L. Kerth, James Coplien, and Norman Kerth. Reading, MA: Addison-Wesley, 1995: 345–352.

[Harrison Coplien 1996] Harrison, Neil B., and James O. Coplien. "Patterns of Productive Software Organizations." *Bell Labs Technical Journal 1*(1), 1996: 138–145.

[Hartley 1992] Hartley, John. *Concurrent Engineering: Shortening Lead Times, Raising Quality, and Lowering Costs*. Cambridge, MA: Productivity Press, 1992.

[Hohmann 1998] Hohmann, Luke. Personal communication, 1998.

[Hsia 1994] Hsia, Pei, Jayaranan Samuel, Jerry Gao, and David Kung. "Formal Approach to Scenario Analysis." *IEEE Software 11*(2), March 1994: 33.

[Humphrey 1992] Humphrey, W. *Introduction to Software Process Improvement*. Pittsburgh, PA: Carnegie Mellon University, Software Engineering Institute, 1992.

[Humphrey 1995] Humphrey, Watts S. *A Discipline for Software Engineering*. Reading, MA: Addison-Wesley, 1995.

[Jacobs 1961] Jacobs, Jane. *The Death and Life of Great American Cities*. New York: Random House, 1961: 68.

[Jacobs 1978] Jacobs, Herbert A. *Building with Frank Lloyd Wright: An Illustrated Memoir.* San Francisco: Chronicle Books, 1978.

[Janis 1971] Janis, Irving L. "Groupthink." *Psychology Today 5*, November 1971: 43–46 and 74–76.

[Jeffries 1999] Jeffries, Ronald E. *C3 Project Terminated.* Located on the Internet at *http://c2.com/cgi/wiki?C3ProjectTerminated.* (Accessed on March 23, 2004.)

[Katz Kahn 1978] Katz, Daniel, and Robert L. Kahn. *The Social Psychology of Organizations*, 2d ed. New York: John Wiley and Sons, 1978.

[Kay 1997] Kay, Alan"The Early History of SmallTalk," in *History of Programming Languages – II,* edited by Bergin, T. J. Jr., and R. G. Gibson. New York, NY: ACM Press, and Reading MA: Addison-Wesley, 1996: 511–578.

[Keil Carmel 1995] Keil, M., and E. Carmel. "Customer-Developer Links in Software Development." *Communications of the ACM 38*(5): 33–44.

[Kendall 2002] Kendall, Kenneth E, and Julie E. Kendall. *Systems Analysis and Design*, 5th ed. Upper Saddle River, NJ: Prentice Hall, 2002.

[Kerth 1995] Kerth, Norm. "Caterpillar's Fate: A Pattern Language for Transformation from Analysis to Design." In *Pattern Languages of Program Design*, edited by James Coplien and Doug Schmidt. Reading, MA: Addison-Wesley, 1995: 293–320.

[Kerth 2001] Kerth, Norm. *Project Retrospectives: A Handbook for Team Reviews.* New York: Dorset House, 2001.

[Kerth Coplien Weinberg 1998] Kerth, Norman L., James O. Coplien, and Jerry Weinberg. "Call for the Rational Use of Personality Indicators." *Computer 31*(1), January 1998: 146–147.

[Kidder 1981] Kidder, Tracy. *Soul of a New Machine.* Boston: Little, Brown and Company, 1981.

[Kilmann 1984] Kilmann, R. H. *Beyond the Quick Fix.* San Francisco: Jossey-Bass, 1984.

[Krakauer 1997] Krakauer, Jon. *Into Thin Air.* New York: Villard Books, 1997.

[Krishnamurthy Rosenblum 1991] Krishnamurthy, Bala, and David Rosenblum. "An Event-Action Model of Computer-Supported Cooperative Work: Design and Implementation." *Proceedings of the International Workshop on Computer Supported Cooperative Work*, Berlin, April 1991.

[Kroeber 1948] Kroeber, Alfred L. *Anthropology: Culture, Patterns and Process.* New York: Harcourt, Brace and World, 1948.

[Kuhn 1996] Kuhn, Thomas S. *The Structure of Scientific Revolutions.* Chicago, IL: University of Chicago Press, 1996.

[Lawler 1981] Lawler, Edward E. *Pay and Organization Development.* Reading, MA: Addison-Wesley, 1981.

[Lave Wenger 1991] Lave, Jean and Etienne Wenger. *Situated Learning: Legitimate Peripheral Participation (Learning in Doing: Social, Cognitive and Computational Perspectives).* Cambridge, UK: Cambridge University Press, 1991.

[Lea 1995] Lea, Doug. *Roles Before Objects*, 1995. Located on the Internet at *http:// gee.cs.oswego.edu/dl/rp/roles.htm.* (Accessed on March 7, 2004.)

[Lemos 1979] Lemos, Ronals S. "An Implementation of Structured Walk-Throughs in Teaching COBOL Programming." *CACM 22*(6), June 1979.

[Linkletter 1968] Linkletter, Art (Compiler). *I Wish I'd Said That! My Favorite Ad-Libs of All Time*. Garden City, NY: Doubleday & Company, 1968.

[Mackenzie1986] Mackenzie, K. D. "Organizing High Technology Operations for Success." *In Managing High Technology: Decisions for Success,* edited by J. R. Callahan and G. H. Haines, Jr. Ottawa, ON: Carleton University, Research Centre for High Technology Management, 1986.

[Manzoni 1984] Manzoni, Alessandro. *The Betrothed*. Translated by Bruce Penman. New York: Penguin, 1984.

[Maranzano 1992] Maranzano, Joe. Personal Communication, 1992.

[Maslow 1987] Maslow, Abraham Harold, Robert Frager, and James Fadiman. *Motivation and Personality*. Reading, MA: Addison-Wesley, 1987.

[McCarthy 1995] McCarthy, J. *Dynamics of Software Development*. Redmond, WA: Microsoft Press, 1995.

[Meszaros 1997] Meszaros, Gerard. "Archi-Patterns." *Proceedings of the Conference on Pattern Languages of Programming, 1997*, Technical Report 97–34. Washington University, St. Louis, Missouri, 1997.

[Meszaros 1999] Meszaros, Gerard. *Artifact Ownership*, April 30, 1999. Located on the Internet at *http://www.bell-labs.com/cgi-user/OrgPatterns/OrgPatterns?ArtifactOwnership.* (Accessed on October 6, 2003 and February 22, 2004.)

[Meyers 1978] Meyers, G. J. "A Controlled Experiment in Program Testing and Code Walkthroughs/Inspections." *CACM 21*(9), September 1978.

[Meyer 2000] Meyer, Bertrand. *Object-Oriented Software Construction*, 2d ed. Upper Saddle River, NJ: Prentice Hall PTR, 2000.

[Morabito Sack Bhate 1999] Morabi, Joseph, Irta Sack, and Anilkumar Bhate. *Organization Modeling: Innovative Architectures for the 21st Century*. Upper Saddle River, NJ: Prentice Hall, 1999.

[Moreno 1934] Moreno, J. L. *Who Shall Survive? Foundations of Sociometry, Group Psychotherapy, and Sociodrama*. Washington, DC: Nervous and Mental Disease Publishing Co., 1934.

[Naisbitt 1984] Naisbitt, J. *Megatrends: Ten New Directions Transforming Our Lives*. New York: Warner Books, 1984.

[Olson 1998] Olson, D. S. "Pattern on the Fly." *PHand* 1998, p. 141–170.

[OMalley 1993] O'Malley, Christopher. "Borland Turns the Windows Page: Quattro Pro for Windows." *PC Sources 4*(1), January 1993, p. 281.

[Papert 1980] Papert, Seymour A. *Mindstorms: Children, Computers, and Powerful Ideas*. New York: Basic Books, 1980.

[Parnas 1978] Parnas, David. "Designing Software for Ease of Extension and Contraction." *Proceedings of the Third International Conference on Software Engineering*, Atlanta, Georgia, pp. 264–277, May 1978. (Also in *IEEE Transactions on Software Engineering SE-5*(2), March 1979: 128–38.)

[Pedersen 2002] Pedersen, Fleming. "Scandanavian Software Development" (unpublished) 2002.

[PCMag 1994] "Editor's Choice." *PC Magazine 13*(1), January 11, 1994: 191.

[Perry 1997] Perry, Betsy Hanes. Personal communication, 1997.

[Princess Bride 1987] *The Princess Bride*. (MGM Pictures), 1987. (Based on [Goldman 1975].)

[Putnam 1992] Putnam, Lawrence H. *Measures for Excellence: Reliable Software on Time, within Budget*, Yourdon Press Computing Series. Upper Saddle River, NJ: Prentice Hall PTR, 1992.

[Recer 2003] Recer, Paul. "NASA Culture Blamed in Columbia Disaster." *Associated Press Wire Services*, August 26, 2003. (Also located on the Internet at *http://www.siliconvalley.com/mld/siliconvalley/6621761.htm.*)

[Reich 2001] Reich, Shalom. "Comments," in *The Risk Management Catalog*, by Alistair Cockburn, pattern 4 "All At Once." Located on the Internet at *http://members.aol.com/ acockburn/ riskcata/allatonc.htm*. (Accessed on March 6, 2004.)

[Riehle 1999] Riehle, Dirk. "Patterns for Encapsulating Class Trees." In *Pattern Languages of Program Design 2*, edited by John M. Vlissides, James O. Coplien, and Norman L. Kerth. Reading, MA: Addison-Wesley, 1995: 88–104.

[Riel 1996] Riel, Arthur J. *Object-Oriented Design Heuristics*. Reading, MA: Addison-Wesley, 1996.

[Rising 2000] Rising, Linda. *The Pattern Almanac*. Reading, MA: Addison-Wesley, 2000.

[Rousseau 1972] Rousseau, Jean-Jacques. *Discours sur l'origine de l'inegalité*, Nouveaux Classiques Larrouse. Paris: Sorbonne Université, 1972.

[Rybczynski 1989] Rybczynski, Witold. *The Most Beautiful House in the World*. New York: Penguin, 1989.

[Sane 1996] Sane, Aamod. Personal communication, 1996.

[Satir 1991] Satir, Virginia, J. Banmen, J. Gerber, and M. Gomori. *The Satir Model*. Palo Alto, CA: Science and Behavior Books, 1991.

[Schwaber 2003] Schwaber, Ken. "Scaling Agile Processes." *Agile Project Management E-Mail Advisor*, April 3, 2003. Located on the Internet at *http://www.cutter.com/project/fulltext/advisor/2003/ apm030403.html*. (Accessed on August 27, 2003; access limited through subscription.)

[Senge 1990] Senge, Peter M. *The Fifth Discipline: The Art & Practice of the Learning Organization,* hardcover edition. New York: Doubleday, 1990.

[Senge 1994] Senge, Peter M. *The Fifth Discipline: The Art and Practice of the Learning Organization,* paperback edition. New York: Doubleday, 1994.

[Stinson 1992] Stinson, Craig. "Quattro Pro for Windows." *PC Magazine 11*(19), November 10, 1992: 162.

[Sutherland 2003] Sutherland, Jeff. *SCRUM: Another Way to Think about Scaling a Project*, March 11, 2003. Located on the Internet at *http://jeffsutherland.org/scrum/2003_03_01_archive.html.* (Accessed July 23, 2003 and February 22, 2004.)

[Sutton Lerner Osterweil 1997] Sutton, S. M., Jr., B. S. Lerner, and L. J. Osterweil. *Experience Using the JIL Process Programming Language to Specify Design Processes.* UM-CS-1997-068, December, 1997. Located on the Internet at *http://www.cs.umass.edu/Dienst/UI/2.0/Describe/ncstrl.umassa_cs%2FUM-CS-1997-068.* (Accessed on February 22, 2004.)

[Sun Tzu 1983] Sun Tzu. *The Art of War.* Ed. James Clavell. New York: Delta 1983.

[Swieringa Wierdsma 1992] Swieringa, Joop, and Andre Wierdsma. *Becoming a Learning Organization: Beyond the Learning Curve.* Reading, MA: Addison-Wesley, 1992.

[Taylor 1999] Taylor, Paul "Capable, Productive, and Satisfied: Some Organizational Patterns for Protecting Productive People," in *Pattern Languages of Program Design 4*, edited by Neil Harrison, Brian Foote, and Hans Rohnert, Reading, MA: Addison-Wesley, 2000: 611–636.

[Vitruvius 1960] Vitruvius Pollio, Marcus. *The Ten Books of Architecture.* Translated by Morris Morgan. New York: Dover, 1960.

[Vlissides 1998] Vlissides, John. *Pattern Hatching.* Reading, MA: Addison-Wesley, 1998.

[Votta 1993] Votta, Lawrence G. "Does Every Inspection Need a Meeting?" *ACM SIGSOFT Software Engineering Notes 18*(5), December 1993: 107–114.

[Votta Staudenmayer 1993] Votta, Lawrence, and Nancy Staudenmayer. Personal communication, 1993.

[Walkenbach 1992] Walkenbach, John. "Opening the Windows on Spreadsheets. (Comparative Review of Excel 4.0, 1-2-3 for Windows 1.1, and Quattro Pro for Windows 1.0.)" *InfoWorld* October 12, 1992: 104–128.

[Walston Felix 1977] Walston, C. E., and C. P. Felix. "A Method of Programming Measurement and Estimation." *IBM Systems Journal 16*, 1977: 54–73.

[Walters 1996] Walters, Joseph. Personal communication, 1976.

[Wasserman 1994] Wasserman, Stanley, Katherine Faust, and Dawn Iacobucci. *Social Network Analysis.* Cambridge, NY: Cambridge University Press, 1994.

[Waters 2000] Waters, John K. "Extreme Method Simplifies Development Puzzle." *Application Development Trends,* July 2000.

[Weinberg 1986] Weinberg, Gerald M. *The Secrets of Consulting: A Guide to Giving and Getting Advice Successfully.* New York: Dorsett, 1986.

[Weinberg 1991] Weinberg, Gerry. *Quality Software Management, Volume 1: Systems Thinking.* New York: Dorset House, 1992.

[Weir 1998] Weir, Charles. "Patterns for Designing in Teams." In *Pattern Languages of Program Design 3*, edited by Robert Martin, Dirk Riehle, and Frank Buschmann, pp. 496–499. Reading, MA: Addison-Wesley, 1998.

[Weiss 1999] Weiss, David M., and Chi Tau Robert Lai. *Software Product-Line Engineering: Family-Based Domain Engineering.* Boston: Addison-Wesley Longman, 1999.

[White 1986] White, William L. *Incest in the Organizational Family: The Ecology of Burnout in Closed Systems.* Bloomington, IL: The Lighthouse Training Institute, 1986.

[White 1997] White, William L. *The Incestuous Workplace: Stress and Distress in the Organizational Family.* Bloomington, IL: Lighthouse Training Institute, 1997.

[Whitehorn 1992] Whitehorn, Mark. "Vorsprung Durch Spreadsheet." *PC User* 195, October 7, 1992: 54.

[Whitenack 1995] Whitenack, Bruce G. "RAPPeL: A Requirements Analysis Process Pattern Language for Object-Oriented Development." In *Pattern Languages of Program Design*, edited by James Coplien and Doug Schmidt, Reading, MA: Addison-Wesley, 1995: 259–291.

[Williams 2002] Williams, Laurie. *Pair Programming Illustrated.* Reading, MA: Addison-Wesley, 2002.

[Yates 1995] Yates, Ronald E. "Employee Empowerment Efforts Found to Be Weak." *Chicago Tribune* December 26, 1995.

[Zachary 1994] Zachary, G. Pascal. *Showstopper! The Breakneck Race to Create Windows NT and the Next Generation at Microsoft.* New York: The Free Press 1994.

[Zuckerman Hatala 1992] Zuckerman, M. R., and Lewis J. Hatala. *Incredibly American.* Milwaukee: AASQC Quality Press, 1992, pp. 81–83.

APPENDIX C

Photo Credits

COMMUNITY OF TRUST (4.1.1): Photograph by Marion Post Wolcott, 1940, Library of Congress, Prints & Photographs Division, FSA/OWI Collection, LC-USF34-053354-D.

SIZE THE SCHEDULE (4.1.2): Photograph by Arthur Rothstein, 1940, Library of Congress, Prints & Photographs Division, FSA/OWI Collection, LC-USF34-029863-D.

GET ON WITH IT (4.1.3, top): Photograph by Russell Lee, 1940, Library of Congress, Prints & Photographs Division, FSA/OWI Collection, LC-USF33-012898-M1.

GET ON WITH IT (4.1.3, bottom): Photograph by Russell Lee, 1940, Library of Congress, Prints & Photographs Division, FSA/OWI Collection, LC-USF33-012918-M4.

NAMED STABLE BASES (4.1.4): Photograph by John Collier, 1942, Library of Congress, Prints & Photographs Division, FSA/OWI Collection, LC-USW3-001418-C.

INCREMENTAL INTEGRATION (4.1.5): Photographed between 1933 and 1945, Library of Congress, Prints & Photographs Division, FSA/OWI Collection, LC-USW33-015690-ZC.

PRIVATE WORLD (4.1.6): Lufthansa German Airlines. Used by permission.

BUILD PROTOTYPES (4.1.7): Photograph by Jack Delano, 1942, Library of Congress, Prints & Photographs Division, FSA/OWI Collection, LC-USW3-000839-D.

TAKE NO SMALL SLIPS (4.1.9): Photograph by Esther Bubley, 1943, Library of Congress, Prints & Photographs Division, FSA/OWI Collection, LC-USW3-038325-E.

COMPLETION HEADROOM (4.1.10): Photograph by Gordon Parks, 1943, Library of Congress Prints and Photographs Division, FSA/OWI Collection, LC-USW-028740-D.

WORK SPLIT (4.1.11): Library of Congress, Prints & Photographs Division, FSA/OWI Collection.

RECOMMITMENT MEETING (4.1.12): Photograph by Russell Lee, 1940, Library of Congress, Prints & Photographs Division, FSA/OWI Collection, LC-USF34-037337-D.

WORK QUEUE (4.1.13): Photograph by Marjory Collins, 1942, Library of Congress, Prints & Photographs Division, FSA/OWI Collection, LC-USF34-100280-D.

INFORMAL LABOR PLAN (4.1.14): Photograph by Russell Lee, 1940, Library of Congress, Prints & Photographs Division, FSA/OWI Collection, LC-USF33-012826-M3.

DEVELOPMENT EPISODE (4.1.15): Photograph by Arthur Rothstein, 1941, Library of Congress, Prints & Photographs Division, FSA/OWI Collection, LC-USF34-024397-D.

IMPLIED REQUIREMENTS (4.1.16): Photograph by Marion Post Wolcott, 1940, Library of Congress, Prints & Photographs Division, FSA/OWI Collection, LC-USF34-055949-D.

DEVELOPER CONTROLS PROCESS (4.1.17): Photograph by Alfred T. Palmer, 1942, Library of Congress, Prints & Photographs Division, FSA/OWI Collection, LC-USE6-D-002685.

WORK FLOWS INWARD (4.1.18): Photograph by Russell Lee, 1941, Library of Congress, Prints & Photographs Division, FSA/OWI Collection, LC-USF34-070365-D.

PROGRAMMING EPISODE (4.1.19): Photograph by Russell Lee, 1941, Library of Congress, Prints & Photographs Division, FSA/OWI Collection, LC-USF33-013079-M4.

SOMEONE ALWAYS MAKES PROGRESS (4.1.20): Photograph by John Vachon, 1942, Library of Congress, Prints & Photographs Division, FSA/OWI Collection, LC-USW3-009386-D.

TEAM PER TASK (4.1.21): Photograph by David Bransby, 1942, Library of Congress, Prints & Photographs Division, FSA/OWI Collection, LC-USE6-D-004089.

SACRIFICE ONE PERSON (4.1.22): Photograph by John Vachon, 1942, Library of Congress, Prints & Photographs Division, FSA/OWI Collection, LC-USF34-065548-D.

DAY CARE (4.1.23): Photograph by Gordon Parks, 1943, Library of Congress, Prints & Photographs Division, FSA/OWI Collection, LC-USW3-034217-E.

MERCENARY ANALYST (4.1.24): Library of Congress, Prints & Photographs Division, Lomax Collection, LOT 7414-F, no. N7.

INTERRUPTS UNJAM BLOCKING (4.1.25): Photograph by John Collier, 1943, Library of Congress, Prints & Photographs Division, FSA/OWI Collection, LC-USW3-034313-C.

DON'T INTERRUPT AN INTERRUPT (4.1.26): Photograph by John Vachon, 1940, Library of Congress, Prints & Photographs Division, FSA/OWI Collection, LC-USF34-060537-D.

SIZE THE ORGANIZATION (4.2.2): Library of Congress, Prints & Photographs Division, FSA/OWI Collection.

PHASING IT IN (4.2.3): Photograph by John Vachon, 1939, Library of Congress, Prints & Photographs Division, FSA/OWI Collection, LC-USF33-001509-M1.

APPRENTICESHIP (4.2.4): Photograph by Alfred T. Palmer, 1942, Library of Congress, Prints & Photographs Division, FSA/OWI Collection, LC-USE6-D-000148.

SOLO VIRTUOSO (4.2.5): Photograph by Russell Lee, 1940, Library of Congress, Prints & Photographs Division, FSA/OWI Collection, LC-USF34-036598-D.

ENGAGE CUSTOMERS (4.2.6): Photograph by Russell Lee, 1939, Library of Congress, Prints & Photographs Division, FSA/OWI Collection, LC-USF34-033032-D.

SURROGATE CUSTOMER (4.2.7): Photograph by John Collier, 1941, Library of Congress, Prints & Photographs Division, FSA/OWI Collection, LC-USF34-081569-E.

SCENARIOS DEFINE PROBLEM (4.2.8): Photograph by Jack Delano, 1942, Library of Congress, Prints & Photographs Division, FSA/OWI Collection, LC-USW3-001663-D.

FIRE WALLS (4.2.9): Photograph by Jack Delano, 1942, Library of Congress, Prints & Photographs Division, FSA/OWI Collection, LC-USW3-000320-D.

GATE KEEPER (4.2.10): Photograph by Russell Lee, 1939, Library of Congress, Prints & Photographs Division, FSA/OWI Collection, LC-USF34-034339-D.

SELF SELECTING TEAM (4.2.11): Library of Congress, Prints & Photographs Division.

TEAM PRIDE (4.2.13): Photograph by Russell Lee, 1942, Library of Congress, Prints & Photographs Division, FSA/OWI Collection, LC-USF34-072474-D.

SKUNKWORKS (4.2.14): Photograph by John Vachon, 1940, Library of Congress, Prints & Photographs Division, FSA/OWI Collection, LC-USF33-001945-M2.

PATRON ROLE (4.2.15): Library of Congress, Prints & Photographs Division, FSA/OWI Collection, LC-USE6-D-009365.

DIVERSE GROUPS (4.2.16): Photograph by Howard Lieberman, 1942, Library of Congress, Prints & Photographs Division, FSA/OWI Collection, LC-USE6-D-004480.

PUBLIC CHARACTER (4.2.17): Photograph by Roger Smith, 1943, Library of Congress, Prints & Photographs Division, FSA/OWI Collection, LC-USW3-031897-C.

MATRON ROLE (4.2.18): Photograph by John Collier, 1941, Library of Congress, Prints & Photographs Division, FSA/OWI Collection, LC-USF34-081012-E.

HOLISTIC DIVERSITY (4.2.19): Photograph by Russell Lee, 1942, Library of Congress, Prints & Photographs Division, FSA/OWI Collection, LC-USW3-003770-D.

LEGEND ROLE (4.2.20): Library of Congress, Prints & Photographs Division, LC-USZ62-103759.

WISE FOOL (4.2.21): Photograph by Russell Lee, 1937, Library of Congress, Prints & Photographs Division, FSA/OWI Collection, LC-USF34-010273-E.

DOMAIN EXPERTISE IN ROLES (4.2.22): Photograph by Howard R. Hollem, 1942, Library of Congress, Prints & Photographs Division, FSA/OWI Collection, LC-USE6-D-007049.

SUBSYSTEM BY SKILL (4.2.23): Photograph by Alfred T. Palmer, 1942, Library of Congress, Prints & Photographs Division, FSA/OWI Collection, LC-USW3-055143-C.

MODERATE TRUCK NUMBER (4.2.24): Photograph by John Vachon, 1943, Library of Congress, Prints & Photographs Division, FSA/OWI Collection, LC-USW3-018497-D.

COMPENSATE SUCCESS (4.2.25): Photograph by Russell Lee, 1942, Library of Congress, Prints & Photographs Division, FSA/OWI Collection, LC-USF34-072226-D.

FAILED PROJECT WAKE (4.2.26): Photograph by Russell Lee, 1941, Library of Congress, Prints & Photographs Division, FSA/OWI Collection, LC-USF34-038817-D.

Developing In Pairs (4.2.28):   Photograph by Arthur Rothstein, 1942, Library of Congress, Prints & Photographs Division, FSA/OWI Collection, LC-USF34-022054-D.

Engage Quality Assurance (4.2.29):   Photograph by Lee Russell, 1939, Library of Congress, Prints & Photographs Division, FSA/OWI Collection, LC-USF34-034109-D.

Application Design Is Bounded By Test Design (4.2.30):   Photograph by William M. Rittase, 1942, Library of Congress, Prints & Photographs Division, FSA/OWI Collection, LC-USE6-D-005139.

Group Validation (4.2.32):   Photograph by Marion Post Wolcott, 1941, Library of Congress, Prints & Photographs Division, FSA/OWI Collection, LC-USF34-057706-D.

Few Roles (5.1.2):   Photograph by Jack Delano, 1942, Library of Congress, Prints & Photographs Division, FSA/OWI Collection, LC-USW3-000678-D.

Producer Roles (5.1.3):   Photograph by Arthur S. Siegal, 1942, Library of Congress, Prints & Photographs Division, FSA/OWI Collection, LC-USW3-009444-C.

Producers In The Middle (5.1.4):   Library of Congress, Prints & Photographs Division, FSA/OWI Collection.

Stable Roles (5.1.5):   Photograph by Marion Post Wolcott, 1939, Library of Congress, Prints & Photographs Division, FSA/OWI Collection, LC-USF34-051788-D.

Divide And Conquer (5.1.6):   Photograph by Russell Lee, 1940, Library of Congress, Prints & Photographs Division, FSA/OWI Collection, LC-USF33-012796-M1.

Conway's Law (5.1.7):   Library of Congress, Prints & Photographs Division, LC-USZ62-77389.

Organization Follows Location (5.1.8):   Photograph by Marion Post Wolcott, 1941, Library of Congress, Prints & Photographs Division, FSA/OWI Collection, LC-USF34-058783-D.

Organization Follows Market (5.1.9):   Photograph by Russell Lee, 1941, Library of Congress, Prints & Photographs Division, FSA/OWI Collection, LC-USF33-013047-M3.

Face To Face Before Working Remotely (5.1.10):   Library of Congress, Prints & Photographs Division, LC-USW33-023716-C.

Form Follows Function (5.1.11):   Library of Congress, Prints & Photographs Division, FSA/OWI Collection.

Shaping Circulation Realms (5.1.12):   Photograph by Ben Shahn, 1943, Library of Congress, Prints & Photographs Division, FSA/OWI Collection, LC-USF33-006275-M5.

Distribute Work Evenly (5.1.13):   Photograph by Russell Lee, 1941, Library of Congress, Prints & Photographs Division, FSA/OWI Collection, LC-USF34-039855-D.

Responsibilities Engage (5.1.14):   Photograph by Marjory Collins, 1942, Library of Congress, Prints & Photographs Division, FSA/OWI Collection, LC-USW3-003591-E

Hallway Chatter (5.1.15):   Photograph by Russell Lee, 1941, Library of Congress, Prints & Photographs Division, FSA/OWI Collection, LC-USF33-011743-M2.

Decouple Stages (5.1.16):   Photograph by Jack Delano, 1943, Library of Congress, Prints & Photographs Division, FSA/OWI Collection, LC-USW3-019552-E.

HUB SPOKE AND RIM (5.1.17): Photograph by Howard R. Hollem, 1942, Library of Congress, Prints & Photographs Division, FSA/OWI Collection, LC-USE6-D-004435.

MOVE RESPONSIBILITIES (5.1.18): Library of Congress, Prints & Photographs Division, Edward S. Curtis Collection, LC-USZ62-117709.

UPSIDE DOWN MATRIX MANAGEMENT (5.1.19): Library of Congress, Prints & Photographs Division, Gottscho- Schleisner Collection, LC-USZC2-4505.

THE WATER COOLER (5.1.20): Photograph by John Collier, 1943, Library of Congress, Prints & Photographs Division, FSA/OWI Collection, LC-USW3-015264-C.

THREE TO SEVEN HELPERS PER ROLE (5.1.21): Photograph by Russell Lee, 1937, Library of Congress, Prints & Photographs Division, FSA/OWI Collection, LC-USF34-030069-D.

COUPLING DECREASES LATENCY (5.1.22): Photograph by Arthur Rothstien, 1939, Library of Congress, Prints & Photographs Division, FSA/OWI Collection, LC-USF34-027252-D.

ARCHITECT CONTROLS PRODUCT (5.2.3): Library of Congress, Prints & Photographs Division, Theodor Horydczak Collection, LC-H814-T-1849-031-A.

ARCHITECTURE TEAM (5.2.4): Photograph by Theodor Jung, 1940, Library of Congress, Prints & Photographs Division, FSA/OWI Collection, LC-USF34-002702-C.

LOCK 'EM UP TOGETHER (5.2.5): Photograph by John Vachon, 1943, Library of Congress, Prints & Photographs Division, FSA/OWI Collection, LC-USW3-025304-D.

SMOKE FILLED ROOM (5.2.6): Library of Congress, Prints & Photographs Division, Detroit Publishing Company Collection, LC-D4-62045.

STAND UP MEETING (5.2.7): Photograph by Walker Lewis, 1944, Library of Congress, Prints & Photographs Division, FSA/OWI Collection, LC-USW3-055963-D.

DEPLOY ALONG THE GRAIN (5.2.8): Photograph by Marjory Collins, 1943, Library of Congress, Prints & Photographs Division, FSA/OWI Collection, LC-USW3-003097-D.

ARCHITECT ALSO IMPLEMENTS (5.2.10): Photograph by Russell Lee, 1942, Library of Congress, Prints & Photographs Division, FSA/OWI Collection, LC-USF34-072428-D.

GENERICS AND SPECIFICS (5.2.11): Photograph by Russell Lee, 1939, Library of Congress, Prints & Photographs Division, FSA/OWI Collection, LC-USF33-012474-M2.

STANDARDS LINKING LOCATIONS (5.2.12): Library of Congress, Prints & Photographs Division, FSA/OWI Collection, LC-USF345-007754-ZA.

CODE OWNERSHIP (5.2.13): Library of Congress, Prints & Photographs Division, FSA/OWI Collection, LC-USF34-14322-D.

FEATURE ASSIGNMENT (5.2.14): Photograph by Russell Lee, 1939, Library of Congress, Prints & Photographs Division, FSA/OWI Collection, LC-USF33-012033-M4.

VARIATION BEHIND INTERFACE (5.2.15): Photograph by Carl Mydans, 1939, Library of Congress, Prints & Photographs Division, FSA/OWI Collection, LC-USF34-000650-D.

PRIVATE VERSIONING (5.2.16): Photograph by Russell Lee, 1937, Library of Congress, Prints & Photographs Division, FSA/OWI Collection, LC-USF33-011316-M5.

Loose Interfaces (5.2.17):   Photograph by Russell Lee, 1939, Library of Congress, Prints & Photographs Division, FSA/OWI Collection, LC-USF33-012300-M1.

Subclass Per Team (5.2.18):   Photograph by Alfred T. Palmer, 1942, Library of Congress, Prints & Photographs Division, FSA/OWI Collection, LC-USE6-D-007624.

Hierarchy Of Factories (5.2.19, top):   Photograph by Arthur Rothstein, 1937, Library of Congress, Prints & Photographs Division, FSA/OWI Collection, LC-USF34-026129-D.

Hierarchy Of Factories (5.2.19, bottom):   Photograph by John Vachon, 1941, Library of Congress, Prints & Photographs Division, FSA/OWI Collection, LC-USF34-063633-D.

Parser Builder (5.2.20):   Photograph by Jack Delano, 1942, Library of Congress, Prints & Photographs Division, FSA/OWI Collection, LC-USW3-004283-D.

Index

Note: References to figures are printed in boldface type.